Happy Xmas 2002

Dear Martin, with

Graham + Vi .

The Short Sharp Life of T. E. Hulme

ROBERT FERGUSON

The Short Sharp Life
of T. E. Hulme

ALLEN LANE
an imprint of
PENGUIN BOOKS

ALLEN LANE
THE PENGUIN PRESS

Published by the Penguin Group
Penguin Books Ltd, 80 Strand, London WC2R ORL, England
Penguin Putnam Inc., 375 Hudson Street, New York, New York 10014, USA
Penguin Books Australia Ltd, 250 Camberwell Road, Camberwell, Victoria 3124, Australia
Penguin Books Canada Ltd, 10 Alcorn Avenue, Toronto, Ontario, Canada M4V 3B2
Penguin Books India (P) Ltd, 11, Community Centre, Panchsheel Park, New Delhi – 110 017, India
Penguin Books (NZ) Ltd, Cnr Rosedale and Airborne Roads, Albany, Auckland, New Zealand
Penguin Books (South Africa) (Pty) Ltd, 24 Sturdee Avenue, Rosebank 2196, South Africa

Penguin Books Ltd, Registered Offices: 80 Strand, London WC2R ORL, England

www.penguin.com

First published 2002
I

Set in 10.5/14 pt Adobe Sabon
Typeset by Rowland Phototypesetting Ltd, Bury St Edmunds, Suffolk
Printed and bound in Great Britain by Clays Ltd, St Ives plc

A CIP catalogue record for this book is available from the British Library

ISBN 0-713-99490-8

To Nina

Contents

List of Illustrations   ix
Acknowledgements   xi
Introduction   xiii

 1 The Whip   ·   1
 2 The Discord Club   20
 3 The Complete Poetical Works of T. E. Hulme   41
 4 The Nightmare of Determinism   67
 5 1911   81
 6 Original Sin   104
 7 Cambridge Revisited   120
 8 The Frith Street Salon   134
 9 Hulme and Modern Art   152
10 Kate Lechmere   172
11 Diary from the Trenches   185
12 Interregnum   209
13 Heroic Values   221
14 The Epstein Book   243
15 Art, Sex and Death   256

Epilogue   271
Notes   277
Bibliography   294
Index   297

List of Illustrations

(Photographic acknowledgements are given in parentheses)
Every effort has been made to contact all copyright holders. The publishers will be glad to make good in future editions any errors or omissions brought to their attention.

TEXT ILLUSTRATIONS

Page 26: Discord Club menu (Paul Hulme)
Page 54: Draft of 'Mana Aboda' (Harry Ransom Humanities Research Center, The University of Texas at Austin)

INSET ILLUSTRATIONS

1. Thomas Hulme (Margaret Myatt)
2. Mary Hulme (David Auchterlonie)
3. Hulme in a school photograph (Newcastle High School)
4. Hulme's mock funeral (Paul Hulme)
5. Hulme in 1912 (Cambridgeshire Collection, Central Libraries, Cambridge)
6. Hulme at the wedding of his sister Kate (Paul Hulme)
7. Hulme with his HAC squad (The Brynmor Jones Library, University of Hull)
8. Hulme relaxing with his HAC squad in France (Imperial War Museum [HU 72867])

9. Sketch of Hulme by Dolly Kibblewhite (The Brynmor Jones Library, University of Hull)
10. Dolly Kibblewhite with Peter and Diana (The Brynmor Jones Library, University of Hull)
11. Walnut Tree House, Rustington (Mary Taylor)
12. Hulme as Second Lieutenant in the RMA (Margaret Myatt)
13. 9.4-in. Mark IV gun (Author collection)

Acknowledgements

Paul Hulme; David Auchterlonie; Wendy Butler at Newcastle-under-Lyme School; Dr Bill Evans of Gratton; Dr Samuel Hynes; Alun R. Jones; Martin Kibblewhite; Ian Harwood; Chris Clayton; Douglas Clayton; Petter Naess; Chris Wildon Bryan-Brown; Ben Read; Helen Burton at Special Collections and Archives, Keele University; Brian Dyson at Special Collections, University of Hull; Dr Ruth Vincent-Kemp; Sister Margaret Truran and Dame Felicitas Corrigan at Stanbrook Abbey, Worcester; Tara Wenger and Avi Santo at the Harry Ransom Humanities Research Center, Texas; Jennifer Graham Jones; Margaret Myatt and Sarah Myatt; Mrs A. Gilman; Ian V. Hogg; Ann Hulme; Susumu Kanetake; Geoff Perkins; David Sexton; Malcolm Underwood at St John's College, Cambridge; David Wildon Carr; Richard Cork; Wendy Baron; Bob O'Hara; Steinar Elstrøm; Chris Jakes of the Local Studies collection, Cambridge Central Library; Adeline Van-Roon and Dr Evelyn Silber at the Henry Moore Institute, Leeds; Juliette Mitchell; David Freedman; Gene M. Moore; Ray Westlake; Joe McKenna; Bruce Swann at the University of Illinois at Urbana-Champaign; Shanon Lawson; Carl Spadoni; Sheila Turcon; Paul O'Keefe; Stephen Crook; Jim Moske; Michael Whitworth; Kathleen Cann; Steve Birks; Gillian Raffles; Tim Groom; Stewart Robinson; Susie Graham-Jones; Lucy Wright at the Manuscripts Room, University College, University of London; Matthew Little, Royal Marines Museum Archivist; Bev and Mary Taylor; Mrs V. Hodnett; Sarah R. Jackson at the Stephen F. Austin State University, Texas; Dr Kathleen Garay; Jonathan Blackwood of Kettle's Yard, Cambridge; Dr David Sutton at the University of Reading; Joanna Kyle at the BBC; Inez Lynn of the London Library; Erin Giordano of the Berlitz Schools;

Ami Oliver-Stilwell at the Tate Gallery Archives; Frank Rickarby; Becky Cape at the Lilly Library, University of Indiana; Alan Wakefield; Chris Farrington; Håvard Johansen; Bernard Hallen; Lynette Madelin; Ruth Vincent-Kemp; Stuart Proffitt; Gloria Ferris; Rivers Scott.

For permission to use and quote from their archives I am grateful to the Masters, Fellows and Scholars of St John's College, Cambridge. My thanks are also due to Dr Samuel Hynes and the University of Minnesota Press for permission to reprint the 'Diary from the Trenches' first published in *Further Speculations*. For permission to quote from letters and papers in their possession I am grateful to the Harry Ransom Humanities Research Center, The University of Texas at Austin; the University Library, Keele University; the Brynmor Jones Library, the University of Hull; Rarebook and Special Collections Library, the University of Illinois at Urbana-Champaign; the Berg Collection, The New York Public Library; the Lilly Library, Indiana University, Bloomington, Indiana; the McMaster University Library, Hamilton, Ontario, Canada; the Tate Gallery Archive.

Introduction

Introducing himself to an audience of London poetry lovers at a lecture in 1908 T. E. Hulme gave them clear notice of what to expect: 'I have not a catholic taste,' he announced, 'but a violently personal and prejudiced one. I have no reverence for tradition.'[1] 'All clear cut ideas turn out to be wrong,'[2] he wrote elsewhere, and I remember the pleasure and relief conveyed to me in youth by another of his aphorisms: 'Why grumble because there is no end discoverable in the world? There is no end at all except in our own constructions.'[3] Hulme was – is – always trenchantly, conversationally quotable. That loose, speaking style is one of his great attractions. I recall, too, how well I savoured the contrast between the anti-romantic nature of his thought and the romantic nature of his personal fate: an early death fighting for his country in the Great War; the entirely posthumous fame based on a tiny legacy of philosophical and critical essays and 'The Complete Poetical Works', five short poems of a striking austerity and beauty. With Rimbaud he shared the distinction of having rejected, at an early age, the adored art of poetry. Reading Alun Jones's biography of Hulme, with its anecdotes of curious and unusual behaviour, only increased my fascination.

But young men are easily fascinated: in the larger scheme of things, was there any substance to Hulme? Does he matter? The answer is, yes, he does. He was one of the half-dozen midwives of the Modernist aesthetic in poetry that was dominant for much of the twentieth century, and his influence on the young Ezra Pound, by personal acquaintance, and on T. S. Eliot, through his writings, has ensured that Hulme's name is never absent from discussions of the development of modern poetry.[4] In the plastic arts he was the first writer in England to provide a convincing intellectual and aesthetic defence of the new abstract art being practised by Jacob Epstein, Wyndham Lewis and David Bomberg, and no history of the birth of British modern art is complete that does not fully recognize his role in the process.[5] As a political philosopher he provided a lucid, passionate and articulate account of why he was so strongly opposed to the liberal humanist belief in moral progress, and why his position could be, properly considered, a source of strength and stability to society rather than the disastrous stasis feared by the political radical. In stark opposition to the intellectual consensus of his time, and while fully accepting the sincerity of the position, he was convinced of the dangers of a pacifist response to the rise of German militarism and provided a sustained and persuasive defence of the need to fight the war in 1914.[6] Like almost everything else he wrote, it was interesting, definite and provocative.

Remarkably, in view of his reputation and influence on twentieth-century British and American culture, at the time of his death Hulme had published no book and his name was unknown except to a small circle of artists and intellectuals in London and to readers of the cultural and literary weekly *The New Age*, with which he was associated as a writer. In 1920 his friend Ethel Kibblewhite handed over a mass of his papers and manuscripts to the critic and writer Janko Lavrin, who passed them on to A. R. Orage, editor of *The New Age*. Orage was convinced that, with good editing, something of value could be salvaged from the 'rick of papers'. His first approach was to the poet F. S. Flint, who declined the task. Orage then offered it to his 27-year-old protégé Herbert Read, the poet and critic, who had been an avid reader of *The New Age* since his student days in Leeds, and an admirer of Hulme's contributions to the paper in particular. Read accepted, and between 1920 and 1922 fragments of Hulme's poetry, aphorisms and writings on the French philosopher Henri Bergson appeared in the pages of the magazine. At some point the idea occurred of having a selection of essays and fragments published in book form, and Read wrote to offer the idea to C. K. Ogden, editor of the *International Library of Psychology, Philosophy and Scientific Method*, explaining that he had 'no interest whatsoever in seeing them published beyond the desire to see work that is, to say the least, provocative and vigorous, saved from complete oblivion'.[7]

Speculations: Essays on Humanism and the Philosophy of Art duly appeared in 1924. It consisted of 'Humanism and the Religious Attitude'; 'Modern Art and Its Philosophy'; 'Romanticism and Classicism'; 'Bergson's Theory of Art'; 'The Philosophy of Intensive Manifolds'; 'Cinders', a collection of aphorisms and *pensées*; and an Appendix consisting of Hulme's introduction to Sorel's *Reflections on Violence*; his 'Plan for a Book on Modern Theories of Art'; and the five short poems gathered as 'The Complete Poetical Works of T. E. Hulme'.

The few reviews it attracted on publication showed what would become a characteristic split in responses to Hulme's writing, between those such as H. C. Minchin in the *Sunday Times* who found it hard to hide their distaste for the views expressed and the manner in which they were expressed, and those such as the anonymous reviewer in the *Times Literary Supplement* who savoured the writer's 'rare gift for forcing people to dissent from him'. *Speculations* did not sell well, but it was nevertheless the volume that created and sustained Hulme's reputation in the interwar years and it became essential reading matter for young British intellectuals of the period.

One of its most enthusiastic readers was the poet Michael Roberts, who in 1938 wrote the first full-length study of Hulme's thought;[8] the initiative came from T. S. Eliot, a director of Faber and Faber. By 1939, Hulme's influence was such that Edwin Muir could open the discussion on 'Criticism' in his history of modern English literature with an assertion that 'the tone of a great deal of it was set by the late T. E. Hulme'.[9]

Speculations also fascinated postwar intellectuals in the anti-revolutionary 1950s. The Marxist critic Raymond Williams devoted a section of the 'Interregnum' chapter in *Culture and Society*[10] to Hulme, expressing an appreciation of his 'major scepticism' and identifying as his main contributions to the thought of the century his rejection of the Romantic idea that man is intrinsically good, but spoilt by circumstance; and his insistence that man was disciplined by order and tradition not towards perfection, but merely towards, in Hulme's own phrase, 'something fairly decent'. Here Williams saw him breaking with a tradition of conservative thought from Burke to Arnold which had associated order with the 'idea of perfectibility – the gradual perfection of man through cultivation'.[11] For Williams, Hulme's death in the war was 'in every way a loss' and he remained 'an extraordinarily stimulating critic'. He distinguished his conservative thought 'essentially' from Fascism.

Frank Kermode spent a chapter tracing Hulme's influence in his history of the *Romantic Image*. While conceding Hulme's 'importance' and 'centrality' in the development of Modernist poetry and crediting him with being the man who gave the image-theory of the first creators of Imagist verse 'a proper philosophical backing',[12] he regarded him as essentially trying to do 'much the same thing' as the nineteenth-century French Symbolist poet Stéphane Mallarmé, and not doing it very well.[13] Along with others who wrote with only *Speculations* as their guide, Kermode's reading of Hulme was conditioned by the fact that Herbert Read's sole aim as an editor had been to arrange a lively collection of pieces of writing, occasionally abridged, into book form. He was not at all troubled by the professional concern a later editor might have felt to present the material in chronological order. The result was that, for those trying to define and discuss Hulme's thought, he frequently appeared to be thinking several contradictory things at once rather than engaging in a distinct process of intellectual change and development. For this reason many critics charged him with inconsistency or, for the sake of convenience, simply reduced him, as Kermode did, to a lifelong Bergsonian.[14]

Too late for Kermode to make use of it, a volume supplementary to *Speculations* and entitled *Further Speculations* appeared in 1955, edited by the American scholar Samuel Hynes. This consisted of a series of short book reviews and philosophical observations on some of Hulme's British and French contemporaries; two accounts of proceedings at the 1911 congress on philosophy at Bologna which Hulme attended; the 'Lecture on Modern Poetry'; the 'Notes on Language and Style'; five essay-reviews on modern art; the 'Diary from the Trenches', and several 'Essays on War'. Apart from the 'Notes on Language and Style' and the 'Lecture on Modern Poetry', both of which had been published as an Appendix to Roberts's book, none of this had appeared in book form before. In 1956 the BBC Third Programme broadcast a documentary on Hulme, 'The Knuckleduster', written and directed by the poet Patric Dickinson.[15] The culmination of this decade of interest was the appearance in 1960 of *Speculations* in a paperback edition and of Alun R. Jones's pioneering biography *The Life and Opinions of T. E. Hulme*. Jones added a fuller account of the life than the single chapter which had appeared in Roberts's study and, like Roberts, brought more of Hulme's writing to light from the obscure magazines in which it had first been published. Overwhelmingly, however, his concern, like that of the literary critics, was with Hulme's thought.[16] By 1964 Hulme's ideas, in particular his definitions of the opposition of romanticism and classicism, had gained such widespread currency that they formed a natural part of the cultural frame of reference of the eponymous hero of Saul Bellow's influential novel *Herzog*.

For the radical and pro-revolutionary generation of the later 1960s, however, the anti-romantic and anti-idealist conservative Hulme was not a natural point of reference. Wallace Martin's *'The New Age' under Orage*, published in 1967, was essentially a biography of Orage's magazine, but devoted considerable space to Hulme and was generous in its assessment of his achievement and influence. Martin understood that Hulme's thought must have developed and changed during his ten years of active intellectual life, and that a proper chronology of the writing would demonstrate this. Michael Levenson's *A Genealogy of Modernism*, published in 1984, made a serious attempt to deal with this problem of dating Hulme, and in particular to dispel the notion that to call him 'a Bergsonian' was to understand him.[17] Karen Csengeri's edition of *The Collected Writings of T. E. Hulme* in 1994 finally brought the full extent of Hulme's writing to public notice for the first time, as well as providing the missing chronology for most of it.[18] A *Selected Writings* appeared in paperback in 1998,[19] and the continuing revival of interest makes it reasonable to suggest that Hulme's reputation is in the ascendant once more.

To write with complete authority about Hulme one would need to be poet, art historian, literary historian, philosopher, political theorist and military historian all at the same time, an almost impossible combination of talents. A more feasible goal, and what I have tried to do here, is to place his work in these various fields in their context, and to trace the style and development of a personality that was able to make lasting contributions across such a broad range of activities.

In doing so I exploit one of the paradoxes of Hulme's position: that the greatest strength of a man who considered the development of personality to be a romantic and humanist decadence, who could in discussion punch a friend on the arm and urge her to 'forget you are a personality', lay precisely in his own abundant personality.

In the purely practical sense of available sources, too, there are difficulties to contend with. In 1954 one of Hulme's friends, the biographer and traveller Richard Curle, was approached with a query about correspondence by Samuel Hynes in connection with Hynes's edition of *Further Speculations*. Curle replied:

I have now found Hulme's correspondence with me, and though there is more of it than I had supposed – thirty communications in all – yet it consists mostly of cards suggesting meetings or giving me his plans and is, as I think I told you, mainly factual. There is only one long letter, full of gossip about himself, his friends and the people he disliked, but apart from the fact that some of it is literally indecipherable – he had the most execrable handwriting – none of it is of any real importance. The fact is that Hulme did not express himself in letters, save in the most superficial manner. At best, they were hurried scrawls, and I doubt whether you will find any of his letters worth reprinting.[20]

What Curle says here holds true for the whole of the small body of surviving correspondence: Hulme's letters and cards to his friends are mostly telegrammatic, almost always undated, and the handwriting is appalling. Less than half a dozen of them could be described as in any way discursive. I have quoted liberally from them, however, on the assumption that *The Collected Letters of T. E. Hulme* is an unlikely project. Family correspondence is also minimal: there are no early letters from Hulme to his family, and from the later years just one to his mother and two to his father, all three written from the Front. One postcard each to his sister and brother survive. There are no surviving letters from members of his family to him. Family relations are thus impossible to depict in the conventional biographical fashion through an exchange of letters.

The traces of Hulme's love life are similarly faded. Ethel Kibble-white, the first of the two women who were close to him in adult life, replied to an approach from Michael Roberts in 1937: 'I am so sorry I didn't keep any of the letters Mr Hulme wrote during the war, but when I left London 5 or 6 years ago I destroyed them, with many other papers.'[21] There are no surviving letters from Hulme to her either, and as a result no direct information at all about their long-standing and important relationship. From the three brief letters written to Michael Roberts, however, it is evident that Ethel Kibblewhite was a discreet woman, so the loss may be more imagined than real.[22]

The most complete surviving body of correspondence is the series of densely erotic letters Hulme wrote from the Front to his lover, Kate Lechmere, during the final two years of his life. Although important in giving us a rounded picture of Hulme as a man these are, with only few exceptions, not discursive in the slightest.

Of the original mass of manuscripts Ethel Kibblewhite handed over, the major survivals are drafts of the published poems, the numerous fragments of poetry, and the 'Notes on Language and Style' which are held at the University Library, Keele. The most notable loss is probably that of the notes from which 'Cinders' was culled. Once he had finished work on *Speculations*, Read returned the bulk of the material to Ethel Kibblewhite, who handed at least some of the papers on to Hulme's aunt, Alice Pattinson.[23] According to Kate Lechmere, who got to know Alice Pattinson after Hulme's death, they included unpublished essays on the relationship between chess and war, and on Go, a Japanese board game akin to chess to which Hulme was addicted.[24] Alice Pattinson died in the early 1930s, well before Roberts began work on his book, and these papers too are lost. In writing the story of Hulme's life I have tried neither to disguise the difficulties presented by the scarcity of primary sources – his two periods abroad, in Canada and in Germany, for example, are almost wholly undocumented – nor to use them as an excuse to speculate on matters of personal relationships concerning which nothing can now usefully be said.

I

The Whip

To T. S. Eliot he was the author of 'two or three of the most beautiful short poems in the English language', his thought 'the forerunner of a new attitude of mind, which should be the twentieth-century mind'.[1] Bertrand Russell called him 'an evil man who could have created nothing but evil'.[2] Forty years after his death Russell remained glad that he had not survived the Great War. To his friends he was Tommy, to his family Ernest, and to the rest of the world, admirers and detractors alike, he is always the austerely initialled T. E. Hulme. He was born on 16 September 1883, the eldest son of Thomas and Mary Hulme, and baptized by the Reverend Bennett Blakeway at Horton Parish Church on 4 November. A sister, Catherine (Kate), was born two years later and a brother, Harold Washington, in 1888.

The family lived at Gratton Hall, not far from Leek, a handsome two-storey brick mansion on a grassy hilltop commanding fine views of the rolling North Staffordshire countryside. On the neighbouring farm, a couple of hundred yards away, lived George Heath, known locally as the Moorland Poet, a writer of folksy ballads and still a man of much greater local renown than Hulme. About all they had in common was an early death – Heath died of consumption in 1869 at the age of twenty-five.

Looking almost due south-west from Gratton Hall it was once possible to see all the way over to Dunwood Hall, the home of Hulme's paternal grandfather, another Thomas. Writing a letter home from the trenches some three decades later Hulme recalled the view, describing his current location as in 'a position very like that of Gratton (on a hill, below another hill) looking at it from Dunwood, but about half the distance away'. Hulme's grandfather died in 1884, but his success as a pawnbroker left his family well provided for. *Kelly's Directory 1892* for Endon listed the principal local landowners as 'the Reverend Joseph Dodd, Wm. Orford Esq. of Wilton Polygon, Crumpsall, Manchester, Mr Thomas Sneyd, Mr Thomas Smith, and the representatives of the late Mr Thomas Hulme'. Endon itself is recorded in the Domesday Book of 1086, and the Hulme family roots go back as far and are realized in the place names Hulme and Upper Hulme, small hamlets that lie some five or six miles to the north and south of Gratton Hall.[3]

Thomas Hulme went into farming as a young man, financially assisted by his father, but the life proved too strenuous for him and while Hulme was still a small boy the family left Gratton and moved into a house on Endon Bank, opposite St Luke's Church. To the 1891 census-takers Thomas Hulme described himself as an 'auctioneer and sales agent', but at some point not long after this he started up in the ceramic transfer business, from a factory at 36 Bedford Street in the suburbs of Newcastle-under-Lyme, supplying the industry of the 'five towns' of Arnold Bennett's novels, Hanley, Burslem, Tunstall, Longton and Fenton. The process involved printing under glaze from engraved copper plates, usually on inexpensive pots produced in large numbers. Thomas Hulme's great interests in life were fishing and shooting, and together with the village blacksmith Charles Perkin he started the first shooting club in Endon. The Hulmes had chauffeurs and gardeners at Endon Bank, but the family had regional rather than Oxbridge accents and there was more social mixing across the classes than was common in the cities. Even so, the local people knew their place: 'Old Tommy Hulme's just gone down the road', the blacksmith might observe to his son. But meeting him face to face it was always Mister Hulme, sir.[4]

The only surviving photograph of 'old Tommy' shows a handsome man wearing a woollen cap and shooting jacket. The soft lines around the eyes and the briar lolling between the lips suggest an easy-going and benevolent nature, which is perhaps misleading: his daughter Kate recalled a man with an explosive temper who was capable of reducing his wife to tears, a remote and hard man whom his children feared and respected. Yet it was Mary Hulme, née Young, always a housewife, who was the disciplinarian in the family, and Kate as well as the boys were not spared the rod for their misdemeanours. Kate recalled her mother as a spirited, independent woman with a good sense of humour and a command of repartee. She enjoyed cycling and on several occasions took her bicycle abroad with her. Anecdotes of family life are sparse, but Kate remembered that Mary enjoyed playing draughts with her son, breaking from whatever work she was engaged in to make some arbitrary move and leaving him alone to ponder his response before returning an hour or so later for her next. Kate was also struck by the fact that, while still a 'mere boy at the top spinning age', her brother had been more interested in the scientific explanation of the phenomenon than in the top itself and had made it his business to read a book on the subject.[5]

The preacher John Wesley travelled in the Endon area in the 1770s and left a legacy of Methodism there, but its real enthusiasts were among the coalminers of the adjacent hamlet of Brown Edge. The attitude of the Hulme family towards religion reflected the moderation of Endon itself; they attended services at St Luke's as a social rather than a pious obligation. The Dunwood Thomas Hulme had been a staunch Liberal and was for many years president of the Burslem Liberal Club. He was also the last chief bailiff of Burslem and the first mayor of the town when the new office was created in 1879. Hulme's father, however, seems to have taken little active interest in local politics.

Hulme had the kind of strong personality that discourages psycho-analysis and suggests instead a generative analysis, one that proceeds from the idea of a man creating rather than suffering his surroundings. Even so, his childhood does offer opportunities to comment on the later development of his personality, as, for example, his expressed attraction to parades and marches, a taste often cited by his detractors as evidence of an innate militarism in his character that compelled him in later life to formulate intellectual arguments in favour of war. It may well be so; but what is quite as likely is that when in adult life he wrote of his delight in a marching band he was simply recalling the pleasures of the annual well-dressing ceremonies of his Endon childhood, a piece of mid-nineteenth-century medievalizing laid to 29 May (Oak Apple Day) in nominal celebration of the Restoration of the monarchy in 1660. By the time the celebrations were formalized in 1868, with a trust formed so that proceeds could be put to use in the village (Hulme's grandfather was among the first trustees), the day had developed into a feast with processions, marching bands, games and dancing. The Endon Friendly Society also arranged, on the first Thursday after midsummer each year, an annual parade that must have delighted any local child. In a procession that could number over 400 in a good year its members marched through the village streets to St Luke's churchyard, directly opposite the Hulmes' house at Endon Bank, in regalia that included a brightly coloured blue sash bearing the motto of the society, and wearing their smartest hats and carrying some sort of wand or staff. To the dismay of the vicar, once at ease inside the churchyard, many of the marchers lit their pipes.

And such days were also, of course, holidays from school for all local children. Hulme briefly attended the church school at St Luke's, but presently transferred to the Newcastle Middle School, a preparatory school for pupils intending to go on to Newcastle High, travelling daily by train to Newcastle-under-Lyme from the station at Endon. His earliest work of literature, a story written on five stiff cardboard pages in a small Victorian book, was probably the result of homework from the Middle School days, though there are no pedagogical comments or markings in the text. The handwriting is neat and joined-up, and although obviously the work of a young boy it is also recognizably that of the man he grew into.

It is a wet and dark evening. Sir Thomas, Lady Eleanor and Miss Austen have to go visiting in a dog cart. As the boy groom, Johnson, is helping Miss Austen up into the cart the horse rears and Miss Austen is thrown to the ground, bringing Johnson down on top of her. She breaks her leg, Johnson gets the blame and is fired. He wanders off down the lane and lies down to sleep under a hedge. Presently he wakes up to hear two tramps plotting a robbery at Sir Thomas's house. 'Now Sam,' says one, 'this is what you have to do, go to Stamford Hall and get into the yard and near the back door you will see a window open, go through it and tap lightly on the wall, then will a boy appear who will conduct you to the room where the silver plate is kept, you get as much as you can and give it to me through the window, Good night.'

Johnson takes a short cut to the Hall and carries out an impersonation of Sam. He gains entrance to the house and is conducted to the plate room. There he pushes the boy to the ground and threatens to thrash him if he doesn't do as he is told. He then impersonates the boy and succeeds in enticing the tramp into the plate room and trapping him there. Sir Thomas and his household are roused and the three robbers overpowered and bound. Johnson gets his job back and the three prisoners are each sentenced to three years' penal servitude.

'Stamford Hall, or The Prevented Robbery', he called it, and signed it 'T. E. Hulme' on the decorated cover. Perhaps its most striking detail is the circumstance of the boy groom's disgrace. There is a suspicion that what upset Sir Thomas most was not his daughter's broken leg but Johnson's lewd presumption in falling 'on the top of her'. If the suspicion is correct then the little story is prophetic, for the adult Hulme would spend much of his short life negotiating his way into and out of sexual scrapes.

Newcastle High School, where Hulme would spend almost a quarter of his life, had been founded only twenty years before he enrolled in January 1894. It was an excellent school, conceived of as the 'new Rugby of Staffordshire', and with a former assistant master from Rugby School itself, F. E. Kitchener, as its first headmaster. The homage extended to referring to the assembly hall as 'Big School'[6] and the prefects as 'Praeposters'; games were played on the 'Close'. During Kitchener's eighteen years there the school rapidly acquired a reputation for excellence and for the particular attention paid to science subjects; but by the time Hulme arrived Kitchener had been succeeded by G. W. Rundall, who at once began urging his staff to 'try to get more literature into the boys' and to ensure that the teaching of geography 'be made stimulating'.

Hulme took the conventional assortment of classes – English, Greek, French, mathematics and science, although for some reason (and uniquely in his year) not Latin – and for the first couple of years usually finished in the top third of his class. His two closest friends throughout his schooldays were F. S. Adams and A. Haigh, both clever lads with a taste for mischief and a willingness to let Hulme lead them into it. Adams, later a doctor, regularly won prizes for his Latin and French and Haigh for his arithmetic, but both boys were slightly in awe of Hulme's intelligence. Adams said later that Hulme had 'more brains than the masters at school' and that he was 'the brightest boy I had met until I went to Cambridge'.[7] Haigh was similarly impressed, recalling him as 'original, humorous and speculative', a boy who 'never seemed to forget a formula that he had ever come across'.[8] Adams didn't notice him showing any particular interest in the arts, but somehow he always produced good essays, which Hulme accounted for by telling Adams that he read a lot, especially Plato. Both Adams and Haigh remember that he never seemed to work hard but always did well in the examinations, and from about the age of fifteen onwards he began regularly winning school prizes for his mathematics as well as scoring highly in physics. In French, however, he was frequently bottom, a circumstance that lends credence to those of his friends in adult life who doubted that the translation of Bergson's *Introduction to Metaphysics* was entirely his own work. His most consistently successful subject at school was the Pitman shorthand they were all taught, in which he rarely came lower than third. In later life his ordinary handwriting was scarcely distinguishable from his Pitman's.

Hulme gradually became an active member of the school. During short-lived experiments at establishing them as school sports he played for his house at both hockey and water-polo, and the rugby team built up a small fixture list of about half a dozen games a year against schools in which he regularly turned out as a front-row forward. From its earliest days Newcastle High produced a school magazine of strikingly high quality called *The Fire-Fly* which reported on the fortunes of the 140 or so pupils on an almost individual basis, and making it possible at times to track Hulme remarkably closely as he makes his lazily brilliant and rather loutish way through his school years. Detailed match reports of all the games are given, including the House games in which Hulme is variously listed as playing for Inner House and Outer House, depending on whether or not he was a boarder at the time. We learn, for example, that in 1901 the XV played an away game against Abbotsholme on 27 October and won 12–3 in 'dull and threatening weather'. On 7 November they beat Tettenhall College at home by one try to nothing on a day when 'rain fell during the whole course of the game'. Hulme was awarded his Colours and the magazine's sport correspondent assessed his efforts: 'A welcome addition to the forward ranks. Pushes well in the scrum, but is rather weak in the open.' The following year, in 1902, the correspondent was disappointed: 'Useful in the line-out because of his reach. Has not improved as much as might have been expected from last year.'

It is unlikely that Hulme took any of this seriously. For both Adams and Haigh he was first and foremost the great debunker, popular with the others for his sense of humour and his awe-inspiring lack of respect. On one occasion he reduced his new maths teacher to tears. The headmaster asked him to apologize and he agreed to do so, but then sabotaged the gesture by writing out his apology in the form of an illuminated manuscript which he insisted on *singing* to the man. On another occasion he was overheard at the school dinner table arguing 'volubly' with his headmaster about the merits of Pearson's *Grammar of Science*. His unpredictability and spontaneity could be alarming. Adams never questioned his brilliance but confessed that he always suspected Hulme 'had a tile loose somewhere'. He was considered trustworthy enough to be made a school prefect in 1899, and in 1900 he and Adams took over the editing of *The Fire-Fly*.

Apart from mathematics, Hulme's most evident talent was for organizing other boys in debates. Much of his importance for the artistic and intellectual life of London in the years between 1908 and 1916 lay in just this ability to organize and control discussion among fiercely egotistical and intelligent people, and the easy authority with which he did so was something he learned while still at school. By the time he became an active member of the Fifth Form Debating Society in 1900 it had been struggling along close to extinction for a number of years. The turnout was rarely more than seven and often it was impossible to obtain a quorum. The general feeling was that the society would shortly disappear like the Chess Club, the Literary Society and the Dramatic Society before it. Hulme and Haigh, however, more or less took it over at the beginning of that year and inaugurated a short, golden age in which the topics of debate were sometimes procedural and sometimes frivolous, but were just as often on major topics of contemporary political and social concern. The debates, extensive records of which have survived, shed considerable light on the development of many of his later positions and responses, often on quite specific issues such as the desirability or otherwise of conscription.

Haigh was elected deputy secretary and Hulme was appointed to a post specially created at his suggestion. As *The Fire-Fly*'s report indicates, his impact was immediate:

The business of the new officer is to induce as many as possible to attend, and to put the names of all those intending to be present on the notice paper before 2.30 p.m. on Mondays. The next thing was to give Hulme a title, and after some discussion they decided to call him the 'Whip'. This measure has already had the desired effect, and the debates are being better attended, thanks to the persuasive powers of the Whip.

At the next meeting Haigh successfully proposed that the words 'Fifth Form' be omitted from the name of the society, after which the whip opened the debate proper. The topic was: 'That some form of compulsory service will be necessary after the [Boer] war', and Hulme's own contributions were summarized in the magazine:

He asked what should we do now, if some of our other colonies were attacked? Almost the whole of our army was in South Africa, with the exception, of course, of that portion of it which could not be moved from India. He said it would mean too much money to increase our regular army, and volunteers, besides being inefficient, can only be had in great numbers in time of war. Therefore we must have compulsory service. He proposed that we should adopt a modification of conscription.

Hulme was opposed by the society's vice-president. Not present himself, he had written out his speech for Haigh to deliver. The gist of his argument was that the British navy provided the country with sufficient protection. The headmaster then joined in on Hulme's side, disagreeing with those who thought England did not need a large army – 'for supposing some great power, having managed to outwit the navy, landed great forces on our coasts. We should then be entirely at its mercy, unless we had a large army of our own.' On a show of hands the motion was defeated by one vote. It was a rehearsal for the argument Hulme conducted seventeen years later in the pages of *The New Age* and the *Cambridge Magazine*.

Hulme presently developed a fascination with words which extended to the use of both violent and bad language, and one sees an early sign of the general attraction to the forbidden which would later land him in serious trouble in his choice of motion for the debate on

26 February: 'That the use of slang is objectionable'. Hulme merely suggested the subject rather than proposed the motion, and on being asked by the chairman which side he proposed to take, laconically replied that he would take neither, that he had only suggested it for someone else to take up. It was Haigh who took it on formally, arguing that most slang 'was introduced by people of a very low class, and that it was unfit to use in Society. Slang expressions were inaccurate, and many involved swearing.' On the contrary, responded one boy, 'slang was very expressive and convenient to express oneself. It was generally shorter than ordinary language, besides being much simpler. And in order to illustrate his speech he concluded by using a few slang phrases.' Hulme expressed the view that, objectionable or not, slang was necessary, and the motion was defeated on a show of hands. According to Haigh this was a memorably amusing session, with the majority of the speakers seizing the opportunity to heap abuse on one another.

Hulme's account of the opposition of romanticism and classicism, first made public after his death in *Speculations*, is one of his most thought-provoking and original contributions to the intellectual life of his times and gives a peculiar interest to the debate held on 6 March that year, when he proposed (at the age of sixteen) 'That the age of Romance has gone'. Characteristically logical in his approach, he began his argument with a definition of precisely what he meant by the word 'Romance' – 'the accounts of the marvellous adventures, the hand-to-hand combats and the love-making of the old days', all of which, he said, had disappeared from 'this utilitarian age'. He ascribed the development to 'firstly, the certainty of modern life, and secondly, the decay of superstition'. The most acute of his opponents were Mr C. W. Gwynne, who argued that chivalry and not love-making was the essence of romance, and that chivalry was far from dead; and Mr Ramsden, a sort of proto-Futurist, who suggested 'the Romance of bicycles and motor cars'. On a show of hands the motion was defeated by four votes.

The last debate of the term was an open discussion on 'The Objects and Benefits of a Debating Society', to which the whip contributed the view that one of the most important functions of debate was education. It was sincerely meant: Hulme was always interested in what others had to say, and particularly interested in those views most strongly opposed to his own.

The Fire-Fly recorded the continuing revival of the Debating Society:

The Debating Society is reasserting itself most vigorously this term, and seems to have entered on a new era of prosperity. A considerable infusion of new blood has brought excellent results; for, while the novelty of the proceedings to many adds to their interest, the unflagging zeal of the Whip and his assistant never fails to secure a good attendance.

Hulme's belief in the value of debate as education is borne out by the regularity and variety of his contributions to these proceedings. They also show that the early political instincts of a man who in later life provided some of the most articulate and clear-sighted definitions of what it means to be a conservative were by no means easy to categorize. Dealing with his opponent's speech 'in detail', he seemed to have inherited something of his grandfather's liberal radicalism in strongly opposing the motion that 'Mr [Joseph] Chamberlain's career is not a creditable one'; but he was silent, or perhaps simply not present, on the occasion when the assistant whip proposed 'That it is desirable to give women the parliamentary franchise'.

In 1901 the school acquired a new headmaster, Frederick Harrison, who at once joined the Debating Society and became an active member. The first meeting of the new year was held on 4 February, at which Hulme provocatively proposed that 'Judging solely from the present state of affairs England cannot last the century'. *The Fire-Fly* reported his prophetic arguments in some detail:

[The Whip] founded his main argument on trade. England was a country which could not produce enough food to support itself, and so was obliged to import. This imported food must be paid for by exported manufactures. He showed by statistics that the export trade of England was steadily decreasing, and the decline of England would necessarily follow. Signs were not wanting that our national character was also declining. Mafeking Night was not in keeping with the Old English quality of self-restraint. He concluded by pointing out that it would not show lack of patriotism to vote for him, as, although judging from the present state of things, England was declining, there was no reason why these conditions should not alter.

The motion was defeated by seven votes. Afterwards the new head-master spoke 'at some length and to great effect'.

The characteristically creative and playful nature of Hulme's intelligence that would in due course enable him to make such fruitful connections across the divide between art and science is always in evidence in his Debating Society speeches. On 21 February the subject for debate was 'That a barbarian is happier than a civilised man', to which he contributed 'an original mathematical theory of happiness':

Happiness was an upward change in prosperity, pain a downward change. The rate of change measured the intensity of the happiness. He compared life to a barometer, for the sum of the upward and downward changes is always zero. So that all men were equally happy, and the civilised man was no happier than a barbarian.

Later that term the evils of drink were debated in the form of a motion 'That the drink traffic unless reformed will ruin England'. The proposer was Mr Taylor, the assistant whip, who had earlier, during Hulme's debate about the terminal decline of England, offered an eloquent denunciation of the drink traffic as the major cause of this decline. Both the whip and his assistant were equally strongly opposed to it. On several occasions in later life Hulme's uninhibited behaviour in public led others to the assumption that he was drunk. In fact he was a lifelong teetotaller whose disapproval of strong drink only increased with the years. His contribution to this particular debate seems to have mixed Darwinism and socialism in equal measure:

The Whip said a thousand years ago France was a great alcohol drinking nation, but now was one of the most temperate. The change was due to the survival of the fittest. The alcohol-drinkers gradually died out, and a race grew up to whom alcohol was repulsive. There was no reason why the same thing should not happen in England. It was chiefly the working people who drank to excess, and they did so because they wanted excitement. If more attention was paid to housing and educating the poor, it would be a far more effective means of reforming the evils of the drink traffic.

Still the popularity of the society increased, and for the debate on 8 October 1901 *The Fire-Fly* proudly reported that thirty-one young men had assembled to discuss the motion 'That the immigration of foreigners should be placed under control'. The general view of the proposer was that 'emigration was encouraged, while immigration was not discouraged. Thus we lost our best blood, and received in return foreigners who made themselves objectionable.' He gave statistics to show that three-quarters of the immigrants were criminals. Mr Reynolds, the deputy secretary, responded by mentioning the Flemish weavers and said that men who were considered criminals in their own countries were not so here, and that England should always be a refuge for the oppressed. A different Reynolds then stood up and complained that the immigrants were chiefly Jews, organ grinders and ice-cream vendors. The Jews had had to be expelled for coin-clipping, the Jesuit immigration of the sixteenth century had done the country great harm, and 'probably many Boer spies had been enabled by our laxity to enter this country'. Hulme's contribution, in a stance that was becoming familiar, offered itself as the dispassionate objective assessment of a difficult and complex situation. He had already acquired an understanding of the fundamental importance for successful argument of using statistics:

The Whip stated that the total number of immigrants per annum was only 150,000, and of these two-thirds were British. Emigration from this country was decreasing, while the immigration of British was increasing. Thus one of the proposer's arguments was disposed of. No Government would be capable of distinguishing between desirable and undesirable foreigners. Restriction of immigration had been tried in America and had not worked well.

The vote was tied at eleven for and eleven against the motion.

On 22 October twenty members attended to discuss the view 'That the general management of the War in South Africa is and has been unsatisfactory', another topic that anticipated a debate Hulme found himself involved in as a grown man. In the 'War Notes' of 1915–16, written while he was recovering from a bullet wound in the arm received in the trenches in 1915, he was heavily critical of the conduct of the war on the Western Front. His adolescent assessment of the way the Boer War was managed was more charitable. Even so it was a characteristically original and elliptical look at the problem in which he maintained that 'if we had been unsuccessful in the war, it did not follow that we had been guilty of bad management'. 'We had done

what no other Power could do,' he contended. Moreover, 'the difficulties were enormous, and the War Office were doing their work very
well'. A youth named Delarue then flummoxed him by giving a speech
in French, which at Hulme's request was translated into English by the
society's president, Mr Gostick, the maths teacher.

The next debate showed the same high consciousness of Britain's
status as an imperial power and anxiety about the dangers of losing it.
A group of twenty-five met to discuss the view 'That naval power is
the most important factor of the greatness and prosperity of a country'.
In the main there seems to have been a good atmosphere at the
Newcastle school, with nice touches of humour in the relations
between boys and teachers. The proposer of this debate was Mr
Pickford, another mathematics teacher. In his reply the chief opposer
opened by complaining despondently that he felt he was fighting an
unequal battle and urging his listeners not to be swayed in favour of
the motion just because Mr Pickford was in a position to award them
good marks in their exams. There is scarcely a Debating Society report
in which Hulme does not speak and on this occasion he advertised a
special knowledge of the Spanish–American war. The motion was
carried by twelve votes.

On 4 February the society had its annual tea, with the expense being
borne jointly by the president, the headmaster and the members, and
on the 19th they discussed an idea of perennial concern to both
conservative and liberal thinkers, 'That there is too great a tendency
at the present day to interfere in the business of other people'. Contemporary issues ('the lead-poisoning question') were raised to demonstrate the 'unwarranted interference of the Government', and 'the great
benefits conferred on Scotland' by Andrew Carnegie cited to oppose
the motion. Hulme's ability to stand back and draw general con-
clusions from particular situations was again in evidence as he proposed that interference was justified in two cases, 'to aid the ignorant
and helpless, and where others would be endangered by our inaction'.
The latter point would later form the basis of his argument against
pacifism during the Great War.

Not all of their debates were on such serious subjects. Hulme
disapproved of the cult of physical education and took the opportunity
in a debate 'That the place of athletics in education is not sufficiently

recognised' to say that he refused to accept the authority of Eugene Sandow,[9] that the importance of athletics was greatly exaggerated, and that a school's chief object nowadays seemed to be to turn out good football and cricket teams. His side lost heavily, however. On 10 December, in the wake of Schiaparelli and Lowell's discovery of 'canals' on Mars, the boys discussed whether or not the planet was inhabited, and Hulme pointed out 'that though the inhabitants of the earth might not be able to live on Mars, other forms of life were quite possible'. In a discussion on the proposal 'That the Government should acquire the British railways by purchase' he expressed the view that it would not work, because Englishmen disliked the rule of officials and that owing to the government's cumbersome way of doing business it would make less profit out of the railways than would private companies.

A falling-off in attendance was reported as Hulme entered the last half-year of his schooldays, but his own debating energies never flagged. On 25 February 1902, in his nineteenth year, he proposed for discussion perhaps the most personally felt of all his proposals, 'That no one can succeed without asserting himself', and used the debate to make a sort of programmatic declaration of both faith and intent. A man's success, he said, depended on the opinion other people had of him, and no one would support a man who did not support himself. Self-assertiveness was necessary both to politicians and tradesmen. Above all, he concluded, it was necessary to schoolboys. Several of his opponents quoted examples of modest men who had been successful, while a boy named Shewell said that boarders must be self-assertive if they were to get fed. The motion was carried by one vote.

In his penultimate debate Hulme again showed his original way of looking at things, of turning questions upside down or viewing them through an intellectual prism in order to shed light on some unsuspected aspect of the discussion. It was often this originality of approach rather than of content that would distinguish his contributions as an art critic and political philosopher in the London years to come. In a discussion of the motion 'That the end justifies the means' he asked them to consider the view 'that the end may be late or soon; if the end is in five minutes it does not justify the means, as the action then profits one person only; but if the end is in a hundred years it may justify the means, as a whole nation may then be profited'.

This valuable period of apprenticeship as a debater and polemicist came to an end with the final debate of the winter term, held on 11 March 1902, on a motion 'That ghosts do not exist'. While supporters of the motion wondered where ghosts got their clothes from, or why they were only ever seen by one person at a time, and opponents offered the usual personal experiences of ghosts as proof of their existence, Hulme spoke a logical and anti-romantic language of his own. Ghosts had no objective existence, he maintained. They were the result of a disordered brain. If visible, they must be material, and if not material then they could not strictly be said to exist. The motion was carried by eleven votes.

Hulme almost single-handedly revived the school's Debating Society during his last two or three years as a pupil there, and he did so very specifically for his own ends – in order to have his say on a wide range of subjects that interested him, and to hear what others had to say on them too. He brought two particular aspects of his personality to the task: the belief that people acting in a group need to be disciplined in order to achieve anything; and the vitality of his own curiosity. The sheer breadth and variety of interests he managed to form and sustain would seem to provide a tribute to the school library, of which he was himself librarian. In a representative term (June 1901) he would have shelved the following new books: *Mammon and Co* by E. F. Benson; *David Harum* by Noyes Benson, *The Jessamy Bride* by F. Frankfort Moore, *Richard Yea-and-Nay* by Maurice Hewlett, *Kronstadt* by Max Pemberton, *A Gentleman Player* by R. N. Stevens, *Elementary Lessons in Logic* by Jevons, *Obiter dicta* series 1 and 2 by Birrell, *Lectures and Essays* 2nd series by Nettleship, *The Renaissance* by Pater, *The Colonisation of Africa* by Johnston, *English Industrial History* by Cunningham and M'Arthur, *First Crossing of Greenland* by Fridtjof Nansen, *The Grammar of Science* by Pearson and *In a Hollow of the Hills* by Bret Harte. The story of Hulme arguing 'volubly' with Mr Harrison at table over the merits of Pearson's *Grammar* confirms that he read at least one book on this list, and his later association of the rise of Humanism with the Renaissance makes it likely that he also read the Pater.

Not quite as forcibly as he represented the Debating Society, but no doubt forcibly enough, he was also a member of the school's Natural

History Society. For some boys, membership was mainly an excuse to go on field-trips in the surrounding countryside or the museums in Manchester. According to Alfred Haigh,

Notices of the Field Club excursions were always displayed on the school notice board, but I never heard of any boy joining them, till one day Hulme suggested to Adams and me that we should go to Manchester with the Field Club, to visit the Victoria University College museum, under the guidance of Professor Boyd Dawkins. This meant asking the Headmaster for leave off for the Saturday morning. Adams and I were sceptical as to getting this leave, but Hulme caused us to muster up our courage, and we went.

As Haigh's memoir suggests, the Natural History Society, like the Debating Society, was in a moribund state by the time the three of them joined it at Hulme's initiative. Appointed treasurer of the society at a meeting on 4 October 1899, Hulme brought his disciplinary skills to bear on things at once, introducing a new rule: 'Whereas several members are in the habit of not paying their subscriptions in the summer term, and whereas most of the collections are made during that term, it is decided to make the aforesaid members pay an entrance fee of a shilling.' On 21 November Adams spoke to the group on 'Bacteria' and on the 28th Hulme addressed them on 'Bees and Bee Keeping', illustrating his talk with slides. Later on he became secretary of the society and on 19 February gave 'a most interesting Lecture on "Weather"', which was illustrated by diagrams and blackboard drawings. He was also a member of the meteorological section of the society.

'Like the Debating Society, the Natural History Society is now in a flourishing condition and can boast a membership of over thirty,' wrote *The Fire-Fly*'s correspondent in March 1901. And if the field-trips had much to do with it, the train journeys, the photography sessions and the teas in country teashops at the master's expense, Hulme's own interest at least was, mostly, serious. 'Original, humorous and speculative', Haigh called him. 'Good fun' and 'a clever boy but not really taken very seriously'. To Adams he was 'a bully and a buffoon' with a great sense of humour. Haigh's account of the field-trip they all went on in the spring of 1899 to a local beauty spot called Mow Cop illustrates all of these facets of his character. Mow Cop was a steep hill with a ruin at the summit, and once they had disembarked from the train at the local station it occurred to Hulme that it ought to be possible to measure the height of the hill by walking up it with his eyes firmly fixed on a point in front of him, and then repeating the procedure all the way to the top, keeping count of the number of repetitions and multiplying it by his own height. Adams and Haigh protested that no one could be certain of keeping his glance level on a slope, but Hulme persuaded them to have a go. He soon lost count (or interest) himself, but according to Haigh this only 'made him all the more anxious that Adams and I should persevere'. He was already an ideas man, as he would later be an ideas man for poets, artists and sculptors. He knew how a thing should be done, but being either physically incapable of doing it himself, or too lazy, he got others to do it for him. He was curious to know how long others were prepared to go on obeying his suggestions as though they were orders. There was no hint of threat or physical violence. It was simply curiosity about the nature and extent of his power as it manifested itself in the reactions of those around him.

There is a stock character in Icelandic saga literature called the 'coal-biter', a big, lazy, loutish youth who spends most of his adolescence hanging around the long-fire gnawing away on a lump of coal. He gets in the way of the women in the house, argues with everyone, and is an object of guarded contempt among the local men. It does not bother him. He does not care what people say of him nor what they think. Then one day, in response to some internal urging, he makes the decision to start trying and is soon astounding those around him with his talents. Hulme was very much this type of character. Content to drift through his early years at school anonymously, once the finishing line of examinations came into view he began making his effort. He won his first prize, the Hawthorn Prize for mathematics, in 1898, and passed through 1899 and 1900 in a blaze of glory, becoming a county council scholar, winning the school's Mayer prizes in science and mathematics and being awarded a Mayer Exhibition. He was runner-up for the history prize and outright winner of the annual Settle Medal for the boy who showed the most aptitude for a career in mining engineering. In 1901, by which time he was boarding at the school, he was made head of House, again won the Mayer Exhibition and the

Mayer Prize for mathematics, and added the Fenton Medal for the best English essay. Finally, in 1902, he was offered a Somerset Exhibition worth £40 to read mathematics at St John's College, Cambridge, and a £30 scholarship to do the same at Queen's College.

There can be few better examples of a young man so obviously straddling the gap between what later came to be known as the two cultures. But institutions of learning never cope easily with this kind of intelligence and Hulme's prowess as a mathematician turned out to be also its own kind of curse, for he was in fact *too good* at it. One of the reasons he seems to stumble so badly through the next few years of his life is that his talent as a mathematician created a set of assumptions in those around him – his parents, schoolteachers, even his own friends – about the nature and direction of his intellectual future: it would of course be mathematical. His debating interests, his reading, his evident philosophical curiosity all paled beneath this blindingly obvious fact.

No one, least of all himself, seems to have known exactly what he was going to do in life. The talent that won him the Settle Prize in 1900 refined his appreciation of Jacob Epstein's *Rock Drill* when it appeared some thirteen years later, but life as a mining engineer in the North Staffordshire coal mines was never a realistic prospect. By the time of his Exhibition to St John's it appears that the school and his father between them had made his decision for him. Mr Pickford recommended his protégé warmly to Dr MacAlister of St John's:

He is going to be Medical ultimately and his people want him to have some time to thoroughly study Science before he 'medicalizes'. He is a very nice fellow, always good-tempered and a solid worker.

Mr Pickford was a prescient man. At the foot of his letter he added an unambiguous postscript warning the authorities what to expect:

Hulme, by the way, will require some attention when he comes into residence. Now that he can get nothing more out of me (or so he thinks) in the way of special assistance in his work, he is giving some trouble in discipline – not serious headaches, but childish defiance of rules, unworthy of a præposter: I think that, unless watched he will think it necessary to celebrate his emancipation, and he is clever enough to do so thoroughly and well. I am trying to steady him with work, which he does not love.

On 22 September, once the offer of a place had been made and accepted and Hulme had sent off his £15 Caution money to the college, he wrote a letter introducing himself to Dr MacAlister:

I should like to have some information about the rooms you propose to give me. If I have any choice could you tell me the various rents, as I want rooms of decent size. Also if I get a fair-sized, should you be able to tell me whether it was well or poorly furnished. So that I might have some idea what to bring with me.

From his tone it was clear that Hulme had every intention of conducting himself in accord with the motion he had defended in debate earlier in the year, 'That no one can succeed without asserting himself'.

2

The Discord Club

Hulme was allocated room C2, in Third Court, overlooking the river by the Bridge of Sighs and next to what was then the main library of St John's. He seems to have picked up more or less where he left off at school, quickly acquiring a circle of friends and joining in the sporting and intellectual activity of the college. One of his closest companions was James Frazer, a choral student who went on to take holy orders. Others, like J. C. (John) Squire and Dermot Freyer, were aspiring poets. Though Hulme himself neither drank nor smoked, many of his friends were, in Squire's words, 'drunken rowdies' who presently made his room the centre of their activities. Most of those who have recalled Hulme do so with a fondness and warmth which also recognizes that he was not to everyone's taste. 'I liked Hulme,' said Frazer, 'though some didn't',[1] and he quickly made his share of enemies among his fellow-students through his disregard of those who did not enjoy constant partying and high spirits. According to Frazer, 'He was always entertaining and kind and at bottom serious. For his first year we were continuously together, spending hours in conversation sitting in his rooms or in my rooms in New Court. No person or subject was "numinous" to Hulme. To me he was the first and the chief of the debunkers. He was far too original and radical to be content to be merely unconventional.'

He took up rowing, joining the Lady Margaret Boat Club and rowing for the college's third-string boat. Not drinking, not smoking, he was even then a great eater of sweets, which partially accounted for the fact that he put on almost a stone in weight between his first and second Lent terms. And as his weight rose so did his interest in the sport decline. A first report in the college magazine, the *Eagle*, on his efforts at number 6 tried to encourage him with praise: 'Has shewn great improvement, and sometimes rows really well. Should cover up his blade more all through the stroke'; but the tone of the report the following year strikes the same note of disappointed censure as the observations on his prowess as a rugby player at Newcastle High: 'Could do quite a lot of work when he wanted to, which was unfortunately not often. Very stiff in the swing.'

His penchant for argument and debate remained his most outstanding characteristic and he did not much mind where or when or with whom. It might be the coach of the boat during an outing, a lecturer in the middle of his lecturing, or the waiter serving him dinner in the college dining hall. On a more formal footing he joined the college debating society, and though the *Eagle* was less thorough in its reporting of the society's activities than *The Fire-Fly* there is plenty of evidence there too of his vocal and provocative presence. The earliest reference to his contribution refers to what must have been his heartfelt opposition to a motion debated on 15 November 1902 'That this house congratulates the University of Oxford on the retention of the study of Greek at Responsions', for Hulme had struggled badly with this part of his entrance examination and was among the reformers who would like to have seen it dropped at Cambridge. As he had done at school he persuaded friends into the society, so that presently Frazer was supporting him when he spoke in favour of a motion 'That the deterioration of the modern novel is marked and deplorable', and John Squire opposing.

St John's was at that time a college strong in subjects which had been studied at Cambridge since the beginning of the sixteenth century – theology, classics, law, mathematics and medicine – and its reputation was no doubt the reason Hulme went there in the first place. But his close friendship with a choral scholar and his informed contributions to a debate on the state of the modern novel highlight once more his intellectual diversity during his adolescence. 'He was certainly interested in mathematics,' Frazer remembered, 'but he cared more for philosophy and art. Though his method of arguing was coldly mechanical, with terms of fixed value, his judgements seemed to be mostly intuitive and aesthetic. He didn't seem to work much at College, but he did talk.'

Frazer's observation is confirmed by Hulme's examination results. He was 'plucked' three times for his Little Go[2] and in his first-year examination in May got no more than a second class. His tutor, Dr MacAlister, formed the impression 'that his mathematics did not appeal to him', and by his second year he was already being given special coaching by a Mr J. G. Leathern at 239 Chesterton Road. The initiative was a disaster. In a plaintive letter to the college of 14 December 1903 Leathern requested payment of his coaching fees, including £28 for Hulme, from whom he despaired of ever collecting the money in person: 'Hulme continues shockingly idle,' he wrote, 'and of course all the money he spends on coaching is wasted. He has brains, but I cannot trust him to do any work.'

Leathern's comments suggest that Hulme may have been beginning to sense a deepening frustration at the limits imposed on his intuition and subjectivity by the study of mathematics. At the same time he was gathering about him a group of young men under the name of 'The Discord Club', with himself the natural choice as their first president, and presently embarked on a campaign of quite strikingly bad behaviour which led with surprising rapidity to his expulsion from the college.

The fateful train of events began with the visit of King Edward VII and Queen Alexandra to Cambridge on 1 March 1904. Throughout the day rumours had circulated around the town that the visit would be celebrated in the evening by a 'rag', a phenomenon described by the *Cambridge Independent Press* reporter as 'any form of violence and disorder in the streets, conflicts between undergraduates and the police, and the wholesale and wilful destruction of private and public property'. To deal with the huge crowds the local police had been reinforced by members of the Metropolitan force, whose manner of dealing with the sporadic eruptions of high spirits that punctuated the day was deeply resented by the crowds. The imported policemen were warned that they would have to 'wait til tonight' if they wanted to know what a Cambridge crowd was really like.

Come evening the students linked arms and, encouraged and abetted by the young men of the town, tried to start a fire on Market Hill. They charged a police line holding the street near the Guildhall and were repelled. The crowd was dispersed by a group of mounted police,

and in the ensuing chaos an 'alien immigrant', as the London reinforce-
ments were called, was isolated and pushed through the window of
Pollard's the confectioners. He made his escape, unharmed, as the
crowd set about looting the shop. Driven off again they split into two
and started fires, one in New Square and one on Parker's Piece, where
Hulme was to be found with other members of the Discord Club. The
evening air was filled with cries of 'Wood! Wood!' as young men
rushed about tearing palings from the fronts of nearby houses,
and looting packing cases from yards and warehouses for the fire.
Wheelbarrows, doors, tubs, benches and shutters went the same way.
Whole trees were uprooted and an attempt to dismantle the wooden
bandstand on Christ's Pieces was repelled only with difficulty by the
police. A great cheer greeted one student who staggered towards the
fire and lobbed the notice board of a local dentist into the flames. It
was followed by a whole sentry box, and presently the entire area
round Parker's Piece was bathed in the glow of the fire as undergraduates, locals, drunks and children joined hands and danced around it
singing. The few police present realized it was futile to intervene and
contented themselves with picking off isolated miscreants, helped by
the university's own proctors and their top-hatted 'bull dogs'. A
number of students had their names taken and were ordered back to
college. One undergraduate, Paul Miller of Pembroke College, was
seen running along the street carrying under his arm a shutter torn
from a shop window. When challenged he was unable to account for
his behaviour and was arrested and taken off to the police station,
struggling violently and shouting 'Rescue! Rescue!' to the group of
friends who followed behind, pelting the police with stones, mud and
pieces of wood.

The following morning Miller appeared before the magistrates
and to the surprise and annoyance of the court offered a defence of
mistaken identity and announced that he was calling several witnesses.
All of these turned out to be members or associates of the Discord
Club, and in their president Mr Raynes for the defence found a stead-
fast and unshakeable witness. Having established that Hulme had
indeed been with Miller on the night in question he proceeded with
his questioning:

MR RAYNES: Was he carrying a shutter?

WITNESS: No, he was not.

MR RAYNES: Did you see one being carried about?

WITNESS: Yes.

MR RAYNES: Are you sure it was not he (defendant) who was taking any part in moving it?

WITNESS: Yes.

MR RAYNES: Was defendant behaving in a riotous and disorderly manner?

WITNESS: No.

MR RAYNES: Not at all?

WITNESS: No.

MR RAYNES: Did you see him arrested?

WITNESS: Yes.

MR RAYNES: Did he protest at all?

WITNESS: No.

Other members of the club stood firm, and when a letter was read from Miller's tutor identifying him as the one man at Pembroke College whom he would have thought absolutely incapable of such an action, his acquittal was assured. As they filed out of the court the undergraduates showed their appreciation of the chairman's discretion with a round of applause.

Among the four magistrates who sat to deal with the procession of rioters and drunks that morning was Mr W. B. Redfern, manager of the city's largest playhouse, the Cambridge New Theatre. Performances at Mr Redfern's theatre had become something of a target for the Discord Club and Redfern and his staff were already familiar with the sight and sound of club members, and of Hulme in particular. Less than two weeks after the rioting, on 13 March, he wrote a letter to the university registrar in which he described in some detail incidents that had occurred during the second act of a performance of *The Prisoner of Zenda* at the theatre. Seated at the back of the dress circle Hulme had annoyed the audience by making noises, 'guying' the performers and loudly correcting their pronunciations. Three times in one week it had been necessary to have him forcibly ejected from the theatre, and on one occasion his conduct in the stalls had been objected to by two ladies, who complained of his use of what they called 'disgusting language'. No action had been taken, since they refused to repeat the words used and declined to give their names. Redfern had tackled Hulme after the Zenda incident:

I said to him last night: 'You would not behave in this way in a London theatre' – to which he replied 'No I would not'. He was quite sober and appears to me to be merely one of a certain class of men who regard the Theatre as a place to make a noise in.[3]

Redfern urged the college to bar him from attending the theatre: 'He is a well-known character here, so such a prohibition on your part can be easily enforced.' He added that Hulme's behaviour was harming town and gown relations, and preventing ladies from attending the theatre.

The registrar passed the letter on to Hulme's tutor MacAlister, who at once contacted Hulme's father. Thomas Hulme replied by return that he had 'written to him strong on the matter, and shall talk to him when he returns home'. A decision to have him rusticated (temporarily sent down from the university) had already been taken, however, at a higher level. Writing to MacAlister the dean said he was sorry for Hulme, 'but there was no other way for it. His father must be a poor creature.' The comment seems harsh, for Hulme had already demonstrated his almost ungovernable resistance to all forms of discipline and authority.

He must have been informed of the decision at once, for on the night of Monday 14 March the members of the Discord Club gathered for an eight-course farewell dinner with their departing president, a sort of Last Supper. Beginning with a choice of Consommé Fleury or Potage Crème Japonaise they went on to Filet de Soles Batelière, Côtelettes d'Agneau à la Nelson, Langue de Boeuf Flamande, Poulets du Printemps rôti, then Pouding au Pommes Moscovite, Tartelettes Agnes, before concluding with dessert and coffee. Much of this would have been a matter of indifference to Hulme, whose favourite dishes were suet pudding and jam roly-poly. Each member of the club had his own printed menu and the cards were passed around to be signed on the back.

The following day, in accordance with an occasional undergraduate tradition, a mock funeral was held to mark his leaving. By common

The menu from the Discord Club's farewell dinner for Hulme in 1904.

consent it was the largest ever seen in Cambridge, and a measure of its rarity, as of Hulme's extraordinary ability to arouse interest in his person, is that the *Cambridge Daily News* saw fit to cover it in detail. Shortly before four o'clock in the afternoon a number of hansom cabs began arriving outside St John's gates. Within minutes there were thirteen of them, stretching from the end of the divinity schools to Trinity College entrance. Alerted to the nature of what was about to happen by the sight of the crêpe affixed to the drivers' whips, a crowd of onlookers gathered, and at four o'clock Hulme emerged with a group of about eighteen young men. All wore large bows of black ribbon in their buttonholes and carried sticks similarly adorned. Hulme's central role in the drama was signalled by the deep crêpe band he wore on his hat and by the ribbons of crêpe that streamed from it. The youths began boarding the cabs. Four who tried to take their places aboard one of them were stopped from doing so by an animal-loving policeman who directed two of them to the next one in line.

With eight of the thirteen cabs filled the procession set off. Hulme sat astride his coffin as it slowly wended its way to the station by way of Sidney Street, St Andrew's Street and Hills Road, the mourners keeping up an incessant barrage of noise, shouting, singing and blowing horns. Just past Sidney Sussex College they stopped to allow a photograph to be taken from a window above a shop on the corner of Sussex Street. Hulme climbed to the front of the cab and posed with one leg dangling casually over the side. The mourners at the back stood up in order to be seen. The clock says twelve minutes past four. Young boys on the pavement grin up at the students. A town man in a flat cap lingers insolently in the roadway, partially blocking the horses, as though to show his contempt for all young toffs who make a joke of being kicked out of university.

Passing the New Theatre a second stop was made to give the mourners the opportunity to express their disapproval of the management's part in the tragedy, and then on they went to the station, where Hulme was carried shoulder high along the platform to the strains of 'For He's a Jolly Good Fellow' and 'Good-bye, Hulme, We Must Leave You'. Once he had entered the carriage the group struck up 'There's a Girl Wanted There', and as the train steamed out of the station in the direction of London the dead man leaned from the window and cried out: 'I'll see you at the Empire!'

The resurrection took place two weeks later on Boat Race Saturday, 26 March. Cambridge won by four and a half lengths that year, and as promised Hulme turned up that night at the Empire Music Hall in Leicester Square. There, clearly still stung by Redfern's taunt that he 'would not behave in this way in a London theatre', he proceeded to cause such an uproar with his catcalling and shouting that the police had to be sent for. After a fierce struggle he was evicted. Once outside, however, he refused to leave the scene. There was more brawling. Two policemen were knocked down. Finally he was arrested and locked up for the weekend at Marlborough Street police station.

On Monday morning he appeared in court, and the *Evening Standard* carried a report of the case on the Tuesday:

MARLBOROUGH STREET

Thomas Hulme, 20, an undergraduate of St John's College, Cambridge, was charged before Mr Kennedy with being drunk and disorderly in Leicester Square. – Sergeant Careless, 2 CR, spoke to having been called to the Empire Music hall on Saturday evening, at about a quarter-past-ten, to assist in ejecting Mr Hulme, who was drunk. When outside he refused to go away, and was taken in charge. – Hulme: I was not drunk. I objected to being taken out of the Empire. – The Clerk read the police-surgeon's certificate, which stated that Mr Hulme was drunk when at the police-station. – Hulme: I certainly was not. I was excited. – The Magistrate: If you wish for an adjournment you may have it, and I will send for the doctor. Have you any witnesses to call? – The Defendant, having declined the Magistrate's offer, and asked that the case might be concluded immediately, was fined 5s., with the doctor's fee of 7s 6d., with an alternative of five days imprisonment.

Aware that they had happened on a phenomenon of some kind the *Cambridge Daily News* ran the story of Hulme's latest escapade, even expressing an admiration of sorts for the way the 'crestfallen reveller' had kept the promise made to his friends at the mock funeral.

In view of this latest scandal several of Hulme's enemies now moved to try to turn his rustication into full expulsion. The composer Cyril Rootham, the college's director of music and organist, enclosed a copy of the *Standard*'s report in his short letter of 29 March to the dean.

I cannot resist cutting this out of today's Standard for your perusal. Cannot the man be sent down on the strength of this? He is ruining my temper at nights, and one of the choral scholar's morals by day and night! I should like to see the man kicked out. Excuse this outburst, but the affair is rather disgraceful.[4]

And on 18 April a Mr Ralph Yearsley of Loughborough wrote to MacAlister: 'It is undoubtedly my duty for the good of many undergraduates in particular to let you know what a disreputable and dangerous person you have in one Hulme of St John's. All I ask is that his moral character at Cambridge and Clerkenwell[5] may be strictly investigated, for I am confident that the result can be nothing less than his immediate removal from the university.' The tone seems unduly strong for catcalling in the theatre and resisting arrest at a music hall, and the suspicion is unavoidable that this Mr Yearsley was the irate father of Claud Yearsley of the Discord Club, one of those who had signed the back of Hulme's menu card at his farewell dinner, and quite possibly the choral scholar whose morals Hulme was said to be ruining by day and night. The protests were accepted and Hulme was duly informed that he was to be sent down.

At once a campaign by the family to get St John's to reconsider its decision got under way. Thomas Hulme wrote to the college on 17 April, begging the authorities not to proceed until he had had an opportunity to talk to them. He and Mary Hulme then urged their most influential relatives to write to the college on Hulme's behalf. An uncle, Edward Hollinshead, wrote to a third party who was a personal friend of MacAlister with the mingled air of affection and exasperation that was characteristic of all the appeals:

I have a nephew who is extremely clever but at the same time foolish, who has got into difficulties at the last boat race in London. It appears that a number of them went to the Empire and with exuberance of spirits got into collision with the police and my nephew, who is a very strong, tall young fellow instead of slipping half a crown into the hands of the policeman put up his back and bowled two of them over.[6]

Regarding the assertion that Hulme was drunk at the time, he supported Hulme's protests, confirming that his nephew was 'not given to drink'. Beyond that, however, he said he had 'nothing to urge for the boy beyond his great cleverness'. 'His obstinacy is something appalling,' he concluded sadly.

Dr MacAlister did not dislike Hulme personally. He found his fault to be only his 'idleness and a tendency to get into foolish scrapes', and he had a sympathetic appreciation of the fact that the mathematics he was studying had in some way turned out to be a disappointment for him. It seems that he briefly allowed himself to be swayed by these appeals and proposed that the punishment of a suspension for one term be restored in place of permanent expulsion.

But those on the receiving end of Hulme's 'foolish scrapes' would have none of it. Getting wind of a possible reprieve, Redfern of the New Theatre wrote again to Dr MacAlister:

April 20 1904

Dear Sir,

It is reported in the town that Mr T. Hulme – who was the cause of much trouble at the Theatre on several occasions last term – is to be allowed to come up again. I venture to hope there is no truth in the rumour, but if it should be true I desire to call your attention to the fact that our officials are instructed not to admit him to any part of the Theatre.

May I ask your kind assistance by prohibiting Mr Hulme from attempting to visit the Theatre, and so prevent any further unpleasantness.

In case you did not see a report of Mr Hulme's conduct when in London I enclose a cutting from a paper of March 29th last.

I remain – Dear Sir
Yours faithfully
W. B. Redfern[7]

Whether this last appeal from Redfern really made any difference and swayed MacAlister's decision, or whether MacAlister himself was overruled, the result was that Hulme was now formally sent down and after five terms in residence his name was 'removed from the Boards' in May 1904 and the first of his two attempts to graduate from Cambridge University ended in failure. He had acquired, however – or perhaps been born with – a code of conduct that required him to cultivate indifference to all such fluctuations in his fortunes, and in calm counterpoint to his spectacularly wilful descent into academic disaster the *Eagle* records his continued attendance at meetings of the college debating society for what remained of the term. They discussed the motion 'That this House would welcome the Establishment of an Academy for the control of English Literature' (Hulme and Squire opposed, motion carried by two votes); and 'That in the opinion of this House, it would be to the advantage of this country to ally itself with France rather than with Germany' (Hulme spoke in favour, motion carried by four votes). Finally, days before his final departure, they discussed the suggestion 'That, as regards the Theatre, the present age is not one of good art', a motion which, with sublime perversity, the scourge of the Cambridge New Theatre opposed.

*

Mr Pickford's warning to the college authorities that Hulme would 'require some attention' once he was up at Cambridge had been in vain. Yet it was scarcely anyone's fault, so furious was Hulme's impatience with authority in these early years. Rebellion is normal in young men, and what makes Hulme's particular experiment remarkable is that he was able to conduct it without the help of alcohol. And experiment is surely what it was, an attempt to see how far the unstoppable force of his personality could expand before meeting the immovable object of society. His rebellion was almost certainly existential in its origins, not neurotic. Many of the drifting and brooding aphorisms contained in 'Cinders', a notebook he may have started as early as these university years, confirm this sense of a mind searching for a meaning in limits, for the authority behind authority:

I am immediately up in arms if a book says a subject can be divided into three parts.

All clear cut ideas turn out to be wrong.

Philosophy is about people in clothes, not about the soul of man.

That great secret which all men find out for themselves and none reveal – or if they do, like Cassandra, are not believed – that the world is round. The young man refuses to believe it.

World as finite, and so no longer any refuge in infinities of grandeur.

Most urgent of all is his Dostoevskyian account of the state of mind of the religiously self-testing young man: 'Jealousy, desire to kill, desire for strong arms and knives, resolution to shake off social convention and do it.' Little evidence remains of Hulme's taste in reading, but he cared enough about William Blake to conduct a stranger to his birth-place one day, and as well as Raskolnikov's dark experiment in godless-ness there is something of Blake's love of spontaneity in this note to himself. It is not difficult to imagine that a challenge of this order rang out through his sober head before every one of those bravely absurd incidents in the theatre, and that he found it more than his self-respect was worth to ignore the challenge.

*

Hulme's expulsion from St John's came as a great blow to his father, and his disappointment was compounded when his son showed no interest in the prospect of taking over the ceramic transfer business. In the long term his failure to fulfil in expected fashion the role of the eldest son placed the burden of succession on young Harold, who accepted it unwillingly and who is said to have harboured an enduring hostility towards his elder brother because of it. The five-year difference in age meant that the two had never been close, and Harold did not begin at Newcastle High School until Hulme was in his final year there. Asked for recollections of his brother some forty years later all he could add to the few details already published in book form by Herbert Read and Michael Roberts was that when he came home from Cam-bridge on vacation he was 'very busy reading all the time as he used to receive a great number of books from The Times Book Club', and that he was a keen walker whose interest in the family's genealogical tree took him on daylong outings to many of the churchyards and cemeteries of North Staffordshire. Hulme's relationship with his sister Kate was closer, but his failure to graduate brought about a partial estrangement between himself and the rest of the family which endured until the fraught circumstances of war rendered it trivial.

In compensation he became increasingly close to a maiden aunt (actually his mother's cousin), Alice Pattinson, who was for a time headmistress of a village school near Alton Towers. One of her pupils was the bird-painter Charles Tunnicliffe, whose talent she recognized and whom she later put through art school at Macclesfield at her own expense. Hulme benefited similarly from her cultural and literary interests and increasingly came to regard Lake House, Macclesfield, as his own home. One of Alice's sisters, Ursula, wrote to Michael Roberts in 1938 that 'my sister could have told you more about him than anyone, for from the time he went to college he was more intimate with her than with any of his relations. He spent most of his holidays with my sister as his own family were not at all sympathetic.'

In the family discussions that followed Hulme's disgrace in 1904 it seems that he tried in vain to bring up the subject of his interest in philosophy. And what, his father wanted to know, was the use of philosophy? 'No use at all in North Staffordshire', was Hulme's glum reply. Alice Pattinson urged that he be given a second chance and it was presently agreed that he would try again, in London this time, where he matriculated at University College London in 1904 to study for a degree in botany and physics. In the botany one might hear a faint echo of his schoolboy interest in beekeeping, but the whole arrangement bears the marks of a doomed compromise between the desire to please his parents and his own persisting and puzzling sense of being in the wrong place at the wrong time pursuing the wrong studies.

The London Library records him as taking out membership in St James's Square as early as August 1903, while still an undergraduate at Cambridge, when his sponsor was Kathleen Lyttleton, the translator of Miguel de Molinos. But apart from the two addresses recorded with UCL, one at 63 Gower Street in his first year and the other at 3 Maida Hill West between 1905 and 1906, he passed through London this first time without leaving any trace of himself. Kate's only memory of the period was of his prodigious feats of walking, and of how he once

33

made the journey from London to Endon on foot, taking three days, sleeping in barns and hedgerows and arriving home filthy and bedraggled 'like the proverbial tramp', a homecoming that veers wildly between penitence and outright rejection. The family refused to have anything to do with him until he had taken a bath. One of his later 'Notes on Bergson' seems to make a reference to this period of long-distance walking. Describing his pleasure at discovering that his own ideas on the nature of the soul were not merely contemporary eruptions of thought but actually links that made him part of a connected chain of similar ideas stretching back into history he wrote that 'the difference it produces in the atmosphere of one's beliefs is like the difference which was produced in my outlook on London in the year when I discovered by actual walking that Oxford Street does actually go to Oxford and that Piccadilly is really the Bath road'.[8]

The marathon walks to Oxford and Bath proved in the end not enough to satisfy Hulme's wanderlust. Once more he scotched his chance of a university degree and with seeming abruptness left London for Canada in July of 1906. Ursula Pattinson understood that it was because his father was putting pressure on him to be 'coached for the civil service' and that, as he told her sister Alice, 'he would rather live on bread and cheese than go on with studies he disliked; and he hated the thought of entering the civil service'. Richard Curle, with whom Hulme became friendly some five or six years later and who knew him as a sexual adventurer, asserted that the trip was made to get away from a woman. Alfred Haigh assumed that it came about 'just for adventure': Canada was an established option for young men wanting to emigrate or see a bit of the world before settling down – fifteen or sixteen had gone out from Haigh's own Potteries village between 1900 and 1907 – and during the time he was at school with Hulme a visiting lecturer had spoken to the boys about Canada, showing magic lantern slides and afterwards handing out pamphlets advertising the country. Given Hulme's spontaneous nature, his choice of destination may have needed no more prompting than some such memory.

According to Adams, Hulme worked his passage out as a ship's steward and came back by cattle boat. In Haigh's version of the story he travelled steerage. Either way he travelled cheaply and quite certainly without his father's approval. Apart from a scattering of impenetrably private references in his notes ('*The two moods in life.* (i) Ill in bed, toothache, W. C. in the Atlantic – the disorganised, withdrawn-into-oneself mood') he left no record of the crossing and few references to his time there. A stray note in 'Cinders' reads: 'The road leading over the prairie, at dusk, with the half-breed. Travel helps one to discover the undiscovered portions of one's own mind', and he seems to have travelled the country working on railroads and in lumberjack camps.[9]

Back in England a few months later, Hulme met his schoolfriend Adams, who was now studying medicine. Adams recalled that he looked to be in very good shape, and with the sort of precision that might explain why Hulme liked him assessed his height at 6 ft 2 ins. and his weight at about 13 st. 7 lbs. He had £70 in his pocket and he told Adams he had taken up the study of philosophy. Adams found him slightly changed. He 'seemed to have lost some of his former aggressiveness, and at the same time some of his sense of humour, of which he used to have a great fund. This short meeting was a great pleasure to me. I never saw him again.'

There could be no question of returning home after this and Hulme apparently hung around London until about the spring of 1907. Again he left no surviving trace of his doings or of his whereabouts. A man who may or may not have been him is glimpsed attending the philosophy lectures at Trinity College, Cambridge given by Sorley and MacTaggart. He is 'tall, fair, of soldierly bearing, obviously a keen earnest student who at that time had already taken some other subjects before turning to Philosophy'. His name is Hulme. The year is 1907. The witness, an undergraduate named Charles Gimblett, never knew him personally but recalls him distinctly.[10]

From here he crossed the Channel to Brussels, where he worked as a teacher of English at the Berlitz School of Languages, attempting in the process to improve his own French and acquire a reading know-ledge of German.[11] The experience reverberates through various of the 'Notes on Language and Style' which he made at the time. The overriding impression made by this scrapbook of ideas and fragmen-tary jottings is of the always fundamental nature of his attempt to discover the rules underlying the uses and effects of language. Hulme was self-taught as a philosopher, and his enquiry typically addresses itself to the problem through concepts and analogies taken from the mathematics in which he had received his formal education. Under the heading 'Analysis of the attitude of a man reading an argument' he writes this:

(i) Compare in Algebra, the real things are replaced by symbols. These symbols are manipulated according to certain laws which are independent of their meaning.

>N.B. At a certain point in the proof we cease to think of x as having a meaning and look upon it as a mere counter to be manipulated.

(ii) An analogous phenomenon happens in reasoning in language. We replace meaning (i.e. *vision*) by words. These words fall into well-known patterns, i.e. into certain well-known phrases we accept without thinking, just as we do the x in algebra.

But there is a constant movement above and below the line of meaning. And this is used in dialectical argument. At any stage we can ask the opponent to show his hand, that is to turn all his *words* into visions, in realities we can see.

As it is in 'Cinders', the atmosphere of the 'Notes' is one of intense privacy and the attraction that of overhearing someone in the actual process of thinking. The half-formulated and fragmentary nature of the writing is at first almost impenetrable; but gradually a sense of what is essentially a poetic connection emerges as one acquires the knack of navigating the spaces between these cindery sentences and interrupted phrases. B. S. Johnson's *A Few Short Sentences* offers consciously the same pleasures of elliptical disjunction as Hulme offered unconsciously, and there is a sense in which both 'Cinders' and the 'Notes' prefigure the literary preoccupations of the Samuel Beckett of 'Breath' or 'Happy Days'. It is easy to imagine Hulme's abrupt and mysterious sentences being staged in the same way as Beckett's fragmentary plays.

Beyond the cryptic, however, the 'Notes on Language and Style' are also studded with aphoristic statements of Hulme's own developing credo which are instantly comprehensible:

Solidity a pleasure

Prose a museum where all the old weapons of poetry kept

All styles are only means of subduing the reader

Impossible to learn anything new in ideas from a book. Must be there beforehand, then joy in recognising it

Literary man always first completely disillusioned and then deliberately and purposely creative of illusions

Literary people work in imaginary land which all of us carry about in desert moments

And in his definition of Literature as 'entirely the deliberate standing still, hovering and thinking oneself into an artificial view, for the moment and not effecting any real actions at all' there is an early formulation of the critique of Beauty as a 'feigned ecstasy' with which he later prefaced his poem 'Mana Aboda'.

The fundamentalist nature of Hulme's thinking leads him in these 'Notes' to attempt to break down and comprehend the workings of language and literature in a way which is at times so cripplingly literal that it is not hard to understand why he never achieved a really extended piece of writing. Contemplating the printed page he experiences an 'uncomfortable vision of all words as line. String lying on paper. Impossibility of getting mystery out of this. Words seen as physical things. Pull gently into rows. Want to make them *stand up*.' Each word he sees has 'an image sticking on to it, never a flat word passed over a board like a counter'. He likens a sentence to a 'hairy caterpillar. Taking each segment of his body as a word, the hair on that segment is the vision the poet sees behind it.' There is a synaesthetic quality to Hulme's imagination. Sentences become worms wriggling on the page. While hymn-singing once he has a vision of music as 'a smooth rolling'. Sound is felt as 'a fluid beaten up by conductor'. In the manuscript of the 'Notes' such observations are often accompanied by small, hurriedly executed sketches of what he is trying to express in words.

Hulme's preoccupation with women and sex is another recurrent feature of the 'Notes':

Watching a woman on the street. Is the idea expressed anything like so –[12]

The two tarts walking along Piccadilly on tiptoe, going home, with hat on back of head. Worry until could find the exact model analogy that will reproduce the extraordinary effect they produce.

Girl hidden in trees passes on other side. How to get this.

Light-haired woman with upturned face in Regent Street.

It is always a passing woman that sets him thinking, never a man. Like Schopenhauer, he was obsessed with the connection between sex and reality and like him found the obsession natural for a philosopher, since human beings are the materialization of sex.

The 'Notes' are less stimulating at points where the suspicion arises that Hulme is writing from a sense of frustration at not being able to discover some logical formula that will enable him to write a novel or play of his own – the trick of it all. Crossed out in the notebook is what looks like an outlined plot for a story: 'mild man doubts his wife's love. Invents a test. Sits at night waiting but she does not come. Waiting for whistle – a light at window.' But even here he is never less than honest with himself. One short section is headed 'Self-delusion':

(i) Whence comes the excitement, the delusion of thinker's creation?
(ii) All inventions spring from the *idea*, e.g. Flaubert and the *purple* bases of Madame Bovary.
(iii) I have a *central* idea like that quite *unworked* out into detail.
(iv) I see a book *worked out* from the same central idea and I unconsciously imagine that I have worked it out myself, and that I could as easily have been the author.
(v) But in the working out is required the multiplicity of detail that I lack. The central idea is nothing.

The nature of his self-appointed task in the 'Notes' he summarizes thus: 'Even my attempt to get to reality (no long words) is in the end only another adjustment of the imaginary toy'; and a graphic expression of his struggle to get to grips with reality and of the sense of wonder investing the struggle is articulated in a solitary, untitled poem:

Over a large table, smooth, he leaned in ecstasies,
In a dream.
He had been to woods, and talked and walked with trees
Had left the world
And brought back round globes and stone images
Of gems, colours, hard and definite.
With these he played, in a dream,
On the smooth table.

Some seven months later, probably early in 1908, Hulme returned to London. From this point onward he becomes if not exactly a public figure then at least a man who gets his name in print because he wants to see it in print and not because he has been hauled before the magistrate at Marlborough Street Court.

*

One of the enigmas of Hulme's personality is that while he could preach the anti-personality doctrines of classicism in art, politics and literature, his way of expressing these views was in itself often very personal. This is true both of his essays intended for publication and of his notes. So if we know that the few months spent travelling and working in Canada had been among the most decisive and formative experiences of his life so far, we do so not from the evidence of any surviving letter nor from conversation recalled by a friend, we do so only because Hulme himself mentions Canada twice, in passing, in his writing. Once it is used to illustrate his idea of the universe as a place too vast to submit to any single theory or explanation: 'Formerly, one liked theories because they reduced the world to a single principle. Now the same reason disgusts us. The flats of Canada are incomprehensible on any single theory. The world only comprehensible on the cinder theory.'

The second reference occurred in a talk he gave to a gathering of poets in London in the year of his return. Having survived the pressure from parents and teachers to be 'medicalised' or in some way to exploit his talent for mathematics, he had decided that what he wanted to do was write poetry. In the lecture he described the role Canada had played in his decision:

Speaking of personal matters, the first time I ever felt the necessity or inevitableness of verse, was in the desire to reproduce the peculiar quality of feeling which is induced by the flat spaces and wide horizons of the virgin prairie of western Canada.[13]

Elsewhere one of his notes states that 'the fright of the mind before the unknown created not only the first gods, but also the first art'[14], a perception that seems related to this epiphany in Canada. It is as though his mathematically inclined mind, used to dominating its surroundings by the imposition of logic, suddenly lost its bearings when confronted with the structureless immensities of the Canadian prairie and was compelled to some kind of modesty. And from this experience began the slow formation of a vision of the world as an essentially chaotic place, beyond any but the partial organizing powers of men, which he would spend the remaining nine years of his life refining, working out a constant system of values to accompany it, discovering confirmation of it in his successive studies in the spheres of poetry, philosophy, politics, the plastic arts. It was to be most conclusively confirmed in war, where the shattered mudscapes of Flanders in 1915 would show him what can only have seemed like irrefutable proof of the truth of his understanding.

Canada gave him the fright of the mind which neither his father, his schoolteachers, his university professors nor yet the magistrate at Marlborough Street Court had been able to induce in him. He grew up. And though the date of its composition cannot be established, it is tempting to suppose that the short poem 'Above the Dock' might have been written at about this time, and that in it Hulme was consciously taking leave of his childhood:

> Above the quiet dock in midnight
> Tangled in the tall mast's corded height,
> Hangs the moon. What seemed so far away
> Is but a child's balloon, forgotten after play.

3

The Complete Poetical
Works of T. E. Hulme

The cultural and political scene in London in 1908 was dominated to a striking extent by issues in which Hulme already, through the debating clubs at school and university, had shown a lively interest. Abroad, the Boer War had ended in 1902 but the delicate task of harmonizing relations between South African Boers and Britons was still going on. In Europe, the traditions of 200 years were being altered as the British regarded with growing unease the militarism and expansionist ambitions of Germany and looked with increasing favour on friendly relations with France. At home, Edward VII had been on the throne for seven years and the outstanding features of the political landscape continued to be shaped by the Liberal landslide in the election of 1906. Campbell-Bannerman's Cabinet included David Lloyd George, Sir Edward Grey, Winston Churchill, whose first post this was, and Herbert Asquith, who became Prime Minister on Campbell-Bannerman's resignation in April 1908 on grounds of ill-health, and who remained in office until 1915. Among plans already announced were those to curb the power of the hereditary peers in the House of Lords, which caused constant division between the two Houses over the next three years. The bitterness of the dispute symbolizes the general intensification of class tensions that had taken place since the formation of the Labour Party as the 'Labour Representation Committee' in 1900, and the increasing penetration of liberal and socialist ideas into the middle and upper classes. The Liberal majority turned increasingly to the nascent Labour Party for many of its radical ideas. Mrs Pankhurst's 'Women's Social and Political Union' was formed in 1903 and between 1906 and 1914 campaigned vigorously and often violently for votes for women in another indication of a growing impatience with tradition and the parliamentary process. The issue of tariff reform, first raised in 1903 by Joseph Chamberlain as a way of securing imperial preference for British trade but latterly favouring moderate protection for British industry in the face of severe German competition, was among the contributing factors in the embarrassment of the Conservatives in the 1906 election; but the idea remained a divisive issue after that because of suggestions that money for social reforms be raised in this way. The question of Home Rule for Ireland was another of the government's major concerns. This had been addressed for the first time by Gladstone's bill in 1886, which was defeated in the Commons. A second bill in 1893 passed the Commons but was rejected by the Lords; a third, put to the House in 1912, was ultimately a beneficiary of the Parliament Act of 1911. Anxiety among the Protestants in Ulster that they would be dominated by the Catholics in Dublin led Ireland to the verge of civil war by the time of the bill's third reading in May 1914, but the whole issue was put on hold with the outbreak of the First World War three months later.

In the world of British arts this was above all a golden age of music, with Elgar, Vaughan Williams, Delius, Holst and Frank Bridge all active. Literature more directly reflected the political climate of the times, and in particular two movements. One was the Fabian Society, a pressure group founded in 1886 which derived its name from the Roman general Quintus Fabius Maximus and his tactic of advancing slowly and inexorably rather than dramatically and as a result of direct and possibly fatal confrontation. The society's ultimate aim was a government run on socialist lines and it attracted numerous writers who in greater or lesser degree propagandized for its radical views. The two most outstanding in Hulme's day were H. G. Wells and George Bernard Shaw. The title of Wells's novel *New Worlds for Old*, published in 1908, exemplified the sort of idealism involved.

The other movement was more properly a tendency of the time. The 'Celtic Twilight' aimed to bring about an Irish literary renaissance, to affirm the independence of Celtic culture and to dispel the influence of English literature on the Irish. It was most closely associated with W. B. Yeats, whose collection of folk tales published in 1893 gave the movement its name, and the publications occasioned by the movement caused the great vogue for Irish drama and poetry prevalent in London in the years immediately after the turn of the century. The racial mystique involved was an offshoot of the strong current of interest in mysticism and spiritualism abroad in London at that time exemplified by the popularity of Madame Blavatsky's teachings. Yeats had been a member of her Theosophical Society until he was expelled in 1890, and he was also a member of a related organization known as the Hermetic Students of the Golden Dawn, founded by the same Madame Blavatsky in 1888 and devoted to the cultivation of occult wisdom and magic through the use of the Kabbalah. A striking number of Hulme's friends were London-Irish, and one of the first he made after coming to the capital, the actress Florence Farr, was closely associated with Yeats in his endeavours to prove that the human mind could make and unmake reality and had the power to control the universe. Hulme, it seems safe to say, never suspected for a moment that such a thing might be possible. But many of his friends apparently did, just as many of them believed in the socialism of the Fabians. Indeed, the political aims of Fabianism and the grandiose spiritual ambition represented by the very existence of a group calling itself the Hermetic Students of the Golden Dawn together formed an atmosphere of idealism the air of which Hulme must have breathed every day of his life after settling in London, and against which he came to pose, with increasing ferocity, a scepticism that would lead him as far as possible in the opposite direction.

Hulme took a room at 100 Sidney Street in Chelsea and began writing poetry himself. For financial support he was dependent on an allowance from his wealthy aunt, Alice Pattinson. Unlike his father, she believed in his talent and his potential. Always a social man, he joined the Poets' Club, an organization headed by a Scottish banker named Henry Simpson. Henry, later Sir Henry, Newbolt, the popular composer of patriotic and nautical verse such as 'Drake's Drum', was joint-president with Simpson; no doubt it was the lustre of Newbolt's name that earned the club a mention in the London press and enabled it to attract guest speakers of the calibre of G. K. Chesterton. Hulme became their honorary secretary and was, according to Simpson, 'an extremely trying one'.[1] Nevertheless it was Hulme, with his organizational talents, who was given the task of drawing up a 'Proposal' for a set of rules to govern the running of the club that showed everywhere his unromantic preoccupation with time and money and his clear understanding of the need of poets for discipline:

RULES 1908

1. The Club shall be called the 'Poets' Club', and shall consist of not more than fifty members.

2. The officers of the Club shall be a President, a Vice-President, the Hon. Secretary, and the Hon. Treasurer.

3. The committee shall consist of five members, including the officers of the Club.

4. The Club shall meet to dine once a month, July, August and September excepted. The place of the meeting to be the United Arts club (above Rumpelmeyer's), 10, St James Street, S.W. The price of the dinner to be 3/6, but members who fail to be present after signifying their intentions to do so, shall incur a fine of half the price of the dinner.

5. After dinner:
   (i) The Chairman shall invite members of the Club to read original compositions in verse.
   (ii) There shall follow a paper on a subject connected with poetry by a member or guest of the Club, its delivery being limited to twenty minutes.

6. At the conclusion of the paper, the subject shall be open for discussion by all present, speeches not to last more than five minutes. No member shall speak more than once unless called upon by the Chairman.

7. The Club shall endeavour to promote the publication of the poems of such of its members as shall be deemed to possess exceptional merit.

8. Members shall give three days notice to the Hon. Secretary of their intention to be present at a dinner.

9. Each member shall be entitled to bring two guests to each dinner.

10. Once in each year, at least, there shall be a general business meeting of the Club.

11. The Annual Subscription for membership shall be 5/-, payable upon joining, and in January of each year. Members more than two months in arrears shall not receive notice of the monthly meeting.

12. The election of new members shall be in the hands of the committee. All candidates to be proposed and seconded by members of the Club.

St James's Street was in the very heart of London's clubland: the Thatched House Club, the Conservative Club, the Carlton, Arthur's, Brooks's, Boodle's and White's all had premises there. The United Arts Club, where the poets were to meet, shared No. 10 with the Junior Army and Navy Club.

Hulme's 'Lecture on Modern Poetry', not published until 1938, was probably delivered there in November 1908, and this may have been the first occasion on which his trenchant North Staffordshire voice was heard in public. Hulme was proud of the accent, and proud of the fact that Dr Johnson, whom he considered the greatest scholar in England, came from the same area. When he interrupted performances at the Cambridge New Theatre in 1904 to correct the pronunciation of the actors it is likely he was hoping to persuade them to adopt a diction more like his own.

Later accounts of other lectures describe Hulme's stage presence as poor and mumbling, in striking contrast to the articulate and persuasive flow of his private conversation. According to Wyndham Lewis he was 'a very large and imposing man, well over six foot, broad-shouldered and with legs like a racing cyclist. He had an extremely fine head, which it was his habit to hold on one side, as if listening (a bird-like attitude) really rather reminiscent of an antique bust.' His lecturing manner, however, was 'crabbed and harsh to the last degree, and rendered grotesque by the sort of accent that has made the fortune of Gracie Fields'.[2] His pronunciation of the word 'art' particularly amused Lewis, sounding as though it were 'wrung out of his mouth' and giving it a 'nonsensical quality to the English ear'. Perhaps suspecting that many of his London listeners would find him the same sort of bucolic curiosity as Lewis, Hulme seems to have played up to it, using the direct and earthy image of the farmyard to make his first point:

I want to begin by a statement of the attitude I take towards verse. I do that in order to anticipate criticism. I shall speak of verse from a certain rather low but quite definite level, and I think that criticism ought to be confined to that level. The point of view is that verse is simply and solely the means of expression. I will give you an example of a position exactly opposite to the one I take up. A reviewer writing in the *Saturday Review* last week spoke of poetry as the means by which the soul soared into higher regions, and as a means of expression by which it became merged into a higher kind of reality. Well, that is the kind of statement that I utterly detest. I want to speak of verse in a plain way as I would of pigs: that is the only honest way. The President told us last week that poetry was akin to religion. It is nothing of the sort. It is a means of expression just as prose is and if you can't justify it from that point of view it's not worth preserving.[3]

Before settling down to a simple and forthright account of his vision of what poetry should be he goes on to use about five minutes of his allotted twenty to make further gruff threats:

I have not a catholic taste but a violently personal and prejudiced one. I have no reverence for tradition. I came to the subject of verse from the inside rather than the outside. There were certain impressions which I wanted to fix. I read verse to find models but I could not find any that seemed exactly suitable to express that kind of impression, except perhaps a few jerky rhythms of Henley . . .

And in a final pre-empting flourish he warns his fellow-poets that 'I don't want any literary criticism, that would be talking on another level. I don't want to be killed with a bludgeon and references to Dante, Milton and the rest of them.'

The lecture proper then proceeds with a logically constructed theory of why poetry thrives at certain times and not at others. Hulme's explanation, in which he leans heavily on an account given by the French poet Gustave Kahn in 1897,[4] is that the cycle is connected with the appearance of a new poetic form which attracts people to its use, like a new toy, or a new dress for a girl. After a while the new form itself is exhausted and ceases to attract practitioners and the search for a replacement must begin.

The purpose of his lecture is to announce that he has discovered such a replacement for outworn forms in *vers libre*, a form born in France out of the decay of the verse style associated with Monde, Sully-Prudhomme and others of the Parnassian school of the second half of the nineteenth century. Again adapting a description from Kahn, Hulme characterizes the principles of the new school as 'the denial of a regular number of syllables as the basis of versification.

The length of the line is long and short, oscillating with images used by the poet; it follows the contour of his thought and is free rather than regular.' Some three years after this lecture, in a review of a book by Tancrède de Visan entitled *L'Attitude du lyrisme contemporain*, Hulme mentions having read in about 1905 or 1906 André de Beaunier's *La Poésie nouvelle*, published in Paris in 1902, which introduced him to the work of a number of poets including Kahn, Laforgue and Rimbaud whom he credited with a revitalization of French poetry which took place between 1885 and the turn of the twentieth century.[5] In addition to preferring *vers libre* to metric regularity the other defining characteristic of this school was, says Hulme, their preference for the symbol, in contrast to the Parnassian cultivation of a precise and clear description of external things. Returning to Kahn for the genealogy, he traced the life-cycle of such symbols or images: born in poetry they descend into prose and finally die 'a long lingering death in journalists' English'.

The ancients accepted that all was flux, he continues, but finding the flux fearful they fell into the trap of trying to create an art which would stand outside time. They caught 'the disease, the passion for immortality'. His analysis leads him to attack the recurring spectre of an *ars perfecta*:

Now the whole trend of the modern spirit is away from that; philosophers no longer believe in absolute truth. We no longer believe in perfection, either in verse or in thought. We shall no longer strive to attain the absolutely perfect form in poetry. Instead of these minute perfections of words and phrases, the tendency will be rather towards the production of a general effect; this of course takes away the predominance of metre and a regular number of syllables as the element of perfection in words. We are no longer concerned that stanzas shall be shaped and polished like gems, but rather that some vague mood shall be communicated. In all the arts we seek for the maximum of individual and personal expression, rather than for the attainment of any absolute beauty.

One newspaper, he mentions, had described their club as a present-day version of the Mermaid Club that met in Elizabethan times at the Mermaid Tavern in Friday Street and included Shakespeare, John Donne and Ben Jonson among its members. But they were not mere revivalists, he objected: 'We are a number of modern people and verse must be justified as a means of expression for us.' He called his a 'standpoint of extreme modernism', maintaining that poets now were writing a poetry that was finished with heroic action and had become modest and introspective, and quoting with approval Chesterton's observation that where once poetry dealt with the Siege of Troy, its task now was to express the emotions of a boy fishing. For poets who were attempting to capture and convey a fleeting and momentarily glimpsed impression of reality, a 'tentative and half-shy manner of looking at things', to use regular metres would be like forcing a child into a suit of armour. Although he calls for a new poetry his grounds are pragmatic, not romantic, and he makes no attempt to back his call with a claim that the new will be in some absolute sense 'superior' to the old. It will only do a more efficient job of communicating contemporary reality.

But if there is innate pessimism and perhaps even a hint of regret in Hulme's analysis, these defer to his stoic acceptance of the changed state of things. And while he dismisses entirely the club president's claim that poetry is 'akin to religion' he holds it in high regard for a different reason: that poetry is the direct language from which the indirect language of prose feeds.

As he enters the last of his twenty minutes he brings his lecture to a close:

A shell is a very suitable covering for the egg at a certain period of its career, but very unsuitable at a later age. This seems to me to represent fairly well the state of verse at the present time. While the shell remains the same, the inside character is entirely changed. It is not addled as a pessimist might say, but has become alive, it has changed from the ancient art of chanting to the modern impressionist, but the mechanism of verse has remained the same. It can't go on doing so. I will conclude, ladies and gentlemen, by saying that the shell must be broken.

In January 1909 members of the Poets' Club produced a small booklet of verse, *For Christmas MDCCCCVIII*. Hulme was represented by 'Autumn' and 'A City Sunset'. In a hastily scribbled note to his Aunt Alice in Macclesfield, datable to December from the reference to Robert Ross's[6] dinner, he wrote:

Dear A

I have been very busy this week and so unable to write but will write tomorrow. Have two things to tell you about

    1) the dinner to Rob. Ross

    2) lecture by Padraic Colum at the Irish Literary Society.

I'm hoping that you will have sent my allowance on *Monday* as if you haven't I shall have nothing at all. The poem I finally sent in is on the other page. Feeling very restless, can't write tonight, will tomorrow. But do send allowance at once.

Yrs E

The poem 'on the other page' was 'A City Sunset':

> Alluring, Earth seducing, with high conceits
> is the sunset that reigns
> at the end of westward streets . . .
> A sudden flaring sky
> troubling strangely the passer by
> with visions, alien to long streets, of Cytharea
> or the smooth flesh of Lady Castlemaine . . .
> A frolic of crimson
> is the spreading glory of the sky,
> heaven's jocund maid
> flaunting a trailed red robe
> along the fretted city roofs
> about the time of homeward going crowds
> – a vain maid, lingering, loth to go . . .[7]

There are a number of drafts of this poem. What must be one of the earliest begins

> Earth seducing, with high conceits
> is the sunset. Thaumaturgic, presenting . . .
> at the end of westward streets
> a sudden flaring sky
> troubling strangely the passer by

Lower down it has

> A frolic of crimson
> is the glory of the sky, erubescent
> Heaven's wanton, clothed provocative
> with meshed wind rippled scarves of carmin'd cirrus

and the almost wilfully lugubrious vocabulary shows how far Hulme was prepared to range in his experimenting before finally settling on the version that was published. What is unusual about 'A City Sunset' is not the syntax, which remains too striking to accord with his own theories, but the theme, which reflects them well, being a wilfully provocative 'attack' on the sentimental exaltation of the sunset by poets throughout the ages. In his desire to maintain his poetic consciousness at a 'low but quite definite level' Hulme experimented elsewhere with such inversions of the clichés of romance. Seen against the background of a cloud, for example, the lark is not for him the ascending miracle of Meredith and Vaughan Williams but a thing that 'crawls on the cloud/Like a flea on white body'. He wrote a second, rather better poem than this, in only partial censure of the sunset, which he did not choose to publish in his lifetime. This version of 'I love not the Sunset' was written on the back of a bill from the Grosvenor Hotel made out to a family friend, Madame Meylan, on 26 May 1908:

> I love not the Sunset
> That flaunts like a scarlet sore
> O'er half a sick sky,
> That calls aloud for all to gape
> At its beauty
> Like a wanton
>
> But Sunset when the sun comes home
> Like a ship from the sea
> With its round red sail
> Shadowed against a clear sky,
> Silent, in a cool harbour
> At eve,
> After labour.

'Autumn', probably the earliest of Hulme's poems, is more clearly than 'A City Sunset' a demonstration of his theories:

A touch of cold in the Autumn night –
I walked abroad,
And saw the ruddy moon lean over a hedge
Like a red-faced farmer.
I did not stop to speak, but nodded,
And round about were the wistful stars
With white faces like town children.

With its strongly visual content 'Autumn' is a good example of where Hulme deviated from Gustave Kahn in his use of *vers libre*. Kahn's aim in breaking from regular metre was to leave the poet free to find a rhythm that was original, individual and personally satisfying. Hulme seems to have been less concerned with cultivating the individuality of the poet. He sought, as he said in his lecture, a poetry that 'appeals to the eye rather than the ear. It has to mould images, a kind of spiritual clay, into definite shapes. This material is [. . .] image and not sound. It builds up a plastic image which it hands over to the reader, whereas the old art endeavoured to influence him physically by the hypnotic effect of rhythm.'[8] Prophetically, he described the new verse he was trying to create as resembling 'sculpture rather than music'. In a surviving variant of 'Autumn'[9] the sole significant difference is the omission in the penultimate line of 'wistful', which is the only emotive word in the poem. Both versions seem to work, the variant requiring only a longer vowel in 'stars' which would have sounded quite natural to Hulme's Staffordshire ear. The communication of reality is quick and direct; we hear the sound of the poet's footsteps along the country lane and see his breath vaporize in the moonlight. There is a childlike simplicity to 'Autumn', an obscure but pleasing sense of contentment, and a tiny symbol of the thought behind Hulme's whole intellectual project in the modest simile with which he closes the poem, regathering stars from the infinity to which generations of romantic poets have scattered them and holding them firmly in the cup of a human hand.

Besides Hulme's contributions to the Christmas volume there were two poems by Selwyn Image, six by Lady Margaret Sackville, four by Henry Simpson, one by Marion Cram, six by F. W. Tancred and two by Hulme's Cambridge friend Dermot Freyer. Francis Tancred's

'A Brief Account of Myself' was both a brief account of himself and a rollicking celebration of his fellow club-members, including Hulme:

> With Phoebus and Favonian Hulme in league
> I keep frail bliss, unchequered by fatigue.
> Now in my Burlington twill waistcoat dressed,
> courting the ladies with punctilious zest.

The publication was reviewed in the pages of *The New Age* by F. S. Flint, a young London poet familiar with the literature of ten different languages, with a special interest in modern French verse. Flint was scathing both about the club and its booklet. The other main subject of his review was a two-volume edition of *Poètes d'Aujourd'hui* and he used the French poets to bludgeon the English. *Poètes d'Aujourd'hui* was 'the flower of thirty or more years' conscious and ardent artistic effort, the work of pioneers, iconoclasts, craftsmen and artists who fought for their art against ridicule, who chose even ludicrous names to isolate themselves in their art, and who listened week by week to the noble phrases and philosophies of the Maître, Stéphane Mallarmé'. The Poets' Club was, by comparison, 'apparently a dining-club and after-dinner discussion association. Evening dress is, I believe, the correct uniform; and correct persons – professors, I am told! – lecture portentously to the band of happy and replete rhymesters – and one or two poets, accidentals.' In the mandarin tone of youth (he was twenty-three, Hulme twenty-four) Flint singled out Lady Margaret Sackville's lush verses as 'the most notable poems – almost the only poetry' in the entire collection. 'Autumn' was patronized in passing as a 'quaint conceit'. 'I think of this club and its after-dinner ratiocinations,' he continued, 'its tea-parties in "suave South Audley Street"; and then of Verlaine at the Hôtel de Ville, with his hat on the peg, as a proof of his presence, but he himself in a café hard by with other poets, conning feverishly and excitedly the mysteries of their craft – and I laugh.' His damning conclusion was that 'the Poets' Club is death'.

Hulme's response appeared in *The New Age* the following week, 18 February 1909:

BELATED ROMANTICISM

When Mr Flint compares the unclassed lyric assembly of the Poets' Club with that of Verlaine and his companions in obscure (sic) cafés – he laughs. I can hear that laugh: sardonic, superior, and rather young.

When, oh when, shall we finish sentimentalising about French poets in cafés! One hoped that with Mr George Moore's entry into middle-age the end of it was nigh. But now comes Mr Flint, a belated romantic born out of due time, to carry on the mythical tradition of the poètes maudits. Nurtured on Mürger, he is obsessed by the illusion that poets must be addicted to circean excess and discoloured linen.

With all the sentimentality of an orthodox suburban, he dwells with pathetic fondness on perfectly ordinary habits, and with great awe reminds us how Verlaine hung his hat on a peg. We, like Verlaine, are natural. It was natural for a Frenchman to frequent cafés. It would be dangerous as well as affected for us to recite verse in a saloon bar.

Mr Flint speaks with fine scorn of evening dress. It is time to protest against this exclusiveness of the Bohemian, that exotic creature of rare and delicate growth. Why should we be treated as outcasts by the new aristocracy of one suit?

Historically, Mr Flint is inaccurate. The founders of the modern 'vers libres' were Kahn and Laforgue, the latter a court functionary 'épris de ton londonien,' Kahn entertained at a banquet where Mallarmé (alas for the granitic flint) in evening dress formally proposed his health.

I hereby invite Mr Flint to come to the next dinner, on the 23rd, in any costume that suits him best, when that 'correct person' – Professor G. K. Chesterton – will lecture 'portentously'.

T. E. Hulme, M.P.C.

Café Tour d'Eiffel.

Flint was unrepentant. His short rejoinder to the letters column of *The New Age* concluded:

A tree is known by its fruit, and the Poets' Club seems to be able to manage no more than an occasional poem, and then only by grafting. I advise the members to go on eating.

Despite the tone of his reply, Hulme seems to have been impressed by what Flint had to say and he made it his business to contact him privately almost at once. The two struck up the friendship that marks

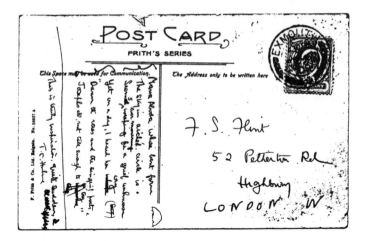

A draft of 'Mana Aboda'. Hulme and Flint were the prime movers in the short-lived Poets' Club, where there was, in Flint's phrase, 'A lot of talk and practice [. . .] of what we called the Image'.

the real beginnings of the 'breakaway' group of the Poets' Club of 1909, the group that seceded from Simpson's club to form the more informal organization that is probably the one Flint was referring to in his well-known but confusing 'History of Imagism', published in the *Egoist* on 1 May 1915. There he recalled an evening 'somewhere in the gloom of the year 1908' when Hulme, 'excited by the propinquity, at a half-crown dance, of the other sex [. . .] proposed to a companion that they should found a Poets' Club. The thing was done, there and then.'

Hulme's first letter to Flint invited him to call at No. 5 Inverness Place, off Queen's Road in Bayswater, where he was lodging by then, and enclosing a little map showing the nearby station at Queen's Road:

Dear Mr Flint

It struck me after I left you that perhaps Sunday afternoon about 4 would suit you better than Tuesday next. If so could you let me know. If you have a copy of the book of verse by 'Storer' (in loose metres) that you reviewed some time ago, could you bring it along, as I've never been able to see it anywhere.

Yours sincerely
T. E. Hulme

And while he was still addressing him formally as 'Mr Flint' he had asked him to come along to the Tour d'Eiffel at seven-thirty on Thursday, assuring him that there would be 'only poets this time' and promising him Ernest Radford, Ernest Rhys, Seosamh Mac-Cathmhaoil, Storer (whom he seems to have hunted up himself) as well as '4 or 5 other versers'.

Gathering for the first time on 25 March 1909 Hulme, Flint, Storer, Tancred and MacCathmhaoil, whom the others presently referred to as Joseph Campbell, the English form of his name, along with Dermot Freyer and Florence Farr, the actress, poet and mystic, were soon meeting regularly at the Tour d'Eiffel on Percy Street, off Tottenham Court Road. With the exception of Miss Farr, who was almost fifty, all were in their mid-twenties. Others who were intermittently present at what was essentially the birth of the Imagist movement in modern poetry were Desmond Fitzgerald and Padraic Colum. The bond that united them was dissatisfaction with the poetry then being written.

Besides these regular Thursday evenings the group frequently met, always at Hulme's initiative, at the premises of the London branch of Yeats and Rolleston's Irish Literary Society, at 20 Hanover Square in Mayfair, a choice of venue probably explained by the fact that Freyer, Farr, Colum, Campbell and Fitzgerald were all Irish: 'Could you come up to tea Sat. I.L.S at 4-30. There will be several people up there,' he writes to Flint, asking him to pass the message on to Storer and telling him that 'Miss Farr is back and I'm asking her up.'

In another card he tells Flint, 'I showed your poem to Miss Farr. She liked the line about poppies', and Florence Farr's presence and Hulme's obvious concern for her interest and opinion are indicative of the open nature of the group. Farr was one of the original New Women of the 1890s, an actress who had played the leading role in plays by well-known champions of women's rights such as Ibsen and Shaw. She had advanced ideas on the political and sexual rights of women, and took many lovers. Although creatively a revolutionary Hulme was a conservative in social matters and his views on most issues concerning the role of women in society would have been quite unlike hers. Apart from the fact that he simply liked her, the attraction for Hulme might have been her celebrity and her closeness to Yeats, Shaw and other members of the fashionable Irish literary presence in

London, something that would have given him and his young friends a sense of being, however peripherally, a part of what was happening in the capital.

There was evidently a real workshop atmosphere to these club sessions and friendships, a pooling of intelligence and talent and a determination not to let oversensitivity get in the way of useful criticism. Enclosing a batch of new poems for Flint to look at, Hulme asked, 'Could you suggest any improvement?', and urged him to be completely honest in his response: 'If you think what I've sent is rot (the enclosed poems I mean) just say so. Tancred says one is. So should be confirmation.'

Flint later recalled how Tancred and Hulme 'used to spend hours each day in the search for the right phrase'.[10] They studied the techniques of *vers libre*[11] and *haiku* as well as Chinese poetry. The title of one of Tancred's six contributions to the first Poets' Club booklet, 'On finding Selwyn Image not at home when calling upon him at lunch' is a direct echo of Li Po's 'On visiting a Taoist master in the Tai-T'ien mountains and not finding him home'. All of them wrote *haiku*, while Campbell specialized in poems in a sacred Hebrew form, and Hulme pursued the path of rhymeless verse.

The question of plagiarism came up for discussion several times. Hulme, who in his lecture on poetry had freely and without accreditation borrowed the words of Gustave Kahn when these seemed to him to express beyond improvement exactly what he was trying to say himself, took a relaxed view of the problem, assuming that all writers are guilty of it at one time or another, consciously or unconsciously. During a stay in Exmouth in the autumn of 1909 he wrote a letter to Flint referring to an article he was writing on Campbell (apparently for use in Flint's own *New Age* poetry column):

I don't think I shall say anything about Campbell and my poem for the reason he may not have intended [it]. From my knowledge of Campbell I should say he imitates everyone. I came up to the I.L.S. one afternoon with a new pair of a particular kind of brown boots, and the very next day Campbell had on a new pair of the same kind.

He went on to point out that in one of Flint's own recent poems the phrase 'sounds echoing in your head' occurred:

I looked through the famous note-book that contains the stack of my poems and saw one written at Hampton Ct. about 2½ years ago:

> Round the pillars of my head, the sound
> Echoes and eddies
> By then a young and bloody

– and so on. Now I didn't imitate you and you didn't imitate me, for you hadn't seen it. So poor old Campbell.

And to make the point absolutely clear he quoted from a poem of his, begun some time ago, 'called it "Young Sex" or Puberty, something of that kind', which included the line 'Mirage – in the cool caves of your eyes I rest'. Having recently bought a copy of Shakespeare's sonnets he had come across several that were new to him, including one which seemed to express exactly the same idea. If he ever got around to finishing it, he wondered, would he be obliged to call it 'Homage to Sonnet CLI'?[12]

He found the trip to Exmouth stimulating and productive and attributed his industry to the fact that it was so very cold down there. He jotted down an inspiration for Flint on 'your favourite subject of the stars': 'And shall the stars smell sweet/ As an August clover field' and sent it to him with the question, 'shall I continue?' He also advised him that a man called Wills, connected with the family who made Woodbine cigarettes, was reviving *The Thrush*. This was a magazine that had appeared briefly in 1901 and was now, greatly to Hulme's surprise, apparently willing to pay for poetry.

Only a month lafter the inaugural meeting, on 22 April, the group was joined by Ezra Pound, who was then twenty-four years old. Pound had been in Europe since 1908 and already published two volumes of poetry, *A lume spento* at his own expense in June 1908, and *Personae* in April 1909. Through his friendship with Ford Madox Hueffer (later Ford) and W. B. Yeats he was already a familiar figure on the London literary scene. What he brought to the club was a thorough knowledge of the traditions of European and especially medieval French poetry. What he derived from it was a jolt to his assumption that not much of the French poetry after Ronsard was worth bothering about. Flint recalled that 'he was very full of his *troubadours*; but I do not remember that he did more than attempt to illustrate (or refute) our theories occasionally with their example'.

Pound's poetry in the days of *A lume spento* was as flamboyant as his personal style and he and Hulme probably found each other equally exotic. In Hulme he saw 'the outward image of a Yorkshire farmer – the Pickwickian Englishman who starts a club'.[13] What impressed him most was Hulme's 'solidity, honesty – determination to get at the facts. He never dodged fact, never kidded himself; even Santayana wasn't so free of bunkum.' If Yeats discovered a phrase he liked he would shift his ideas to fit it. Hulme, by comparison, was intellectually uncompromising. Pound's characterizations of other members of the Eiffel Tower group were brusque.[14] Flint he called 'the last pastoral mind in a Cockney body, the Keatsian ideal, but without the grip'; Francis Tancred was Hulme's 'creature' ('Hulme thought he had invented Tancred – he could have had no prior existence') and a 'satellite', as were Flint, Storer (nicknamed Custard) and Joseph Campbell. Neither Padraic Colum nor Desmond Fitzgerald (father of Dr Garret Fitzgerald) who later joined Sinn Fein and was, according to Pound, 'the only martyr of the Troubles not shot', was a member of this class. Hulme was a firm opponent of Home Rule for Ireland and he and Fitzgerald must have had many political discussions on the subject. Pound wrote a canto to the two of them entitled 'To Hulme (T. E.) and Fitzgerald (A Certain)' that seems to have little to do with either man and uses, for some reason, an extremely well-caught Scottish voice.

Hulme wanted a poetry that was intimate and half-shy and composed to be read in private. Pound did not, and on his first evening with them at Percy Street he roared out 'Sestina: Altaforte' until the tables shook and the cutlery rattled and the proprietor, Mr Stulik, had to place a screen around them for the protection of the other diners. Yet despite the great differences between them these two strong personalities remained on civil terms until not long before Hulme's death, when a quarrel over the complexities of the sculptor Henri Gaudier-Brzeska's estate, involving the two of them and Sophie Gaudier-Brzeska, wearied Hulme out of the relationship. Pound felt Hulme's greatest quality was that he never treated an inferior as an equal, and certainly Hulme did not find it easy to respect people. He was once asked for how much longer he would be willing to put up with Pound and replied that he knew exactly when he would have to kick him downstairs.[15] He never did kick him downstairs, but was on occasions capable of a low-key sarcasm to which Pound seemed oblivious. By his own account Pound 'spoke to him one day of the difference between Guido [Cavalcanti]'s precise interpretative metaphor, and the Petrarchian fustian and ornament, pointing out that Guido thought in accurate terms; that the phrases correspond to definite sensations undergone'. Hulme 'took some time over it in silence', and then finally said: 'That is very interesting. That is more interesting than anything ever said to me. It is more interesting than anything I ever read in a book.'[16] Hulme was not anti-intellectual, but Pound did not wear his learning lightly.

The Poets' Club published a second volume of the group's verse at Christmas 1909, to which both Flint and Pound contributed. Hulme was represented by 'The Embankment' and 'Conversion'.

'The Embankment' makes good use of an image that seems to have occurred to Hulme for the first time while in Canada. It appears in his notes as:

> Somewhere the gods (the blanket-makers in the prairie of cold)
> Sleep in their blankets

In 'The Embankment' he gives it a human context, subtitling the verse 'The fantasia of a fallen gentleman on a cold, bitter night':

> Once, in finesse of fiddles found I ecstasy,
> In the flash of gold heels on the hard pavement.
> Now see I
> That warmth's the very stuff of poesy.
> Oh God, make small
> The old star-eaten blanket of the sky
> That I may fold it round me and in comfort lie.

Much of the literary-historical interest around 'The Embankment' concerns the extent to which Pound was involved in its composition, specifically in the making of its second line. The version actually printed in *The Book of the Poets' Club* had 'the pavement grey'. By the time the poem reappeared in *The New Age* of 25 January 1912 this had evolved to 'pavement hard', and in the version printed as an

Appendix to Pound's *Ripostes* in October of the same year to 'hard pavement'. Of these, 'grey' picks up 'gold', but does so weakly, while 'hard' shifts the reading weight back on to 'heels' but is too far removed from it. The right effect does not emerge until the reversal of the old-fashioned inversion. Several writers on Hulme have suggested that Pound was responsible for this improvement[17] and that with 'grey' Hulme had been following Yeats in 'The Lake Isle of Innisfree' ('While I stand on the roadway, or on the pavements grey') until the more modernist sensibilities of Pound prevailed. Pound's recollections on the score are several. In a letter to Michael Roberts in 1937 he wrote, 'I was learning how Yeats did it. I believe that T.E.H. (if you dig up ms/you can verify) referred in verse to "the pavement grey" or gray, don't remember his spelling,'[18] which suggests that Pound was responsible not for 'hard' but for 'grey'. This interpretation seems to be confirmed in the note Pound wrote about the matter to Samuel Hynes in 1954:[19] 'Believe he resisted gray pavements/which I wanted.'[20] Whatever the exact facts of the matter, Pound had a strong sense of the individuality of Hulme's voice. In a BBC radio interview with D. G. Bridson in 1959 the conversation turned to Hulme. Pound said:

I came on six lines of Hulme's the other day – no importance unless you think that it is important that a guy who left only a few pages of poetry should have a style so unmistakable that you come on it and know that it's Hulme's.[21]

James Frazer's comment that 'no person or subject was numinous to Hulme' is borne out by 'Conversion'. Like 'A City Sunset' it takes the form of an unexpected and startling attack on Beauty. The early draft is little more than a bald expression of the idea itself:

> I walked into the wood in June
> And suddenly Beauty, like a thick scented veil,
> Stifled me,
> Tripping me up, tight round my limbs,
> Arrested me.

An intermediary stage was recorded from memory ('the poem runs something like this') in a note to an unknown recipient, possibly Alice Pattinson:

I walked into the valley wood –
in the time of hyacinths.
Sudden Beauty, like a scented cloth
(Thrown or Cast) over me. Stifled me, and tripped me up.

Now go I to the final river
Ignominiously in a sack
As any peeping Turk to the Bosphorus.[22]

In its final form this becomes the considerably more sophisticated:

Lighthearted I walked into the valley wood
In the time of hyacinths,
Till beauty like a scented cloth
Cast over, stifled me. I was bound
Motionless and faint of breath
By loveliness that is her own eunuch.
Now pass I to the final river
Ignominiously, in a sack, without sound,
As any peeping Turk to the Bosphorus.

Despite the archaic reference to a form of execution in the final line, 'Conversion' seems to have something of the same modernist horror of Nature as Munch's 'Scream' does. But Hulme was not neurotic and his target was not beauty itself but the kitsch and almost pornographic appreciation of beauty, the onanistic way in which we will visit beauty in order to excite our aesthetic sensitivies. Eliot's longer poem on a similar theme, 'The Death of St Narcissus', was inspired by a reading of Hulme's verse.

'Autumn', 'Above the Dock' and arguably 'The Embankment' all show a formal correspondence with Hulme's expressed theories of the way poetry should be written. In 'Conversion' and in 'Mana Aboda', the last of the five poems that make up the legendary 'Complete Poetical Works', he was more concerned to make a provocative aesthetic point. 'Mana Aboda' was another product of that chilly sojourn in Exmouth in late 1909. On 7 September 1909 Hulme sent an early draft of it on a postcard to Flint:

> Mana Aboda whose bent form
> The sky in archéd circle is
> Seems ever mourning for a grief unknown
> Yet on a day, I heard her cry
> 'Damn the roses and the singing poets
> Josephs all, not tall enough to try.'

'This is truly inspiration, quite sudden,' he added at the bottom, and the crossings out and emendations make it impossible to doubt him. The revised version published in *The New Age* in January 1912 was prefaced with a statement that made the attack on the abuse of the beauty-instinct quite specific:

Beauty is the marking-time, the stationary vibration, the feigned ecstasy of an arrested impulse unable to reach its natural end.

> Mana Aboda[23], whose bent form
> The sky in archèd circle is,
> Seems ever for an unknown grief to mourn.
> Yet on a day I heard her cry:
> 'I weary of the roses and the singing poets –
> Josephs all, not tall enough to try.'

Although by no means all of the poetry that Hulme wrote, these four verses – 'Autumn', 'Mana Aboda', 'The Embankment' and 'Conversion', along with 'Above the Dock' – were all that he cared to see in print. He seems to have lost most of his interest in the writing of poetry after this, though not in poetry itself. A passing reference in one of his 'Notes on Bergson' in February 1912 suggests he might have become disillusioned with the whole notion of a poetic revolution by that time, at least where such a revolution was predicated on the idea that a 'glorious new kind of poetry' might emerge if only poets could 'emancipate' themselves from the 'hampering restrictions of rhyme, metre and form generally'.[24] Adapting Burke's dictum that the restraints on men as well as their liberties are to be reckoned among their rights, Hulme seemed by then to be urging that it was a romantic pathology among poets to regard as restricting rather than liberating the discipline imposed by formalities such as rhyme, metre and form. In July 1912, by which time his analytic interest in the spirit of his own times had expanded to include philosophy and art, he delivered a lecture in Clifford's Inn Hall on 'The New Philosophy of Art as Illustrated in Poetry';[25] but by that time the sub-section of the Poets' Club known variously as 'the Secession Club', 'the School of Images' and 'the Forgotten School of 1909' had already, in Frank Flint's words, 'died a lingering death at the end of its second winter'. Hulme's intellectual enthusiasms were in the end probably simply too various to be contained by a poetry group, and it was left to the dedicated poets Flint and Pound to advance the specific and technical ideas of the movement elsewhere.

*

'The covers of a book are responsible for much error,' Hulme noted in 'Cinders'. 'They set a limit round certain convenient groups of ideas, when really there are no limits.' Something similar might be said of names of movements in art and literature generally, but from a member's point of view a movement in art has two important practical functions that outweigh the constrictions of belonging. The first is to allow it to identify and explain itself to a public that is often indifferent and downright baffled; and the second is to provide support in the face of conventional critical hostility. At one time or another Imagism thus provided a safe haven for poets as various as Pound, Amy Lowell, Marianne Moore, D. H. Lawrence, H. D., Richard Aldington, F. S. Flint and William Carlos Williams. Every such movement needs a leader with enough vision and self-assurance to hold it together long enough to carry through its break with tradition, and in its infancy Imagism had such a figure in Hulme. Whether it was an Imagist poem or not is neither here nor there; 'Mana Aboda' with its cool disdain for the 'singing poets' of tradition was a challenge and a rousing call to arms to all younger poets to break with the outworn gestures of romanticism and start creating something for their own time.

Hulme, though he never used the word himself, was Imagism's catalyst. In his 1915 article in the *Egoist*, published after the appearance in 1914 of *Des Imagistes*, the first anthology of overtly Imagist poetry, Flint was concerned to establish the order of precedence in the history of the Imagist movement: 'In all of this,' he wrote, referring to the discussions of the role of the image, the experimentation with form, and the analyses and dissections of each other's verse, 'Hulme was the ringleader. He insisted too on absolutely accurate presentation and no verbiage. [. . .] There was also a lot of talk and practice among us, Storer leading it chiefly, of what we called the Image. We were very much influenced by modern French symbolist poetry.'

It was Pound, with his sharp journalistic instinct, who imported the word into the language in the spring of 1912 in its French form, *imagistes*, largely as a way of promoting the poetry of Richard Aldington and H.D. to Harriet Monroe's magazine *Poetry*. Later that same year he used the word again in the foreword to a selection of his verse entitled *Ripostes*, where he explained that he was reproducing Hulme's five poems 'for good fellowship' and because they recalled 'certain evenings and meetings' with Hulme and his friends in the Tour d'Eiffel café. 'As for the future,' he prophesied, 'Les Imagistes, the descendants of the forgotten school of 1909, have that in their keeping.' Flint had followed Pound into the new group and in 1913 formulated the three tenets of Imagism, all of which agree closely with his own account of how Hulme led the discussions of that 'forgotten school of 1909':

1. Direct treatment of the 'thing', whether subjective or objective.
2. To use absolutely no word that does not contribute to the presentation.
3. As regarding rhythm: to compose in the sequence of the musical phrase, not in sequence of a metronome.

These Imagists proper produced four annual anthologies between 1914 and 1917, a Manifesto in 1915, and a final nostalgic fifth volume in 1930. Yet the movement has acquired an importance out of proportion to the quantity of its productions, not least because of the critical belief articulated by T. S. Eliot in 1953 that 'the *point de repère* usually and conveniently taken as the starting-point of modern poetry is the group denominated "imagists" in London about 1910'.[26] At its simplest level this is a way of saying that up until about 1910 all poetry had to rhyme, and that afterwards it did not. Eliot's own admiration for Hulme was well documented and enduring and in the first instance rested entirely on the five poems of 'The Complete Poetical Works of

T. E. Hulme', collected and published for the first time in *The New Age* of 25 January 1912, and reproduced later in the same year as an appendix to *Ripostes*. 'I cannot remember reading any of Hulme's essays in *The New Age*,' he wrote, 'and the first of Hulme that I read outside of the poems appended to Pound's *Ripostes*, was in the volume entitled *Speculations*.'[27] Apart from the well-known observation in his *Criterion* article in April 1924, about Hulme's having written some of the 'most beautiful short poems in the English language', Eliot wrote privately to Mary Hutchinson, 'I am not sure whether you thought that Hulme is a really great poet, as I do, or not? I can't think of anything as good as two of his poems since Blake;'[28] and in his 1917 essay 'Reflections on *vers libre*' he praised the technical skill shown in 'The Embankment' as an example of 'the skilful evasion of iambic pentameter'.[29] That he should have gone on, after reading the essays in *Speculations*, to praise Hulme so spectacularly as 'the forerunner of a new attitude of mind, which should be the twentieth-century mind',[30] shows how deep he felt the affinity between them to be, and highlights the over-arching consistency in Hulme's poems and essays and its root in his rejection of romanticism.

One final poem appeared during Hulme's lifetime, the one Pound included in his *Catholic Anthology* in 1915 under the title 'Trenches: St Eloi', with the subtitle: 'T.E.H. Poem: Abbreviated from the Conversation of Mr T.E.H.'. Pound met Hulme in London at a time when the latter was convalescing from a bullet wound. On that occasion he had for Pound's benefit 'recited a poem but refused to write it down',[31] and this was presumably the genesis of 'Trenches: St Eloi'. Though it feels like poetry, 'Trenches: St Eloi' looks like prose, and the mere fact it could be considered a poem at all is a mark of the triumph of the poetic revolution Hulme had helped to start just seven years earlier:

> Over the flat slopes of St Eloi
> A wide wall of sand bags.
> Night,
> In the silence desultory men
> Pottering over small fires, cleaning their mess-tins:
> To and fro, from the lines,
> Men walk as on Piccadilly,

Making paths in the dark,
Through scattered dead horses,
Over a dead Belgian's belly.

The Germans have rockets. The English have no rockets.
Behind the line, cannon, lying back miles.
Before the line, chaos:

My mind is a corridor. The minds about me are corridors.
Nothing suggests itself. There is nothing to do but keep on.

4

The Nightmare of Determinism

Hulme's exchange with Flint over the Poets' Club marked his first appearance in the pages of *The New Age*, the weekly magazine which rapidly became his main forum of expression and to which he continued to contribute for all but the last year of his life. *The New Age* was founded in 1894 by Frederick A. Atkins as an independent weekly with a leaning towards Christian liberalism and socialism. Its subtitle, 'A Weekly Record of Culture, Social Service, and Literary Life', was changed the following year to 'A Journal for Thinkers and Workers'; during this phase Ramsay MacDonald was among the contributors. Though always clearly Liberal in its sympathies, the magazine failed to establish itself and a succession of editors presided over a steadily declining circulation that reached a nadir in 1907, when it had to be sold to cover its debts to the printer.

The figure most closely associated with it thereafter was Alfred R. Orage, a young Yorkshireman. With the writer Holbrook Jackson, whom he met in Leeds through a shared interest in Nietzsche, Orage founded the Leeds Art Club in 1903, and through its guest speakers, who included Belloc, Shaw, Yeats and Chesterton, he came in contact with some of the most important writers of the day. Both men were socialists of the less dogmatic sort and felt that the Fabian Society was paying too little attention to the role of philosophy and art in socialism, and to the relationship between culture and economics, so, early in 1907, soon after arriving in London, they started a Fabian Arts Group.

The moribund *New Age* was bought to serve the interests of this group. Holbrook Jackson had published a book on George Bernard Shaw in 1907, and on the strength of personal acquaintanceship Shaw was persuaded to put up £500 towards the purchase. Another £500 came from Lewis Wallace, a merchant banker with an interest in theosophy, and the combination of radical literary, political and spiritual interests was to remain consistent throughout this particular incarnation of the magazine. Wallace continued to offer unobtrusive financial support, but Shaw's direct involvement with the paper was limited to the initial loan. He did, however, become an enthusiastic contributor.

The revitalized *New Age* appeared for the first time in May 1907 under the joint editorship of Orage and Holbrook Jackson. They gave the magazine a new subtitle, 'An Independent Socialist Review of Politics, Literature and Art', and promised their readers that they would not be operating according to 'any specific formula, whether of economics or of party'.[1] It was widely assumed that the reincarnated paper would be a Fabian organ, reflecting the Fabian commitment to a slow and hopefully inexorable push towards socialist government. But Jackson left in January 1908, and for the next fifteen years Orage edited the magazine alone and according to principles of ideological independence. In so doing he created a paper whose mercurial and often brilliant unpredictability made it, especially in the years just prior to the outbreak of war, the most important cultural forum for the young in the capital, filling a gap created by the sheer venerability of nineteenth-century survivals such as the *Athenaeum*, *The Spectator* and *The Cornhill Magazine*, and providing a breadth of coverage not met by the relatively new specialist magazine the *Times Literary Supplement*. Its only real competitor during this golden age was Ford Madox Ford's *English Review*, and once Ford had left the *Review* in 1910, *The New Age* virtually had the field to itself. At its height its weekly circulation was about 20,000 copies.

Orage's brand of socialism was a very mixed bag indeed. In a much quoted passage he once gave his own outline of the evolution of the movement in Britain since the 1890s:

[Socialism was then] a cult with affiliations now quite disowned – with theosophy, arts and crafts, vegetarianism, the 'simple life', and almost, we might say, with musical glasses. Morris had shed a medieval light over it with his stained glass *News from Nowhere*. Edward Carpenter had put it into sandals, Cunninghame Graham had mounted it upon an Arab steed to which he was always saying a romantic farewell. Keir Hardie had clothed it in a cloth cap and red tie. And Bernard Shaw, on behalf of the Fabian Society, had hung it with innumerable jingling epigrammatic bells – and cap. My brand of socialism was, therefore, a blend or, let us say, an anthology of all those.[2]

His editorial practices reflected this lack of dogmatic insistence. He wanted discussion and controversy from his writers, and a readership that was provoked and stimulated rather than placated and confirmed in its prejudices. There was room for socialists and Catholics, liberals and conservatives, Home Rulers and anti-Home Rulers, suffragettes and anti-suffragettes, Nietzscheans and Christians. Hulme, like Eliot, Pound, Hamsun, Lawrence and many of the most outstanding figures in the creation of Modernism, was conservative and traditionalist in his personal views but artistically a revolutionary. This fertile mixture of sympathies, coupled with the eclectic nature of his interests, made him the ideal *New Age* writer. Orage recognized this and never made any attempt to tamper with his writing. Hulme's boyhood friend Alfred Haigh recalled a conversation in the course of which Hulme remarked that he was more than a conservative, he was a reactionary. 'Then why,' Haigh wondered, 'do you write for a socialist paper like *The New Age*?' Hulme's reply was simple: 'Because *The New Age* will print anything I write. Any other paper would cut and edit it, and I couldn't stand that.'[3]

But if *The New Age* became a platform for Hulme it never became a living. The paper was run on a shoe-string and contributors were often poorly paid or not paid at all. Some called it 'The No Wage', and for his daily bread Hulme remained dependent on the small allowance from his aunt in Macclesfield.

*

From 1909 until early in 1912 Hulme used the forum of *The New Age* to write almost exclusively on the subject of Henri Bergson and his philosophy. Bergson was a Frenchman, son of an English mother and a Jewish father who was a musician. He was a mathematical prodigy and by the age of eighteen had published in a scholarly journal of mathematics. In 1889, at the age of thirty, his doctoral thesis, *Essai sur les données immédiates de la conscience* (*Time and Free Will: An Essay on the Immediate Data of Consciousness*), was published to immediate acclaim and in 1900 he was appointed professor of philosophy at the Collège de France in Paris. Other books, *Matière et mémoire* (*Matter and Memory*) in 1896, *Le Rire* (*Laughter*) in 1900 and especially his major work *L'évolution créatrice* (*Creative Evolution*) in 1907, brought him to the attention of a public far beyond the confines of academia. His beliefs, coupled with his ethereal appearance and lecturing manner, made his lectures intellectual tourist attractions to which aristocratic Parisian ladies would dispatch their servants hours in advance in order to secure them a seat. In the years leading up to the Great War he achieved a personal celebrity in Europe that of his recent contemporaries among intellectuals perhaps only Henrik Ibsen could have matched. His ideas had considerable influence on contemporary literature. The theory of time that invests Proust's *À la recherche du temps perdu* is derived from him, and Shaw's preface to *Back to Methuselah* repeats it in digested form.

Hulme probably came across Bergson's name for the first time while teaching at the Berlitz School in Brussels. He was only twenty-four and perhaps the fact that the famous philosopher was a mathematician like himself was enough to pique his curiosity. He told F. S. Flint that he actually read him for the first time sitting on a Dorset cliff top in 1907.[4] The book was the *Essai sur les données immédiates de la conscience* and its effect was dramatic. Describing it four years later he wrote of how Bergson's thought entered his life as 'a kind of relieving force', putting an end to 'an intolerable state'. The 'mental explosion' delivered him from 'a previously existing state of siege' and he experienced 'the exhilaration that comes with a sudden change from a cramped and contracted to a free and expanded state of the same thing' and 'the sense of giddiness that comes with a sudden lifting up to a great height'. The almost religious exhilaration in these accounts is reinforced by his description of Bergson as 'heaven-sent', and it is evident that his response was rooted in a highly personal need that went well beyond the disinterested response of the trained philosopher. He at once embarked on a voyage of discovery, reading not only everything written by Bergson but everything about him too. 'I thought,' he wrote later, 'that I could ensure in this way that I should not, from a too hasty picking out of that one of Bergson's ideas which I had understood most easily, jump to the conclusion that this was the central and essential part of Bergson.'[5] In the end he could find no other use for his labours but to hand the whole bibliography over to F. L. Pogson, who appended it to his authorized translation of the *Essai sur les données* into English in 1910.

Bergson's thinking, lecturing and writing were ranged against the determinist-materialist view of human beings that had been gaining ground since Spinoza and had prevailed almost unopposed among European intellectuals since the middle of the nineteenth century. This view proceeded from a perception that the cumulative effect of scientific discoveries from the Renaissance onwards had been to extend the dominion of matter and causation into areas previously regarded as belonging properly to religion, most notably the idea that there is an immaterial spirit or soul residing within each person. Belief in God and the existence of an individual soul were rejected as irrational and untenable superstitions, and human beings were seen as predictable flesh-and-blood machines incapable of spontaneous activity. The point was made with immodest fervour by the eighteenth-century French mathematician and astronomer Pierre Laplace:

An intellect which at a given instant knew all the forces with which Nature is animated and the respective situations of the beings that compose Nature – supposing that the said intellect were vast enough to subject these data to analysis – would embrace in the same formulae the motions of the greatest bodies in the universe and those of the slightest atom; nothing would be uncertain for it, and the future, like the past, would be present to its eyes.[6]

Like Hulme, Bergson was more than half an artist himself,[7] and in many ways his arguments and beliefs are most fruitfully approached through the medium of Hulme's writings, for Hulme's personal and intense way of describing his discovery of Bergson provides a rarely compelling description of a mind grappling with what used to be called, in a phrase deriving from Thomas Huxley, 'the Nightmare of Determinism'. In a series of five long 'Notes on Bergson' for *The New Age* that ran from 19 October 1911 to 22 February 1912 Hulme formalized the views scattered across two dozen or so earlier contributions, in the form of book reviews and letters to the editor, on the subject of his favourite philosopher, using a remarkably modern and informal 'speaking' style that enabled him to articulate this nightmare and the fears it inspired in a way that can still evoke its horrors.

The essence of Hulme's opposition to what he referred to as 'Laplace's famous boast' was that in what had once been a fair fight between competing views of the soul, the discoveries of science had been appropriated by humanist philosophers in order to turn the determinist option into a compulsory purchase:

The balance of evidence is on the materialist side, but not sufficiently so to turn it into a nightmare. The arrival of the mechanistic view changes all this. It turns the open question into a closed one. It settles the thing definitely in favour of materialism. It is not merely that you may believe that this is the true view, but that you have to. The honest use of your reason leads you inevitably to that position.[8]

The critical word is 'honest'. Hulme was mathematician and logician enough to concede the state of affairs, and it led him to one of his most acute psychological observations, that beliefs are also forces 'and it is possible for one view to compel you to accept it in spite of your preference for another'. In the unopposed triumph of determinism he saw a philosophical equivalent of the *ars perfecta* periodically announced in music, an intolerable state of affairs in which aspirant composers are assured that the highest reaches of their discipline have already been attained and their only concern henceforth can be the maintenance of the work of composers who came before them. His abhorrence of such situations – whether in poetry or philosophy – led him later to his critique of the role played by personal 'satisfaction' in the formulation of philosophical theory and to an unusual and original series of analyses of the psychology of belief and conversion in political and philosophical thinking.

The explanation for Hulme's passionate pursuit of Bergson is that as a youth with a particular gift for abstract and mathematical thinking he had taken quite the opposite view of determinism:

It is, perhaps, necessary to point out that at a certain stage this prospect does not appear to be a nightmare to us. At a certain stage of one's mental evolution the delight in finding that one can completely explain the world as one might solve a puzzle is so exciting that it quite puts in the shade the disadvantages of the conception from other points of view. [. . .] One delights in it so much that one resents any attempt to interfere with it or to show that it is not a fact but merely an hypothesis. I recall quite vividly the emotion I felt when I looked, in my school library, at Stallo's quite harmless little book which makes fun of the conservation of energy. I positively detested the sight of the book on the shelves, I would have liked to have it removed from the library.[9]

With a hindsight afforded him by Bergson he recognized the cause of his adolescent alarm: 'my toy would have been taken away from me'. Yet the very ferocity of his response to Stallo's book indicates that beneath his adolescent pride he was much less happy than he thought he was in knowing the solution to the riddle of creation. At what point the fiercely guarded complacency of acceptance turned into a perception of the mechanistic universe as a nightmare is unclear. Possibly it was part of that epiphanous moment on the Canadian plains, when man's puniness and the helplessness of his little constructions before the fact of a vast and inexplicable wilderness were revealed to him and for the first time he felt the 'fright of the mind before the unknown'.

While fully in sympathy with it, he could not be content with what he called 'the commonsense view that such assumptions are nonsense to everyone but a theoretician of reality'. The vital point about the Bergsonian awakening was that it won him over by persuading the logic of his mind, not his heart:

The growth of the mechanistic theory during the last two centuries has put a weapon of such a new and powerful nature into the hands of the materialist, that in spite of oneself one is compelled to submit. [. . .] A candid examination of one's own mind shows one that the mechanistic theory has an irresistible hold over one (that is, if one has been educated in a certain way). It isn't simply a question of what you would like to win. It is a matter simply of the recognition of forces. If you are candid with yourself you find, on examining your own state of mind, that you are forcibly, as it were, carried on to the materialist side. It is from this frank recognition of forces that comes my excitement about Bergson. I find, for the first time, this force which carries me willy-nilly to the materialist side, balanced by a force which is, as a matter of actual fact, apart from the question of what I want, able to meet on equal terms the first force.[10]

The two crucial factors in these 'equal terms' were Bergson's conception of time as a subjective 'flux', and of 'intuition' as the tool of inward reflection. Mechanists and determinists were guilty of a failure to distinguish between description and definition, map and terrain. They mistakenly took the functional conveniences of analytic thought to reveal something fundamental about the nature of reality itself. But description and measurement are not definition, a river is not the measurement of its volume and rate of flow, and because the hands of a clock move does not mean that time consists of a series of discrete 'moments' strung together to create an illusion known as 'time'. The mistake we make is to 'place ourselves in the immobile in order to lie in wait for the moving thing as it passes, instead of replacing ourselves in the moving thing itself, in order to traverse with it the immobile positions'.[11] Reality is too subtle and fine-meshed to be captured by such crude methods. It must be taken by surprise. 'Intuition', or 'intellectual sympathy' as he also called it, was the tool Bergson suggested for this task of placing ourselves 'in the moving thing'. In the 'Notes' Hulme defended Bergson against suggestions that this made him merely an over-articulate advocate of views put forward more succinctly hundreds of years earlier by philosopher-poets such as Lao tzu and Chuang tzu or by Heraclitus, who said that a man can never step into the same river twice. Novelty is never one of the requirements of philosophy, said Hulme:

It is as impossible to discover anything new about the ways of man in regard to the cosmos as it is to observe anything new about the ways of a kitten.[12] The general conceptions we can form are as limited in number as the possible gestures of the dance, and as fixed in type as is the physiology of man himself. The philosopher who has not been anticipated in this sense of the word does not exist [. . .]

That being so, he asks rhetorically, why bother investigating even the relatively new? Because

the phrases of dead philosophers recorded in print are to most people as dead as dead kittens. In order that they appear alive they must be said over again in the phraseology of the moment. This, then, is the only originality left to the philosopher – the invention of a new dialect in which to restate an old attitude.

This, then, is the sense that I might safely say that Bergson had presented a new solution to an old problem. I should restate the thing, to avoid any suspicion of romanticism, in this way: Bergson has provided in the dialect of the time the only possible way out of the nightmare.[13]

Elsewhere in the 'Notes on Bergson' he dealt with the question: why not just ignore determinism? This was the commonsense view and the view of the mystically inclined, like W. B. Yeats. Ignore it and it would simply go away. But if comfort was the characteristic indulgence of the nineteenth century, it was not Hulme's. 'It is not by ignoring mechanism that you will arrive at anything worth having, but by struggling with it,' he wrote. And in a phrase which placed rigour at the heart of his approach to metaphysics he referred to 'some things which you have to conquer before you have any right at all to any spiritual view of the world'.[14]

Without this wrestle with the intellectual tyranny of rationalism Hulme would probably have remained the prisoner of his mathematical talents and never felt free to embark on the creative and open-ended studies of metaphysics and aesthetics which went on to preoccupy him for the rest of his life. From the intellectually distressing position in which Hulme found himself in 1907, uncomfortably straddling the line between science and art, Bergson helped him to take a firm step over into the world of art. He helped him to see rationalism in perspective and to distinguish between its uses and abuses, including 'the abuse of the power of translating the flux of immediate experience into a conceptual order'. His example gave Hulme the will and the intellectual means to embark on the campaign of fierce resistance to the colonization of the spirit by science and to the spreading idea of metaphysics as a science and not an art which becomes one of the most amusing and enjoyable features of his career.

In a very direct sense as well Bergson's views influenced Hulme's own writing. His entry into Hulme's life coincided roughly with the formation of the Poets' Club and his meditations on the value and function of the image influenced Hulme's own thoughts on the subject. In the *Introduction to Metaphysics* Bergson wrote that if images cannot represent the inner life, abstract concepts are even less able to do so. The image can neither reproduce the exact feeling of the flow of conscious life nor replace the intuition of duration. But if its aims were more modest then the value of the image could be great. It kept things concrete, and a judicious borrowing of images from very different orders of things could, when assembled, 'direct consciousness to the precise point where there is a certain intuition to be seized',[15] a descrip-tion that illuminates the club members' fascination with the revelatory brevities of Japanese *haiku*. Hulme's 'Lecture on Modern Poetry' in 1908 seems to contain echoes of Bergson's writing, where he speaks of the 'piling-up and juxtaposition of distinct images in separate lines' in a poem, and of the way in which 'two visual images form what one may call a visual chord' and unite to suggest an image which is different from them both.[16] As a writer of prose too he learned much from Bergson, not least the virtues of a lucid style which make it possible for a philosopher to communicate his beliefs to an intelligent but untrained thinker, and the frequent and enlightening use of metaphor and simile to illustrate points and arguments.

Hulme attempted to serve his developing passion for metaphysics in the same way as he had served his interest in poetry, by starting a club. A letter to *The New Age* on 23 June 1909 announced that, 'in response to a good many suggestions, privately made, it has been decided to form a group for the discussion of the main points of metaphysics'.[17] The meetings were to be purely conversational and informal, and would be held bi-monthly 'in some central room in London'. Subscrip-tions would be nominal. Those interested were invited to contact him at the Hanover Square address of the Irish Literary Society. Hulme was the sole signatory, and it seems he did not get many takers, for a year later a second letter containing a similar proposal appeared under the same heading, 'A Metaphysical Group'. This time the signatories were three – two secretaries *pro tem*, Hulme (inverted by a printer's demon to 'E. T. Hulme') and J. Stuart Hay, and a chairman *pro tem*, Ernest Belford Bax. Bax was one of the fathers of English Socialism and an associate of William Morris, with whom he founded the Socialist League. A supporter of Orage and Holbrook's Fabian Arts Group and a published writer some thirty years older than Hulme, his presence as a co-signatory to the letter is testament both to his tolerant good humour and to Hulme's considerable personal charm, for the two had earlier clashed through several editions of *The New Age*. Hulme's first article for the journal, entitled 'The New Philosophy', had appeared on 1 July 1909. Ostensibly a review of William James's *A Pluralistic Universe*, what evidently interested him most about the book was James's confession to having had an experience very similar to his own in reading Bergson, of personal liberation from a philosophical nightmare. A half page in praise of James's confessional style of writing, which he found 'very engaging', was sufficient before he moved on to deliver his own account of Bergson's main ideas.

Bax responded to the article with a claim that the ideas found in Bergson had previously appeared in a book of his own published in 1892, at a time 'when Bergson was not heard of'. Hulme replied firmly, pointing out that the order of priority was clear, all of Bergson's books were essentially developments of ideas first stated in 1889 in the *Essai sur les données immédiates de la conscience*. As part of a brief series of three he did for the paper that year under the general heading 'Searchers After Reality', Hulme followed this up the next week with a more detailed article looking at Bax's claims, basing his piece on ideas expressed in Bax's most recently published book, *Roots of Reality*. The opening paragraph is a fine example of his irreverent approach to debate, and of why to his younger contemporaries his seemed such a refreshing voice in the conventionally restrained world of philosophical debate:

When the clown at the circus puts his head through the paper disc, he appears framed in a ring of torn paper. This is the impression I have of Mr Bax's position after reading the 'Roots of Reality'. He has certainly put his head through a previously unpenetrated system, but he still remains surrounded by the ragged edges of the medium he has destroyed. His original views appear surrounded with pieces of Kantian tissue paper.[18]

Evidently Bax did not hold Hulme's own literary clowning against him.

Hulme's love of an argument with the sleeves rolled up was lifelong, and being a passionate defender of Bergson gave him plenty of opportunities to indulge it over the next three years, usually in the pages of *The New Age*. When presently he acquired the rights to translate Bergson's *Introduction to Metaphysics* into English, probably as a result of a meeting with Bergson in July 1910,[19] his mission to defend acquired a solidly materialist basis. Much of what he wrote earned him the ridicule of the professional philosophers, for whom Bergson's widespread popularity was in itself a sign of his triviality; but as Haigh observed of Hulme in reference to his unfashionable interest in the school Debating Society, he was never one to be affected by the dictates of fashion.

'That no one can succeed without asserting himself' was the last topic he had suggested for debate before leaving school in 1902; but despite the enormous self-confidence with which he was presenting himself to London's intellectuals and artists as a philosopher, Hulme remained an untrained thinker. He made up for it by an aggressive and sarcastic way of dealing with those who sent letters to *The New Age* questioning his enthusiasm for Bergson. A Mr Simmons wrote in claiming that Aristotle had said it all before. Hulme may have agreed in a general sense that true originality is impossible in philosophy but did not wish to agree with Simmons and denounced him as an 'ingénue'. When Simmons wrote in again he was brusquely informed that his letter was a 'pathetic document'. A German reader 'irritated' him (a favourite word) by his claim that Bergson owed his ideas on perception and the unity of consciousness to William James ('sheer nonsense'), and that Anatole France's dismissal of Bergson was in the spirit of Montaigne and Rabelais and represented the attitude of the true French intellectual – Bergson, after all, was only half-French. Hulme dismissed this scoffingly as 'racial romance':

All this racial gossip about philosophers is a little tedious. Philosophy is always a special activity appealing only to a few, and to those who have been through its special kind of discipline; Bergson has brought a new conception which will remain a permanent part of it. This is the important thing about him. For people who like gossip it may be equally interesting to know that not only is he half English, but that he wears elastic-sided boots.[20]

Bertrand Russell was the object of one of the most striking examples of Hulme's rudeness. In the context of an account describing the different ways of responding to the nightmare of determinism, he held up Russell as an example of one of the 'tougher people who have realised the problem' and attempted to respond to it. But he disapproved of the nature of

Russell's response, and accused him of being only the latest exponent of an attitude previously associated with Huxley:

Consciousness generally, and ethical principles in particular, are supposed to be mere by-products of a world-process which produces them accidentally and which will in time inevitably destroy them. Yet we are to act as though these ethical principles had an absolute value. The world has no purpose; our ethical values do not, as a matter of fact, correspond to anything in the nature of ultimate reality, and yet we are to act as though they did. The fact that it all leads to nothing is supposed to give an added dignity to man's ethical endeavours.[21]

Hulme's view was that even though Bergson had put it in its place, logic still had its uses and still carried with it an intellectual obligation to act upon the consequences of one's beliefs. He felt that philosophers such as Russell betrayed this obligation and he derided the 'glamour' and 'melancholy dignity' of their belief that the world is without purpose. As the 'Note' closed he whipped himself into a verbal fury in contemplation of the dishonesty of Russell's position: 'Occasions may arise when the natural expression of one's emotions can only be accomplished by the incoherent use of the words "filth", "sewerage", and the rest of it. My annoyance demands physical expression. I want to do something dramatic with the printed page. I find myself muttering: "You think that, do you? You –!"'

In all likelihood it shows only that his pleasure in the use of violent language survived undiminished from his undergraduate days. Yet the response might also recall the growling horror with which he had once contemplated Stallo's little book on physics on the shelves of his school library, and suggest that Hulme did not yet feel as secure in his Bergsonian salvation as he would like to have felt. 'Beliefs are also forces,' as he had noted himself, and it may be that he dreaded the appearance of an analytic intellect, formidable enough to compel his respect and propounding beliefs contrary to his own with sufficient force to destabilize them and send him tumbling back down into the nightmare again.

*

Twenty-one months before this outburst, on 6 June 1910, Hulme had been admitted as a member of the Aristotelian Society of London. Founded in 1880, the society met monthly from November to June to hear papers and discuss philosophical ideas. The annual fee was one guinea. At the time of Hulme's joining the president was Samuel Alexander. Russell replaced him the following year. The honorary secretary was Herbert Wildon Carr, a wealthy stockbroker who was for a time secretary of the London Stock Exchange Council. Like Hulme, Carr was a self-taught philosopher and an admirer of Bergson, on whom he delivered several papers over the years at the rooms of the Royal Asiatic Society in Albemarle Street where the society met. Bergson himself was among the society's corresponding members.

In his own writings Hulme makes only one reference to the society, a half-comic description of an episode at the 1910 annual meeting, when a naïve young man stood up and proposed that the society pick a topic ('Neo-Realism') and discuss it over and over again 'until the truth had actually been discovered'. G. E. Moore was a member but had no recollection of ever meeting him. Neither Russell nor D. L. Murray, the writer and later editor of the *Times Literary Supplement* who was elected to the society at the same time as Hulme and who later attended the Bologna Conference with him, recalled seeing him there, nor is there any record of Hulme's delivering a paper or participating in the discussions. It may well be that he attended only rarely; or, if he did attend regularly, his awareness of the fact that he was among trained philosophers might have accounted for his keeping such an unusually low profile. His membership of the Aristotelian Society indicates his growing desire to formalize his interest in philosophy. One unexpected consequence of it was to involve him presently in a second nightmare, this one brought on by the determinism of sexual desire.

5

1911

Since settling in London in 1908 Hulme had led a peripatetic existence, lodging in temporary addresses or with friends. By 1911, at the age of twenty-eight, he was tiring of this way of life and had taken rooms of his own at 35 Manchester Street in central London, between Manchester Square and Paddington Street. More importantly, he established in the same year a relationship with Ethel Kibblewhite, one of the two women of enduring importance in his adult life.

Ethel, or Dolly as she was universally known, was the oldest daughter of a stained glass manufacturer named Thomas Figgis Curtis and his wife, Mary. Born in London in 1873, she was a handsome, dark-haired woman ten years Hulme's senior. She bore a passing physical resemblance to his mother, but her features were rounder and more feminine and reflected the general impression she gave of being a warm and selfless person. She had a sister Dora, three years younger, to whom she was close despite dissimilarities of character. Both girls studied drawing in London under Fred Brown, and when Brown was appointed professor at the Slade, followed him there. Dolly emerged a painter of watercolours and flowers in oils. Dora later worked as a book illustrator and designer of fabrics for Tootal, Broadhurst and Lee. She was the adventurous one, an expeditionary who travelled with missionaries in China and Siberia – for the company, not from religious motives. During the war she enlisted in the French Army as a driver and was awarded the Croix de Guerre. Not long afterwards she was killed in a swimming accident, diving off a rock into shallow water in the Canary Islands and fracturing her skull.

Dolly was the more traditionally feminine of the two. Richard Curle described her frankly as Hulme's 'slave, with no thought of herself'.[1]

Yet she cannot have been lacking in spirit. When she and Hulme met she was already the mother of two small children and had walked out of her first marriage, to Gilbert Kibblewhite, a Wadhurst man four years her junior. After marrying in London in 1900 she and Kibblewhite had gone to live in the West Sussex village of Storrington, where Kibblewhite had been installed as manager of a dairy farm bought for him by his father. He turned out to be a man with a violent temper and on a number of occasions Dolly had to flee from him for her own safety. It was during one such separation, while staying with her parents in London, that her first child Peter was born.

The marriage broke up in 1903, shortly after the birth of her second child Diana, when in a fit of rage with a recalcitrant horse Kibblewhite shot and killed the animal. Fearing for her own life Dolly gathered together a few possessions and fled with the two children to Walnut Tree House, the Curtises' country home in Rustington, a few miles south of Storrington.

Not long afterwards Kibblewhite turned up in Rustington and demanded to see her. Dora refused to admit him, and in a wild, Hardyesque gesture of revenge he torched a wooden outhouse which the sisters sometimes used as a studio. The family cat Johnnie escaped with his life, but all that remained of Thomas Curtis's eight beehives, ranged alongside in the shelter of the studio, was 'a pitiful line of charred timber and dead bees'.[2] Curtis, the mildest of men, threatened legal action against his son-in-law, and not long afterwards Gilbert was persuaded by his family to leave the country for Australia. The whole business was clearly a dreadful trauma for Dolly and the children. The shame of separation meant that the recent past was never spoken of, never discussed. What had happened was a 'terrible thing'.[3] Thereafter the two children spent part of each year at Walnut Tree House, where they were raised by a combination of grandparents and nannies.

After her separation Dolly worked for a time as a designer for the Royal School of Needlework, in Exhibition Road, an institution founded in 1872 with the aim of restoring ornamental needlework to the high place it had once held among the decorative arts, and returned to live in the Queen Anne house owned by her father at 67 Frith Street on the corner of Soho Square. The four floors of the house were linked by a remarkable spiral staircase that ran from top to bottom, with landings giving access to the rooms on each floor. Each tread, about four feet wide, was cantilevered out from the wall of a circular well, with no other support. Thomas Curtis ran the firm of Ward & Hughes, Ecclesiastical Stained Glass Manufacturers, from the first floor of the house, where he and his clerk Mr Guyton each had an office, and the family occupied the remaining three floors. Their immediate neighbours were Louis Poirier's Wine Importing business at No. 65 and Ferdinand Monti's laundry at No. 63. Curtis's main supplier of glass had a warehouse just round the corner in Soho Square. At the back of the house was a yard, approached by a narrow drive-in from Dean Street, and a long, ramshackle lean-to against a high wall which housed Curtis's three glaziers. The household consisted of Thomas and Mary Curtis, Dolly and the two children, the peripatetic Dora, a cook and a housemaid.

Even before Hulme's time No. 67 was a centre of cultural activity. The Curtises were friendly with a branch of the musical Dolmetsch family who lived in Rustington, and on his visits to London to research into the history of early music at the British Museum Arnold Dolmetsch frequently took tea with them at Frith Street. The connection stirred little Diana Kibblewhite's interest in the lute, and in later life, as Diana Poulton, she became an outstanding lutanist and author of a standard work on the composer John Dowland.

Dolmetsch provides the one tenuous connection that links Hulme, Kibblewhite and Frith Street. He knew Florence Farr, who was a member of Hulme's Secession Club in 1908 and 1909, and had made for her a sort of lute called a psaltery, which Farr used in recitals designed to demonstrate some theories of W. B. Yeats' about the delivery of verse to musical accompaniment. There is therefore a possibility that Hulme came to know Dolly through Farr or Dolmetsch, but there is not a shred of documentary evidence to prove it. The painter Kate Lechmere, who got to know Hulme early in 1914, said that Gilbert Kibblewhite 'had tried to kill' Dolly and without being specific about how added that Hulme had 'put a stop to this'.[4] Hulme was not given to dramatizing things – rather the opposite – and as this information must have come from him it is probably reliable. But whether this intervention was the occasion of their meeting or later on in the relationship, is impossible to say. Wherever and however they met, it seems safe to assume that at least part of the attraction Dolly felt to Hulme was on account of his physical strength and easy accept-ance of aggression between men that made her feel safe from a violent husband. Hulme in turn would have been moved by her vulnerability and need of his protection. Whatever the chronology of their begin-ning, they were evidently close by the winter of 1911, when Hulme published 'A Personal Impression of Bergson' in *The Westminster Gazette* and used as his *nom de plume* an improvisation based on her name, 'T. K. White'.

Hulme seems to have glided happily into the role of a de facto husband and father within the family and from 1911 onwards made the house at Frith Street the base of his activities, never living there but having at his permanent disposal a large room where he was able to write and study. Summers and weekends would be spent with the children at Rustington, Hulme and Dolly taking the train to Littlehampton and walking the mile across the fields to Walnut Tree House. Hulme loved the company of children and there are photo-graphs of him in the garden at Rustington with the two of them clinging on to his back like little monkeys. Diana's skill at making his favourite suet pudding was such that he swore he would marry her when she was old enough.

Hulme and Dolly were companions as well as lovers. He taught her to play Go, and they could sit for hours absorbed in a game. All her life Dolly remained a keen cyclist, and if Wyndham Lewis's description of Hulme as having 'legs like a racing cyclist' can be related to her hobby then it was probably at Rustington they did their cycling. She made pencil sketches of him, the only one to survive a sensitive drawing that captures in the heavily lidded eyes the brooding inwardness of mood which was one of his two characteristic manifestations. In the other, harder to capture in a sketch, the look was said to be sharp and projecting.[5]

The relationship with the Kibblewhite family endured for the rest of Hulme's life. It did not, however, domesticate him. The playwright Ashley Dukes, who was from 1909 the drama critic for *The New Age*, was one of several friends who knew Hulme in his late twenties and whose reminiscences of the period show a man still in vivid revolt against authority and convention. One particularly striking memory was of a day when Hulme was apprehended by a policeman while urinating in broad daylight in Soho Square. 'You can't do that here,' he was told. Still buttoning his trousers, Hulme turned to him and replied, 'Do you realize that you're addressing a member of the middle class?' The policeman then apologized and walked on. Connoisseurs of the episode assume that Hulme was caught short after a night's drinking, but Dukes states expressly that the incident took place 'in broad daylight'.[6] Hulme, moreover, remained unshakeably teetotal. If a rational explanation is possible a clue might be that note in 'Cinders' in which he referred to the 'resolution to shake off social convention and do it', a compulsion he apparently experienced so strongly at times that he called it 'the knife order'. It may be that Hulme was performing his devotions to the god of the knife order that day in Soho Square, and that he urinated where and when he did precisely *because* there was a policeman standing nearby.

In sexual matters Hulme was equally addicted to risk. The novelist David Garnett described him as 'someone who was, by his own account, a man of astounding sexual prowess, always trying to pick up women in places like the British Museum and enjoy their favours in the most unsuitable places'. He recalled one occasion on which Hulme suddenly broke off a conversation while talking with a group of friends at the Café Royal. Pulling out his watch he remarked that he had an urgent engagement in five minutes' time and hurried out into the street. Twenty minutes later he was back, sweating lightly and complaining that the steel staircase of the emergency exit at Piccadilly Circus tube station was the most uncomfortable place in which he had ever copulated. Richard Curle found it normal and healthy behaviour in a young man, but Garnett and Richard Aldington were uncomfortable with it. 'I didn't like it, being what they called a womaniser,' Aldington said, and with the hindsight of forty years of Freudian thinking consoled himself with the thought that if death had not intervened Hulme would inevitably have turned to homosexuality and sodomy.

Dukes's reaction to Hulme's philandering was, like that of Aldington and Garnett, an unease amounting almost to distaste, offset only by his great liking for Hulme and enjoyment of his company. The girls, he recalled, 'were all casually met and mostly of the shopgirl class'. For some reason he believed that Hulme's Staffordshire accent made them 'take him for a German' and that this, coupled with his 'Prussian' looks, was the partial explanation of his success. Like Aldington, Dukes had to assure himself that it cannot all have been as straightforward as it looked and decided that Hulme was 'not really attractive to them though, they thought him older than he really was'. His theory was that this was why girls trusted him not to get them pregnant. Hulme was well known among his friends for his intimate knowledge of the streets and suburbs of London and once explained it as a result of all the travelling involved in his pursuit of sexual adventure.

Some of the notes in 'Cinders' reflect on Hulme's interest in promiscuous sex, dignifying it as part of the quest for a meaning in life: 'The pathetic search for the *different*. Where shall they find it? Never found in sex. All explored sex is the same'; and he refers to his idea of 'the real level-headedness: to be able to analyse a pretty girl at first sight, not to be intoxicated with clothes'. A surviving fragment of a letter to Alice Pattinson regrets the lack of 'body poetry' being written, and complains that when poets 'deign to refer to the body it is always "Soft white limbs" by poets who wear tight boots'. The rather rambling fragment seems to be in response to something she wrote to him about her spiritualist beliefs, or perhaps it was part of a general exchange of views about theosophy. 'If the mind is immortal,' it concludes, 'the body must be too, for they can't exist apart – so that sex shall endure.'[7] Sexual ethics, he once wrote, as usually presented to young people, contained very little that could be called ethical, 'but only taboo, custom, expediency and good form'.[8] But though it later played a part in the formation of his tastes and judgements in matters of art, his obsessive interest in sex did not often lead him to philosophize on the subject in public.

*

In April 1911 Herbert Wildon Carr travelled to Bologna in northern Italy as the official representative of the Aristotelian Society at the Fourth International Congress of Philosophy, taking with him his daughter Joan, a Roedean schoolgirl. Other English philosophers attending the congress, held between 6 and 11 April, were Dr F. C. S. Schiller, A. W. Benn, D. L. Murray, Miss E. E. Constance Jones, principal of Girton College, and T. E. Hulme. The major attraction for both Hulme and Carr was certainly Bergson's presence.

Hulme, who travelled alone, had planned his trip a year in advance. He left England early and took the opportunity to pay two visits on his way through France, the first to the French philosopher Jules de Gaultier in Dieppe. Eighteen months earlier he had written about de Gaultier in *The New Age* as part of the 'Searchers After Reality' series, taking his eminence along with that of Bergson as a sign that the centre of interest in philosophy had shifted from Germany to France. In that article he had praised the style of contemporary French philosophers generally. They wrote like gentlemen, not like pedants, even when writing 'metaphysics of a very subtle and distinguished kind'. And for all the complexity of what he was writing about, de Gaultier was able to communicate in an 'extremely personal way, expressing often views of violent originality'. Hulme's temperamental affinity with such a man is obvious. The explanation for the 'charmingly lucid' manner in which these philosophers wrote their philosophy was that they, by contrast with the Germans, 'always seem to me to treat it, either explicitly or implicitly, not as a science but as an art'.[9] De Gaultier was bracketed with Bergson as another of those who had rescued him from the prison of science and kept philosophy as an art.

He had discussed his planned visit to Bologna with Bergson at their meeting in the summer of 1910, when Bergson had responded with guarded scepticism to the whole notion of such gatherings of philosophers. He did, however, allow that 'sometimes when you have been puzzled by a man's philosophy, when you have been a little uncertain as to his meaning, then the actual physical presence of the man makes it all clear'.[10] De Gaultier was accordingly appraised as a performer and judged as a personality at the meeting in Dieppe. Hulme was honest enough to admit that really he had no choice in the matter: 'I had not spoken French for so long,' he wrote, 'that all my uprisings of interruption were stifled automatically.' The result was that he had what must have been for him a rare experience, that of sitting face to face with another philosopher and listening in complete silence as he expounded his metaphysics.

From Dieppe Hulme travelled to Paris to visit the writer Pierre Lasserre, whose anti-romantic *Le Romantisme français* he had read and much admired. He was curious to know why a writer with whom he felt in such sympathy should recently have chosen to launch an attack on Bergson: 'I was in agreement with both sides, and so I wondered whether there was any real inconsistency in my position.'

The essence of what Lasserre said to him at their meeting was reproduced as one section of an article for *The New Age* of 9 November entitled 'Mr Balfour, Bergson and Politics'. In Lasserre's analysis the Revolution of 1789 was a romantically inspired disaster for the country, and romanticism itself was 'an awful disease from which France had just recovered'. The aim of socialism was to bring about a situation in which the individual was able to enjoy the institutions of society in such as way as to procure the maximum good for himself, and the socialists proposed to achieve this by the government of the individual, leaving it to the will of the majority to decide the fate of institutions. The result, according to Lasserre, was not democracy but 'a regime which can be defined as an oscillation between two apparent contraries, the despotism of the State and general anarchy' which ensured the contentment of none and the suffering of all.

As Lasserre now saw it, Bergson's invidious role in all this was to provide socialists with a potential justification for an irresponsible tampering with institutions. Socialists and democrats were able to argue that his definition of time denied the validity of the idea that there are 'necessary laws governing societies, and more particularly that these laws can be discovered from past history',[11] for he had shown that the present was always a unique present, having no parallels with what had come before. Time is real, so there can be no repetition. This interpretation provided the Left in France with an argument for rejecting the belief that the past can or should provide a model for the present; and a further argument for the consequent need to structure the development of society along idealistic lines through the application of theory.

Lasserre's counter-argument was essentially the same one put forward by Burke in his essay on the French Revolution, that a society which failed to understand and respect the past as symbolized in the functioning of its time-honoured institutions was flirting with political and social disaster. This was an argument Hulme must have listened to with particular interest, for political life in Britain since 1908 had been witness to just such an attack on one of the country's historical institutions in the struggle between Asquith's elected Liberal majority in the House of Commons and the entrenched Conservative majority in the House of Lords which effectively blocked every piece of reforming legislation passed up to it by the Lower House. The matter was not settled until 1911, when the Parliament Act deprived the Lords of all power over 'money bills' and restricted it to a suspensive veto on other legislation of two successive sessions. The House of Lords was compelled to pass the bill. Had it not done so, George V would have created the 250 peers necessary to ensure its passage. This was just one of many signs (the reappearance of abstract art would be another) that convinced Hulme he was living through a time of dramatic and little-understood change.

This meeting with Lasserre was thought-provoking. Not only did it convince Hulme that it was possible to use Bergson's teachings to provide an apology for democracy and the pursuit of political idealism; it also forced him to consider for the first time the possibility that even the 'pure' Bergsonism not warped by this socialist interpretation was, in fact, 'nothing but the last disguise of romanticism'. 'If I thought this was true,' he wrote, almost as though preparing himself for a day when he would, 'I should be compelled to change my views considerably.'

*

Once in Bologna Hulme's informal observations of the place and the conference were noted down and sent for publication to *The New Age*, where Orage expressed himself delighted with them:

No better notes on the congress could be written and I am much impressed by their genius. I'm delighted, too, that you are meeting everybody. You must give me a whole evening's reminiscences when you return. Meanwhile, I shall be happy to receive as many more sets of Notes as you feel inclined to write.[12]

At the top of the letter is Hulme's scribbled reminder to himself, 'Cheque was enclosed with this. Don't *lose* this.'

As his 'Notes' made clear, the city pleased him: 'In so far as philosophers are still peripatetic and like to walk the road gesticulating,

Bologna seems to me the ideal place for them to meet in,'[13] he wrote. A street should be a street, a place for strolling and talking in, and with its compact little piazzas flanked by arcades with never a broad straight street nor an open vista in the whole place, Bologna answered his needs perfectly. In particular he approved of its wall. He felt that the conventionally drawn polarity between town and country, with the progress of events tending to spread the one to the ruination of the other, was mistaken. Proposing instead a theory that the country is not the raw material out of which townships evolve, he maintained that there were two perfect correlatives of artificial and deliberate construction, the compact walled town, and the country: 'You feel always, though you may never see it, the bracing feeling of a disciplinary wall keeping it all up to the ideal pitch of town I require, and never allowing it to sprawl into desert. It is a quadrangle and cloister raised to the highest power.' The touch of self-mockery is a reminder that he was still uneasy about the idea of being serious, the characteristic noted by Haigh back in the days of the school Debating Society when he would end all his sentences with a sort of mocking 'snigger'. Obviously, in *The New Age* he was writing for a particular audience of interested amateurs who wanted also to be entertained, and a thoroughly sober account of the philosophical proceedings appeared in the journal *Nature* of 18 May, unsigned; but for the next twelve months or so Hulme does seem to have been trying to establish himself professionally as a journalist and lecturer, and the emphasis in his articles is often on entertainment no matter what his subject.

On the morning of 6 April, the opening day of the conference, Hulme was in his hotel room writing letters when he was disturbed by the sounds of shouting and music. From his window he saw troops of soldiers marching past, and heading out to the centre of town to see what was happening, he came across a huge crowd of Italians in the Piazza Vittoria Emanuelle assembled beneath great red banners that hung from the brick Renaissance palaces that lined the square. 'Surrounding each man,' he noticed, 'was a large space occupied by his cloak.' He was filled with a puzzling sense of admiration for this crowd, and presently discovered why: 'It had achieved the impossible. It was a crowd without being a crowd. It was simply an aggregation of people who managed the extraordinary feat of coming together without becoming that very low class multicellular organism – the mob.' The experience was almost enough to make a democrat of him: 'If anyone could invent a kind of democracy which includes, as an essential feature, the possession of large and sweeping brown cloaks, then I will be a democrat.' Anxious to discover the cause of the fuss he bought a copy of the *L'Avvenire d'Italia* and from the banner headline 'Filosofia' discovered to his amazement that it was nothing less than the conference on philosophy, specifically the welcome for the Duke of Abruzzi who had come from Rome to open the congress on behalf of the king.

The situation presented him with a dilemma: after the official opening the academic side of the conference was due to get under way at ten o'clock in the Archigynasio, where the president of the congress, Professor Enriques, would be reading his paper on '*Il problema della realtà*' to the 500 delegates. A voice whispered in his ear that if he meekly turned up to hear all this he would miss everything else that was going on in the streets outside, the wonderful procession with the soldiers riding by in their sweeping blue cloaks, the marching bands, the cheering of the crowd. Standing there on the pavement he rehearsed the arguments in favour of truanting: inside, he knew, they would only talk of progress, but the only form of progress he recognized was that of princes and troops, 'for they, though they move, make no pretence of moving "upward". They progress in the only way which does not violate the classical ideal of the fixed and constant nature of man.' And once inside all the talk would be of the 'all' and the 'whole' and of the harmony of the concert of the cosmos, in none of which he believed. His every instinct told him to stay and watch; but his intellect would not permit it:

Finally inward ridicule decided the thing. To cross Europe with the sole purpose of attending a congress, and then to watch a procession instead, would be too much of a comic spectacle. To my lasting regret I went in. I missed a spectacle I shall never see again. I heard words I shall often hear again – I left the real world and entered that of Reality.

And once inside things were not quite as bad as he had feared. Passing down long, arched corridors lined by policemen, soldiers and firemen ('I shall return to the subject of the enormous number of firemen which guarded us later') he found himself in the 'Salla di seduti generale' among 'great numbers of pretty women', whom he fervently hoped were not philosophers. 'Surely,' he said to himself, 'this cannot be the world of Reality.'

General meetings of the congress were held in the large hall of the Archigynasio, where papers were given in German or English. The specialized work was divided into sections for General Philosophy and Metaphysic; History of Philosophy; Logic and Theory of Knowledge; Ethics; Philosophy of Religion; Juridical and Social Philosophy; Aesthetic; and Psychology.[14] In the report written for *Nature* Hulme sticks closely to the proceedings themselves and makes no mention of a story he told John Squire on his return, which he swore was true, that at one session of the Ethics section a free fight had broken out. He provided instead short and sober accounts of papers by, among others, Bergson, Poincaré and Durkheim before summarizing the contributions by the English contingent – eleven papers out of a total of 200. His report that a paper on 'Error' by the Oxford Pragmatist F. C. S. Schiller provoked a lively discussion was confirmed by Wildon Carr in his formal report to the Aristotelian Society, who said that Schiller's paper was followed by 'the most animated debate of the session'. Hulme would have agreed with one of what Carr identified as the two main points to emerge from the congress, that philosophy was no longer in any sense a national pursuit; but perhaps not with the other, that philosophy was a body of knowledge that was advancing, growing and progressing. Hulme concluded his article in *Nature* by announcing that the next such conference would be held in London in 1915, and that he hoped it would arouse greater interest than similar previous initiatives had among the English.

An attack of toothache kept him in touch with the everyday realities and he visited a Bolognan dentist, a voluble man who took the chance to practise his English on him, informing him that he had trained in London, at the Royal Dental Hospital in Leicester Square. Hulme was much impressed by this dentist. In a humorous article written later he claimed that he carried out his work using a complex arrangement of mirrors, 'like that by which velocity is measured, some inside my head and some outside', in which Hulme was able to study an image of his own tooth 'about a foot long'. This was one of many references to toothache scattered across Hulme's notes. Evidently it was a recurring affliction, and in a man addicted to eating boiled sweets, an inevitable one too.

After the conclusion of the congress on 11 April he remained in Italy for a few weeks, travelling south as an independent tourist. A postcard to his brother Harold described with exemplary brevity a day spent in Pompeii:

I have just been to Pompeii for the day. This is a dig exactly as it was caught and preserved in the lava 2000 years ago. Yrs Ernest.

He sent a longer card to his sister Kate on 6 May after a visit to Assisi:

This church in Assisi is very interesting, for it was practically the beginning of all modern art. It was in the decoration here that people for the first time began to paint things they saw instead of the kind of conventional patterns which had done for Christ and for the Saints for about 10 centuries. This one is by Giotto. Of course, it doesn't look much, but when you see the kind of thing that came before it you realise how wonderful it was.[15]

His notion of 'the kind of thing that came before' was based on what he had seen at Ravenna during an outing arranged for the delegates at the congress. There, in the mosaic of the Empress Theodora in the church of San Vitale and in the dome of the fifth-century Baptistery of the Orthodox, he had seen for the first time the art of the Byzantines. The heavily stylized religious art, which had survived remarkably unchanged from about the middle of the sixth century to the fall of Constantinople in 1453, aimed to give artistic expression to a body of controlled and largely unchanging religious dogma. Its tools were uniformity and anonymity. Byzantine architects and painters pursued perfection within their tradition, eschewing the path of variation according to individual artistic whim. One of their purposes was to lift the spiritual life out of the contamination of the mundane and to fix it beyond reach of the vagaries of time and the corruption of personality. From the last sentence of his postcard to Kate it is obvious that Hulme initially found Byzantine art primitive, that he believed in progress in art and by extension in humans, and that an artist like Giotto seemed to him to demonstrate the truth of these beliefs. Within two years, however, his views would change dramatically, and he would be using the stylized and enduring art of the Byzantines as the intellectual basis for an aesthetic theory of his own on the origins and social purposes of art with which he prophesied and defended the work of his London contemporaries such as Jacob Epstein, Henri Gaudier-Brzeska, Wyndham Lewis and David Bomberg.

Walnut Tree House had been extensively renovated that year, with a new stable, coach house and pig sties, and Hulme may well have spent the summer holiday there with Dolly and the children after his return from Italy. He was, however, in London to catch a performance of Diaghilev's Ballets Russes at Covent Garden. In a very short space of time the company had changed the status of ballet in England. From being a low-brow form of entertainment mainly associated with the music hall it had risen to the heights of a command performance at the coronation gala for the new king and queen in June. The season of public performances that year lasted from 21 June to 11 August, and at one of these Hulme met again by chance D. L. Murray, with whom he had been at Bologna. Aside from his enthusiasm for brass bands, Hulme was not a music lover, and from their conversation Murray recalled that his interest and enthusiasm seemed to lie rather in the attempts being made by Diaghilev and Nijinsky to 'bring the plastique of ballet into line with the non-humanist ideals that inspired Egyptian, archaic and Polynesian art',[16] an indication that the Ravenna mosaics were now beginning to work inside him. The Italian trip had been a fruitful one for Hulme. Besides Murray he kept up with others he had met there, including E. E. Constance Jones and the mathematician E. S. Russell. He also began a correspondence with Wildon Carr's young daughter Joan.

*

Hulme published seventeen assorted articles and book reviews in 1911, most of them about Bergson and most of those in *The New Age*. But his circle of journalistic contacts was expanding and as well as his account of events at Bologna for *Nature* he had five articles on general political topics published in a short-lived weekly social and political review called *The Commentator*, in addition to the Bergson article in *The Westminster Gazette* for which he had used the name 'T. K. White'. To readers of *The Commentator* he was 'Thomas

Gratton' (twice, because of a misprint, 'Thomas Grattan'), the reason
for these pseudonyms being probably nothing more than his sheer love
of secrecy. Murray, who after the meeting at Covent Garden saw
Hulme quite frequently, apologized to Alun Jones for being unable to
offer him letters for use in his biography, adding that 'he was, I think,
an essentially secretive man about his private life and I never knew
anything worth mentioning about it'.[17] Yet the choice of his *Commentator* name is interesting, harking back, presumably with pride, to his
birthplace Gratton Hall.[18] The use of 'T. K. White' must have been
flattering for Dolly Kibblewhite, though he seems not to have used it
again. A relic of the article, entitled 'A Personal Impression of Bergson'
and published on 18 November, is a card Hulme sent home to his
father:

If you get tomorrow a Monday's Westminster Gazette you will find an article
'Bergson a personal impression' signed under pseudonym T. K. White which
is by me and might interest you. Yrs affct. Ernest[19]

The note suggests that Hulme was not actively prolonging any
estrangement from his father; that his father's approval was not a
matter of indifference to him; and that, this being an article on a
subject contentious in Endon (philosophy), it was also a way of telling
old Tommy Hulme that philosophy might, after all, have its uses if a
man could make a living as a journalist from it.

A few days later he would have been able to show his father even
clearer proof that he had been right to hold out for philosophy. On
28 November the publisher T. Fisher Unwin wrote to 'T. K. White'
c/o *The Westminster Gazette* with a flattering offer:

My dear Sir
I have read your article in the Westminster Gazette of November 18, with
very much interest, as a Publisher. I have often been connected with volumes
from H. Bergson's pen. I do not know whether you are writing more on the
subject or whether you may be editing or translating any of his works, but,
if at any time you have a Manuscript which you desire printed or published,
I should be very happy to hear from you.

Yours very truly,
T. Fisher Unwin

Hulme was in fact already under contract both to write a book about the philosopher and to translate Bergson's own *Introduction to Metaphysics* for the Covent Garden firm of Stephen Swift and Co., and he was entitled to think that at last a degree of seriousness had entered his life, that he was close to acquiring publication credentials and a reputation. He already had three years worth of journalistic material which he could reshape into book form, and he had spent much of the autumn preparing a series of four lectures aimed at introducing Bergson to a lay public in clear and simple terms, which would also take him halfway towards a completed book. A prospectus was published giving some idea of the content of the four lectures he was offering:

1. Introduction. Method of Exposition to be adopted. The problem of contemporary philosophy. Bergson's new 'method'. The conception of an intensive manifold. Application of this (A) to mental life. Real duration. Restatement of problem of free-will. 'Time and Free-will'.
2. (B) to the question of the relation of mind and body. The Nature of perception. Memory. 'Matter and Memory'.
3. (C) to the problem of nature of life. Vitalism. The theory of evolution. The Élan Vital. Instinct. The nature of 'intuition'. 'Creative Evolution'.
4. (D) to the theory of art. The literature of the subject. Bergson's influence. Two disciples – Le Roy the Catholic, and Georges Sorel the Syndicalist.

His final world view and its relation to mysticism and religion.[20]

A notice on the back page of *The New Age* on 9 November advertised the event:

> The Philosophy of Henri Bergson
> During the last 2 weeks of November &
> the first 2 of December a Course
> of Lectures on the Philosophy of Bergson
> will be given by
> Mr T. E. Hulme
> At 6 Scarsdale Villas, Kensington
> (Two minutes from High Street 'District' station)
> (by kind permission of Mrs Franz Liebich)

The lectures will commence at 4.45 on
Thursday, November 23 and 30th, and
December 7 and 14th

Tickets 10/6 for all 4 from
Mrs F. Liebich; F. W. Tancred Esq
29 Westbourne Gardens;
Miss Florence Farr,
20 Glebe Place Chelsea.[21]

These lectures and publications in 1911 were all part of the effort Hulme was making that year to establish himself, to secure a measure of financial independence from his aunt, and to prove himself to his family. In a professional sense what he had to offer was Bergson. But intellectually his enthusiasm for Bergson had by now run its course and, under the influence of his conversation with Lasserre, Hulme had begun the process of extricating himself from an identification with his hero that had become oppressive.

Hiding behind a smokescreen of humour he articulated his unease in an article for *The New Age* of 2 November, before the lectures at Mrs Liebich's house and halfway through his five-part series of 'Notes on Bergson' for the same paper. Mindful of the harm such an admission might do to his developing career as a professional Bergsonian he used the 'Thomas Gratton' pseudonym for his account of the lectures Bergson gave at University College London, between 20 October and 28 October 1911.

Though he had received in private Bergson's own assurance that he found his celebrity status in London slightly risible, Hulme was still disturbed by what he felt to be the absurd level of intellectual security surrounding the lectures, in particular the way in which applicants for tickets were required to submit their academic credentials before being allowed to buy them. Approaching the lecture hall he half-expected to be challenged by a guard of university eunuchs demanding to see his graduation papers – 'I meditated getting in the night before through a window and hiding under the platform.' Once inside he was dismayed to see that 90 per cent of the audience consisted of women, all with their heads lifted in an 'Eager Heart' attitude of expectation. 'If these are the elect,' he wondered, *'what were the rejected like?'*

As he sat waiting for the speaker to appear a fit of depression overcame him. It was followed by an experience of 'the profoundest and blackest scepticism – a scepticism that cut right down to the root of every belief that I had hitherto fancied I held as certain and fixed'. He recapitulates his discovery of Bergson and the great service Bergson did in liberating him from determinism. He admits openly that he has been Bergson's 'disciple' – 'His phraseology formed, indeed, the spectacles through which I have seen everything; but the spectacles were not external to me, fixed on my nose, removable at will, but were – if I may extend the metaphor illegitimately – fixed right in the middle of my mind, where I was not even aware of their existence.' Nothing, he felt, could have shaken him out of his hard-won Bergsonian certainties. Why, then, did he suddenly feel bereft? Because the presence of 400 equally adoring other people had brought about a 'complete reversal of feeling':

I was filled by a sentiment of most profound disgust and depression. My mind began at once, almost unconsciously, to feel that what these people thought about Bergson was entirely wrong. More than that, I passed on to the further belief that Bergson himself was wrong. The whole structure of beliefs so carefully constructed fell down like a house of cards. Something inside me determined, quite independently of my own volition, that it would set about and prove that in Bergson was not the 'truth', but a bubble soon to be burst. What these people agreed on could not be right. It is not in the nature of truth to be grasped so easily or so enthusiastically.[22]

From this point onward in the article Bergson is forgotten and Hulme turns in fascination to an analysis of his own disappointment. He finds it has subjective, trivial causes. Bergson's celebrity means that 'there was no longer any mild kind of distinction in knowing someone of whom the rest were ignorant'. Fully conscious of the absurdity of the situation, he registers the 'extraordinary distaste we feel for sharing even our most cherished beliefs with a crowd'. For him, 'being a Tory by disposition', as he describes himself, the root cause of the problem is that 'I have been exposed to this awful situation by the fact that 400 people have been allowed to come together to listen to a philosopher':

The type of mind represented by my childish repugnance at this moment is not new. It has always existed, and it has always been provided for. The ancients knew what they were about. They never allowed these kinds of emotions to come to the surface. They prevented it by a most simple device, which it will be necessary for us to return to if we are to preserve ourselves from this most dangerous form of scepticism. They knew how foolhardy it was to violate the Cosmos's feelings of delicacy. Violate that delicacy by bringing 400 people to see her undressed, and she is sure to revenge herself by sowing these seeds of blighting scepticism. We must, then, re-establish the old distinction between the public and the esoteric doctrine. The difficulty of getting into this hall should have been comparable to the difficulty of getting into a harem, not only in appearance, but in fact.[23]

Trivial and subjective though its causes may have been his disappointment was real enough and it was now really only a matter of time before he withdrew his interest from Bergson completely.

*

The metaphor Hulme discovered to convey his ignorance of his own prejudices, that of a man wearing a pair of spectacles without being conscious of the fact, turned out to be a persuasive and versatile tool for undermining the self-confidence of any readers of his articles who had thought themselves secure in their beliefs. He introduced it to particularly good effect in a series of short political articles which expanded on that passing reference to himself as a 'Tory by disposition', written between 1911 and 1912 for The Commentator. With such titles as 'The Art of Political Conversion', 'On Progress and Democracy' and 'A Tory Philosophy', Hulme seemed to be harking back to the 'Chesterbelloc' debate that raged through the pages of The New Age for much of the winter of 1907–8, where Arnold Bennett wrote on 'Why I am a Socialist' and G. K. Chesterton responded with 'Why I am not a Socialist'. Their occasion, however, was contemporary, being Hulme's interest in what he considered to be perhaps the most remarkable feature of the constitutional crisis of 1911 over the reform of the House of Lords: why was it that so many middle-class people were attracted to radical views in general? What was the cause of the landslide among the intellectuals to the socialist side?

In his articles he tried to identify the Conservative Party's main problem in dealing with the rise of socialism. Being opposed to the very idea of an ideology, conservative philosophy is condemned to define itself always as a response to attacks on specific institutions (the Church, the monarchy, the House of Lords), the stability and continuity of which Tories know to be essential to the good functioning of society. Compared with the premium put on theory which can be articulated by the socialists, this state of affairs will always make it appear as though conservatives have no ideology and stand for nothing in particular.

Hulme looks for possible ways of reversing the strong drift to socialism among the middle classes. Particularly ripe for conversion (or re-conversion) are those students and intellectuals who have, 'under the influence of a certain environment, adopted a theory which is not at all the expression of [their] own prejudices'. He likens them to people wearing blue glasses to whom everything will appear blue until the glasses are removed. Once such a person's true prejudices are revealed to him it should be possible to effect a conversion, so Hulme's task is to persuade blue-spectacled socialists like these of the dishonesty of socialist idealism.

He sets about it with relish. He terms such idealism a romantic pathology based on the delusion that man is born good. The villains are Goethe and Rousseau. He quotes from a letter by Rousseau: 'The fundamental principle of all morality is that man is a being naturally loving justice. In *Emile* I have endeavoured to show how vice and error, foreign to the natural constitution of man, have been introduced from outside, and have insensibly altered him.' Such a view, says Hulme, leads the romantic to suppose that things can be accomplished only by breaking rules and so to the prospect of a society with an addiction to endless and ultimately pointless revolution.

Against this tendency he offers the potential convert a quite different view of man according to which:

Man is by his very nature essentially limited and incapable of anything extraordinary. He is incapable of attaining any kind of perfection, because, either by nature, as the result of original sin, or the result of evolution, he encloses within him certain antinomies. There is a war of instincts inside him, and it is part of his permanent characteristics that this must always be so. The future condition, then, will always be one of struggle and limitation. The best results can only be got out of man as the result of a certain discipline which introduces order into this internal anarchy. That is what Aristotle meant by saying that only a god or a beast could live outside the State. Nothing is bad in itself except disorder; all that is put in order in a hierarchy is good. Moreover, man being by nature constant, the kind of discipline which will get the best out of him, and which is necessary for him, remains much the same in every generation. The classical attitude, then, has a great respect for the past and for tradition, not from sentimental, but on purely rational grounds. It does not expect anything radically new, and does not believe in any real progress.[24]

Having exposed the idea of progress as a romantic addiction he concludes his argument with an attempt to persuade the potential convert that an unchanging society is not something to fear; that to the contrary it can be a source of comfort and great beauty. H. G. Wells, Lowes Dickinson and A. W. Benn are all quoted as examples of thinkers for whom a constant society is axiomatically a bad, even nightmarish thing. Hulme is disappointed that none of them even feels the need to argue the point:

It is easy to see here that it is this repugnance to the idea of fixity which is at the bottom of a great many political ideals. But if you once face this repugnance in its nakedest form, you will find that it vanishes. Why should the idea of a constant, continuous, and endless progress be any more rational or satisfactory than the idea of constancy? Either the progress attains its end (when it is finished with), or it never attains its end, and then it is still more irrational; for progress towards an end which constantly recedes cannot be said to be a satisfactory view of the world-process [. . .] It is quite as easy and natural for emotion and enthusiasm to crystallise round the idea of a constant world as round the idea of progress. An extraordinary solidarity is given to one's beliefs. There is great consolation in the idea that men have always thought as we think now. It gives to religion a great stability, for it exhibits it as a permanent part of man's nature, and the nature of man being constant, it places these beliefs beyond all change.[25]

Clearly one of the most effective ways to demonstrate the truth of what Hulme was saying would be the appearance of some great art that embodied it, and when presently he began to take a serious interest in aesthetics this was one of the ideas uppermost in his mind, that he was looking for an art with the 'romantic' attractions of seeming both strange and revolutionary that was yet deeply rooted in the view of human nature as something fixed and constant.

Twice in the course of these political articles Hulme makes the surprising claim that he was a socialist himself in his youth: 'It so happens,' he says, discussing the power of the slogan and the catchword in politics, 'that the days when I was a Socialist are not so far away that I have forgotten the kind of emotion that moved me then.'[26] At greater length but to the same end he relates an anecdote based on the claim:

Some years after reading Menger's big book[27] on the juridical aspect of Socialism, I tried, with the enthusiasm of youth, to explain some of the ideas in it to a typical suburban dweller who was travelling up to his business in an early morning train. After listening to me for some time with an amused and tolerant expression, he suddenly leaned over his *Daily Telegraph* and said, 'My dear fellow, these things may be all right in theory, but they would be very different in practice.' The fatuous complacency with which this remark was uttered, and the unction with which he pronounced the word 'theory', drove me to a pitch of frenzy in which I would willingly have destroyed him instantly with a blow from the heavy book which had started the discussion, and which lay ready on my knees.[28]

It is hard to judge whether this claim was a debating ploy or sincerely meant. The use of such a ploy would not have been beyond him; but as Orage's description indicates, early twentieth-century socialism was a very mixed bag indeed. Orage's own version of it included an admiration for Nietzsche which he found not at all inconsistent with his appreciation of *Das Kapital*. Georges Sorel, whose *Refléxions sur la violence* Hulme later translated, is to some modern analysts an anti-democrat and a seminal figure in the evolution of European Fascism; to many of his contemporaries, however, his was the true voice of socialism and *Refléxions* an original and timely critique of democracy. Readers of *The Commentator* might well have credited Hulme's assertion without automatically assuming that it was a claim once to have been a follower of Karl Marx and Keir Hardie. He might have been looking even further back than this, to his schooldays and the debate on the drink problem, where he had taken the socialist and 'idealist' position that the solution lay in better housing and education for the poor. If not a ploy then the socialist past he was referring to might have resulted from the same adolescent fidelity to a logically compelling system that had also turned him into a determinist. But no political equivalent of Bergson as his rescuer from the socialist delusion is ever mentioned and he evidently never felt trapped by the logic of socialism as he had by that of determinism. True or not, the claim enabled him to address his readers from the point of view of one who has made the same mistakes as they, but has seen the light.

*

After the prolonged chaos of his adolescence Hulme seemed by 1912, at the age of twenty-eight, to have found himself. He knew who he was: a polymath philosopher. But where was the proof? Where were the papers? One of his complaints in 'Bergson Lecturing' about the difficulty of gaining entry to the lecture was that 'when I applied for a ticket I received a note asking for *full* particulars of my qualifications', the exasperated italics again a reminder that he did not have the annoying little bit of paper that would *prove* he was a philosopher.

But on other fronts things were more certain. He was established in a small family arrangement with the Kibblewhites and had a base with Dolly at 67 Frith Street. He had French translations to be getting on with, Bergson's *Introduction to Metaphysics* and the Sorel book to which he had at some point also acquired the rights, as well as a book of his own on Bergson to write. Contemplating this stability, it occurred to him that now was the right time to return to Cambridge, take his degree in philosophy, get that piece of paper and make a fresh start to his life. To do that he had to persuade the authorities at St John's that he was now a reformed character.

6

Original Sin

Hulme's task was probably more correctly to prove to the college authorities that he had become a disciplined character, for discipline and not reform was the only option for someone who believed as firmly as he now did in the reality of original sin. The references to the doctrine which appeared in his political articles for *The Commentator* were repeated in almost everything he wrote at this time, and it went on to form the basis of most of his thought for the remainder of his life and to symbolize more than anything else exactly what he stood for. In the years following his death and the publication of *Speculations* it became so firmly identified with his name that in *Blasting and Bombardiering* Wyndham Lewis humorously dubbed him 'Hulme of Original Sin'. Although his personal discovery of the doctrine is not documented in the same way as is his release from the nightmare of determinism, it is still possible to take an educated guess at its genealogy.

'Impossible to learn anything new in ideas from a book,' he had observed in 'Notes on Language and Style'. 'Must be there beforehand, then joy in recognising it', and this was probably always true for Hulme, even where the book in question turned out to be the Bible. Moreover, he was an amateur thinker, not an academic philosopher picking and choosing his way through a history of ideas, and an obvious reason for the attraction of the doctrine is that it corresponded closely to his own observations of himself and the people around him. He was, in addition, a young man with a strong element of that youthful snobbishness that likes to be ahead of the game, and having been one of Bergson's first readers and apologists in Britain he found, as we have seen, that the growing popularity of Bergson's ideas made them suspect. Despite his gratitude to Bergson for the part he had played in his intellectual development and his continuing professional involvement as his translator, it seems clear that by 1912 Hulme no longer needed the support of his ideas to the same extent and was actively searching for something more challenging to believe in. In original sin he found it. It had no taint of romanticism or populism to it and in its austerity it was unlikely ever to appeal to those huge audiences of women with their heads lifted in 'Eager Heart' attitudes of expectation that he had experienced at Bergson's lectures.

Another factor in his decision to introduce the dogma into his articles and lectures at this time may hark back to the 'Chesterbelloc' debate already referred to, which occurred at just the time when Hulme was becoming an actor on the London cultural scene. Though it pitted the Fabians Shaw and Wells against the Catholic conservatives Chesterton and Belloc, the debate was only nominally about socialism. Its real theme was human nature and how this ought to be assessed in the light of evolutionary theory, and in the course of the discussion the merits and otherwise of Roman Catholicism were frequently touched upon. It marked a watershed in the relationship between Catholics and liberal idealists which many Catholics up until this time had assumed to be a natural political alliance. Hulme, a man with strong journalistic instincts and a natural controversialist, must have noted the emerging polarity and been engaged both by the views expressed and by the degree of interest aroused by the debate. Twice in the course of the debate *The New Age* was completely sold out.

More specifically there is Hulme's enthusiasm for the French social-ist thinker Georges Sorel. Sorel published his most famous book, *Refléxions sur la violence*, in 1908 and Hulme seems to have been among its first English readers. After an exchange of letters with the author he had obtained permission to translate it, but had initially been unable to interest a publisher in the idea.[1] By late 1911 he had revived the project and persuaded Stephen Swift to take it on. Problems of various sorts, however, delayed publication in England until 1916, by which time both Sorel and Hulme had moved on from their respect-ive original positions.

After working for most of his life for the French government as a civil engineer, Sorel had retired at the age of forty-five to devote himself full-time to writing. His influences included Nietzsche, William James, Bergson, Marx, Vico and Proudhon, and in the course of his thinking he moved swiftly between a variety of ideologies in all of which he sought an adequate response to the puritan sense of disgust he felt at the corrupt and degenerate state of French society. He was at various times a Marxist, a royalist, an anti-royalist, and, after the Russian Revolution of 1917, a supporter of Lenin and the Bolsheviks. At the time he wrote *Reflections on Violence* he was a revolutionary syndicalist,[2] and the book is full of a ferocious impatience with what he saw as the dilatory, compromise-ridden state of the socialist movement at the turn of the century. He identified as socialism's main problem the crippling effect on the movement of its intellectual theorists and those who believed, like the Fabians in England, that the road to eventual success lay by way of democracy and the constitutional process. The solution he offered involved the vigorous promotion of an anti-intellectual form of socialism which should have as its most powerful weapon the 'myth' of a general strike. That such a strike might not be practicable was not the point, it was the myth itself that was important. The adoption of such a myth would imbue the working class with an irresistible sense of its own power and would act as the motor for violent socialist revolution. Sorel applied to religious history to support his theory, citing the faith of the early Christians that Christ would return at the end of the first generation to banish corruption and establish the kingdom of heaven on earth. This did not happen, Sorel observed, but the power of the 'mythic belief' gave the movement the inspiration and sustenance it needed to survive and eventually prosper. Another example, 'even more striking', according to Sorel, came from Catholicism:

Catholics have never been discouraged even in the hardest trials, because they have always pictured the history of the Church as a series of battles between Satan and the hierarchy supported by Christ; every new difficulty which arises is only an episode in a war which must finally end in the victory of Catholicism.[3]

Sorel neither expected nor wanted socialist intellectuals to understand his theory of myths. He likened them to those educated Catholics who were horrified when they discover that the ideas of Joseph de Maistre have helped to encourage the ignorance of the clergy, which did not attempt to acquire an adequate knowledge of a science which it held to be accursed; to these educated Catholics the myth of the struggle with Satan then appears dangerous, and they point out its ridiculous aspects; but they do not in the least understand its historical bearing.[4]

Syndicalism, in adopting his 'myth', would rid the socialist movement of the 'stream of confused commentaries' that came from its intellectuals and rendered it impotent:

The Syndicalists solve this problem perfectly, by concentrating the whole of Socialism in the drama of the general strike; there is thus no longer any place for the reconciliation of contraries in the equivocations of the professors; everything is clearly mapped out, so that only one interpretation of Socialism is possible. This method has all the advantages which 'integral' knowledge has over analysis, according to the doctrine of Bergson; and perhaps it would not be possible to cite another example which would so perfectly demonstrate the value of the famous professor's doctrines.[5]

Two paradoxes quickly emerge in considering Hulme's enthusiasm for Sorel. The first is that while Sorel defined Bergson's position as an anti-intellectualism in which he exulted, Hulme valued Bergson precisely because he had used an intellectual approach to cure intellect of its delusions of grandeur. He took pride and pleasure in his ability to conduct philosophical and ethical debates with opponents on their own terms, and the anti-intellectualism that lay at the heart of Sorel's theory cannot possibly have appealed to him.

The second follows on from this: Sorel was a socialist and Hulme was not. Whatever form of the ideology he had in mind when he referred to 'the days when I was a socialist' in his *Commentator* article, Hulme was by 1912 not only describing himself as 'a Tory' but was actively seeking effective ways of converting people from socialist to Tory beliefs. The resolution of the paradoxes is that Hulme's attraction to Sorel was philosophical and not political. It was Sorel's ethics, not his political views, that attracted him. As he wrote to C. K. Ogden:

Personally I find Sorel a great deal more interesting than Syndicalism itself. I think that after Bergson, he is the most interesting person writing at this present time. I think it is a mistake entirely to get at him merely as a writer on Socialism. He is much more a person of Nietzsche's stamp, whose main interest is in general ethical criticism.[6]

It was the 'general ethical criticism' Sorel offered along the way in his exposition of the theory of 'myths' that was the attraction. It included the view that man is not born good; that man does not naturally seek happiness; that 'nature' is an inscrutable and entropic chaos which can be controlled only by the discipline of will-power; and that the values of comfort, hedonism and materialism are inherently contemptible – all assertions that struck a profound chord in Hulme.

In like fashion, his enthusiasm for the right-wing, royalist French pressure group Action Française between the years 1909 and 1912 needs to be seen as an enthusiasm for the ethical views of the group rather than a shared interest in their specific political aims. Pierre Lasserre, the writer Hulme had visited in Dieppe on his way to Bologna, was one of its ideological leaders, along with the group's founder, Charles Maurras. The aims it pursued were a revival of the monarchy in France; the return of conservative values; and an intense patriotism and a submission to authority that led Maurras – a freethinker – to promote the view that France needed Catholicism. Hulme already lived in a monarchy, and his conservative instincts were not constantly chafed by reminders of a great liberal revolution in his country's recent history. Nor did he share the perverted form of nationalism that led to anti-Semitism within the group. What attracted him was the way Action Française had revived conservative fortunes in France and even made conservatism fashionable. When he recommended the group generally and Maurras and Lasserre in particular to Ogden, it was for the chief virtue of their 'very precise and lucid Anti Romanticism'.[7] And the most trenchant form of this was, for him, the insistent rejection of the idea that men are born good.

The spirit if not the letter of Roman Catholicism hovers around both these francophile enthusiasms of Hulme's late twenties. He once told Ashley Dukes that if he were French he would, as a good nationalist, also profess Roman Catholicism.[8] Not being French, however, 'he always said he was a member of the Church of England', Dukes recalled, though he never saw him at any kind of religious devotions.[9] If nothing else, his use of the Catholic term 'original sin' was a good marketing ploy, giving the dramatic authority of religion to a view of human nature that might have seemed less striking had he contented himself with the statement that men are born bad.

And yet, scattered across Hulme's notes and letters are references that hint at a real interest in Catholicism. Insofar as his conception of the doctrine can be placed in a religious context at all his pessimism seems to have been less complete than that of Augustine and closer to the conditional pessimism of Aquinas, who held that original sin was transmitted not as the personal fault of the first man but as a condition of human nature. Aquinas's conceptions supposed a division in the first man between man's own pure nature and the supernatural privileges that directed him towards his supernatural end. With the Fall he lost these supernatural privileges, but by divine grace was allowed to retain the natural powers of his reason, will and passions. In a letter of response to a criticism of Bergson that had appeared in *The New Age* Hulme mentions Aquinas and advises the critic to read R. P. Sertillange's book on the saint for its discussion on the physics of Aristotle.[10] He also recommends that he read a work by De Tongedet[11] for its account of Bergson 'from the Catholic point of view'.

In the same letter Hulme refers to an encounter with a 'professor of philosophy at a Catholic Seminary with whom I discussed these things years ago' (and whom he claims assured him that Aristotle wrote in Latin); the recollection may provide a clue to how Hulme, from a non-Catholic background, came to be so preoccupied with the religious formulation of the anti-romantic doctrine of the badness of man.

Since being sent down from Cambridge in 1904 he had come to regard the Pattinsons of Macclesfield as his real family and Alice Pattinson's home, Lake House, as his real home. He was also a regular visitor to Stanbrook Abbey in Worcester, where Alice's two sisters were members of a Benedictine order, and which may well have been the site of his conversation with the professor. A friend recalled that Hulme 'constantly went to visit them',[12] although the only direct evidence of such visits are two notes of characteristic brevity he wrote during the war to Richard Curle.[13] The first reads:

My dear Curle,

I enclose 10/-. I don't know exactly what I owe. I'm off to Worcester today. Expect to be back in town about Saturday.

Mrs K. W. returns on Wednesday.

Yrs

T. E. Hulme

And the follow-up:

Selbourne Rd

Worcester

Dear Curle,

I expect to be in town to-morrow *Monday* afternoon. Will you come in to tea at Frith Street if you have nothing else to do.

Yrs

T. E. Hulme

Both these women, whose company Hulme sought out so regularly, were graduates of Newnham College – the sort of paradox that seems to crop up in the life of every intelligent male supremacist. The first to take holy orders was Helen, who entered Stanbrook in 1887 at the age of thirty-one and was given the name Barbara. She assumed the title of Dame[14] the following year. Dame Barbara was a gifted icon painter and a translator of Catholic texts including the *Letters of the Blessed John of Avila*, published in London in 1904, *The Interior Castle, or the Mansions of St Teresa* and *The Way of Perfection* in 1925.

She was joined at Stanbrook in 1893 by Florence, who was given the devotional name Ursula. From Hulme's point of view perhaps one of the most striking facts about the sisters is that both were converts to Roman Catholicism, and in Ursula's case at least the conversion was in the face of strong paternal disapproval. Her father, Thomas Pattinson, even went to the lengths of sending her to Dr Stubbs, the great historian of Anglo-Saxon England and Bishop of Oxford, in the hope of deterring her. In the light of his struggles with his own father as a youth an episode like this can only have struck a sympathetic chord in Hulme, and the fact that both women insisted on taking the most important decisions of their lives for themselves must have given their example great authority in his eyes.

Of Barbara the abbey's own 'House Chronicle' said, on her death in 1924, that 'she was a convert and her ideas of religious life were not always quite from a Catholic point of view. We always called her "a man of desires", as she was continually longing for something, for the garden, her books, etc, and her desires were nearly always fulfilled in an extraordinary way – for she had great confidence in prayer.'[15] This strong independence of mind obviously made her a stimulating intellectual companion for Hulme in his own search for truth; and the same is probably true of Ursula.

The Pattinson sisters were all in their different ways interested in art. Besides supporting the outcast philosopher-poet Hulme within her own family Alice later helped the struggling young painter Tunnicliffe through art college. Ursula was remembered for the great beauty of her mezzo-soprano voice, taught drawing in the convent for many years and was a designer and embroiderer of vestments, a tapestry weaver, gardener and designer of furniture for the abbey. She lived just long enough to see the appearance of Michael Roberts's book on her nephew and wrote to him after publication with one or two stories of Hulme's early life that came too late for inclusion in Roberts's biographical sketch. In her letter she recalled Hulme's visits to Stanbrook and how on one visit he had bought a penny catechism. All in all, the more one forms a picture of this Pattinson side of Hulme's family the more one is inclined to find here the steady drip of a theological influence that eventually crystallized into a belief in original sin.

*

One of Hulme's earliest public uses of the term, trumpeted with all the force of recent discovery, was in the opening sentence of the *Commentator* article of 3 April already described: 'It is my aim to explain in this article why I believe in original sin, why I can't stand romanticism, and why I am a certain kind of Tory.' At about the same time as this appeared he travelled up to Cambridge to lecture to university undergraduate groups and on 25 February addressed a philosophical society presided over by C. K. Ogden known as 'The Heretics'. He had written to Ogden a few weeks earlier seeking guidance on what to talk about:

Do you want to know also the title of the paper? – I am still undecided myself as to what it will be. I don't know quite the kind of thing you like. Do you want a paper on somebody else, Sorel or L'Action Française for example, or shall I trot out some of my own theories? I have got two in mind, 'Anti Romanticism and Original Sin' or another on 'Dolls, Idols and Idealogues'. But if you are in London before the 23rd December, will you come and see me here and we could talk about it?[16]

The choice fell on 'Anti-Romanticism and Original Sin' and the *Cambridge Magazine* carried a lengthy précis of the lecture, from which it seems that this was one of three slightly different versions of one and the same piece of writing Hulme was working on at this time. The second was the lecture entitled 'The New Philosophy of Art as Illustrated in Poetry', which he delivered at Clifford's Inn Hall in London on 15 July that year; and this was in turn almost certainly the basis for the essay 'Romanticism and Classicism' reproduced in *Speculations*.[17] Ogden provided a précis of Hulme's lecture for the *Cambridge Magazine* which shows that it mixed political elements of the *Commentator* article with provocative statements about the reality of original sin and the failings of romanticism:

He emphasised the importance of certain words – words of power – in the formation of prejudices and ideals, and the general clouding of our judgement. Repeat the word 'Progress' often enough and it is easy to delude oneself into denying the truths of the doctrine of Original Sin amidst the mess of hypocritical Utopias, which ignore the principle of the constancy of Man. It never occurred to the Classicists to have any illusions about Progress; and here Mr Hulme launched forth a diatribe against Lady Welby, Goethe, Mr Lowes Dickinson, Mr Alfred Benn, and all those who take the Spiral as the symbol of the Nature of Man, and declared that if he were ever made a Peer he would take as his insignia a particularly lively Wheel, chastising a complacent Spiral.[18] Let no-one think he denied Progress in the sense of change. Obviously there is change; but what he did most certainly deny was the particular kind of Progress which was responsible for the particular kind of emotion characteristic of the professed Romantics of the 'New Heaven and a New Earth' sort.

The Deity has many aliases, and the time had come to write an Odyssey of his wanderings up and down the alphabet. *Dynamic, Vibration, Rhythm* ('They even have a paper'[19]) were words which he abhorred.[20]

'And on this note of abhorrence,' Ogden writes, 'the paper came to a close.' It was followed by a long and lively discussion 'in which Mr Hulme expended much energy in convincing the uninitiated that their questions were irrelevant'.

The slightly ironic tone of Ogden's report suggests that for his audience of undergraduate Heretics Hulme consciously added a leavening of the caustic and provocative style of his *New Age* persona. This is less conspicuous in 'Romanticism and Classicism', which, given its consistent focus on the implications of his analysis for poetry rather than any other form of expression, was perhaps even identical with the lecture delivered at Clifford's Inn Hall. On 25 January 1912 'The Complete Poetical Works of T. E. Hulme' had been collected and published for the first time in *The New Age*, and it may have been this revival of interest in Hulme's poems that led to the invitation to lecture on verse. The talk was part of a short monthly series that began in May with Harold Monro, soon to open his Poetry Bookshop, on 'Modern Poetry', and continued in June with Darrell Figgis ('Michael Ireland') on 'The Sanction of Poetry'.

Although it covered the same ground as 'A Tory Philosophy' its focus on poetry made it almost certainly Hulme's first attempt to synthesize all his important ideas so far in the fields of literature, politics and philosophy on the basis of original sin; it is one of his best-known pieces of writing and the *locus classicus* of his polarizing definitions of the terms 'classical' and 'romantic' that have inspired and exercised writers and critics from T. S. Eliot to Saul Bellow, from Read himself to Raymond Williams and beyond. Writing in 1957 Frank Kermode referred to the 'extraordinary celebrity' of the paper. So familiar has it become that reading it now is almost like reading a compendium of quotations:

Man is an extraordinarily fixed and limited animal. It is only by tradition and organisation that anything decent can be got out of him.

You don't believe in a God, so you begin to believe that man is a God. You don't believe in Heaven, so you begin to believe in a heaven on earth. In other words, you get romanticism.

The amount of freedom in man is much exaggerated.

It is essential to prove that beauty may be in small, dry things.

Hulme states his purpose in the opening lines of his paper: 'I want to maintain that after a hundred years of romanticism, we are in for a classical revival, and that the particular weapon of this new classical spirit, when it works in verse, will be fancy.'[21] He explains in introductory remarks that he is aware of the pitfalls in using the words 'classic' and 'romantic', that they can represent five or six different kinds of antitheses and that he runs a risk of being misunderstood. But he does so, he says, because it enables him to conform to the practice of the 'group of polemical writers who make most use of them at the present day' – Pierre Lasserre, Charles Maurras and other leading members of Action Française. In their active pursuit of a return to classical values these writers had requisitioned the two words and 'almost succeeded in making them political catchwords'. The observation underlines a point made in the Heretics lecture, that it was the failure of the conservatives in England to provide catchwords like these, catchwords which had the power to combat the attractions of a word like 'progress', that was responsible for their losing so much ground to socialism.

The second of Hulme's two pairs of oppositions, that between Imagination and Fancy, is derived from Coleridge and turns out to be the poetical echo of that between romanticism and classicism. Until 1817, when distinctions between the two conceptions were drawn by Coleridge in *Biographia Literaria*, the words had been used virtually interchangeably in the context of writing on the creative process by, among others, Hobbes, Dryden and Locke. Coleridge insisted that they were two distinct and different faculties. 'Fancy' he regarded as the faculty that receives images ready-made from the senses and restructures them without altering their content. 'Imagination' was the faculty involved in the making of real poetry. It actively 'dissolves, diffuses, dissipates' the sensory impressions it receives 'in order to re-create'. Fancy seemed to him self-evidently the lesser of the two faculties: 'Fancy . . . has no other counters to play with, but fixities and definites. The fancy is indeed no other than a Mode of memory emancipated from the order of time and space.' But it was for precisely these qualities – of dealing in fixities and definites and of confining its intervention to a modest restructuring of the spatial and temporal order in which its images were originally received – that Hulme intended to propose its superiority to Imagination, and to show why it was Fancy and not Imagination that would be the defining virtue of poetry in the new period of classicism he was prophesying.

The primary opposition to establish, however, was that between romanticism and classicism, and before going on to talk about verse he set about it. Hulme used these two words to describe the two basic human temperaments. The classical was the original temperament. According to this view man is a limited creature of finite capabilities. Innately lazy and not disposed to do good, he must accept and exercise discipline if he is to raise himself from the level of a beast and achieve anything at all. As a way of looking at human beings in their relationship to the cosmos it was a view well conveyed by the doctrine of original sin, and Hulme simply borrowed it from Catholicism and placed it in the secular context of a debate about literature to support a philosophical definition. In making use of it in this way he adds a note that seems almost like an aside to himself as he contemplates the odd possibility that in affirming the truth of this teaching he is merely exchanging one kind of determinism for another. 'It would be,' he observes, 'a mistake to identify the classical view with that of materialism. On the contrary it is absolutely identical with the normal religious attitude. I should put it this way: That part of the fixed nature of Man is belief in the Deity. This should be as fixed and true for every man as belief in the existence of matter and in the objective world. It is parallel to appetite, the instinct of sex, and all the other fixed qualities.'[22] But in the main his interest in the dogma at this point in his argument and in his life does not appear to have been strongly religious. In passing ('One may note here') he says that the Church is to be counted among the forces of classicism in society 'since the defeat of the Pelagian heresy[23] and the adoption of the sane classical dogma of original sin'; but an acceptance of this identification of the beliefs of the Church with his ideas of what 'classicism' means for the purpose of his discussion is all he is really after.

By Hulme's analysis the classical view of man was usurped in modern times by romanticism. Later on he would date this change to the fifteenth century, Pico della Mirandola and the beginnings of the Renaissance; but for the purposes of his paper on poetry he locates it to the early years of the nineteenth century. This is close enough in time to allow him to use the French Revolution of 1789 as a way of bringing out clearly the difference between the two attitudes of mind he is trying to describe. In analysing why the revolution succeeded as an idea – as opposed to the separate material causes involved which produced only the forces – he finds that it was fired by the teachings of Rousseau that man is by nature good and only spoiled by the circumstances of bad laws and customs and the oppression of order. The seduction of these teachings was so great that those elements in society which might naturally be expected to have opposed it did not do so. Hulme explains why this was so:

This always seems to be the case in successful changes; the privileged class is beaten only when it has lost faith in itself, when it has been penetrated with the ideas which are working against it.[24]

The assumption underlying the reference to the revolution is, presumably, that anyone looking at subsequent developments in France will see very clearly that romantic ideas about the innate goodness of man were simply not borne out. The wheel merely went round, not forward. He then offers a pithy summary of the position:

Put shortly, these are the two views, then. One, that man is intrinsically good, spoilt by circumstance; and the other that he is intrinsically limited, but disciplined by order and tradition to something fairly decent. To the one party man's nature is like a well, to the other like a bucket. The view which regards man as a well, a reservoir full of possibilities, I call the romantic; the one which regards him as a very finite and fixed creature, I call the classical.[25]

Two completely different types of poetry are produced by these two completely different temperaments. According to Hulme, the poetry characteristically produced by those of a romantic temperament is damp, insistently grandiose in its choice of theme and immodest in its depictions of man's place in creation. It indulges the intemperate imagination and measures its success by the degree and intensity of emotion produced. With great disapproval he quotes from the second volume of John Ruskin's *Modern Painters*: 'Imagination cannot but be serious; she sees too far, too darkly, too solemnly, too earnestly, ever to smile. There is something in the heart of everything, if we can reach it, that we shall not be inclined to laugh at.'[26] It is the kind of romantic pessimism that produces a 'sloppiness which doesn't consider that a poem is a poem unless it is moaning or whining about something or other'.[27]

The classical cast of mind, on the other hand, will produce something quite different – new verse that will prove 'that beauty may be in small, dry things'.[28] Its virtues will be substantially those that Hulme and his friends in the Secession branch of the Poets' Club tried to cultivate – directness, simplicity, thematic modesty and technical exactitude. 'Subject doesn't matter,'[29] he says, and the romantic trick of 'dragging in the infinite'[30] will no longer be sufficient to define a poem as a poem. The vital question will not be *where is the infinite in this?* but 'Is there any real zest in it? Did the poet have an actually realised visual object before him in which he delighted?'[31] As for the subject, 'It doesn't matter if it were a lady's shoe or the starry heavens.'[32] Plain speech will be used, but plain speech made rich and accurate by the use of new metaphors. Fancy will reclaim the high ground from Imagination by its insistence on precision in its new metaphors – 'It is only by new metaphors, that is, by fancy, that it [plain speech] can be made precise.'[33] The poet's skill in the technically difficult task of fitting the metaphor exactly to the thing described will be the measure of his success, not the size of his subject matter or the intensity of his emotions. He cites the traditional Irish ballad 'On Fair Kirkconnel Lea' as a good example of the direct simplicity he mentions. Unlike the morbid ballad, however, and quite unlike the sort of poetry of which Ruskin would approve, the classical verse to come will be 'cheerful, dry and sophisticated'.[34] Nor will the new poetry be filled with wonder, for wonder can only ever be a passing phase, never 'a permanently fixed thing'.[35]

Hulme attempts a rough categorization of individual writers within his general scheme. Horace, most of the Elizabethans and the writers of the Augustan age are 'classical'; Lamartine, Hugo, parts of Keats, Coleridge, Byron, Shelley and Swinburne are 'romantic'. Shakespeare seems to be both. The list points up an obvious weakness in his presentation, that he is unable to mention any living poets whose work could be used to demonstrate the imminence of the classical revival. Hulme deals with this lack of 'any new efflorescence of verse' by saying that movements in art have life cycles. They get old, decay and die. Every school of poetry creates a corresponding attitude of response in critics that tends to linger on after the poetry itself has become mori-bund and ceased to satisfy the poets themselves. Thus contemporary criticism still applies the same outmoded standards in judging what is and what is not good poetry, and would be functionally incapable of recognizing good classicist verse even if it appeared. It was an argument similar to the one he would shortly repeat in the field of aesthetic criticism in trying to argue the same point about romanticism and classicism. Poetry would have to wait for Eliot to confirm the accuracy of Hulme's vision, but in the plastic arts living sculptors and painters were already producing work which he could use to support the theory of an imminent change in the *Zeitgeist*.

Here and there in the course of his paper Hulme makes some trademark lurches from high objectivity into rough subjectivity. He claims that one sure indication of the coming classicism is 'the increas-ing proportion of people who simply can't stand Swinburne', and that it was 'precisely that quality in Pope which pleased his friends, which we detest'. By 1912 his well-documented fondness for strong language had become a matter of principle and a part of his loathing for the 'vagueness' of romantic poetry and more general disapproval of 'the person with catholic tastes' and his sympathy with the aims of Action Française and the French classicists generally was also admiration for the passion which they were prepared to support their beliefs. 'The best way of gliding into a proper definition of my terms would be to start with a set of people who are prepared to fight about it,' he says at one point, and describes with approval the French classicists who cared enough about long-dead Racine to start fights 'all over the house' at a lecture at the Paris Odéon a year previously, provoked by the lecturer's disparaging remarks about Racine's 'dullness' and 'lack of invention'. 'Passion without action is but the anger of a child' was one of Hulme's own aphorisms in 'Cinders'. He admired commitment like this intensely, hence the provocative rhetorical haymakers in his lecture about how he 'hates', 'abhors', 'detests' and 'can't stand' romanticism. He wants his listeners and his readers to know that he believes strongly in what he is saying. And he wants to know, do those who disagree with him care as much about their own views? Are they willing, as he implicitly declares himself willing, to put up their fists and fight for them?

'Each field of artistic activity is exhausted by the first great artist who gathers a full harvest from it,' Hulme observed in his lecture. He was not a great artist, but he gathered a full polemical harvest from the simple stroke of genius that suggested to him that he pick out the disturbing notion of original sin from its religious context and wave it under the nose of an increasingly secular society that would have liked nothing better than to forget all about it. Wyndham Lewis was among those contemporaries who relished the sight. 'But I can see all this will seem gibberish to you,' he wrote in *Blasting and Bombardiering*,

unless by good luck it has been your hobby to instruct yourself in all these highbrow goings-on. All I can really tell you is that it *was* extremely original of this Mr Hulme – especially living as he did in Mr Polly's England – to pick out this stuffy old doctrine of Original Sin and rub everybody's nose in it. He was a very rude and truculent man. He needed to be. And he greatly relished rubbing his countrymen's noses in the highly disobliging doctrine in question.[36]

One is left with the general feeling that, despite a sympathetic interest in the Catholic religion, Hulme's adoption of the term original sin at this time was largely provocative, and his broadcast approval of it an expression of the general conservative belief in the value of the Church as a social institution. But by the time he returned specifically to it in 'A Notebook' four years later, older and under the urgent pressure of war, he had outgrown the need to provoke and his interest was both deeper and more personal.

7

Cambridge Revisited

Hulme's first approach to L. K. Bushe-Fox, Dr MacAlister's successor as philosophy tutor at St John's, had been made in a letter of 28 February, while he was still in Cambridge after lecturing to the Heretics. He made it clear that he was keen to get his degree and wanted to supplement his reading of philosophy with two 'specials' in psychology and mathematics. Concerning his previous experience as an undergraduate at the college he was open but not effusive, preferring to let his potential and actual achievements since that time speak for his new seriousness of purpose: 'Two books of mine have been announced and will shortly appear, one an authorised translation of Bergson, and the other a critical exposition of his philosophy.'[1] The former was of course the *Introduction to Metaphysics*, and the latter the book advertised to appear after the lectures at Mrs Liebich's house. Swift had been advertising this regularly in *The Granta* and the *Cambridge Magazine* at a price of 7s 6d, as compared to 2s 6d for the translated essay. A synopsis in Swift's advertisement, obviously written by Hulme himself, indicates that the intention was to 'develop at some length a part of Bergson's philosophy which has been written about very little, and which may prove the most interesting part to many people – his *theory of art*' and that the book was 'not technical' and was 'intended for the general reader', and advertising the author's personal acquaintance with Bergson.

MacAlister had gone to Glasgow University and Bushe-Fox wrote to him there for his account of what had happened in 1904. MacAlister's reply was reassuring. Hulme's faults were 'idleness and a tendency to get into foolish scrapes'. He could recall nothing against the young man's moral character, and nothing in his conduct that he could not redeem if he awoke to his responsibilities. My impression was that his mathematics did not appeal to him. Now he seems to have found his line in philosophy, and if you are satisfied that he has given up his vexatious pranks, I should raise no objection to his readmission.[2]

At about the same time Hulme arranged for a number of testimonials to be sent to the college in support of his application. One was from his father, who wrote that he had seen his son several times each year for the past few years and that 'for the whole time since he left his behaviour has been good'. Two more were from clerics. Reverend Morris wrote from Endon Vicarage to confirm that since the 'painful occurrence' Hulme had been under his 'close observation'. It was gratifying for him to be able to report that 'his conduct and mode of life have been in every way excellent. Not once has he shown signs of frivolity.' A maternal uncle, the Reverend T. A. Duncan, wrote of his nephew's 'steady and reputable life' since leaving university, and Dolly Kibblewhite's father, Thomas Curtis, submitted a similar report.

Along with these conventional expressions of good faith Hulme was able to provide what must have been a most impressive document in 1912, a letter of warm personal and professional recommendation from the most famous living philosopher, Henri Bergson, dated 6 March from Villa Montmorency, in the Auteuil district of Paris:

Je me fais un plaisir de certifier que je considère Mr T. E. Hulme comme un esprit d'une grande valeur. Il apporte, à l'étude des questions philosophiques, de rares qualités de finesse, de vigueur, et de pénétration. Ou je me trompe beaucoup, ou il est destiné à produire des oeuvres intéressantes et importantes dans le domaine de la philosophie en général, et plus particulièrement dans celui de la philosophie de l'art.[3]

Bushe-Fox gave his approval on 15 April and the following day Hulme was formally readmitted as a student at St John's. He lived out of college, renting two rooms for the Easter term at 5 St Andrews Hill from a Mrs Hobson. The rent was £10 for the term, and food, shoe-cleaning, hire of crockery, coal for heating and gas for lighting brought the sum up to £14 1s 5d. Hulme described his new life in a postcard to Alice Pattinson's brother Thomas in Macclesfield:

Dear Mr Pattinson,

I was very glad to hear from you. It seems very strange to read in a letter 'I knew Cambridge in the forties'. I was telling this to the editor of the Cambridge Magazine, & he at once with the editorial instinct said 'Couldn't he give me some reminiscences'!

Don't bother to send the 3/6 for the book. I meant it as a present. It is very pleasant being up here. Of course being older I know a very different set of people to those I did when I was up before. I know more of the dons and very few of the undergraduates. I am not living in College this time but outside in rooms, as having a good deal of work to be done I want to be quieter.

An American judge I know came up to Cambridge to see me the other afternoon. He said that he thought he had never been in such a beautiful town.

A great many addition [sic] new courts have been added since you were up but I think you would find the general aspect of the place the same. I expect you would find however that the undergraduates were a good deal more negligent in their attire. Hoping that you will soon completely recover and enjoy the summer.

Yours affectionately,
Ernest Hulme[4]

Older he may have been and in some respects wiser, but the 'appalling obstinacy' once noted by his uncle Edward Hollinshead had not changed at all, and within a few short weeks of taking up residence at 5 St Andrews Hill Hulme had driven his new landlady to the verge of hysteria. The problem arose because of the style in which the rooms were furnished, one that Hulme admitted most people would have described as 'nicely furnished'. The bedroom, where edifying texts flourished and he was exhorted to 'Watch and Pray' as he shaved, flanked by photographs of the seafronts at Bournemouth and Margate, seemed to him just about tolerable. The sitting room was the problem. It had an overmantel containing one large and eight small mirrors; a sideboard with further mirrors, and a free-standing mirror that was simply a mirror by itself. Dotted about the room were some two dozen vases of differing shapes, sizes and colours as well as fern and ordinary pot plants, and coating the walls twenty or thirty framed photographs of pictures hanging in clusters of four. The tables and chairs were of bamboo. These were the first to go, banished to the corridor outside his room. Mrs Hobson protested. Hulme's response was to have the sideboard removed the next day. There were more protests, which Hulme met by removing four or five other pieces of furniture, including the piano. When she protested that there was no room for the piano in the corridor he suggested that she try storing it under the bed.

Hulme chose to interpret this struggle as essentially aesthetic. He supposed that Mrs Hobson had an 'ideal' formed by a fusion of her own original working-class tastes (represented by the bedroom texts and seafront photographs) with those of the long succession of under-graduates who had passed through the rooms. It was a conflict of ideals, concealed and disguised as one of practical motives. When he was able to counter her protest that there was no room in the corridor for the furniture she simply changed tack and said that it would be very difficult to re-let the rooms once they had been 'despoiled' in this way. In writing the whole thing up as a humorous article for *The Granta* Hulme described this as a familiar 'feminine manoeuvre' and gave another example:

If you are trying to persuade a lady to meet you at a certain time, and she gives as a reason for refusing the fact that she has to call that afternoon at a certain shop for a book, it is no use urging that you will have a messenger sent for it: a new reason will be given. All argument on reasons given is absolute waste of time, for the real reason is something not given.[5]

From this he deduced that Mrs Hobson had an ideal of what a room should look like, and that each time she came into his room to lay the table she suffered at the sight of the damage done to it. The conflict came to a head one afternoon when he requested the removal of what seemed to him yet another superfluous bamboo object. She left the room, only to return moments later with tears in her eyes to inform him that she wanted him out, he was to look for new rooms at half-term. Indicating the walls with a despairing gesture she said: 'You see, sir, it's like this: I'd rather see my rooms *empty* than *bare*.'

Hulme the humorous columnist affected to find in her phrase a confirmation of the most cherished beliefs of Hulme the philosopher:

The perfection of its self-revelation is such that by it she raised herself from out of this sordid world of change and flux, where the individual landlady passes away like the snows of yester-year, and placed herself by the perfection of her self-expression amongst that timeless world where things are eternal because they are universal and typical. So shall she stand through all the shifting ages, fixed, immutable, a Cambridge moment caught in amber.[6]

Hulme having made his point – if indeed that was the object of the exercise – he and Mrs Hobson buried the hatchet and for the remaining weeks of his second career as a Cambridge undergraduate St Andrews Hill remained his address.

Hulme was evidently enjoying himself very much by now. On the same day as his account of this duel appeared in *The Granta* he had a letter published in the *Cambridge Magazine* under the heading 'A Prophecy', which he signed 'One Who Is Very Sorry He Can Read'. This consisted of a facetious listing of forthcoming books and 'papers' from the academic industry including 'Bergson and the Working Man' by Reverend W. Tudor Jones, 'New Light on God' by Amos C. Bulbous, and 'The New Infinite and the Homoousion' by Professor Hiram B. Honk. Herbert Wildon Carr was among those spoofed.

*

Bergson, of course, remained a major feature of his life and the translation of the *Introduction to Metaphysics* continued to occupy at least some of his time at Cambridge. Frank Flint, whose French was so much better than Hulme's, was sent pages for editing and correction. Indeed, according to Ezra Pound, it was Flint – with a little help from Dolly Kibblewhite – who did most of the spadework on the finished book.[7] Hulme was supposed to be paying him, but he was hard up himself and it seems there were disagreements over money that threatened to end the friendship a few months later when Hulme again approached Flint for help with the translation of *Reflections on Violence*. Yet another whom Hulme cajoled into helping was Sir John Squire, who told Michael Roberts that 'Hulme's French wasn't very good; he depended on me for his translations from Sorel and Bergson.'[8] He seems to have regarded Hulme's casual attitude to the whole thing as just another aspect of his incorrigibly mischievous personality. Whatever the facts of the matter, the final hand on the English prose was unmistakably Hulme's own, and the *Introduction* in translation reads remarkably like a piece of his own writing.

Promoting the forthcoming book seemed to him just as important as translating it, and perhaps more fun too. On 26 February, the night after his lecture to the Heretics, Hulme had spoken on Bergson at the invitation of Miss E. E. Constance Jones to the women of Girton College. Given that Bergson does not seem to have been among the options offered to Ogden for his talk the night before, his choice was probably influenced by his awareness that this was a philosopher who appealed particularly to women. The compiler of Girton's 'College Notes' in the *Cambridge Magazine*[9] duly noted that 'On Monday evening the majority of average intellects in the College were mystified by a lecture on "Bergson" by Mr T. E. Hulme'; his talk, however, was 'highly appreciated by the initiated'. Hulme had appreciated both the invitations and the helpful plug Ogden had given in the Heretics report to his 'two forthcoming volumes on Bergson, which we shall await with interest, now that we have had a taste of his method'. In a letter of thanks from Frith Street he said that he had enjoyed his visit very much and regretted that he would not be able to come up and hear Bertrand Russell, who was booked to deliver the next lecture to the Heretics. This turned out to be an extended critique of Bergson, a paper which did much to establish Russell's reputation. The attack, coming in the wake of a similar one in Russell's opening address as president of the Aristotelian Society in the autumn of 1911, had exacerbated the harm already done to Bergson's reputation in academic circles by his popularity, and it was perhaps becoming clear to Hulme by now that on philosophical issues Russell was his natural enemy. Writing from Girton to thank Hulme for his talk and enclosing a small cheque, Miss Constance Jones can hardly have been aware of this emerging polarity: 'People were immensely interested and everyone thought that your lecture was too short and would have liked to hear the other half,' she told him, before recommending 'two little books in the Home University Library which I believe you would be interested in. One is Mr Bertrand Russell's "Problems of Philosophy" and the other is Whitehead's "Introduction to Mathematics".'[10]

The translation of *Introduction to Metaphysics* was scheduled for publication by Swift at the end of the year and in the months leading up to it Hulme was again out and about promoting and defending Bergson and touchily insisting upon the authority of 'his' translation. In April the *Cambridge Magazine* carried an obituary of Lady Welby, whom it referred to as 'probably the first to appreciate the merits of Bergson in England', noting her 'translation of his "Introduction to Metaphysics" (which, although by another hand, is to appear in English before the end of the present year) was completed by her immediately after its publication in France'. Hulme wrote in to point out that she had translated only the last third of Bergson's essay – 'As I have received from M. Bergson sole rights for the translation into English of this essay, you will pardon my calling attention to the matter.' It was probably hardly a coincidence that Lady Welby had been on the list of disciples of Rousseau named by Hulme in his address to the Heretics back in February. And in the wake of the advertisements in the *Cambridge Magazine* for the impending publication Hulme found himself involved in an exchange of letters with anti-Bergsonites in the paper's correspondence columns. A Mr H. M. Lloyd began it, writing a bantering letter in which he claimed to be expressing regret on behalf of the university at 'the translation into English of writings which surely cannot add to its reputation wherever sound philosophy is held in esteem', and citing the adequate dismissals of the whole Bergson cult by Russell, G. E. Moore, W. E. Johnson and James Ward. By way of conclusion he hoped 'that Mr Hulme may be persuaded to desist from his design while there is yet time'.

Hulme responded on 6 May. The attacks had changed nothing, he wrote, adding that 'the work of M. Bergson which I have to translate is at once the shortest and the least expensive of his writings'. This was at best a diffident defence, and in his next letter Lloyd savaged it: 'I cannot be sure what importance Mr Hulme attaches to the fact that he is translating the *shortest* of Bergson's productions: let me assure him that the length of the translation palliates the proceedings only in the slightest degree.' Hulme, ever so slightly lumbered with an obsolescent enthusiasm, let the matter rest there.

*

The return to Cambridge and the steady relationship with Dolly Kibblewhite had given his life a solid structure within which he was able to pursue his varied interests. That *The New Age* should have published 'The Complete Poetical Works of T. E. Hulme' while the author was still alive and not yet thirty years old was, of course, a joke; but as Bergson's reference had testified, Hulme's interests were by now moving away from literature towards aesthetics. His stimulating friendship with Ezra Pound continued, and on 13 August he and Pound sat up until 11.30 at night discussing the metaphysics of art.[11] But given Hulme's enduringly provocative personality there was something deceptive about the calm, and sure enough, a few days later, a letter arrived for him at 35 Manchester Street which tore it to shreds:

> 27 Chancery Lane, W.C.
> 31st August 1912.

Sir,

    We think it right to inform you that our client Mr. H. W. Carr has handed to us a letter of an unspeakably disgusting & horrible character which we are instructed was written by you and sent to Mr Carr's daughter to an address in Cornwall, and the letter bears on the face of it inferential evidence that it is one of a series.

    Our client is considering what steps should be taken in the matter and meanwhile we must warn you against attempting to hold further communication of any kind whatever with our client's daughter.

    If you desire to make any explanation or statement it should be addressed to us,

> Your obedient Servants,
> Radford and Frankland

Hulme's reply, via Messrs Peacock and Goddard, reached Radford and Frankland on 19 September:

> 35 Manchester Street
> Manchester Square, W.

Dear Sirs,

    Will you inform your client that I am leaving London at once. I am at present bound by Contract to finish off a translation of a French Book (by

Sorel) on a certain date. As soon as this is finished which will be in about a couple of weeks I leave England for Germany for a year at least. Will you address anything you have to communicate after this to my Solicitors.

Yours truly,

T. E. Hulme.

In her charming, privately published memoir *On a May Morning* Joan Wildon Carr gives a detailed account of the whole business. She was the eldest daughter of passionate Fabians, liberal and progressive in their ideas on education and upbringing. As Geraldine Spooner, her mother had been courted by George Bernard Shaw, who once said that she had been the model for his Candida, and it was through Shaw that she got to know her future husband. The family were wealthy and had a house in More's Garden in London and a weekend cottage in the West Sussex countryside at a village called Bury. Magazines such as *Mind* and the *Aristotelian News* lay about the house, as well as controversial books such as Freud's *Interpretation of Dreams*, with a notice inside saying that it was for the use of the medical profession only and not for sale to the general public. Joan dipped into it surreptitiously and with the help of a dictionary added words like 'coitus', 'phallic' and 'onanism' to her vocabulary.

Wildon Carr often invited friends of his from the Aristotelian Society as house-guests in the summers at Bury, men whom Joan, with all the arrogance of a precocious sixteen-year-old, found ridiculous. She and her mother called them 'Daddy's old Aristotelians' and found them 'dry as dust'. George Dawes Hicks seemed to typify the entire philosopher breed, with his 'small tottery body and oversized wobbly head, talking always in interminable drooling sentences and seeming utterly unaware of everything round him'.[12] To a man they were small, deaf, unathletic and dull. At Roedean her best friend was a vivacious and stylish girl, Janet Reeves-Smith, whose father was managing director of the exclusive Berkeley Hotel and together they laughed at all the 'boisterous young hockey players' sent to the school by 'rich cotton-picking parents to lose their Lancashire accents', and Joan listened as Janet boasted of all the boys and men who were in love with her, from the lift-boy at the Berkeley upwards, gamely trying to match her with fabricated accounts of her own affairs on holiday in far-off and uncheckable places such as

Egypt. Once, during a holiday stay with Janet at the hotel, Joan even saw her go into a boyfriend's room in the dead of night.

As part of his belief in a liberal upbringing Carr took Joan travelling with him to broaden her education, and it was at the conference in Bologna that she and Hulme met and afterwards began their correspondence. Given her experiences of 'Daddy's old Aristotelians' at Bury Joan must have found Hulme a surprise in every way, from his broad Staffordshire accent to his irreverence and his evident virility. She became infatuated with him, and a correspondence that perhaps began with a pretentious and harmless desire to seem more sophisticated than she really was, at some point escalated into one in which Hulme introduced her to a lot of words she would not have found in her dictionary or even in Freud – hard, clear, direct and unromantic words like 'cunt', 'cock' and 'fuck'.

John Squire provided a striking description of this side of Hulme's personality: 'He led people up the garden path, made them agree to things, and then left them in the cart. He used to twinkle at me across their heads. I couldn't help smiling but I did think "what a bad man you are".'[13] Squire was talking about his experience of Hulme as a persuasive debater, but his attitude towards seduction seems to have been the same, and he was merciless in his willingness to let others take the consequences of their own pretensions. Like Pound and Lewis, he seems to have been deeply uncomfortable with the idea of innocence.

Joan had been made a prefect at Roedean, and about a year after the Bologna congress she came up to London at the end of her summer holidays to buy furniture from Heal's for her study. She had arranged to meet Hulme afterwards and they ate lunch together in Soho and then took a bus to his rooms in Manchester Street. 'What happened then,' she wrote, 'took me completely by surprise.' In the bedroom Hulme apparently began removing his clothes. Joan's façade of sophistication was ruthlessly exposed and away she ran, hatless and coatless. She had almost reached Regent Street before he caught up with her and persuaded her to come back and collect her things. He calmed her down and she had already begun to see things in a rosier light by the time she caught the train back home that evening. Next day she sat down and proudly wrote to her friend Janet about her day in London 'lost in oblivion in Hulme's arms'.

Both the Wildon Carrs and the Reeves-Smiths turned up at the school a few weeks later for one of the prefects' Sunday tea parties. At chapel that evening Janet managed to whisper to Joan that her parents had found the letter about Hulme, and the purpose of their visit was to put an end to this corrupting friendship of their daughter's. Her mother intended to inform both the school and the Wildon Carrs of what they had discovered. Geraldine Wildon Carr was accordingly invited to meet Mrs Reeves-Smith at the Berkeley Hotel and shown the letter. She declined to read it and with magnificent disdain tore it up and threw the pieces into the fire. The two women then began making friends with one another. Photographs of Janet fishing and Janet riding were shown. Geraldine Wildon Carr expressed the hope that such a lovely girl would not be contaminated by her own daughter's encounter with the sinister and unsavoury Hulme, 'the only one of her friends who would take advantage of a young girl's indiscretion'.

Though she was now forbidden to see Hulme any more Joan continued to correspond with him in secret. The prohibition can only have heightened the thrill of the adventure for them both, but Joan soon found that Hulme was taking her way out of her depth. She showed the letters to Janet. One in particular impressed them: 'Oh Joey,' Janet said when she saw it, 'it *is* going a bit far, isn't it. But it's definitely the real thing.' The 'real thing' was a detailed description of the sexual act, explaining the girl's exact role in it. If she really loved the man the girl would reply to him and ask him to perform each stage of the act, just as he had described it to her, and using the words he had taught her. Try as she might, Joan could not bring herself to do it.

In the autumn of 1912 she suddenly got very tired of being a troubled adolescent. Lying in bed one night in the Sussex cottage, wondering if she would still like him, she took out her favourite Swinburne again and read *Atalanta* by candlelight: 'We have seen thee, oh love, thou art fair, thou art goodly, oh love.' To her relief she did. The spell held and romanticism won the day, a triumph that perhaps only the most diehard of classicists would have regretted on this occasion. The following morning she collected all the letters from their hiding places and walked into the beech woods with her sister Ursula and made a bonfire of them. The magical act of burning did the trick and she was able to set about forgetting, for the time being at least, all those hard, clear words Hulme had been teaching her.

She had not been thorough enough, however. Still another cache of letters turned up in London in More's Garden and it was with one of these in his pocket that Wildon Carr visited his lawyers in outrage and fury. Hulme had committed no crime and the advice given to Wildon Carr was to offer him £100 for his signed promise never to write to Joan again. 'I think this was done,' Joan writes in *On a May Morning*, and perhaps it was. But the enraged self-confidence with which Wildon Carr subsequently pursued the matter suggests it would have been unnecessary. He realized he was able to ruin Hulme's hopes of attaining academic respectability as a philosopher, and he did so without hesitation.

After his reply to Radford and Frankland Hulme retreated to Macclesfield and in mid-October wrote to Bushe-Fox about 'certain unavoidable private matters' which unexpectedly necessitated his going to Germany in November and so missing the winter term. He hoped, however, to be able to come up in the usual way for the January term. Suspecting that this might be what he was planning, Wildon Carr wrote to the master of St John's telling him the reason for Hulme's trip to Germany. The master, Forsyth Scott, raised the matter with Bushe-Fox, and Wildon Carr was told that before the college acted it would have to be satisfied that he could substantiate the allegations. Carr at once wrote back telling them that he possessed, and could produce if necessary, a letter proving Hulme to be 'a man of scandalous life and a corrupter of youth'.[14]

On 20 November Hulme was told that he must reply to the charges before he could return into residence. But he had already decided that there could be no question of this and was busily trying to complete the translation of *Reflections on Violence* before he left. As with the Bergson translation, he was again heavily reliant for this on Frank Flint's linguistic skills and goodwill. He wrote telling him that he had to finish the book within a week and asking him to come to Frith Street for four days of intensive work. Flint replied that he was going on holiday soon and could not help. Hulme came close to panic:

Dear Flint

I have just received your wire which upsets me considerably. I have got myself in a position now where I must have a little further help to finish the thing off. I cannot wait until you come back from your holiday. You must *come round tomorrow if only for a couple of hours in order to finish the job off*. Otherwise I shall be left in a most awkward position . . .[15]

Hulme did not hide the fact that this letter was a three-line whip: 'Everything is ready for you, there are only a few difficulties to discuss. Now do make an effort – I really require you.' In reply Flint explained that he often worked overtime in the evenings at the post office, and although he could theoretically exchange one form of paid evening work for another there were three very good arguments in favour of preferring the post office:

(1) The date of pay from the P.O. is absolutely certain; from you uncertain.

(2) The difference in the rate of pay is so little in your favour as to be quite negligible.

(3) I should do only 2½ hours 'work' for the P.O., but 3 hours' *work* for you, with travelling time both ways to be added too.

(1) is important. You are asking me to exchange payment made on a definite date for a payment made god knows when, and I cannot afford to do this. This is important. (2) and (3) are negligible.[16]

But on the grounds that Hulme was 'the most intelligent man I know', he agreed to help him. Hulme's financial position was always precarious, however, and once again he was late in paying Flint. Hulme's somewhat graceless response to Flint's letter of complaint was to send him a pound with a covering letter asking him 'to be a little more careful with the translation. What you have sent me appears to be extremely bad. Of course you can't help it if you are ill, but none the less it is very little use to me. [. . .] I must point out that a translation which gives me almost as much trouble to revise as it would do to do all over again is no use at all.' However, he promised if necessary to borrow what he owed to Flint in order to pay him in full if money still owing to him by Swift for his Bergson translation did not arrive before he left for Germany.

Somehow or other the work was completed in time. On 21 November Hulme collected a new passport, giving 'author' as the 'profession of bearer' and 'travelling in Europe' as his intention, and left England the same day. Tancred sent him on his way with a verse in *The Poetry Review* in which he urged his friend to regard the enforced absence as a well-earned rest:

> Great Hulme! as you by dint of toil have won
> Laurels and cater for your pot, have done
> With fostering verse, lay by Sorel, desist
> From turning your yoked brain-might into grist;
> And let your thoughts like boots long stretched on trees
> Relax where Host Mirth at the Cheshire Cheese
> Plumps a guest's craving for enjoyment with
> Dishes and wines that give lank'd sprites new pith.[17]

The following day Hulme booked in at Pension Mehring, at 81a II Kurfürstenstrasse in Berlin. One of his first acts there was to write to Bushe-Fox explaining that he would prefer to deal with the accusations against him on his return to England, and asking for the return of the Bergson testimonial. 'I find that to attend certain lectures I have to give some proof of ability,' he explained, a wan admission that he now knew he would never acquire a degree. The final bit of tidying-up was a postcard to Bushe-Fox about the return of his Caution money and an unpaid bill to his landlady who, 'as a result of a dispute about the furniture', had given him a half-term's notice which she afterwards withdrew.

Hulme never told anyone in his family the real reason for his leaving Cambridge. At one time he muttered vaguely that he and his tutor had not got on well, at another that it had never been his intention to finish anyway and that he had only reapplied out of bravado. Not even Kate Lechmere, the woman he was closest to for the last three years of his life, ever heard the story of what really happened.[18]

8

The Frith Street Salon

At the station in Berlin Hulme was met by Rupert Brooke, who had arrived a few days earlier to stay with his friend Dudley Ward while working on a dissertation on John Webster which he hoped would gain him a Fellowship at Cambridge. Edward Marsh, a ubiquitous figure in pre-war literary circles who had the same sort of social and entrepreneurial skills as Orage, and to some extent Hulme himself, had introduced them a short while before, probably at the Café Royal. In professional life Marsh was private secretary to Winston Churchill, who was then First Lord of the Admiralty. Three years later, with Brooke dead and Marsh writing a book about him, Hulme recalled some of the details of their intercourse in a letter to Marsh, describing how they frequently discussed problems of aesthetics, art and culture arising from Brooke's work:

I remember once going with him in the train from Friedrichstrasse Station to Zoologische Garten (near where he was living) and he suddenly asked me if I had any ideas about tragedy and what I thought [was] its real nature. He said he was writing something about tragedy in his essay. I then started talking about this particular Einfühlungsästhetik. We had several conversations about it. I remember his saying some days later that 'he always kept before his mind the idea that possibly all such theories were wrong because perhaps the subject was not *one* subject, the unity was that of the word; we called by the name *art* things that might be very diverse in nature and consequently there might be no esthetic at all'. [. . .] I had one conversation with him that I was very interested in at the time. We were talking about the part of esthetic (of which Ribot's book[1] is an example) which is concerned with the psychology by which a work of art is produced. The overhead railway crosses the street by which he used to go home, to Dudley Ward's flat. The trains cross very noisily leaving a trail of smoke about every two minutes. He said he had been thinking about this and would probably write something in which it came, how much better it was to be a train. He said that with him, in writing, the first *direct* step (of crystallisation, as it were, as distinct from mere thought about a subject) was to get hold of one finished line with a *definite rhythm*, that set the mould for the rest.[2]

Hulme was in the habit of dictating his lectures and certain of his letters – such as this one – to Dolly Kibblewhite at the typewriter,[3] with the result that a thinking-aloud sometimes ended up committed to paper as a finished thought. Presumably he understood what Brooke meant by remarking 'how much better it was to be a train', but could Marsh have known what lay behind such a private notion? Perhaps Brooke's idea was that the creative process itself is a noisy, rattling affair but what it leaves behind is quiet and mysterious.

That September Brooke and Marsh had started planning the first of what would eventually be five volumes of 'Georgian poetry', and Brooke's other main activity in Berlin besides the Webster dissertation was to keep Marsh supplied with a flow of possible contributors and ideas for the book. Harold Monro at the Poetry Bookshop had agreed to publish it. Arundel del Re, Harold Monro's friend and associate at the Poetry Bookshop, claims that Marsh was assisted in his choice of contributors to the first volume of Georgian poetry by – in addition to Brooke and Monro – '[John] Drinkwater, [Wilfred] Gibson and T. E. Hulme, whose judgement he greatly respected'.[4] In the same reminiscence he says that, 'in spite of their differences Pound acted as a powerful stimulus to Monro and, together with Flint and, to a lesser extent, Hulme, encouraged and backed the venture as soon as it started'.

Hulme's merely cautious encouragement for the projected volume is understandable. If literary schools are in the main artificial constructions, then the construction of 'the Georgian school' was more artificial than most. The term itself was Marsh's coinage, being an attempt to link a 'new beginning' in English poetry with the ascent to the throne of George V in 1910. But to the extent to which the new grouping had any discernible aesthetic theories at all these were very different from the rigour and precision of Hulme's and Flint's ideas about the role of the image in writing poetry. Monro himself offered a programmatic statement of sorts in an article entitled 'The Future of Poetry' that appeared in the first issue of *The Poetry Review* in 1912:

The poet's modern equipment must include, apart from the natural adoration of beauty, a clear and sound grasp upon facts, and a stupendous aptitude for assimilation [...] [The poet] must work on persistently and delightedly towards an invisible goal. For that goal is nothing less than the final rewelding of metre to meaning: and it cannot, in the nature of things, be achieved until man has attained a second innocence, a self-obliviousness beyond self-consciousness, a super-consciousness; that condition, in fact, produced only by a complete natural form, which, inevitably, will yield only to the spirit able to mould it; form will be as elusive as sunlight, yet enduring as marble [...] In its final majestic simplicity [...] poetry springing from the roots of life, will flower into natural and perfect language, bright with dreams and tense with meaning. Metre will serve substance; form will be one with expression, metaphor with thought; poetry will be the call of spirit to spirit, the very throb of the heart of nature, as expressed in her ultimate manifestation – man.[5]

This is a far cry from Hulme's statement in his 1908 lecture on poetry that he intends to 'speak of verse in a plain way, as I would of pigs', and its damp and yearning conceptions are a world away from the hard, dry and finite modesty of Hulme's Imagism. There were good poets among the Georgians, notably Walter de la Mare and Edmund Blunden; but the majority of them were content to write sentimentally about friendship, love and nature and to cultivate a naïve literary persona along the lines of Housman's Shropshire Lad. The five volumes edited by Marsh and published by Monro between 1912 and 1922 were hugely successful commercially; but the poetry of Yeats and Pound made it seem old-fashioned even as it was being written, and with the appearance of Eliot's *The Wasteland* in 1922 the Georgians' pretensions to be the future of poetry were ruthlessly exposed.

In 1913 Hulme would be one member of the jury to award Brooke's 'Grantchester' a £30 prize for the best poem to appear in *The Poetry Review* the previous year, so he may not have been entirely indifferent to Brooke's talent. But the aesthetic differences between them were great, and the ten days together in Berlin did not lead to a friendship.

Brooke wrote to Marsh that he found Hulme 'an amiable creature and a good talker', and though he was not impressed by him as a 'philosophic thinker' he was struck by his 'extraordinary power of observation' and his 'good memory'.[6] As for Hulme, he seems to have considered Brooke pretentious, and could not resist telling Marsh that 'he was always carrying his Webster (the book) about with him, reading it casually in cafes'. Twenty years later, with both men long dead, the discreet Dolly confessed to Michael Roberts that 'as a matter of fact, and quite confidentially, Mr Hulme didn't like him at all'.[7] Perhaps he found Brooke, as he sometimes found Ezra Pound, too obviously and too publicly 'the poet'.

*

Brooke returned to London on 12 December in time for the publication of the first of the *Georgian Anthologies* and Hulme was left to his own devices. Harold Monro had commissioned him to write a 'German Chronicle' on the poetry of the Berlin avant-garde for *The Poetry Review*, of which Monro was editor at the time,[8] and he set about the task now in his usual laconic fashion:

How do I take my duties as a chronicler? Rather lightly perhaps. My tale will be rather haphazard. I do not intend to make a careful *inventory* of current literature, either by honestly tasting everything, or by collecting current opinions. I shall make no special effort. I shall not read anything on your behalf that I should not naturally have read for my own amusement. I intend merely to give an account of the things which reach me naturally, as I sit gossiping at the Café des Westens.[9]

The dissimulation notwithstanding, his article turned out to be an important general overview of the scene that introduced to a London readership a whole generation of German poets with which it was not previously familiar. Hulme may have disapproved of Germany's destabilizing military ambitions in Europe but he was much too large-spirited to allow this to colour his account of the country's recent literature. In essence the chronicle is a description and review, liberally sprinkled with quotations in untranslated German, of the anthology *Der Kondor*, edited by Kurt Hiller and published in 1912. The poets represented, sponsored by the Expressionist paper *Die Aktion* and mainly associates of Hiller's from his 'Cabaret Gnu' (*Das Gnu*), a secession from the more well-known *Der Neue Club*, are identified by Hulme as the successors to Rilke, Schaukal, Eulenberg and, 'among those who are not, properly speaking, poets, Wedekind, Heinrich, and Thomas Mann'.

He writes with evident approval of the ambience he experienced at the Gnu's monthly meetings at the Café Austria, the fierce self-confidence of the poets, the informality that left patrons free to talk and laugh if they found the poetry undeserving of closer attention – 'it is all much pleasanter than a reading here'. Despite the left-wing and humanist slant of the Expressionist poets he sympathized with the general air of creative dissatisfaction they exuded, discovering in their activities an attempt to use the German language in a new way and to cure it of what seemed to him its vices. He found the language of the Gnu poets terse and elliptical, not soporific like 'the diffuse German of the past', and his attraction to Hiller's editorial protest in *Der Kondor* against poets who 'mistake a metaphysical and pantheistic sentimentality for poetry' is obvious. He quotes from work by Arthur Drey, Ernst Blass, 'the German Rimbaud' Georg Heym, whom he compares to Richard Middleton on account of his early death, René Schickele and Else Lasker-Schüler – the best-known name in the anthology and a familiar figure in the Café des Westens, Hulme remarks, whose short hair, extraordinary clothes and manly stride belied her very feminine prose.

Hulme praises the group's anthology for the fact that none of the poems included could be described as either pretty or sentimentally derivative; but his final position was one of caution. Though the intelligence at work was obviously *constructive* he distinguished this from the superior *poetic* intelligence, finding too much bony intellectual intention showing through the poetry. It was a difficult point to articulate and he goes on to try to explain what he means, not only to his readers but to himself:

To explain in more detail, I assume that the sensibility of the poet is possessed by many who themselves are not poets. The differentiating factor is something other than their sensibility. To simplify matters then, suppose a poet and an

THE FRITH STREET SALON

intelligent man both moved in exactly the same way by some scene; both desire to express what they feel; in what way does the expression differ? The difficulty of expression can be put in an almost geometrical way. The scene before you is a picture in two dimensions. It has to be reduced to verse, which being a line of words has only one dimension. However, this one-dimensional form has other elements of rhythm, sound, etc., which form as it were an emotional equivalent for the lost dimension. The process of transition from the one to the other in the poet is possibly something of this kind. First, as in the case of all of us, the emotional impression. Then probably comes *one* line of words, with a definite associated rhythm – the rest of the poem follows from this. Now here comes the point. This first step from the thing clearly 'seen' to this almost blind process of development in verse, is the characteristic of the poet, and the step which the merely intelligent man cannot take. He sees 'clearly' and he must construct 'clearly'. This obscure mixture of description and rhythm is one, however, which cannot be *constructed* by a rational process, *i.e.*, a process which keeps all its elements clear before its eyes all the time.[10]

The analysis which follows reads like a final expansion of those riddling sentences and half-caught wisps of thought in the 'Notes on Language and Style' on the mysteries of the creative process; and – just as importantly – on the mysteries of the process that looks like creation but is not: what makes one man a poet and another who may be just as intelligent and perceptive not a poet. Hulme has the rigour to make the poetic gift something rare and remarkable, and the courage to try to deny that he is himself in possession of it. It amounts almost to an explanation of why he gave up writing poetry:

The handicap of the intelligent man who is not a poet is that he cannot trust himself to this obscure world from which rhythm springs. All that he does must remain 'clear' to him as he does it. How does he then set about the work of composition? All that he can do is mention one by one the elements of the scene and the emotions it calls up. I am moved in a certain way by a dark street at night, say. When I attempt to express this mood, I make an inventory of all the elements which make up that mood. I have written verse of that kind myself, I understand the process. The result is immediately recognisable. Qualities of sincere first-hand observation may be constantly shown, but the result is not a poem.[11]

The poets he has been discussing are finally not poets, he concludes, and their destiny will be to influence not German poetry but German prose.

The 'German Chronicle' turned out to be Hulme's last word on poetry. By the time he was finished Harold Monro had fallen out with the proprietors of *The Poetry Review* and it appeared belatedly in the June 1914 issue of *Poetry and Drama*, a quarterly Monro had started in the spring, as one in a series of European 'chronicles'.

*

Despite the lively way he described it, the 'literary café' phase of Hulme's life in Berlin turned out to be short-lived and a little frustrating. He wrote to Flint:

> I spent most of my time here between the library and the cafes when I first came. I got myself introduced to the same sort of set as I know in London but it was no use as I was absolutely unable to say anything I wanted, so that at present I live in isolation [. . .] I should very much like to see a lot of people at the present time as I am bursting with theories and haven't the energy to write them down.[12]

In his absence from London it was Ezra Pound, a difficult but generous friend, who, by reprinting his 'Complete Poetical Works' as an appendix to *Ripostes* in both 1912 and 1913, helped to keep his name alive. The only reviewer who actually mentioned Hulme's poems took his cue from the jokey description and dismissed them as 'five scraps by Mr Hulme'.[13] *Ripostes'* London-based publisher, Stephen Swift, was by this time almost a house publisher for Hulme and his friends: he also had Pound, Richard Curle and John Squire on his list, and from 1912 published Middleton Murry's Bergsonian review *Rhythm*. In the winter of 1912, however, the firm collapsed and Swift absconded with all the money that was left, leaving Murry with a debt to his printer of £400, which bankrupted him. Swift reached Tangier before he was arrested.

All three of Hulme's projected publications in England were affected. The Bergson translation did appear in G. P. Putnam's American edition in November 1912 and in Macmillan's London edition in March 1913, price 2s 6d, with a slightly different version of the translator's preface; but the Sorel had to wait two more years for publication, and the *Introduction to Bergson*, confidently advertised by Swift as early as March 1912, never appeared at all. Hulme's already parlous financial situation worsened dramatically, and Flint was again the innocent bystander who suffered. In an undated, incomplete and despairing draft for a letter he presumably did eventually send, Flint wrote:

Dear Hulme
Dem Arbeiter gebürt sein Loln [the worker is due his wage]. You have
not kept your promise to send me *mein Loln* from Germany. But you have
broken so many promises to me that I am not surprised. I am only irritated,
– irritated to think that even the paltry price I was to receive for my work I
cannot get from you. If you had told me frankly that you could not pay me,
I should not have minded so much; but it is your promising to pay and
leading me as you did to spend money on the strength of your promise that
irritates me. I have had to borrow money to replace what I spent.[14]

Hulme apologized, pleading force majeure and confessing that of course he had no idea that the business with Swift would turn into such a disaster. He explained that he had had to pay £65 cash to get his books away from Swift. Hannay was taking over two of the books and 'if Hannay pays me I send the lot, if not another instalment. I am really very hard up myself not only in the relative sense.'

He promised to send Flint a copy of the *Introduction to Metaphysics* once he was back in England, but expressed disappointment that it 'has not yet had one serious review'. Its most extensive notice was in *The Quest*, a more self-consciously highbrow version of *The New Age*, with a strongly theosophical profile. The reviewer was the editor, G. R. S. Mead, who welcomed its appearance, opening his discussion with warm words of praise for the translation: 'We are very glad to welcome Mr Hulme's excellent version of this important essay.'[15]

Hulme's curiously idle form of restlessness, or restless form of idleness, intensified as the months passed. By April he had moved further down Kurfürstenstrasse to Pension Engels at No. 55, from where he wrote apologizing to Flint for not having written more often – 'I have for the past month felt most unusually and extraordinarily lazy and this is the only letter I have written for weeks. I can't sit down for a minute.' But by then he already knew that the torment would soon be over: 'I shall be back in England definitely on the fifteenth of May,' he wrote, and so he was. 'A year at least', he had told Wildon Carr's solicitor he would stay away. No doubt he meant a Bergsonian year, one that felt like a year even when it was not. Inevitably there was a rumour of 'trouble in Berlin' attaching to his return, something unspecified that 'might have started with Hulme's outspokenness and ended with the police'.[16] But Paul Selver, a *New Age* writer on literary matters who was the source of the story, conceded that this might have been 'just gossip'. Hulme, in any case, knew the date of his return weeks beforehand.

The dapper Ashley Dukes, now on the editorial staff of *Vanity Fair* and reviewing plays for the *Star*, had a top-floor flat at 21 Mortimer Street and Hulme moved in with him, living in a small front room for which he paid Dukes rent, 'usually six months in arrears' as things turned out. Dukes remembered with great pleasure how he would sit for hours 'unwinding, as it were, general ideas, with expansive gestures which began and ended in the region of his chest'.[17] He seldom went to bed before three in the morning, slept until about noon and then read for a couple of hours before getting up for lunch. His idea of a good dinner was a steak and kidney pie and if a friend decided he wanted a chop Hulme would protest, 'But that costs sixpence more!' In his personal habits he was a careful, frugal man who objected to extravagance and kept a record of his expenses. He was proud of his frugality and claimed that by neither drinking nor smoking he could afford to buy an extra book a week. Perhaps he meant 'order' an extra book a week, for in a draft of his Foreword to *Speculations* Jacob Epstein, the American-born sculptor with whom Hulme had become friendly, recalled with gratitude how Hulme 'bought works of art for which he could not afford – [sic] though he owed vast sums of money for books which he could not afford'.[18] In the afternoons he would go round to Frith Street to read, write, dictate letters to Dolly or play Go with her. On evenings when Dukes was not at the theatre he would sometimes join him at Frith Street at about tea-time. Later the two of them would leave to dine at a chop-house called the Sceptre, behind the Café Royal. Hulme had returned from Germany with a passionate interest in new art, and they were often joined at the Sceptre by Epstein and another sculptor who was to some extent Epstein's protégé, the twenty-year-old Frenchman Henri Gaudier-Brzeska; by painters including Robert Bevan and C. R. W. Nevinson; and by Richard Curle and the Spanish writer Ramiro de Maeztu, who was married to an Englishwoman.[19] After dining their conversation would continue at the Café Royal, an artists' café with a function similar to that of the Café des Westens in Berlin, where the practice of 'table-hopping' readily led to the formation, extension and extinction of groups linked, usually temporarily, by shared artistic ideals or ambitions.[20]

The discussions started in the Sceptre and the Café Royal were often carried over to Hulme's regular Tuesday evening meetings in Soho at 67 Frith Street, held in the sumptuous salon on the first floor, among 'First Empire mirrors and chandeliers'. The atmosphere was informal but serious, nothing stronger than beer was drunk and there were never any problems with drunkenness. Richard Aldington, then in his early twenties, estimated that on a regular basis 'at least fifty young men came there' while the women, 'a tiny minority', sat and 'growled' with Dolly. Knowing his own weakness for women, Hulme had better reason than most to fear their disruptive effect on the company and Epstein, who once described Hulme's as an 'erotic' personality,[21] understood the prohibition on women at Frith Street to be a form of sexual self-censorship. Moreover, Hulme had an unflattering view of the ability of women to take part in rational discussion. Dukes, like so many of his friends a sometime Fabian alternately resisting and embracing liberal and progressive views, often took issue with him about this and challenged him with the names of obviously intelligent women whom Hulme would airily dismiss as 'just misplaced whores'.[22] There was a strong element of the *enfant terrible* in Hulme and the response will have owed at least something to his compulsion to shock and tease the right-thinking among his friends. No doubt the more Dukes insisted the worse Hulme became.

One aspect agreed on by all those who recall the Tuesday evenings was the high degree of freedom and openness tolerated in the discussions. This was not a gathering of like-minded people intent on validating each other's views but a gathering of those whom Hulme for one reason or another liked and respected and with whom he wished to exchange opinions. The debate was genuine, an attempt to hear and say something new, to have your own views challenged and to challenge the views of those who opposed you. Hulme's talent to organize such a gathering of creative and intelligent minds and prevent their discourse from degenerating into riot and venom was a rare and valuable one: 'However rigid and narrowly defined his own philosophy was,' D. L. Murray wrote, 'he never lost his intellectual interest in all manner of systems, beliefs, art theories and personalities, loved listening to ideas the most opposed to his own, and demolishing them with a ferocity too jovial to take offence.'[23] Aldington recalled that he saw him close to losing his temper only once, during a discussion that was being constantly grounded by the facile contributions of an unidentified man. Hulme dealt with the situation by proposing a dummy adjournment to another location and resuming the discussion once the offender had been tricked off the premises. On another occasion he was observed hanging over the railings of the central spiral staircase and shouting down to Henry Simpson of the Poets' Club, who had just entered the panelled lobby, that if he made any attempt to climb upstairs he would be thrown back down again; but that was hardly a show of temper, more an example of Hulme's boisterous and still undergraduate sense of humour.

In a gladiatorial, status-conscious world of competing intellects such as this there were naturally those who wanted to see the king of the castle taken down a peg or two. Richard Aldington was one, a man who seems always to have felt uneasy about his liking for Hulme. One evening Ezra Pound brought a fellow-American named Henry Slonimsky to Frith Street. Slonimsky was a Hebrew scholar and 'proper' philosopher who had recently taken his Ph.D at Marburg on Parmenides and Heraclitus. Aldington recalled with some satisfaction how Hulme had 'injudiciously challenged Slonimsky on Plato and – well, the floor was wiped'.[24] Slonimsky remembered the occasion too, likening Hulme's debating tactics to those of 'a boxer who is not very quick on his feet but packs a powerful punch if and when he can land it'. Hulme took his floor-wiping like a man and in the course of the evening befriended Slonimsky:

There was a strange assortment of oddities and notables present, milling around and babbling, but Hulme and I managed to sit apart for a good while, and later when I left for home (my lodgings were in Bayswater) he walked with me part of the way, up Regent St and out Oxford St. I remember his turning aside from Regent St. to show me Golden Square where Blake was born. The hour was late and the streets were quiet, and Hulme walked and talked in his leisurely definitive way, and made a singularly pleasant impression on me. The very bulk and health of the man were reassuring, and his secure self-assured self-centred quiet manner seemed to me the very epitome of English staying power. Of his actual talk on that occasion only two remarks stuck in my memory because of their novelty. He thought Swift the supreme model of English prose writing. And he declared Arthur James Balfour a poor leader for the English Tory party, because a leader should be feared and hated by his opponents, whereas Balfour was liked and admired by Asquith and the Liberals.[25]

'He had the most wonderful gift of knowing everyone and mixing everyone,' wrote C. R. W. Nevinson. 'There were journalists, writers, poets, painters, politicians of all sorts, from Conservatives to New Age Socialists, Fabians, Irish yaps, American bums and Labour leaders', the whole gaggle of 'oddities and notables' held in check by the 'genially aggressive' personality of the host. Among those Nevinson recalled seeing there were Epstein, Gaudier-Brzeska, W. L. George, Douglas Ainslie, Rupert Brooke, Dukes, Orage, Beatrice Hastings, Edward Marsh, Robert Bevan, Harold Monro and F. S. Flint.[26] There were Germans, Italians, Frenchmen and Spaniards. Aldington's list included Flint, Pound, Curle, D. L. Murray, Shanks, Squire, Ralph Hodgson, 'and most of the Georgian Anthology except Flecker'. H. D. was also there, of course. H. J. Massingham, a former Fabian who edited *The Daily Chronicle* and *The Nation*, recalled seeing the poet Hodgson, the guild socialist Arthur J. Penty, Aldous Huxley ('I think'), George Moore, Epstein and Brzeska,[27] while Ashley Dukes picked out 'Epstein, Brzeska (Gaudier), Wyndham Lewis (seldom) and the painters Bevan, Gilman, Ginner. And the poet Flint'. Middleton Murry was another. Pound brought along the Imagist poet Allen Upward one evening and Upward regaled the company with 'scandalous facts about the deity and the Jerusalem council etc with great solemnity in the midst of uproarious laughter'.[28] Epstein, who figures on most lists of re-membered guests, kept a low, watchful profile:

The company, mostly workers in intellectual fields, included Ford Madox Hueffer as he was then called, later Ford Madox Ford (I remember him a very pontifical person), Ashley Dukes, A. R. Orage, editor of the *New Age*, Douglas Ainslie, Richard Curle, Sir Edward Marsh, Wyndham Lewis, Ezra Pound, Richard Aldington, Ramiro de Maeztu, who later became Spanish Ambassador to the Argentine, and many others. Among artists, Charles Ginner, Harold Gilman, Gaudier Brzeska, and Spencer Gore, Madame Karlowska and Robert Bevan. I remember having an amusing argument with Stanley Spencer concerning a statue of Buddha on the mantelpiece. When Spencer was asked what he thought of it, he shuddered and said he knew nothing of Asiatic art, as he was a Christian. I asked him what part of the world Christ came from. Spencer was of that school of philosophers who will not drink coffee because it is not grown in England. Hulme, to attract so large and varied a company of men, must have had a quality, I should say, of great urbanity, and his broadmindedness, I maintain, only ceased when he met humbug and pretentiousness.[29]

As Epstein points out in his illuminating mockery of Spencer's parochialism, at a time when the London art world in general was focused on the insular visions of the Arts and Crafts movement and in the world of music on Vaughan Williams's, Butterworth's and Holst's reworkings of English folk-song, Hulme was keenly cosmopolitan, and these Frith Street guest lists reflect a man actively inviting foreign influence on his thinking, enthusiastically absorbing whatever he found to be good in it and in many cases being a leading importer into England of intellectual goods, in the form of French *vers libre*, Bergson's dignified and dignifying metaphysics, and the artistic theories of the German aestheticians Worringer, Lipke and Volke which thoroughly irrigated the rich but rather closed artistic world of pre-war England and in many important respects established the direction in which British art was to develop in succeeding decades. Nor did Hulme share with many of his contemporaries the idea that there was something innately comical about Americans and their preoccupations; Epstein's fascination with the art of native and primitive peoples introduced him to a new aesthetic world which he very shortly made his own.

Harold Monro, who features on most of the Frith Street lists, was another of those gifted entrepreneurs like Orage and Marsh without whom, in the world of artists, things would simply never get done. One of the most attractive and interesting initiatives of this period was his Poetry Bookshop at 35 Devonshire Street, Theobalds Road. The shop was in a four-storey Georgian building in a slum area not far from the British Museum. It sold nothing but verse, offered regular evenings of readings and lectures, and published the *Georgian Poetry* series, edited by Marsh, in 1912, 1915, 1917, 1919 and 1922, as well as *Poetry and Drama*, a magazine edited by Monro himself between March 1913 and December 1914, a well-written, independent publication that in the short span of its life managed to reject Eliot's 'Love Song of J. Alfred Prufrock', handed to Monro by the visiting Conrad Aiken and returned by him to Aiken with the comment that it was 'absolutely insane, or words to that effect'.[30]

Monro's shop had a homely, club-like atmosphere that encouraged people to linger. He had a cat that came and went as it pleased, and in winter there was always a coal fire going. The offices of *The Poetry Review*, which Monro edited for the Poetry Society, were up on the first floor, poetry readings were given in a room on the second floor, and the two small attic rooms at the top were rented out to any congenial soul in temporary need of a place to stay, at a rent of 3s 6d per room with the option of a cooked breakfast for a further 3s 6d. Among those who stayed there at various times were Epstein, Lascelles Abercrombie, M. Willson Disher, Edward Thomas, Isaac Rosenberg, Robert Frost and, for a time, in the early spring of 1914, Hulme himself.

The runaway success of the first volume of Monro and Marsh's *Georgian Poetry*, which had sold 9,000 copies by the end of 1913, seems to have given the old Poets' Club members something to think about. The theories and ambitions of the Imagists (or *Imagistes* as they were by then, post-Pound) were out of sympathy with the poetry of the Georgians, which seemed to them to tend towards a resurgent romanticism; yet some of them were unhappy about not being a part of this successful new venture. Marsh wrote to Rupert Brooke, the star of the new anthology: 'Wilfred tells me there's a movement for a "Post-Georgian" Anthology, of the Pound–Flint–Hulme school, who don't like being out of *GP*, but I don't think it will come off.'[31]

Marsh was mistaken. A *Des Imagistes* anthology appeared in New York and London editions in the spring of 1914, with eleven poets represented including Pound, Flint, Ford Madox Hueffer, William Carlos Williams, H. D. and James Joyce; but not Hulme. His brief but influential career as a poet was already over. But his interest in the writing of verse remained intense and an encounter with Robert Frost in 1913 attests to the status he retained among contemporaries as an important theoretician of the art.

Frost was another of that remarkable generation of American poets and writers including Pound, Aiken and Eliot who established a fertile relationship with literary London in the years immediately prior to the outbreak of the war. Drifting along the London streets one dark morning Frost had chanced upon the opening of the Poetry Bookshop:

I found myself pausing before the window of a shop where a clerk was arranging volumes of current poetry. A notice announcing the opening, that night, of Harold Monro's Poetry Bookshop. I went in and asked if I might return for the evening. The assistant told me guests were 'Invited'. But I might try.[32]

Frost returned and struck up a conversation with Flint, who promised to introduce him to Pound. Pound was an influential man and a celebrity by then, a mark of his stature the fact that *Punch* had printed a joke about him and the *Bookman* a photograph. The meeting took place, but it seems Frost never quite managed to trust Pound and the two did not get along. He had more success with Hulme, whom he met through Flint not long after Hulme's return from Germany in May. In a letter to Flint of 19 June Frost refers to some of his poems in manuscript which Flint had passed on to Hulme for his appraisal, and a few weeks later wrote to him again:

Do you suppose you could get Hulme to listen with you some night to my theory of what would be pure form in poetry? I don't want to talk to a salon, but to a couple of clear-heads who will listen and give my idea its due. I will be greatly helped in what is before me by a little honest criticism. You would advise as metrical expert and he as philosopher. Do I ask too much.

R. Frost

Be sure not to force Hulme. I wouldn't put him to sleep for the world.

A meeting duly took place on 1 July and Frost seems to have been pleased with the results. On 6 July he wrote to Flint from his rented house in Beaconsfield to arrange a further session:

I don't know but that I have delivered the best of what I had to say on the sound of sense. What more there may be I will be on hand to talk over with you and Hulme at five, Tuesday. My ideas got just the rub they needed last week.[33]

What Frost was showing Flint and Hulme at these meetings were drafts of the poems that went to make up his early masterpiece *North of Boston*, published in 1914, and the remark about his ideas getting 'just the rub they needed' is a nice tribute to the stimulation his work received from the two Englishmen. However, Hulme's advice to him to call the volume *Yankee Eclogue*, on the grounds that an English readership would assume he was referring to the Lincolnshire town, was ignored.

Another poet on whom Hulme may have exerted indirect influence at this time was Isaac Rosenberg. In the latter half of 1913 Rosenberg was becoming increasingly preoccupied with the task of writing a more modest and precise kind of poetry, an idea of Hulme's that may well have been transmitted to him by their mutual friend, the painter David Bomberg.[34] Hulme and Rosenberg seem to have met only once, at the Café Royal on 10 November, where the introductions were handled by Mark Gertler. The ubiquitous Edward Marsh was also present that night. But not all these attempts at literary matchmaking were successful. Richard Curle had begun to correspond with Joseph Conrad at about this time and was moved to set up an introduction to Hulme. One can see the logic of his thinking, but after they exchanged stilted pleasantries for half an hour in a hotel south of the Strand the meeting broke up and Original Sin and the Heart of Darkness went their separate ways.[35]

When W. H. Davies recalled the Tuesday evenings 'at a lady's house in Frith Street' to which he was taken by a 'popular young intellectual, who was doing all he could to get interesting people together' and noted that 'it was mostly for artists, and not so much for literary people',[36] he was in his ingenuous way correctly assessing what had become, by late 1913, Hulme's idea of 'interesting people': painters and sculptors. Apart from those who owed their loyalty to Roger Fry and the Bloomsbury set, almost every London-based painter and sculptor of interest made his way to Frith Street at some point or other during this immediate pre-war period. Hulme in turn was a regular at salons elsewhere organized by and largely for artists, notably Robert Bevan's Sunday evenings at his home at 14 Adamson Road in Hampstead, and Walter Sickert's Saturday afternoon teas in Cumberland Market. That his main interest now lay in the work being done by painters is obvious, making it likely that theories of painting and sculpture formed the basis of much of the discussion at Frith Street between 1912 and 1914. The talk would have been of Marinetti and the Futurist movement; of the predominantly French artists introduced at the two Post-Impressionist exhibitions by Roger Fry, but including Picasso and Van Gogh. Hulme's own contributions would certainly have included enthusiastic explications of the theories of his favourite German aesthetician Wilhelm Worringer, whose seminal book *Abstraktion und Einfühlung* (*Abstraction and Empathy*) was published in 1908. He seems to have been one of the few men in London in 1913 to have heard of Worringer.[37] David Bomberg went so far as to say that Worringer was 'unknown, except to Hulme'.[38]

Hulme liked painting, but loved sculpture. Perhaps it had something to do with admiration for the sheer force involved in shaping stone to a thought with the bare hands, and the degree of commitment required to practise a form of expression which by its nature afforded no second chances to correct a mistake; as well for the endurance of sculpture through time, a condition that answered well to his idea of man himself as a fixed and unchanging creation. It was not surprising that his first attempt to articulate his aesthetic theories in public should have been occasioned by sculpture, specifically by Jacob Epstein's first one-man show, held at Mrs Smith's Twenty-One Gallery at the Adelphi in London, which opened in December 1913 with ten pieces of sculpture and drawings.

Hulme reviewed the exhibition twice. His original review was probably written for *The New Age* but seems never to have been published.[39] Less than 1,000 words long, it contains a statement of his principal belief about art and includes a version of his original idea of using the analysis of a work of art to identify the onset of hidden, major change in the *Zeitgeist*. 'Mr Epstein is certainly the most interesting and remarkable sculptor of this generation,' he opens. 'I have seen no work in Paris or Berlin which I can so unreservedly admire.' After this bold fanfare, however, the piece degenerates into a dull and unassured piece of writing.

Perhaps he would have submitted it anyway had not something happened that caused him to withdraw it and write a completely new review at something like five times the length. This was the appearance in *The New Age* of a review of recent exhibitions by Anthony Ludovici, a writer and lecturer with a particular interest in Nietzsche and a devotee of the sculpture of Auguste Rodin. Ludovici was a cultural and social conservative who dismissed abstract modern art as a sign of decadence. In his round-up he wrote at some length about exhibitions at the Carfax and Suffolk Street galleries, limiting his observations on the sculptures and drawings exhibited by Epstein at the Twenty-One to the concluding paragraph of his review. It is worth reproducing in full, both as a background to the reaction it elicited in Hulme, and because it provides a good statement of precisely what Hulme did *not* believe about art:

To understand what I think of Jacob Epstein is not difficult. When the plastic arts can no longer interpret the external world in the terms of a greater order or scheme of life, owing to the fact that all great schemes or orders are dead, they exalt the idiosyncrasy or individual angle of the isolated ego. But the only two factors in common between a plastic work of art and the people to whom it is supposed to appeal, have always been these: (1) the portion of the external world selected; and (2) the terms of the great order or scheme of life, shared by all, and revealed in the interpretation. Now, when the minor and non-creating ego is as isolated as he is today, the second factor falls out altogether, and leaves only the first. When, therefore, the first ceases to be pure transcriptism, the art has no interest whatsoever, save for cranks and people who have some reason of their own in abetting or supporting purposeless individualism *à outrance*. To these, the particular angle of vision of a minor personality has some value – to me it has none.[40]

The effect of this dismissal on Hulme was to provoke him into one of his most passionate, articulate and controversial displays of verbal aggression.

9

Hulme and Modern Art

A token of Hulme's growing interest in theories of aesthetics was his return to Berlin in the late autumn of 1913 to attend the *Kongress für Ästhetik und allgemeine Kunstwissenschaft* (Congress on Aesthetics and General Art Theory) hosted by the University from 7 to 9 October. The trip had been planned during his first visit, when he had written to Flint of his intention to return in October in order to learn German properly. He travelled with Edward Bullough, the Cambridge aesthetician, who was to deliver a paper on '*Genetische Ästhetik*' ('Genetic Aesthetics'). At the conference he heard Wilhelm Worringer lecture on '*Entstehung und Gestaltungsprinzipien der Ornamentik*' ('The Origins and Shaping Principles of Ornamentation'), took copious notes of Moritz Geiger on '*Das Problem der ästhetischen Scheingefühle*' ('The Problem of the Aesthetics of Appearance') and once back in England in November asked the conference chairman, Max Dessoir, to send him copies of Charles Lalo's '*Programm einer soziologischen Ästhetik*' ('Programmme for a Sociology of Aesthetics'), Richard Hamann on '*Ästhetik und allgemeine Kunstwissenschaft*' ('Aesthetics and General Art Theory') and Charles Myers's '*Ein Beitrag zum Studium der Anfänge der Musik*' ('A Contribution to the Study of the Origins of Music').

Of these it was Worringer's views that made the greatest impact,[1] and it was Worringer's ideas on the origins and social and psychological purposes of art that he now made the starting point for his own. By his 'horse's mouth' view of the relationship between a philosopher's theories and his physical presence he also made it his business to meet Worringer personally in Berlin. Characteristically open, he never made any secret of the debt he owed to his mentor: 'What follows is practically an abstract of Worringer's views', was how he introduced the section on aesthetic theory in a lecture delivered to the Quest Society on 'Modern Art and Its Philosophy' early in 1914.

But as he had also written in 'Notes on Language and Style', it is 'Impossible to learn anything new in ideas from a book. Must be there beforehand, then joy in recognising it.' The Byzantine mosaics he had seen at Ravenna in 1911 had sown the seeds of a new understanding of the significance of the abstract art being produced in London by his friends Epstein, Lewis, Gaudier-Brzeska, David Bomberg, William Roberts and Lawrence Atkinson. But the understanding did not come to fruition until he read Worringer's *Abstraction and Empathy* and experienced the joy of recognition in finding an intellectual expression of something he had always known instinctively to be true. Worringer analysed artistic sensitivity in human beings as polar, exhibiting at different times in history mutually exclusive needs for an art that engages the empathy and identification of the beholder (*Einfühlung*), and that discourages both responses (*Abstraktion*). His description of the conditions that give rise to abstract art meant much to Hulme:

Let us recapitulate: the original artistic impulse has nothing to do with the imitation of nature. It is an impulse in search of pure abstraction as the only means possible of obtaining rest amidst the caprice and confusion of the organic world, and beginning with itself it creates a geometric abstraction. This creation is the realization and sole expression possible for man of his liberation from the arbitrariness and temporality of the image of the world.

On Worringer's analysis, the history of art is a barometer showing the continual confrontation and alternation between a need to identify with the object of contemplation and a need to withdraw from it. The idea that there is progress in the field of artistic expression is mistaken, and the mistake arises from a failure to understand the nature of the contrast between the simple techniques used by primitive peoples to produce abstract art and the technically sophisticated techniques used to make the representational art of the Western tradition. The art made by the Egyptians, Indians, Byzantines and Africans was abstract and stylized because these peoples wanted it to be so, not because they were incapable of anything more complex. Hulme might also have seen this for himself during his visit to Pompeii, where the graffiti on the brothel walls depict in a wholly naturalistic and 'modern' way men and women in erotic embraces; but if so he did not fully understand the significance of what he had seen until he encountered Worringer's analysis.

Worringer had formulated his idea as a way of interpreting late Antique and early Christian art. In his view the aim of abstraction was to transcend nature by the denial of space in representation as a response to what was ultimately the same sort of perceptual agoraphobia Hulme had experienced on the plains of Canada in 1906. However, Worringer regarded 'abstract' and 'stylised' as synonyms. He used both terms to describe any art which was anti-naturalistic and which did not appeal to empathy as its means of expression, whether it be Gothic architecture, primitive ornament or ancient relief sculpture. He would not, for example, have applied the term 'abstract' to the sort of non-objective work being produced by Hulme's artist friends in London.

Hulme did. What he added to Worringer was an application of his perception to modern times. He 'Hulmified' it and slotted it into his own developing *Weltanschauung*, relating it to the truth of original sin and using it as further proof of his theory that progress was a myth. Because of the role in it of abstract art, his highly personal synthesis might also be said to have stabilized and repaired his damaged relationship with his first love, the mathematics, and especially the geometry, of his Newcastle-under-Lyme schooldays. Beyond that it gave him the method and the self-confidence to deal with those, like Ludovici, whom he felt to be dangerously obstructive of the truth of the new vision.

In Jacob Epstein he found the artist who has little knowledge of such theories but whose instincts and interests have already assimilated them thoroughly. The son of Jewish-Polish parents who fled the pogroms in 1870, Epstein was born in 1880 and raised in the ethnic and cultural melting pot of Manhattan's Lower East Side. His exceptional artistic talent showed itself early on and the strength of his self-belief enabled him to resist his father's attempts to have him educated as a lawyer or a doctor and travel to Paris late in 1902 to study at the École des Beaux Arts. Six months later he left, finding he 'could not continue there with any advantage'. It was at this time that he began his trawl through the art galleries and museums of Paris that led him to the discovery of the African art that was to influence his own early works so greatly and, through them, to foster Hulme's own interest in the organic art of tribal peoples working in a different time and culture from his own European tribe.

After one or two short trips across the Channel Epstein finally settled in London early in 1905. Late in 1910 he applied for British citizenship on the advice of Bernard Shaw, who had submitted his name as sculptor for the Shakespeare Memorial Theatre, hinting at the same time that he would stand a better chance of landing the commission if he were a British citizen. In the event the commission for the job at Stratford went to another, but Epstein's application for citizenship was granted, a circumstance that he would have cause to regret with the outbreak of war four years later.

Hulme knew that Epstein was a frequent visitor to the primitive sculpture galleries in the British Museum and an active collector of African art, Easter Island figurines and Polynesian sculptures, and that he was allowing these art forms to influence his own work. Epstein recalled that it was at his studio in Cheyne Walk, while he was working on the Oscar Wilde monument, that he first met Hulme, which puts the meeting at some time late in 1911. Epstein's inspiration for the monument was the Assyrian sphinx, and he recalled that as soon as Hulme saw it he 'immediately put his own construction upon my work, turned it into some theory of projectiles'.[2] In the Quest Society lecture Hulme identified perhaps this very first sight of the Wilde monument in Cheyne Walk as the moment in which he realized that the Renaissance era in European history had at last come to an end: 'Finally,' he said, 'I recognised this geometric character re-emerging in modern art. I am thinking of certain pieces of sculpture I saw some years ago, of Mr Epstein.'

The rapport between the two men was strong and instantaneous and owed not a little to their common interest in the subject of sex. Epstein had already been at the heart of a public controversy over the explicit nature of his work. In 1908 London newspapers pilloried him for the frieze for the British Medical Association building in Agar Street, a series of wholly naturalistic nudes that studded the exterior wall of the building with their genitals easily visible from the pavements below. Eric Gill, a man sexually obsessed himself, described Epstein as exactly that, and the perception was shared by Mark Gertler, who visited him at Bay Point and wrote to tell Dora Carrington that he was hating his holiday there because Epstein had 'a filthy mind and he always has some girl living with him, *including* his wife. Now he has a horrible black girl. She tells me she's at the Slade. She's like a Gauguin.'[3] Robert Frost, older and more sophisticated than Gertler, was content to describe Epstein as an artist 'whose mind runs strangely on the subject of generation',[4] while Wyndham Lewis defended his 'heroic preoccupation with Human Birth'.

In thematic terms this interest manifested itself in Epstein's enthusiasm for the openly erotic art of African and other tribal peoples, which he quickly communicated to Hulme, who found himself especially drawn to the subject of phallic worship. Epstein's figure for the Wilde monument had not only wings but a penis, and when this looked like causing controversy in the French press prior to the official unveiling in Père Lachaise cemetery, Hulme set about organizing a petition of support for him among European and American artists. The American writer John Fletcher recalled meeting him one day in Orage's office at *The New Age* and being asked if he would sign. 'Passion is action, and without action but a child's anger' was one of Hulme's own aphorisms in 'Cinders', and he felt passionately about Epstein's art. He had already publicly praised the way Racine's French admirers had rioted during a lecture which attempted to belittle their hero, and Ludovici's dismissive review of Epstein in *The New Age* now gave him the chance to show that he cared every bit as fiercely about his favourite art as the French did.

The rewritten review of the one-man show was entitled 'The Critics and Mr Epstein' to reflect the altered focus. It began with a preamble which more or less conceded the impossibility of writing about the plastic arts at all but excused his own 'clumsy, hurriedly-written and unrevised notes' on the grounds that his real aim was to 'protect the spectator from certain prejudices which are in themselves literary'. The particular kind of instinct possessed by an art critic, he maintained, did not enable him to tell good from bad art but to recognize someone who could. It left the field vulnerable to charlatans whose technique was to adopt a 'tag' and repeat it as they passed from picture to picture.

1. Hulme's father, Thomas, known locally as 'Old Tommy'. Hulme was Ernest to his family, a name he disliked. After leaving home he dropped it and became 'Tommy' himself.

2. Mary Hulme, Hulme's mother.

3. 'His obstinacy is something appalling': Hulme aged about twelve in a school photograph at Newcastle High from 1895.

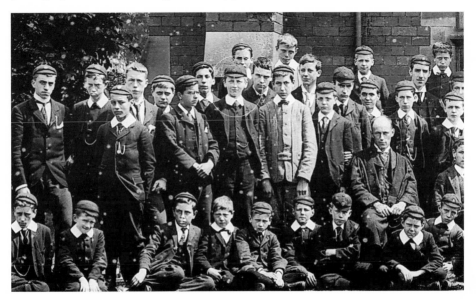

4. 15 March 1904. The largest mock funeral ever seen in Cambridge makes its way down Sidney Street towards the railway station. Hulme sits on the left of the foremost cab. His coffin is further back in the procession.

5. Hulme in 1912, at the start of his second period as a Cambridge undergraduate. At the time he was attempting the seduction, by post, of Joan Wildon Carr.

6. Hulme on the left, in the uniform of the RMA, at the wedding of his sister Kate in Endon on 8 April 1916. Kate Lechmere stands beside him.

7. Hulme with his HAC squad, probably in training in Belhus Park, Aveley.

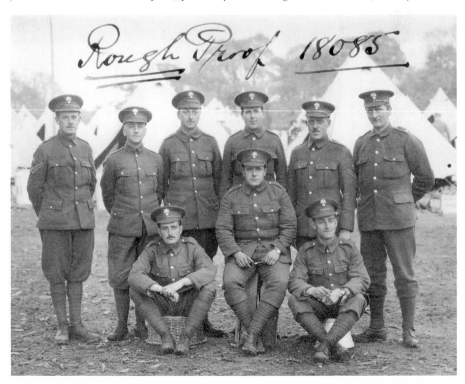

8. 'We had breakfast outside the cobbler's cottage & in the afternoon went up to the Inn on the hill & they all drank wine outside.' Diary from the Trenches, 10 February 1915. Hulme is in the centre, below the window.

9. A pencil sketch of Hulme by Dolly Kibblewhite. Both she and her sister Dora studied at the Slade under Professor Fred Brown.

10. Dolly Kibblewhite at about the time she met Hulme, with Peter and Diana, the two children of her marriage to Gilbert Kibblewhite.

11. Hulme and the Kibblewhite family spent their summers away from London at Walnut Tree House, Rustington in West Sussex.

12. Hulme as Second Lieutenant in the RMA. The war aged him dramatically

13. A 9.4-in. Mark IV gun of the type being manned by Hulme when he was killed on 28 September 1917.

Ludovici's 'tag' was the insistence that 'great art can only appear when the artist is animated by the spirit of some great order or scheme of life'. In Hulme's world of rigour a critic who had learned to repeat a tag – for example, something about 'balance' in a painting – ought to be made to stand in front of a picture and demonstrate with his finger the specific lines which constituted the 'balance' he was talking about.

Hulme's primary concern in the article was to provide an intellectual justification for the kind of art Epstein was producing and in so doing he dealt with other negative criticisms besides those of Ludovici. Many critics had been embarrassed and repelled by *Carvings in Flenite*[5] and suggested that a modern, Western artist had no business borrowing formulae from other civilizations in his work. Even if these did express something inside him, the expression could only be unnatural for a modern citizen of the Western world. Hulme replied that to criticize the Flenites as 'deliberate imitations of Easter Island carvings' was to misunderstand the idea of artistic formulae. The real problem was that such critics did not 'approve' of the sort of feelings an artist such as Epstein was trying to express and so claimed that they were, at best, leftovers from 'dark ages as distant from modern feeling as the loves of the Martians'. 'Modern feelings be damned!' was Hulme's response to this. 'As if it was not the business of every honest man at the present moment to clean the world of these sloppy dregs of romanticism.'

His own definition of a formula followed:

Man being constant, there are certain broad ways in which certain emotions must, and will always naturally, be expressed, and these we must call formulae. They constitute a constant and permanent alphabet.

This gave him the bridge to bring up his own discovery, 'that in the peculiar conditions in which we live, which are really the breaking up of an era, it has again become quite possible for people here and there to have the attitude expressed by these formulae'. The 'peculiar conditions' were the breakup of the Renaissance tradition. He seems to have been alone in identifying this development. Marinetti and his Futurists reacted to the peculiar and unnerving experience of being switch-flicking barbarians in a world of technological wonders (light bulbs, telephones, motor cars) that few understood by choosing to worship the technology and trying to imitate it in their art. Hulme found that the artists he liked showed a better way of dealing with what would later be termed alienation. In line with his realization that 'revolution' means something that goes round and not necessarily forward he identified the rise of abstract art as in fact the *return* of abstract art, and that this was taking place in response to the same inner prompting that had called it forth in the Byzantines, the Africans and the Indians – a desire to withdraw from the vagaries of social time into something permanent. Modern Western man, in the confusion and uncertainty of changing times, was experiencing a return of this need and modern Western artists answering it by producing art that rejected the appeal to empathy and replaced it with the remoter appeal of abstraction.

Hulme saw all the anthropocentric art of Europe, from the time of Pico della Mirandola onwards, as an aberration, a self-satisfaction that had lost touch with the truth of original sin and fallen into the delusion that man was a harmonious part of nature. Hulme somewhere referred to 'the state of slush in which we have the misfortune to live' and a man so resolutely out of sympathy with the spirit of his own age had a huge intellectual and personal interest vested in the success of the new art of Epstein and like-minded artists. It was this that fuelled the ferocity of his response to those, like Ludovici, who attempted to hinder the progress of the one artistic development that seemed to him to hold out hope of a more appropriate and honest future for his society. In 'The Critics and Mr Epstein' he called this analysis a 'by-path', but it remains one of the most succinct statements of his position:

I think that in this way we can force these people back on to the real root of their objection, the second prejudice I mentioned, the feeling that it is unnatural for a modern to have the kind of emotion which these formulae naturally express. In getting at this, one is getting at something that is really fundamental in modern life. I do think that there is a certain general state of mind which lasted from the Renaissance till now, with what is, in reality, very little variation. It is impossible to characterise it here, but it is perhaps enough to say that, taking at first the form of the 'humanities', it has in its degeneracy taken the form of a belief in 'Progress' and the rest of it. It was in its way a fairly consistent system, but it is probably at the present moment breaking up. In this state of break-up, I think it is quite natural for individuals here and there to hold a philosophy and to be moved by emotions which would have been unnatural in the period itself. To illustrate big things by small ones I feel, myself, a repugnance towards the *Weltanschauung* (as distinct from the technical part) of all philosophy since the Renaissance. In comparison with what I can vaguely call the religious attitude, it seems to me to be trivial. I am moved by the Byzantine mosaic, not because it is quaint or exotic, but because it expresses an attitude I agree with. But the fate of the people who hold these views is to be found incomprehensible by the 'progressives' and to be labelled reactionary; that is, while we arrive at such a Weltanschauung quite naturally, we are thought to be imitating the past.

Critics and admirers alike, each for their own reasons, have made much of Hulme's aggression – too much, according to Kate Lechmere. Yes, she conceded, he carried a knuckleduster. But it was essentially a piece of sculpture made for him by Gaudier-Brzeska, one of numerous small pieces Gaudier made to commission for friends, and which were generally referred to as 'toys'. Ezra Pound, Wyndham Lewis and Kate Lechmere all carried a pocket-sized Gaudier 'toy' about with them. Another was the door-knocker he made for Dolly Kibblewhite. All of Hulme's friends knew that he carried his particular 'toy' on his person, for in conversation he had a habit of taking it out of its leather case and playing with it. 'I never heard it referred to as a knuckleduster,' said Dermot Freyer, and Hulme's later description of it to Kate Lechmere, and the use he made of it with her, indicate that it was primarily a sexual toy, and its major significance for him was connected to the sexual act and the female orgasm. The association with violence remains, however, and will hardly be changed now. Patric Dickinson entitled his BBC Third Programme about Hulme in 1956 'The Knuckleduster', and the image of a man capable of using the threat of violence to win an argument was the key to the way in which Hulme was presented. Dickinson ended his programme with the assertion that Hulme philosophized 'with a knuckleduster'. What is not in dispute is his fondness for violent language, well-documented in the debate at Newcastle High School on swearing and in the outrages at the Cambridge New Theatre where the use of bad language was more or less the direct cause of his being sent down in 1904.

Having provided an intellectual defence of Epstein's art, the second-ary aim of 'The Critics and Mr Epstein' became to subject Ludovici to the same kind of ridicule as that to which Ludovici had subjected Epstein. Much of what Hulme wrote to this end was merely impolite, as when he likened him in his inability to see the larger picture to a dog out walking that smells only other dogs; or to the Red Indian visiting a large town for the first time who sees nothing but horses. A year or so earlier Ludovici's book *Nietzsche and Art* had been passed on to Hulme for review, and though he does not appear to have reviewed it then he did so in passing now, calling it 'a very comical little book' and comparing Ludovici's understanding of Nietzsche to that of a four-year-old who has been taken to the theatre to see a tragedy about adultery. The contentious lines followed:

That a man should write stupid and childish things about Nietzsche does not perhaps matter very much; after all, we can read him for ourselves. But when a little bantam of this kind has the impertinence to refer to Mr Epstein as a 'minor personality – of no interest to him', then the matter becomes so disgusting that it has to be dealt with. The most appropriate means of dealing with him would be a little personal violence.[6]

The history of cultural life has many examples of artists taking issue with critics, from the angry wit of Erik Satie's postcards to the critic 'Willy' informing him 'through God' of his displeasure with his reviewing to Henrik Ibsen's letter of ferocious rebuke to his colleague Bjørnstjerne Bjørnson for his failure to 'knock senseless' a critic who had disliked *Peer Gynt*. Hulme's threat, like Satie's, was made publicly and in defence of someone else's honour. He at once defused it, adding that he would be doing nothing of the sort, in thrall as he was, Nietzsche notwithstanding, to the 'unworthy sentiment of pity for the weak'. The directness and honesty of Hulme's attack exposed the fact that there are ways and ways of being civilized. Ludovici's contempt touched not only Epstein but all of those who believed Epstein to be an important artist. He gambled on bolstering his own reputation by thinking he could offload a little contempt on to a minor figure in the guise of criticizing his work and get away with it.

Later on in the article Hulme seems almost to be giving Ludovici a lesson in the etiquette of criticism when he directs at the established figure of Augustus John the sort of harsh criticism that Ludovici had only dared make of a young foreigner like Epstein whose reputation was still in the making. Even there he was careful to distinguish between his attack on John as pointing merely to 'a degeneration, temporary perhaps, of a great talent', and Ludovici's wholesale dismissal of Epstein. But it was the observation about violence that characterized the review and for the next few weeks Ludovici, Wyndham Lewis and others debated the appropriateness of Hulme's tone in the letter columns of *The New Age*.

There is a final point to be made about the Epstein review. Something that went unexpressed in this exchange about the work on show at the Twenty-One Gallery but that seethed underneath the reactions is that many of the exhibits were highly sexually charged. The *Venus* of 1913 showed a nude with parted legs and a clearly defined pudenda standing on a pair of mating birds; and the *Flenite Relief*, which Hulme sub-sequently bought and paid for in weekly instalments, depicted on one of its sides a woman's hand clasping an erect penis. Hulme was also an admirer of the many small erotic and pornographic studies done by Gaudier-Brzeska and his interest in the purely genital aspect of sexual relations might account for at least some of the passion in his defence of Epstein. Like many Edwardians he seems to have suffered in a sort of fierce silence from the way Victorian attitudes lingered on into the new century, discouraging any public expression of the fact that humans are sexual beings and that fertilization and reproduction happen in such and such a matter-of-fact way. Without ever saying so specifically Hulme wanted and encouraged more openness about sex, although D. H. Lawrence's literary efforts to do so failed to satisfy him. 'I remember his astonishment,' Epstein wrote, 'when a book of D. H. Lawrence appeared which was entirely concerned with sex. To his mind this was inexplicable.'[7] Lawrence was briefly associated with Pound and Flint and the *Des Imagistes* volume, and Hulme must have known him, if only slightly, for Epstein to record that he 'attributed the book, not without reason, to a lack of virility on the part of the author'. He was unable or unwilling to recognize in Lawrence the attempt to portray sex as only one part of a more complex relationship. Indeed the very possibility of a complex sexual relationship is some-thing Hulme seems to have excluded until close to the end of his life.

Epstein's sculptures were to his mind a much more satisfactory way of bringing sex into the open than Lawrence's.

Inspired by his experience at the Berlin Congress and given a flying start by Ludovici's criticism, over the next six months Hulme went on to write an important series of articles on modern art for *The New Age*. Roger Fry's First Post-Impressionist Exhibition in 1910 had introduced the British public to painters like Cézanne, Gauguin, Van Gogh and Manet. Cézanne, Matisse and Picasso were particularly well represented at a second exhibition in 1912, which also had an English section that included works by Eric Gill, Stanley Spencer, Spencer Gore, Duncan Grant, Wyndham Lewis, Edward Wadsworth, Vanessa Bell and Fry himself. These initiatives had identified Fry in the public mind as a prophet of the new direction in art. Not so, said Hulme: 'It has become increasingly obvious that Mr Fry and his group are nothing but a kind of backwater.'[8] When the Grafton Group of painters under Fry's leadership exhibited at the Alpine Club, Hulme's review on 15 January was dismissive of the work in general and Roger Fry's in particular. Confining his remarks to the English painters represented in the show, he wrote of an 'anaemic effect showing no personal or constructive use of colour'. Fry's own landscape displayed his 'inability to follow a method to its proper conclusion' and his use of colour was 'always rather sentimental and pretty'. Duncan Grant's 'Adam and Eve' took elements from the 'extremely intense and serious Byzantine art' and made use of them in an 'entirely meaningless and pointless way'. This was the 'feeble imitation' of archaism, not a sign of the genuine re-experiencing of 'Byzantine' values. Hulme identified what he called a 'typically Cambridge sort of atmosphere' hovering about the whole exhibition, a negative quality associated with over-refinement, urbanity, lack of seriousness and a too literary self-consciousness. He dismissed it as chocolate-box art that was destined, like the art of the Pre-Raphaelites, to find its proper home in the fabric department at Liberty's. The only exemptions he allowed were a drawing by William Roberts and a piece of sculpture by Gaudier-Brzeska. 'The Lewis group have got hold of the *New Age* critic and he's written an amazing thing which I send to you,' Fry wrote to Grant. 'Please send it back.'[9]

Though Hulme's planned career as a lecturer had been abandoned by this time he did give one last talk on the subject of the new art, addressing the members of G. R. S. Mead's Quest Society at Kensington Town Hall on 22 January. Mead's was a London-based theosophical group that had broken with the international body under Annie Besant over the reinstatement of a cleric named Leadbetter, who had been forced to leave the movement for teaching small boys the benefits of daily masturbation. Mead then started a quarterly, *The Quest*, which rapidly became an excellent forum for debate on artistic and religious issues of all kinds, and Hulme's lecture to the group on 'The New Art and Its Philosophy'[10] was in keeping with its adventurous, open-doors policy. In this he gave a fuller account of his view that the values, metaphysics and art associated with the Renaissance since its beginnings with Pico were coming to an end, and that the rise of a new abstract art was the proof of this. He argued that the vital, humanist art of the past four centuries had come about because Renaissance man, like the ancient Greeks, no longer possessed any religious intensity and had become happily the measure of things himself. 'The change which Copernicus is supposed to have brought about is the exact contrary of the fact,' he said. 'Before Copernicus, man was not the centre of the world; after Copernicus he was.' Artists were not turning away from 'vital', figurative art towards abstraction because of the mental fear of space that led primitive people to abstraction, but from a sense of disharmony or separation between man and nature. As with so much of what Hulme said and wrote, one of the pleasures of this lecture is the distinct sense it conveys of a mind in the almost visible process of discovering problems and trying to solve them. He understood and tried to think through the natural objection to abstract art, that to the average man it seems without meaning or relevance, and made clear the connection between 'vital' and abstract art:

A perfect cube looks stable in comparison with the flux of appearance, but one might be pardoned if one felt no particular interest in the eternity of a cube; but if you can put a man into some geometrical shape which lifts him out of the transience of the organic, then the matter is different. In pursuing such an aim you inevitably, of course, sacrifice the pleasure that comes from the reproduction of the natural.[11]

And he contemplated the vexed question of the extent to which the tendency to abstraction was or ought to be influenced by machinery:

As far as one can see, the new 'tendency towards abstraction' will culminate, not so much in the simple geometrical forms found in archaic art, but in the more complicated ones associated in our minds with the idea of machinery. In this association with machinery will probably be found the specific differentiating quality of the new art. It is difficult to define properly at the present moment what this relation to machinery will be.[12]

It had nothing to do with the idea that machinery must be beautified. When Roger Fry spoke of machinery being 'as beautiful as a rose' this showed something that was already obvious from his work, said Hulme, that Fry had 'no conception whatever of this new art' and was 'a mere verbose sentimentalist':

The point I want to emphasize is that the use of mechanical lines in the new art is in no sense merely a reflection of mechanical environment. It is a result of a change of sensibility which is, I think, the result of a change of attitude which will become increasingly obvious.[13]

But Hulme was sometimes loudest when he was least sure of himself and he seems still to have been uncertain about the degree to which abstract art could exist and be meaningful if it were to sever completely its roots in realism. The two preceding quotations are close to contradicting each other. In the first his analysis is similar to Lewis's idea that the rise of abstract art is environmentally conditioned by daily exposure to an urban landscape in which the rigid lines of streets and houses and rooftops create a different kind of consciousness in the artist from the soft, rounded, irregular contours of the rural landscape. In other words, the nature of their modern art was ultimately a product of social factors such as the industrial revolution, the growth of cities and depopulation of the countryside. Like Marinetti's, this was an essentially passive account. Things, discoveries, inventions greater than man himself are at work on man, changing him. Man is squeezed by his environment and a new kind of art is produced. Hulme's second quotation expresses something closer to his heart's desire than this passive logic. He seems to want his artists to be *choosing* to work in this way, to be deliberately withdrawing from a distressing and unimpressive present moment and re-establishing their links with a higher, long-neglected world of unchanging response.

Hulme's exposition was summarized and applauded in the *Observer* by the paper's art critic P. G. Konody, who said that he was grateful at last to be given 'a really lucid and logical explanation of this "new geometric art"'.[14] He remained convinced, however, that it had no evolutionary possibilities and contained within itself the seeds of its own decay.

In the third of his articles for *The New Age*, following on the defence of Epstein and the Grafton Group review, Hulme replied to a complaint similar to Konody's made by the artist Charles Ginner, that what Ginner called 'the adoption of formulae' must lead to the decay of an art. Much of the article was devoted to demonstrating that it was Cézanne who had initiated the break-up of realism in modern art and provided the material for an abstract art which Picasso then took over and organized; but to answer Ginner he revived the point made in his political writings, that what we think of as 'our' ideas are very often no more than the set of social, cultural and aesthetic assumptions of the society into which we are born, and that these assumptions colour our vision and dictate our responses as surely as someone born wearing a pair of blue-tinted spectacles will believe the world to be blue until the glasses are removed. Ginner's inability to understand geometric art was due to the fundamental but unnecessary belief that it was entirely the artist's business to represent and interpret nature, and to his assumption that, even if it were not the artist's duty to represent nature, he was compelled to do so for the practical reasons that away from nature his invention was bound to decay. It was as if Ginner thought abstract art resulted from trying to paint what one saw with eyes shut tight rather than being an attempt to simplify to essentials the complexities of the organic world. In their way these objections resembled Ludovici's, but Ginner was a practising artist whom Hulme admired and he treated his views and his person with scrupulous respect. His conclusion provided a striking image of how seriously he took the new art: both realism and abstraction could be engendered only out of nature, he wrote. But while realism's only idea of living seemed to be that of hanging on to its progenitor, abstract art had cut its umbilical cord.

His fourth article, published on 26 March, was a review of the inaugural exhibition by the London Group of painters at the Goupil

Gallery. He took his already traditional passing swipe at 'Roger Fry and his friends' and their 'faked stuff' and was kind, but not corruptly so, to those of his friends such as Robert Bevan who belonged to the group but were not abstract artists. The most interesting part of the article was that dealing with a development in geometric art represented by the paintings of Wassily Kandinsky, whose art seemed to him to express a new idea, that 'abstract form, i.e., form without any representative content, can be an adequate means of expression'. In this style a 'scattered use of abstractions' replaced the 'hard, structural work' of an artist such as Picasso. Hulme's attachment to logic made it hard for him to take this kind of art seriously. In contrast to Fry, who praised Kandinsky's most abstract work as 'pure visual music', he missed 'the controlling sensibility, the feeling for mechanical structure, which makes use of abstractions a necessity' and he called the development a 'romantic heresy'.

This business of the root of geometrical art in the real structure of machinery was becoming a sticking point. Commenting on a drawing by William Roberts he claimed that 'no artist can create abstract form spontaneously; it is always generated, or, at least, suggested, by the consideration of some outside concrete shapes'.[15] Yet he objected to Ginner's insistence on the realist's need for a real-world visual inspiration in his art while seeming to echo it in his own insistence that the forms characteristic of the new art would be the more complicated ones associated in our minds with machinery.[16]

Thus the 'beauty of banal forms like teapot-handles, knuckledusters, saws, etc.', was being perceived for the first time. Along with his acceptance of the art of primitive peoples the observation is also evidence of the fact that he was the first art critic to accept the *relativity* of artistic norms. The typically provocative assertion drove one *New Age* reader to send in a letter of despairing protest – 'Conspuez le Cubisme. Life and Ludovici forever! Quack! Quack!'

For the remainder of his article Hulme considered the work of individual members of the London Group. He was distinctly critical of the direction Wyndham Lewis was taking in his painting, but it was at least specific criticism. Lewis's forms in the 'Eisteddfod' were not controlled enough: 'Long tranquil planes of colour sweeping up from the left encounter a realistically painted piece of ironwork, which, being very large in proportion to the planes, dwarfs any effect they might have produced.' He was more fond of Lewis's drawing 'The Enemy of the Stars'. In varying degrees he praised Edward Wadsworth, C. J. Hamilton, Frederick Etchells, Nevinson and Gaudier-Brzeska, and in a concluding paragraph recycled from the unpublished review of Epstein at the Twenty-One reiterated his claim that Epstein was the greatest of them all. Epstein possessed 'that peculiar energy which distinguishes the creative from the merely intelligent artist'. A letter Epstein wrote to Hulme after the London Group review appeared showed how keenly the artists involved felt about Hulme's judgement. Slightly misremembering Hulme's actual praise, fulsome as it was, he wrote that 'Lewis seems mostly to feel the fact of your calling me a "genius" and him "merely intelligent". It was this that seemed to rankle and he naively asked me if under similar circumstances that is if the names were reversed, I would not resent it?'[17] It was at around this time that Lewis began repeating his glum mantra 'Hulme is Epstein, Epstein is Hulme'.

Hulme was sufficiently sure of his tastes by now to present between 19 March and 30 April a series of 'Contemporary Drawings' in *The New Age* by Gaudier-Brzeska, David Bomberg, William Roberts, C. R. Nevinson and Edward Wadsworth, with his own comments. His direct, informal and unpretentious approach to the business made him excellently suited to the task of presenting difficult, new art to a sceptical public: 'You have before you a movement about which there is no crystallised opinion, and consequently have the fun of making your own judgements about the work,' he told his readers. Brief as they were, his comments had the inestimable virtue to public and artist alike of being specific. Even where an artist might feel that Hulme's specifics did not tally with his own memory of his intentions in a painting, of his understanding of the fundamental principles that lay behind a work there could be no doubt.

In one of his *New Age* articles Hulme revealed, almost in passing, the order of precedence in his vision, how he had started from a conviction that the Renaissance was breaking up and then found that he was able to illustrate it by the change in art, not vice versa. It was important for him that his whole synthesis of poetry, philosophy, psychology and aesthetics hang together. But from a feeling of being ahead of the game the work of painters like Kandinsky and, in particular, David Bomberg now obliged the honest critic to confess that it was becoming a struggle even to stay abreast of it. In what turned out to be his final article on abstract art, a review of David Bomberg's show in July at the Chenil Gallery in Chelsea, he admitted the difficulty openly. He had devoted some space to Bomberg's giant painting *In the Hold* in his earlier review of the London Group's exhibition in March, referring with grudging approval to 'the real fanatics of form' who rejected, 'as savouring of literature and sentiment', the use of abstract form to convey even general emotions, and required appreciation of their work to begin and end with form itself. On that occasion he had concluded that Bomberg's chequer-board fragmentation of the image was a 'reduction ad absurdum' [*sic*] of this heresy about form' and that no development was possible along such lines; but that Bomberg himself was an artist of 'remarkable ability' whose future work he looked forward to with interest.[18]

Reviewing a whole exhibition of Bomberg's work returned him to the early doubts he had aired in that first Epstein article in 1913, about the feasibility or even the desirability of writing about modern art at all. He was quite certain about Bomberg's individuality and talent, but

that does not make it any easier for me to write an article about it. An article about one man's pictures is not a thing I should ever do naturally. The only absolutely honest and direct and straightforward expression of what I think as I go round such an exhibition would be a monotonous repetition of the words 'This is good or fairly good. How much does that cost?' for I would certainly rather buy a picture than write about it. It seems a much more appropriate gesture. Any more rotund or fluent expression than these short sentences must, however admirable, be artificial. Only the expert art critic can prolong the gesture of admiration artificially by cliché – that, of course, is his métier. I wish I could do it myself.[19]

But, he concluded, 'as an outsider in this business', he did not have these clichés at his command in order to write about Bomberg's pictures, and would have to use 'the only form of incense natural to me: I can get up an argument about them – which I therefore proceed to do'. Bomberg prefaces his catalogue with the statement that the object of all his painting is the construction of 'pure form', and Hulme admits his attraction to the work, he concedes Bomberg's success. He finds the drawing *Zin* remarkable for containing 'hardly any representative element at all'. In the upper, best part of the drawing 'there are no recognisable forms at all, but only an arrangement of abstract lines outlining no object'. That Hulme should be fascinated by this is obvious. The logician in him feels that abstract art *must* have its origins in the reality of the shapes and curves of machine parts; what Bomberg's work hints at is something Hulme simultaneously wants to be true but shies away from, and that is the deeper independence of an artist's mind which seems to have direct knowledge of geometrical shapes as pure form, before conscious intention interferes to make use of them in the creation of artefacts. It obliges him to ask himself the question: is pure form alone a sufficient basis for interest in art? He accepts without question the validity of the subjective response that says, Yes, I feel the same interest in abstract form as another man does in atmosphere or landscape. What he denies is that the conclusion to be drawn from such a response is that there is an independent, specific 'aesthetic emotion' and that its sole function is to respond to the contemplation of form. The emotions produced by abstract art are, he insists, merely our familiar, everyday emotions produced in a different way. But to prove this he finds his emotional logic leading him inexorably back to the *Einfühlung* which was the staple of the old, humanist, 'vital' art which he is counting on abstraction to replace. 'After all,' he writes, 'this possibility of living our own emotions *into* outside shapes and colours is the basic fact on which the whole of plastic art rests.' His strong concern that the layman be able to understand and accept the new art leads him to insist that 'there is nothing esoteric or mysterious about this interest in abstract forms':

Once he has awakened to it, once it has been emphasised and indicated to him by art, then just as in the case of colour perception and impression the layman will derive great pleasure from it, not only as it is presented to him organised in Cubism, but as he perceives it for himself in outside nature. He will feel, for example, probably for the first time, an interest in the extraordinary variety of the abstract forms suggested by bare trees in winter (an interest, I must repeat, which is really an interest in himself as these forms, by an obscure psychological process, become for him the bearers of certain emotions) or in the morning, he may contemplate with interest the shapes into which his shirt thrown over a chair has fallen.[20]

Coming from Hulme this is almost idealism, and predictive of Anthony Burgess's passionate conviction that Joyce's *Ulysses* was just the book for the man in the street if he would only learn to like it. He insists on the possibility that abstract art is art for everyone.[21] He recalls that he went round Bomberg's exhibition in company with 'a very intelligent painter of an older school',[22] who objected that though he found the drawings extremely interesting, 'I feel abstract work would become tiring when one continually saw it in a room.' Not so, counters Hulme:

Personally, I think I should find drawings in which your imagination was continually focused in one direction by a subject more fatiguing. The proportions of a room or the shape of a good window, though they exercise a definite effect on one, do not become tiresome. And the pleasure to be got from good abstract art is of the same kind, though infinitely more elaborate, as the pleasure you get from these other fixed elements of a room.[23]

Hulme's attention gave the sensitive and difficult Bomberg a great lift and was largely responsible for the healthy state of his reputation in London in the pre-war years. Afterwards, through the long years of obscurity before his genius was again recognized, Bomberg retained his sense of gratitude for Hulme's support at a time when abstract art was considered strange rubbish by all but a few:

At the time Hulme began to write the 'New Age' articles for Orage, there had been only journalistic criticism of painting in this country with the exception of Walter Sickert and George Moore, Roger Fry and Clive Bell. These, though the most eminent, had not the remotest idea what we were doing. Hulme had and wrote about it, and in this way he became the spokesman for the innovators in the first exhibition of the London Group. And he did me much honour. [. . .] There was no valuation whatever for Imagist poetry or Abstract painting, there was no critical circle here or elsewhere who understood the language. [. . .] I have always wondered why acknowledgement as the first of the new philosophical approach or it might be termed the scientific approach to literary and art criticism – the explanation is, that insufficient capital has been sunk in making known the works of Hulme before he was killed, and no one came forward to risk any more capital after his death.[24]

Hulme, with his championship of Bomberg and Epstein, and Pound, who made writing about Gaudier-Brzeska his speciality and secured Gaudier's reputation after his early death, were the only critics writing seriously about the abstract art of the years that mark the true beginning of Modernism in England. Hulme's support for Epstein is particularly remarkable. The status of the sculptor at that time was considerably lower than that of the painter. He was seen as an artisan who had to suppress his individuality and do the bidding of his commissioners, usually corporate or public bodies. The public at large were not interested in his work and the response of the critics was to treat it as an art dependent on architecture and to use the same critical vocabulary to describe it. Hulme's insistence that Epstein was an artist of the first rank who was not merely decorating society but expressing it forced a change in these perceptions that promoted sculptors from the 'arts and crafts' ghetto into the realms of fine art and began the rise and rise in their status which continued unabated throughout the twentieth century. After Hulme's death Bomberg made a sketch for a memorial to his name, with a sword laid flat across a plinth and a soldier in attendance nearby with head bowed.[25] He may sometimes have been an arrogant man, but 'with artists he was always humble and willing to learn', as Epstein said of him, and it was his real love of art and admiration for artists whom he knew to be genuine that made him so well-remembered by Epstein, Bomberg, Lewis and the other abstract painters whose work he wrote about with such warm and intelligent sympathy during those first six months of 1914, arguably the most important of all the cultural interventions of his short life.

10

Kate Lechmere

By February 1914 Hulme was occupying one of the two small attic rooms above Monro's Bookshop in Devonshire Street and had become friendly with Wyndham Lewis. Lewis had a flat two doors down from Rudolf Stulik's exclusive Eiffel Tower Restaurant in Percy Street, where Hulme's branch of the Poets' Club used to meet in 1909–10 to discuss Imagist theory. It is quite possible the two men knew each other as early as this, and that Lewis was the first serious, practising artist Hulme got to know personally. The bonds between them were many. There was pre-eminently a shared interest in the new geometric art, as well as a shared hostility to Roger Fry's Bloomsbury group. Hulme's hostility seems to have been aesthetic, Lewis's both personal and aesthetic. He had been on cordial terms with Fry and members of the group, but broke with them after an episode involving the Ideal Home Exhibition in 1913. The *Daily Mail* was sponsoring a modernist room as part of the exhibition and P. G. Konody, who had been impressed by the decor Lewis and Spencer Gore had provided for the walls of Frida Strindberg's nightclub the Cave of the Golden Calf, suggested to the paper that they ask Gore to decorate its walls. Gore was too busy to accept the invitation and passed it on to Lewis. Lewis and several of his friends were at that time loosely associated with Fry's Omega Workshops project at 33 Fitzroy Square, a co-operative workshop and showroom inspired by the ideals of William Morris and John Ruskin and dedicated to the production of painted furniture, textiles and artefacts. Lewis was not at Fitzroy Square when Gore called in to give him the good news, and a message was left with Duncan Grant. Grant later confessed that he 'may have forgotten' to pass it on to Lewis, but he did pass it on to Fry. According to Lewis,

Fry at once appropriated the commission for himself and his friends. He informed Lewis that no decorations of any sort were to be placed on the walls of the room and invited him instead to carve a mantelpiece. 'Shortly after this,' wrote Lewis, 'Mr Lewis went away on his holidays, and on his return in September, found large mural decorations, destined for the Olympia Exhibition, around the walls of the workroom.'[1] A few days later Lewis met Gore and heard the full story of what had happened. He at once confronted Fry at the Omega. There was a heated exchange and Lewis broke with him and the other members of the Bloomsbury group. Friends and sympathizers such as Wadsworth, Etchells, C. J. Hamilton, William Roberts and Gaudier-Brzeska left with him and presently formed the London Group, which shortly afterwards evolved into the Vorticists.

Lewis shared Hulme's admiration for the ideas of Georges Sorel, as well as the conviction that idealists and humanists such as H. G. Wells and the Fabian intellectuals were misguided in their faith that man was a being of infinite capabilities who needed only the right set of circumstances to proceed to a state of social grace. With a mixture of admiration, irritation and melancholy Lewis devoted several pages of his autobiography, *Blasting and Bombardiering*, to Hulme. 'All the best things Hulme said about the theory of art were written about my art,' he wrote, and maintained that as artist and critic they were made for each other. 'What he said should be done, I *did*. Or it would be more exact to say that I did it, and he said it.' Lewis's claim is understandable, especially in view of the fact that Epstein abandoned abstract art even before the end of the war, but it was pre-war Epstein, along with David Bomberg, who provided the best examples of the kind of geometric art Hulme wanted to see establish itself. And of the three of these it was Epstein the sculptor, the carver in stone, whose imagery was so often erotic (*Venus*) and at times pornographic (the Flenite reliefs), whose work gave him the deepest spiritual and sensual satisfaction. For the ambitious and talented Lewis, having made enemies of the powerful Bloomsbury set, it must have given further cause for distress to realize that he was always going to stand in Epstein's shade whenever Hulme wrote about modern art. 'He was unquestionably Hulme's man (or perhaps I should say Hulme was Epstein's man) upon the social plane,' Lewis wrote. 'They were great friends, where I never stood in that relation to Hulme at all.'[2] Hulme's devotion to Epstein seemed to him 'doglike'. Epstein and Hulme both were aware of Lewis's unease about their friendship. The *Schadenfreude* in Epstein's letter to Hulme describing Lewis's response to being called a 'merely intelligent' artist indicates just how vulnerable Lewis felt in the situation, as well as signalling the extent of Hulme's authority in London art circles at that time. The relationship always had this undercurrent of unease. Epstein recalled an occasion when Hulme and Lewis met in the street. At some point in their conversation Lewis said, 'I suppose your article about Epstein is going to be just an advertisement,' infuriating Hulme. The conversation grew heated. Lewis raised his umbrella in a threatening gesture but then backed down and their fight was postponed to a later date.[3]

These professional spats apart, for a while at least the sodality was fair and the Bloomsburys an enemy that demanded a united front. Another competitor who had to be dealt with was the Italian Filippo Marinetti. Marinetti was a frequent visitor to European capitals in the last years before the outbreak of war, preaching the gospel of Futurism wherever he went, the veneration of machines, speed and anything that could be described as 'dynamic', and bent on 'liberating' words from the restrictions of grammar and syntactical order. In Berlin in the spring of 1913, while Hulme was still there, he had given a show, or 'lecture' as he called his public appearances, at the Expressionists' favourite Café Josty, and in the summer of 1914 he was in London again for a second or third time, seeking converts and stealing the newspaper headlines. He and C. R. W. Nevinson ('always a dark horse', according to Lewis), inserted in the *Observer* of Sunday 7 June a stentorian manifesto that damned every recent trend in British cultural life, from Maypole dancing to Oscar Wilde, and requisitioned for the glory of the Futurist movement the cream of non-Bloomsbury British artists including Etchells, Wadsworth, Lewis, Hamilton and Roberts. Quite apart from the ideological differences involved there was offence in the very act of appropriation and five days later, at a quarter to nine on the evening of 12 June, as Marinetti began his advertised lecture at the Doré Galleries in Bond Street, the doors burst open and ten of the aggrieved artists and their supporters entered. The group came direct from a hearty meal at Lewis's flat in Greek Street and included Epstein, Hulme,

Gaudier-Brzeska and Edward Wadsworth. Lewis described how Marinetti 'put down a tremendous barrage in French as we entered. Gaudier went into action at once. [. . .] He was sniping him without intermission, standing up in his place in the audience all the while. The remainder of our party maintained a confused uproar.'⁴ In more formal protest members of this same group were among the signatories to a letter that appeared in the *Observer* the following Sunday dissociating themselves from the 'futurist' manifesto of 7 June.

With his love of rowdy fun Hulme would have greatly enjoyed the evening at the Doré; but there were serious differences of attitude at stake too. Marinetti was fired by an impetuous desire for a break with the past which was very different from the painstaking and respectful efforts being made to do the same thing honourably by Hulme in his aesthetic theory, Lewis in his painting and Pound in his poetics. Most of the names requisitioned by Marinetti for his *Observer* manifesto were now so-called Vorticists, a name coined for the group by the public relations genius of Ezra Pound, and associates of Lewis at his Rebel Art Centre at 38 Great Ormond Street: to add insult to injury Marinetti and Nevinson had used stationery from the centre to give authority to the manifesto sent to the *Observer*.

The Rebel Art Centre was a studio started by Lewis and Kate Lechmere following Lewis's break with Fry and the Bloomsbury group over the Omega room decorations. Lewis and Lechmere had met for the first time in 1912 at a dinner party given by Robert and Stasia Bevan at 14 Adamson Road in Hampstead and Lewis had fallen in love with her. Early in 1914 she wrote to him from France suggesting that she finance the hiring and running of an arts centre along the lines of those popular among Parisian artists, and when the Rebel Art Centre opened in March that year it was her money that had paid for the refurbishment and the rent. The plans were to give instruction, invite interesting lecturers and hold exhibitions of work by Lewis himself, Gaudier, Etchells, Wadsworth, Roberts, Nevinson and other Vorticists. Epstein, though never strictly a Vorticist himself, was a frequent visitor. So was Hulme.

Spring and early summer of 1914 was probably the period when Hulme and Lewis came closest to being friends rather than acquaintances. Certainly they spent enough time in each other's company for

Lewis to give in *Blasting and Bombardiering* an excellent pen-portrait of Hulme:

In private life there was no 'severity' about Hulme. He was a very talkative jolly giant, arrogantly argumentative, but a great laugher. He laughed painfully, coldly, but heartily, always wrinkling his nose as if about to sneeze, and as if he had a bitter taste in his mouth.

'Among other things he was very fond of girls,' Lewis wrote, 'his conversation mostly bore upon that subject.' Since Lewis too was fond of girls there was no doubt an element of sexual competition in the repetitive choice of topic. Hulme's ideas on how the sexual life should be conducted were apparently both specific and didactic, though Lewis does not record them in *Blasting and Bombardiering*. Instead he says that for Hulme 'St Thomas Aquinas presided, when it was a statue, and Bergson when it was the living flesh'.[5] At some length he relates the story of Hulme's frustrated attempts to seduce a young female assistant at what he describes as 'the only bookshop in London at which he could obtain books on credit':

The proprietor of the bookshop worked upstairs. But unfortunately he had a hole cut in the ceiling, and whenever this discoverer of Original Sin was getting on rather nicely with the beautiful assistant, there would be a frantic stamping, as of an enraged horse, upon the ceiling overhead, and a Mormon-like eye would appear in the aperture.

Lewis does not go into detail in his published account, but the shop in question was almost certainly Harold Monro's Poetry Bookshop and the assistant Monro's beautiful Polish fiancée, Alida Klemataski, part of a curiously insistent Polish element in Hulme's circle that included Gaudier-Brzeska's companion Sophie and Robert Bevan's wife Stasia. 'The beastly Hulme is in the shop,' Alida wrote to Monro in one letter of March 1914. 'I am writing to you and not taking any notice of him. He has just got a remarkably irritating female in to talk to him. Why does he need to put his arm around her in the shop?' Her resistance was enough to make her an obsession for Hulme and Lewis described how he 'sneered, with a painful twisting of the nose, whenever he spoke of it'. And because the availability of credit compelled him to use Monro's shop,

He was exposed incessantly to this dilemma – his purse, his sex, his intellect all contributing. The lot of Tantalus was his, a cunningly-contrived frustration: and he could see no way out of it at all.[6]

For Lewis's amusement Hulme clowned the situation as a philosophical conundrum. He outlined the various changes of circumstance which might release him from the impasse: Monro might become less trusting as a bookseller and stop giving him credit, thus relieving him of the need to use the shop any more; or he might become as a man more trusting and simply stop peering down through his peephole; a change in reading tastes or the appearance of a competitor might cause him to modify his policy on credit, or to invest in more lightweight stock and cease catering for the sort of tastes represented by a customer such as Hulme. Alida herself might resolve the matter simply by abandoning her resistance to him. But none of these things transpired, and the awful stasis continued. He was an excellent gossip, Lewis concluded, recalling the way Hulme's 'nagging, nasal, North-country voice' induced in his listener an overwhelming sensation of 'the cussedness of things'.

*

Hulme and Lechmere saw each for the first time in January 1914, when she accompanied Lewis to Kensington Town Hall to hear him, Pound and Hulme talk on modern art. Hulme's contribution was the lecture on the reasoned basis for geometrical art which Konody of the *Observer* found so enlightening. He was not a natural performer and throughout his talk Lewis criticized his stage manner to Lechmere, pointing out how he mumbled and failed to hold his head up. When his own turn came to speak he made exactly the same mistakes himself. As a piece of entertainment the evening was only rescued by Pound. Foppishly lounging on the podium in velvet jacket and floppy hat, reading from his own and Hulme's poetry he looked every inch the poet of popular perception. Lewis gracelessly explained to Lechmere that the only reason the audience liked him was because he was an American. Just as Hulme's strong regional accent seemed to him comical so Lewis confessed that he found it 'rather a joke hearing poetry read by an American'.[7]

A few weeks after this, in the late spring, Lewis brought Hulme along to the Rebel Art Centre to show him some paintings. Lechmere had a lunch appointment and he was not expecting to find her there. The appointment had been cancelled, however, and when they arrived he was obliged to introduce Hulme to her. In her own word, they 'clicked'. Lewis sensed it immediately. Once Hulme had left he asked her insistently 'What do you think of Hulme?' 'Hulme is Epstein, Epstein is Hulme,' he repeatedly told her, as though he thought it might lower her opinion of Hulme.

Lewis's anxiety served only to further arouse her curiosity about Hulme. That same evening she was dining with Ashley Dukes and began to question him about his erstwhile room-mate. Who was he? What did he do? Dukes proudly replied that his friend was a real philosopher and that if they went along to the Sceptre chop-house they might well find him dining there. They did so and there she and Hulme met and were able to talk free of Lewis's jagged scrutiny.

The clicking got louder. Hulme invited her to join him for dinner with some friends on the Saturday night. Lechmere mentioned this to Lewis, and Lewis's unease grew. It also fuelled a streak of paranoia in him and he began to entertain the unfounded fear that Hulme intended to supplant him as leader at the Rebel Art Centre. His response to her news was a repetition of that woeful 'Hulme is Epstein, Epstein is Hulme.' Lechmere recalled:

Poor dear Lewis quite lost his head and when he accused me of this Hulme attachment I said he had shown little attention to me of late and his remark was that it was not good for a woman to have too much notice taken of her. It only proved that Lewis was of a suspicious and jealous nature and certainly later developed a mild persecution mania.[8]

Second best in art and now second best in love, with Hulme responsible for both relegations, the brooding Lewis presently cracked and set out one day in pursuit of his tormentor. With a despairing cry of 'What are you doing to me?' he burst into the house at Frith Street and went for him. A great brawl ensued. Lewis was dragged down the stairs, out into the street and over towards the park in the centre of Soho Square. Lewis, himself a six-footer, managed to get his hands round Hulme's throat and tried to strangle him. Hulme broke free, lifted him up and brought the fight to an abrupt end by hanging his opponent upside down by his trouser turn-ups from the iron railings surrounding the park.[9] Every window of No. 67 afforded a view of the square and all of this must have been clearly visible to any guests present at the time.

The fight brought about a complete break between the two men, and Lewis never spoke to Hulme again. Since Hulme was part of the group that supped with Lewis before going on to disrupt Marinetti's lecture at the Doré on 12 June the fight must have taken place after that date. It may even have been the following week, for when the first issue of Lewis's seminal magazine *Blast: The Review of the Great English Vortex* was published by John Lane on 20 June Hulme was neither a contributor nor a signatory to the Vorticist Manifesto. Lewis had originally asked him to write an essay on Epstein and Hulme had agreed.[10] Its pages contained contributions from many of his friends – Gaudier, Pound, Aldington, Wadsworth and Hamilton. Given his sympathy for the broad aims of the movement his name can be absent only because of the personal animosity of *Blast*'s editor. Not even during the war, when the two men were stationed within walking distance of each other in Flanders, could Lewis bring himself to make contact with his old friend and rival, a fact which Hulme's death caused him to regret profoundly. As he told Kate Lechmere after the war, Hulme was 'the one man he would have been interested to meet.'[11]

How did Hulme explain the scene in Soho Square to the mistress at No. 67? Without difficulty, one suspects. And once his affair with Kate Lechmere was properly under way (she recalled that on their first kiss she was 'fervently implored never to drink whisky'), he assured her that, though he continued to have a close personal relationship with Dolly and to call Frith Street his home, they were no longer lovers. Dolly, however, remained unaware of this latest development in Hulme's life, and for the following three years the affair was conducted in secrecy.

Kate Lechmere was four years younger than Hulme, born in Herefordshire in 1887 into a moderately wealthy family. After attending Clifton College in Bristol she studied art in Paris and at Westminster Art School under Sickert. She was particularly friendly with Lawrence

Atkinson, one of the more obscure names in the Vorticist movement, and studied the piano with him in Normandy, where she spent much of her time. She had a cheerful, sensual, rather chubby face and strong white teeth. At the time she and Hulme met she was wearing her dark hair short.

The early months of 1914 were a period of particularly intense activity by the suffragette movement. Houses were burnt down in Scotland, a bomb planted on Yarmouth Pier, and an attack made with a meat cleaver on the *Rokeby Venus* at the National Gallery. Although not an active suffragette, Kate considered herself very much a modern and 'enlightened' woman, a freethinker in religious matters and in sexual matters an opponent of the double standard that winked at the rogue who took several lovers but scowled at the whore who did the same. The attraction of such a woman to a man such as Hulme is one of the glories and mysteries of love, for on the basis of his views alone Kate should have detested him. Early on in their relationship he informed her that a woman's place was at home and that the only reason a woman had for travelling was to find a husband. Women should have plenty of children, he said, to keep them from thinking too much about themselves – 'He told me he wanted five,' she remembered, 'but he meant ten.' Motherhood and domesticity were the only logical roles for women, he explained, since women 'cannot enter the pure realms of reason'.[12]

As she later told Michael Roberts, 'anyone, man or woman, would flounder badly on first acquaintance with Hulme'. Under the influence of an aunt she had imbibed a few 'agnostic teachings' in her adolescence, and having no idea that his belief in original sin was a part of his everyday mind she chanced one day to make a dismissive remark about the Fall in his presence. Hulme took Gaudier's little toy out of his trouser pocket and 'once again my buttocks were severely attacked by Hulme and his K.D. and the safest thing was to encourage Hulme's kisses'. In later years what she remembered was the intensity of the sexual attraction between them. 'It is rather difficult for me to tell you much that can be published about Hulme,' she explained to Roberts. 'Our relationship was so completely as that of man and woman and I had his love.' They called each other K.D. and almost from the start signed their letters to each other K.D., a practice that seems to mingle their secret knowledge of the device with Hulme's own nasal pronunciation of her first name (Katie):

The Knuckleduster had a very special image concerning sex – it had no other interest for him, except as an abstract design. He also got G.B. [Gaudier-Brzeska] to design other K. Dusters but the one he carried about with him was the usual old antique brass one with 5 holes for the fingers to go through.[13]

He explained the symbolism of the device to her: the two horizontally projecting pins were her legs, the central space was her vagina, and the array of finger holes represented the tossing of her head in the moment of orgasm. She found him 'a very healthy, natural normal man' with a 'great interest in sex', liked the way his hair curled at the front and what she called a 'certain stand-easy laziness-insolence about him'. His eyes 'could have a quick almost projecting gaze and also the lids could become heavy and the eyes veiled when in contemplation'. 'He did not intellectualise sex,' she remembered, 'but he himself was well sexed.'[14]

The most difficult side of the relationship was his overpowering personality. He wanted to 'make everyone he met into a little Hulme' was how she put it. For a time she tried to stay away from him, but found herself unable to. Most difficult of all was his insistence on keeping their relationship secret. Some of Hulme's friends, such as Ashley Dukes, considered that he and Dolly Kibblewhite were effectively a married couple and made no secret of their disapproval of his betrayal of her trust.

Lechmere was kept in one of the many compartments of Hulme's private life, welcome in some circles, forbidden to others. She was never allowed to meet what she called 'the Kibblewhite gang'. It meant, for example, that she was not among the group of friends including Hulme, Dukes, Curle and Ramiro de Maeztu who had a day out at the Epsom Derby on Wednesday 27 May 1914. This was the first time Hulme had been to a racecourse and the experience did not greatly excite him. Paraphrasing a remark made by the Shah of Persia on declining an invitation to attend the Derby during a recent state visit, he assured Dukes he was already aware of the fact that some horses can run faster than others. But the nationalist and the monarchist in him was pleased by the sight of King George flanked by the peerage and numerous members of the House of Commons, and the mathematician in him fascinated by the skill of the bookmakers in adjusting the changing odds. A 20–1 outsider, Durbar II, won that year, three lengths ahead of Hapsburg at 33–1, with Peter the Hermit a length and a half away at 100–1. According to the *Daily Telegraph*'s racing correspondent there was widespread disappointment that the king's horse Brakespear had not won. He called the race 'one of the most unsatisfactory and disappointing in history' and claimed that 'no cheering was heard as the winner passed the post'. Afterwards they took the train back to London. In a newsy, brooding letter Hulme received a few weeks before his death Curle recalled the outing as a last untroubled day before the outbreak of war: 'Where is Dukes,' he mused, '– where Maxwell?[15] When shall we all be at another Derby?'[16]

Some two months after Derby Day Hulme was sitting in the Café Royal with David Bomberg when news broke of the declaration of war on Germany. Less than a week later, on 10 August, he volunteered for service at Armoury House in Finsbury, the headquarters of the Honourable Artillery Company. He chose the HAC, according to Dukes, because of its traditions as the oldest regiment in the British Army and the senior regiment of the Territorial Army. He may also have become interested in the regiment during his second short spell as a Cambridge undergraduate in 1912, when the HAC struck up a liaison with the university, possibly as part of its recruiting drive, and sent a team to challenge the Officers Training Corps in a Grand Assault-at-Arms which included boxing, bayonet fighting, sabre fighting, gymnastic displays and, for the grand finale, a Singlestick Mêlée between two teams of six men. It is notable that Hulme, with his capacity for leadership, did not apply for a commission, suggesting that his deep-rooted ambivalence towards constituted, as distinct from natural, authority had still not fully resolved itself. The perfunctory medical examination established his apparent age as 30 years and nine months, his height as 6 feet 1 inch and his chest measurement as 42 inches, including the 4 inches range of expansion. He was then enlisted, signing a Certificate of Attestation in which he promised to serve for four years and giving his trade or calling as 'author'. Richard Aldington, who applied to join with him, was turned down. Hulme expressed pleasure and relief. 'War is not for sensitive men,' he told him. Recalling the occasion in later life Aldington added that 'he thought he was tough. He was, I think.'[17]

At the time the HAC nominally consisted of a half-battalion, two batteries of horse artillery and two ammunition columns with a combined strength of approximately 740 men. All these were alike in being under their establishment; several years of recruiting drives had failed to remedy the situation. Now, almost overnight, the regiment found itself inundated. The volunteers arrived in their thousands and tents sprang up covering every available inch of the field at Armoury House, including the cricket pitch in the middle. Before the end of the month authority had been obtained to increase the strength of the infantry from half to a full battalion by adopting a 'double-company' formation, and when that proved insufficient to form a second battalion. Hulme was assigned to B Company in the First Battalion as Private No. 1305.

He remained in London until mid-September, and was with Epstein, Aldington, Tancred and Dolly Kibblewhite in the group which turned up at Charing Cross station to wave goodbye to Gaudier-Brzeska, who was leaving London to enlist in the French Army. 'Your friend Brzeska is going to enlist if there is a war, displaying bloodthirsty sentiment,' Hulme had written to Richard Curle in the summer.[18] Hulme and Gaudier had only known each other for about two years but Hulme genuinely liked Gaudier's work and admired his fighting spirit. D. L. Murray recalled seeing them together at the Café Royal after the fighting had started, 'bubbling over with delighted anticipation' at the prospect of joining in.[19] 'People said that the War could not possibly last more than two months and that we need not worry,' wrote the artist-socialite Nina Hamnett.[20] No doubt Hulme and Gaudier shared the view that it would all be over within a matter of weeks and that their personal survival was not in question.

Sophie Brzeska, Gaudier's soul sister and closest companion, was at the station too. After meeting Gaudier in Paris she had followed him to London, but in two years of living there had made few friends. One was Nina Hamnett, who recalled some of Sophie's many eccentricities in her memoirs: her horror of the moon and how she would insist that when they went out on moonlit evenings they walk sideways or with their backs to the moon in order to avoid its evil influence; her habit of wearing the same clothes all the time; her obsessive making of jam. She was twenty years Gaudier's senior, a poet who had failed to persuade others of her talent and who had invested all her love and her faith in his genius. She sobbed helplessly throughout the leave-taking and her distress left Gaudier pale and shaken.

Hulme, meanwhile, had temporarily lost contact with Kate, and as soon as he heard that B Company were being sent for training to Belhus Park, at Aveley in Essex, he wrote to arrange a meeting:

Dear K.D.

I have joined the Hon. Artillery. Co. about a month ago as soon as the war started. We never know from one day to another whether we shall be free but could you call here to-morrow *Wednesday* at 5.30 and ask for me. I shall probably be returning from a day's march so come inside and wait. If you can't do this wire me an appointment for later in the evening.

Private Hulme

B Company

Hon. Artillery Co.

Armoury House,

Finsbury Pavement E.C.

At Belhus Park there was bayonet training, training in trench warfare, weapon training and waiting. Hulme was not among the first detachment of troops sent to Flanders – 'too fat, I suppose' – he suggested laconically to Kate. But he did not have long to wait. A note to her scribbled on a page torn out of his field-service notebook gave her the news:

Southampton

Just off to France at last. My address will be

    K.D.

    H.A.C. (Infantry)

    No.2 Company

    (1st Draft)

    Expeditionary Force.

Do write to me dear. We are I believe going near *Ypres* in Belgium.

Yr K.D.[21]

I I

Diary from the Trenches

Dec. 30th, 1914[1]
We left Southampton about 4 p.m., after marching down the principal street, all out of step, and all the girls waving from the windows. (On the way down on Sunday, people waved to us from the back windows; all the troops go down that line so they have formed a habit.)

We had a very smooth crossing, 700 of us in a tramp steamer which was fitted out to carry cattle or horses. We slept in the stalls hurriedly whitewashed to make them clean, with notice painted over our heads 'This is for urine only not for dung.' It sounds dreadful but it's really all right.

We were accompanied all the way by two English destroyers, as escort, got to the port I said we should come to about 4 a.m., but did not leave till about 9. As we entered the harbour, some French soldiers, drilling on the quayside in white trousers looking from the distance exactly like penguins, called out 'Air we down hearted.' We marched then, with all our equipment up a fearful hill about 4 miles to what is called a Rest Camp, a fearful place, deep in mud, where we have to sleep in tents which makes me very depressed. I hope we shan't stay here long. All my clothes are wet through with sweat.

I am writing this in a little cafe, by the camp. Crammed full of Tommies of all sorts, where we are eating tremendously. We are all dreading the night for we are 12 in one tent and it looks like rain. The town seems absolutely empty but for the soldiers in red trousers, of all ages.

I thoroughly enjoy all the events, like being seen off at the dock, except that there were only about 10 people to cheer us as the ship left the side, but its all very amusing – and the girls at the windows.

We are in one of a series of similar Rest Camps on the top of a hill.

Send the first part of this letter to my Aunt.[2] Ask her to send me a large pair of chauffeurs gloves, line with felt. (Any socks must be long in the leg). Also a piece of soap and a night light each week.

Jan. 5th, Tuesday. Rest Camp

We are leaving here to-day. A wire came at midnight that we were to be ready. I shan't be sorry to leave this mud. You must imagine a large space of clayey earth, no grass, like an undeveloped building plot, all pulped up into mud and covered with tents with large trenches round them. We get up at 5:30 and march down to the docks, as a rule without breakfast. Here we do [. . .] work in an enormous shed. Here is the base for the army and here is all the food. The shed is 5/8 of a mile long and 79 yrds wide. On one side are the ships coming in and on the other a luggage train of [. . .] covered in vans and the same length as the shed. Each truck is marked with chalk with the amount of stuff that has to go in. So many boxes of corned beef, pepper, salt, bran, hay, oats etc. We work in gangs and have to fill so many trucks from the piles inside the shed. The train goes off in 4 parts each night, to feed the whole army. The shed inside is quite nice, as it's quite new, all light iron work and has of course immense distances in it, men and horses at the end of long avenues, between the mountains of boxes looking quite tiny. There are two cafés inside the limit of the camp (otherwise we have no leave) and we go and talk to the Tommies there. There are all people from all kinds of regiments, some wounded, some lost etc., a kind of sorting camp. We spent one evening with some Belfast Tommies, men about 35, who had rejoined, very simple people with faces like pieces of wood, who told us fearful stories of this sort. Some Ghurkas were left in charge of German prisoners. In the morning all the Germans were found with their heads off. Asked for an explanation, they opened their haversacks, each of which had a German head in it and said, 'Souvenir Sahib.' All this in the most wonderful accent you ever heard. – Three men have been sent back with pneumonia already and I'm not surprised. In the enormous shed we worked in, were batches of English prisoners, people sent back from the front for various reasons, a sergeant 5 years for cowardice, another 15 years for looting. At one end of the shed was an enormous cage, in which all the rum was kept. This was to keep it from being stolen by the A.S.C. men, who are really London dockers enlisted for the war. It was really impressive to see all the piles of food, all done up into cases a convenient size for men to handle. It makes the word 'base' and 'lines of communication' seem much more real to have seen it. It was all guarded by English Territorials who slept in a little enclosure made of packing cases in the middle. All the men doing clerks work live in little houses made of packing cases put together. They say that when the Germans were 12 miles off some months ago they had to shift the whole contents in a day.

Monday. I was called off suddenly at this part of the letter, as we were told we must fall in to leave at once for Rouen. We left about 12, marched 7 miles to the station got here about 8 and then they left us in a railway siding till this morning. We did not know where we were going – it's rather amusing travelling in this way. It was a fearful night however. I woke with a pain behind my right back and could hardly walk. However after going about 200 yds it passed off. We marched off in the morning about 7 miles to an enormous camp up here, through acres of mud, but finally to quite a dry new camp, where we are again under canvas, but much more comfortable. I've got a bad headache so can't write much – am writing this in the Y.M.C.A. shed, there are dozens of them about the camps. I expect we shall be off to-morrow, or in a few days, to the trenches. We have had our fur coats issued to us – I have a kind of goat or wolf skin, look like a bear, great long fur stretching out all over from me. I haven't had my clothes off since I left Southampton. I have chucked my extra pair of boots away, as I couldn't stand the weight. With these heavy packs we perspire like anything on the march, though we go very slowly, very different to marching in England. This camp is on a kind of plateau on the hills outside Rouen and is enormous.

Sunday Jan 10

My dear Father
I received the letter you sent to Southampton yesterday. Letters have been delayed as we have been moving up gradually. We leave here Rouen tomorrow, Monday. I expect we shall have a long journey this time, 30 or 40 in cattle trucks for a day or so. I don't know where we are going but I suppose we shall shortly be in the trenches. We have been under canvas here in a big camp on the height above the town. It has poured nearly the whole time and most of us have fearful colds. We have had no leave at all, and they have passed the time giving us odd jobs to do, sweeping roads, packing up old fur coats off wounded men, carrying planks etc. However we move off tomorrow and that's an end of that kind of work. Now I suppose we shall see the real thing, so whether we shall like it or not when we do, I don't know.

Your affectionate son
Ernest.

Tuesday, Jan 12th
We did not have such a long journey as I expected. We left about 4 p.m. and arrived here at the frontier (and the front) about 10 this morning. We travelled up in wagons between 30 and 40 in closed horse or cattle trucks. They are fitted up inside with rough seats down the centre. We marched down to the station, to a kind of railway siding where the cattle train was waiting for us. They kept us standing about for 3/4 hour, so that we should be thoroughly uncomfortable and then we had to scramble in, everyone of course fighting for the corners. As it got dark people dug their clasp knives into the sides of the truck and fastened their candles to them, so the whole place looked dark and mysterious eventually, with little groups playing cards under the candles. Trucks as you know are fastened with a kind of iron sliding door. It was fearfully uncomfortable. The rain made the floor a pool of black mud and the few of us who could get down to sleep there had to do it in the mud with continually feet fighting all the night.

As we got near here, we saw on the flat kind of horizon lines of cavalry on horseback, exercising their horses I suppose. When we got here we were marched up into a kind of greenhouse for grapes. It's a very large one and there are about 300 or 350 of us sleeping in it. It's a steel thing, looking like a small Olympia. We have strict instructions not to hang anything on the vines. Just now when everyone is writing letters or getting to bed it looks like the opening of one of the scenes of the 'Miracle.' I have just been outside the greenhouse now 7:30 p.m. You can hear all the heavy guns going off. It's like the sound of summer thunder a long way off. We are only about 8 miles from the firing line here and from the part of the trenches, we shall probably march to to-morrow. To continue, every now and then on the horizon, you see a flash, its a kind of illuminating shell used to light up things so that the artillery can fire at anything they see moving. If you listen carefully you can hear from time to time, quick firing by the men's rifles in the trenches. The men are standing watching it by [. . .] fire outside, as if it were a fireworks exhibition. We have just met some men I used to know in the 1st Battalion. They are very gloomy about the trenches. An officer and two men have just been killed by snipers. We shall either move up to the trenches to-morrow, or else in 6 days time when the rotation comes round again. We have not rejoined the regiment who are in billets 3 miles nearer the fighting line. There's no doubt about us actually being at the front at last.

Wednesday, Jan 13th
We left the place I last wrote from on Wednesday. It was pouring with rain and we had to march about 6 miles altogether I should think. It sounds very little but when you have all your equipment and very heavy packs it becomes very tiresome. We were told before we set out that we should, in a few miles, be inside the area of shell fire. The roads are simply fearful with mud and you keep meeting supply motors and carts which push you to the side of the road in the mud. All you can think of on the march, is various ways of shifting the weight of your pack from one shoulder to another, every now and then you rest and you bend down something like this in order to save the weight of your pack on the shoulders. You look reflectively at your feet and the patterns of the mud as you do this, and that will be the predominant

impression I shall carry away from this war. The first thing that looked at all characteristic of war (in the old Boer War sense) was when we were overtaken by a transport wagon taking food, guarded by men on horseback with rifles slung across their shoulders. These we met at the corner of a road where we seemed to have lost our way. Our feet of course were all wet through. About midday we passed through a village, where a lot of our H.A.C. men were resting and people recognised each other. They kept us standing here 20 min. without letting us take our packs off, every man swearing. Finally about a mile further on, after the man on horseback who was supposed to be guiding us, had cantered up to various farmhouses, one about 100 yards off the main road was pointed out to us as the one where we were to eat. There was a big barn there, where we could shelter from the rain. We waded across a field and through a farmyard with mud above our ankles, only to be turned back by a staff officer who said we had made a mistake. This was the last straw – some of us wandered off by ourselves and found a little cowshed where we took off our packs at last and ate bully beef. When we got a 1/4 mile from the village we were making for, we had to stop and wait till dusk, as it is rather exposed to shell fire. We heard fearfully unpleasant noises of guns going off, but they were our own batteries just behind us. After dusk we got in the village where our men were. About half the houses have one side or a roof missing, as this place has often been bombarded and there are great holes at the side of the road made by Jack Johnson shells.[3] All the houses in this place are empty, a few of the whole and shelled houses being used as a billet for our men. We could see some of them asleep and some washing as we came in. There is a very incongruous bandstand in the centre, surrounded by barbed wire entanglement ready to be moved to the trenches.

We were marched up to some large schools where we were billeted. In the evening I went round to see some of the people I used to know in the 1st Battalion. All looked very different, their faces and clothes a sort of pale mud colour, all very tired of it and anxious to get back.

Thursday, Jan. 14th
We had to mend the holes in the road made by the shells, great holes
that are very dangerous at night.

Friday, Jan 15th
We had to dig a deep trench to clear away the water from a lot of dug
outs (holes made as a protection from shell fire). All the time we were
doing this the Germans were dropping shells onto a hill above us. One
fell about 70 yds away, by the bandstand. You hear a noise like a train
high up in the air appearing to go very slowly, then you see a thick
cloud of black smoke going up where they have burst, then you hear
the bang, then after that the whistling noise seems to end.

Nobody is in the least frightened because they are all being aimed
at a point a few hundred yards away, where they think an English
battery is. Everybody stopped digging when they heard the first whistling noise in order to run to a place where they could see them burst.
How we should behave if they started shelling us I don't know. This
village has several times been bombarded and probably will be again,
only the Germans don't know we are here. In order that they shan't find
it out, no fires are allowed at night, all candles must be kept on the floor
and window spaces blocked up. A regiment near here neglected this and
got a shell in the middle of their place, killing about 10 men.

Friday, Jan 15th
They have not amalgamated us yet with the 1st Battalion, so we did
not go into the trenches with them. I wanted to see what the trenches
were like, so I volunteered to go as one of a party which was going up
to the trenches at night, to take up large bundles of wood to put at the
bottom of them for the men to stand on. These parties go up almost
every night. They are fairly safe, though it so happened that the party
that went the night before had one man killed. But they go night after
night and nothing happens. There were about 100 of us. We wore our
overcoats and carried rifles. We were formed up about 5 o'clock when
it was dark and to load our rifles and then we filed past a barn where

each man drew a long bundle of faggots about 8 ft long. We then went off in single file, down a long road lined with poplars, nearly all the way. The Germans kept firing off rockets and star shells. These latter hang in the air for a few minutes and light up the whole road. We were told that whenever one of these went off we were to stand still and bend our heads down so that the white of our faces could not be seen. After a time we began to hear bullets whizzing over our heads all fairly high. All that worries anyone is the uncomfortableness of the faggots. Also I had not put the sling of my rifle on properly and was wondering all the while whether it would not slip off my shoulder on to the ground and draw attention to me personally and my clumsiness. After about a mile along the road we turned off along the fields and made for the trenches. Here the uncomfortable part started. It seemed to be absolutely all mud. Its bad enough walking over uneven ground in the dark at any time when you don't know whether your foot is landing on earth or nothing the next step. Every now and then you fell over and got up to your knees in the mud. As the trenches here are rather this shape [. . .] you got bullets flying over your head from the German trenches in all directions. Nobody worries about these however, all you can think of is the mud. What makes it infinitely worse is that, every now and then you lose sight of the man in front of you. The line ahead of you runs over a rather more dangerous part and you must keep up at all costs, though it's all in the dark and you are floundering about all the time. You simply must keep up, because if you once lost the man in front, you wouldn't know what on earth to do, you might even walk up to the German lines. We finally had to cross a series of great ditches of mud and deposit the faggots under the shelter of some rising ground about 40 yds behind the trenches. Its fairly quiet up in the trenches, and all we heard was an average of about 20 a minute and as we were a short distance behind the trenches they were flying over our heads all the time. The only thing that makes you feel nervous is when the star shells go off and you stand out revealed quite clearly as in daylight. You have then the most wonderful feeling as if you were suddenly naked in the street and didn't like it. It isn't that really but the impression it makes on you, as if you were walking across a flat heath or common at night and along a long line in front of you the lights were shooting off all the time silhouetting all the trees and bushes. It's really like a kind of nightmare, in which you are in the middle of an enormous saucer of mud with explosions and shots going off all round the edge, a sort of fringe of palm trees made of fireworks all round it. One thing I forgot to mention, when you do lose the man in front of you, if you crouch down low in the mud you can see the profile of the men in front of you, but with these faggots in a sort of frieze – like the procession in Scheherezade, or rather very unlike it. It took me the *whole* of the next morning to scrape the mud off my clothes, it was all over my coat up to my waist.

Saturday, Jan 16th
At 7 o'clock on Saturday we had to parade in the road outside the school where we lived, to march back in the dark, some 3 or 4 miles to a place further back from the firing line, out of range of shell fire, for 4 days rest. After that we shall go back for 4 days in the firing line again and so on. It was an awful confusion as we marched out in the dark, as the other regiments to take our place were entering the place and we got mixed up in the road with another regiment also leaving for the night. We seemed to be about 3 different regiments abreast going different ways. We marched in single file all the way, it was pitch dark. When we got to the next town we were told off to different cottages where we were billeted. There are 36 in the room I'm in. Here in the time during the 4 days rest, I'm spending all my time with my old section and am really quite comfortable. They have been here for weeks and know the ropes. They have things sent them out from England, have made friends with a Flemish cobbler and we all 12 of us, sit in their back room all day, cooking our meals ourselves on the stove that all the villages have here. You must feed well these days of rest in order to keep well in the trenches. Here is where we find a little money useful. We can buy ourselves eggs etc. and all kinds of things. The bully beef gives everyone bad dysentery. In the afternoon we go up a hill where we can see for miles our own and beyond the German lines, the flash from an English gun, and then later see, it seems miles away, the white smoke of the shell bursting. Then you see all over the landscape the white puffs from which German shells are bursting over our trenches. We can see a town about [...] miles away that was

bombarded. I can't go into details about anything or the letter would be torn up.

To-morrow, Wednesday we go back to the trenches for 4 days. It so happens however that the next 4 days, all No. 2's officers are away on leave, so to my annoyance my company will not go to the trenches this time, but will act as reserve, but we shall probably go up to the trenches to carry up things.

Jan. 27th
I have had a very uncomfortable time this week. As I told you last week after 4 days rest we go down to a place near the trenches. We marched off there last Wednesday, late in the day so as to get there after dark, or we might be shelled on our arrival. We never know whether we shall get a good or a bad billet when we arrive there, it's always different. We were led into the chapel attached to a school and our section managed to get a corner by the altar. It looks very curious to see a lot of troops billeted in a place like this, rifles resting on the altar, and hanging over statues of the saints, men sleeping on the altar steps. (You had better leave this part out in sending it to Stanbrook).[4] It was rather cold as all the windows were smashed and we have no blankets now. We lit a brazier, i.e. an old bucket with holes knocked in it, burning charcoal and coke. We had nothing to do the first night, as it was some other company's turn in the trenches. Next morning one of the men went out and dug up some vegetables from a deserted garden and made a kind of stew without meat. We get no cooked meat in the 4 days. The next night we went up to a kind of circular reserve trench. You go up a long file, as I described in my last letter. We were challenged at the entrance and then entered a narrow passage going down to the level of the trenches. I don't think I've been so exasperated for years as I was in taking up my position in this trench. It wasn't an ordinary one but was roofed over most of the way, leaving passage about 4 ft: absolutely impossible for me to walk through. I had to crawl along on my hands and knees, through the mud in pitch darkness and every now and then seemed to get stuck altogether. You feel shut in and hopeless. I wished I was about 4 ft. This war isn't for tall men. I got in a part too narrow and too low to stand or sit and had to sit

sideways on a sack of coke to keep out of the water. We had to stay there from about 7 p.m. till just before dawn next morning, a most miserable experience. You can't sleep and you sit as it were at the bottom of a drain with nothing to look at but the top of the ditch slowly freezing. It's unutterably boring. The next night was better, because I carried up a box to sit on and a sack of coke to burn in a brazier. But one brazier in a narrow trench among 12 men only warms about 3. All through this night, we had to dig a new passage in shifts. That in a way did look picturesque at midnight – a very clear starry night. This mound all full of passages like a mole hill and 3 or 4 figures silhouetted on top of it using pick or shovel. The bullets kept whistling over it all the time, but as it's just over the crest of a hill most of them are high, though every now and then one comes on your level and it is rather uncomfortable when you are taking your turn at sentry. The second night it froze hard, and it was much easier walking back over the mud.

In reality there is nothing picturesque about it. It's the most miserable existence you can conceive of. I feel utterly depressed at the idea of having to do this for 48 hours every 4 days. It's simply hopeless. The boredom and discomfort of it, exasperate you to the breaking point.

It's curious to think of the ground between the trenches, a bank which is practically never seen by anyone in the daylight, as it is only safe to move through it at dark. It's full of dead things, dead animals here and there, dead unburied animals, skeletons of horses destroyed by shell fire. It's curious to think of it later on in the war, when it will again be seen in the daylight. We had to do this for every night for 12 hours. Next week we shall be in the firing line, in two periods of 24 hours each. On our way down we generally meet someone being brought up wounded or killed to cheer us up.

Feb. 10th
The last day of the last 4 days rest here was like summer. We had breakfast outside the cobbler's cottage and in the afternoon went up to the Inn on the hill and they all drank wine outside. A regular who was up there said 'Who says there's a war now' and it certainly did

seem absolutely remote from it, though we could see here and there the [. . .] of heavy artillery firing at the Germans. The same evening we marched straight from here up to the trenches. We went to the firing line again. But this time it was not a new properly constructed trench like the last one I told you about but an [. . .] average trench. We had to spend the night in the open air as there were very few dugouts. There was a German rifle trained on a fixed part of the trench just where we were. It's very irritating to hear a bullet time after time hit the same spot on the parapet. About lunch time this rifle continually hitting the same place, spattered dirt from the parapet over my bread and butter. It gets very irritating after a time and everybody shouts out 'Oh stop it.' It showed however that it was a dangerous corner and the next day another company of our regiment took our place in this trench, a man in exactly the place where our section was, getting curious at the repetition of a shot in the same spot, got up to look with his field glasses. He stayed up a second too long and got shot through the head dead. Field glasses are rather a temptation, they make you stay up too long. Towards the end of our [. . .] the same day, the Germans started to shell our trench. It was a dangerous trench for shelling because it was very wide so gave no protection to the back. Our N.C.O. told us to shift to a narrower part of the trench. I got separated from the others in a narrow communication trench behind with one other man. We had seen shells bursting fairly near us before and at first did not take it very seriously. But it soon turned out to be very different. The shells started dropping right on the trench itself. As soon as you had seen someone hurt, you began to look at shelling in a very different way. We shared this trench with the X regiment. About 10 yds away from where I was a man of this regiment had his arm and 3/4 of his head blown off a frightful mess, his brains all over the place, some on the back of that man who stands behind me in the photograph. The worst of shelling is, the regulars say, that you don't get used to it, but get more and more alarmed at it every time. At any rate the regulars in our trenches behaved in rather a strange way. One man threw himself down on the bottom of the trench, shaking all over and crying. Another started to weep. It lasted for nearly 1½ hrs and at the end of it parts of the trenches were all blown to pieces. It's not the idea of being killed that's alarming, but the idea of being hit by a jagged piece of steel. You hear the whistle of the shell coming, you crouch down as low as you can and just wait. It doesn't burst merely with a bang, it has a kind of crash with a snap in it, like the crack of a very large whip. They seem to burst just over your head, you seem to anticipate it killing you in the back, it hits just near you and you get hit on the back with clods of earth and (in my case) spent bits of shell and shrapnel bullets fall all round you. I picked up one bullet almost sizzling in the mud just by my toe. What irritates you is the continuation of the shelling. You seem to feel that 20 min. is normal, is enough – but when it goes on for over an hour, you get more and more exasperated, feel as if it were 'unfair.' Our men were as it happened very lucky, only three were hurt slightly and none killed. They all said it was the worst experience they have had since they were out here. I'm not in the least anxious myself to repeat it, nor is anyone else I think. It was very curious from where I was; looking out and over the back of the trench, it looked absolutely peaceful. Just over the edge of the trench was a field of turnips or something of that kind with their leaves waving about in a busy kind of way, exactly as they might do in a back garden. About 12 miles away over the plain you could see the towers and church spires of an old town very famous in this war. By a kind of accident or trick, everything was rather gloomy, except this town, which appeared absolutely white in the sun and immobile as if it would always be like that, and was out of time and space altogether. You've got to amuse yourself in the intervals of shelling and romanticising the situation is as good a way as any other. Looking at the scene the waving vegetables, the white town and all the rest of it, it looks quite timeless in a Buddhistic kind of way and you feel quite resigned if you are going to be killed to leave it just like that. When it ceased and we all got back to our places everybody was full of it. We went back that night to a new billet in a barn, so near the line that we weren't allowed to have light at all, but spread our bread and butter in the dark, or by the intermittent light of electric torches pointed down. The next night we went up to new trenches altogether. This time we weren't in the firing line, but in a line of dug-outs, or supports.

These dugouts were about 2 ft deep, so you can imagine how comfortable I was. They put me in one by myself. It felt just like being in your grave, lying flat just beneath the surface of the ground and covered up. And there I had to be for 24 hours unable to get out until it was dark next night for we could be seen from the German lines. – We were relieved very late and altogether were out 30 hours instead of 24. We had a couple of men wounded on the road up, so we went back by a safer way across the field. A man I know quite well had a bullet entered one side of his nose and came out near his ear. They have sent him back to England and say he will remain.

I'm getting more used to this kind of life and as long as I don't get hurt or it doesn't rain too much, don't mind it at all.

February 11

My dear Father,

I am sorry I have been unable to reply to your letter before. I am now in the town a few miles from the trenches where we go for our 4 days rest. Our last few days in the trenches were very unpleasant as we had the worst shelling that the regiment has had since they were out here.

I won't tell you much about that as you will read it in the letter Cousin Alice will forward you, probably the thing that will most interest you will be the shooting. In the ordinary time in the trenches that is the long interval between attacks there is very little rifle shooting. In the night the observers i.e. the men who take it in turn to keep awake let off their rifles to show they are awake. The Germans do the same. It is these accidental bullets aimed at nothing which often wound men on their way up to the trenches. Occasionally too in the day time, putting our heads above the parapet for a moment, we see Germans showing their heads, working at repairing the top of their trenches and we have a shot at them.

There is another kind of shooting however. The Germans have rifles trained on certain points probably clamped on tripods and they fire these off occasionally; last Saturday when we were having our lunch in the trench, every minute almost a bullet hit exactly the same spot on a sandbag on the parapet and spattered earth all over my bread and butter. This happened more than a dozen times. It's very irritating but we naturally didn't put our heads up above to see where it came from.

The next day another company of our regiment was in the same trenches; the same thing happened at exactly the same place, and a man stood up to examine with field glasses, stood up a second too long, got shot through the head and killed at once. Most of the wounds in the trenches are fatal for they are all through the head, your only chance of getting a comfortable wound which will get you invalided home is on the way up to the trenches at night.

The German trenches are only 80 yards away from us, so if they ever do try to advance here the shooting required from us will be of a very simple character. We have our rifles always loaded on the parapet of the trenches, and on the same day a man in the same section as myself had about 6 inches of the wooden casing that surrounds the rifle shot right away, leaving the barrel itself quite exposed.

We have moved to a new line of trenches a little further north. I had to spend Monday night not in the firing line but in some dug out as a reserve. I had to spend 24 hours lying in a little hole by myself just under the ground. I noticed that during the day there were more shots fired by the artillery than by the rifles.

Our rifles get covered in mud and it is a great nuisance cleaning them – the bolt particularly gets choked up with mud and we generally cover the black part up with an old stocking well oiled. We don't always go up to the actual firing trench but [. . .] the support which are about 60 yards behind the first trenches. We don't always go in the same trenches and they vary very much in the amount of mud they contain.

We are brigaded with 4 regular regiments, one from a neighbouring county, with whom we get on very well, doing exactly the same work as they do.

It's a very monotonous and depressing life now, always the 4 days in and the 4 days out. I hope that in the Spring we shall be let off a bit. We lose 4 or 5 men every time we go down. I think it will be an impossible life for Harold[5] for the exposure would be sure to make him ill. I don't know how he will like the job of despatch rider, for the roads here are frightful, just a path in the centre and the rest all mud.

I shall be very glad indeed when the whole thing is over. I hope Mother remains well and is quite cured. I heard from Aunt Sara today saying that Kate[6] is staying with her.

I will write you again in about a fortnight.

Yr affectionate son Ernest.

Feb. 20th

We went down to the trenches on a Saturday. We form up at dark in the one street of the town here. There is generally a lot to be done on the last day as we have to clean up all our billets ready for the other brigade marching up after their 4 days at the trenches. While we are formed up there in the street waiting, some of the other regiments of our brigade who go to the trenches at the same time as we do are sure to march past. A regiment on the march here is a very curious sight. In spite of the fact that they have to clean themselves and their clothes in their 4 days of rest, they all look a general pale, washed out, dusty muddy colour. The officers march on foot generally at the head of their platoons, looking very little different to their men, except that they generally carry a roughly trimmed piece of wood, about as long as a shepherds crook, as a walking stick. They find these useful in the muddy paths up to the actual trenches. Very few are in any kind of step and they slouch along generally two deep, for only the centre of the road is really passable. The exception to the slouching is an occasional section when the two front men play a mouth organ or bones, when they march well together. Their packs look a good deal lighter than ours, they don't get so many parcels. At intervals come the officers' horses, generally unmounted (they ride them however at the end of 4 days when they are coming *back* from the trenches and are more tired). At the end come the mules carrying extra ammunition, the transport and finally the field kitchens, usually boiling something and stuffed up with odd bits of wood ready for fuel and the cooks leaning on them as they walk behind. This time we did not go straight up to the trenches but into 'closed billet' for the night. This is a large barn. It's comfortable except that it's well within range and if only the Germans one day find out we are here, they will drop a shell on us, and then we should most of us be done for. On the morning of the next day we had all suddenly to get ready and come downstairs, because shells were falling uncomfortably near. We always have a guard outside to report aeroplanes and the nearness of shells for this purpose. None of us are ever allowed out in the daytime. How near it is to the trenches may be judged from the fact that this time one of our sentries was shot dead by a stray bullet. The next night we went up to the trenches. I think I told you in my last letter that we are now holding a different part of the line, a mile or so N of our old trenches, worse trenches and a worse path up to them. Last time we went up to them by a road but we had one man wounded (there are too many stray bullets passing over it) so we went up by a new way over the fields. Suddenly when we were going up a fearfully muddy field by the side of a wood in a long line and single file, a shell whizzed over us and burst a few yards behind the last man. I happened to be looking backward when it burst. Being night it was very bright and looked more like a firework than anything else. We at once got the order to lie flat in the mud on our faces and although it isn't pleasant to be flat on your face in pure mud, yet the presence of the shells makes us do it without any reluctance. I didn't see much after that, for I had my head down flat, but they put about 20 shells over us, rather smallish shells they must have been which seemed to go whizz-bang – very quickly. They fell all along the line of the 50 men, but all a little wide. We got bits of earth flung over us but nothing more. They all thought their last hour had come for to be caught and shelled in the open like that is the most dangerous thing that can happen to you. You have no protection like you have in a trench. It was soon over however and then we got up and continued our walk to the trenches, most of us expecting suddenly to hear the same explosion again. We had to cross several shell and Jack Johnson holes full of water bridged by a single plank and in the dark most of us fell in once before we got there. We got to miserable trenches where we were not allowed to have a brazier and we sat there absolutely wet through up to the pips for 24 hours. That's the worst of getting wet here, it isn't like after a day's shooting when you can get home and change. The next night when we got back, an attack from the Germans was expected. We had to sleep in our boots etc all night and couldn't take anything off. That made 48 hours thoroughly wet through. The extraordinary thing is that it doesn't hurt you. It hasn't hurt us at any rate, though when the regiment last spent 3 days in the trenches before Xmas they lost 250 men and 11 officers through sickness. It makes you very depressed however and weakens you – it gave me diarrhoea. This last 6 days have been unusual for all kinds of things have been happening to the N of us of which we hear rumours. We are told over night that further up the line certain trenches are to be retaken and next day we hear they have been taken. I expect you have read all about it in the papers and of course as it is only a few miles from us, it affects us. We have to be ready for a counter attack. That first night we were up we could tell that something was up. It was a pitch black night, one of those nights that exasperate you because you are afraid of losing the man in front of you. All the heavy guns on both sides were firing, never a minute without a report and you could see the flashes from the muzzles all round the horizon. In the trench that day (it couldn't properly be called a trench, just a ditch with sandbags on the top) we sat all day and watched shells burst in the field behind us. Fortunately never nearer than 20 yards. In the next trench, a different company of our regiment in, they killed one man and wounded 15 that afternoon. The most annoying part of being in the trenches is the waiting for the 'relief.' You get ready long before it comes. Sometimes it comes hours after you expect it. You listen and think you hear voices and feet. At last it's coming. Then it turns out that you were mistaken. Finally a German star shell reveals them to you half-way across the field. They are all standing immobile in the middle of the field bent down. It is curious how this continuous shelling and the apprehension of it has altered some men. They keep very quiet all day long and hardly say anything. This day in the trenches I should think 50 or 60 dropped in the one field making holes all over it like a sort of smallpox. It is these holes filled with water which make walking up the roads at night so annoying. The 4 days when we came back we were told we shouldn't be relieved for some days. However we were relieved after 6 days and marched back very late to our rest town, everyone fearfully exhausted. I have written much too long a letter. I want to post it at once so that it won't be delayed like the others were I can't tell you much, but as a result of the recent fighting there are all kinds of changes. We are now in a different brigade etc.

[NOTE BY CENSOR. Please inform sender next letter of this length will not be passed. H. P. G. M.]

March 2nd

The first time up we went back again into the trenches where we were
shelled. This is a bad trench in which you just have to sit out in the
open all night. It froze hard and all the rifles were white in the morning.
The next time it was our turn to have a rest, but they gave us (the
platoon about 40 men) a fatigue up to the trenches, carrying up hurdles
and barbed wire. Except for the danger from stray bullets, this is
compared to going into trenches, a pleasure trip. You are very light
carrying only a rifle. It was a bright moonlight night, and the way up
to the trenches is a straight narrow road. There were far too many
men to carry the stuff and 4 of us carried one hurdle ragging each
other all the way up, suggesting that the fat man should sit on top of
it and we would carry him up. Half way up we met the stretcher
bearers, carrying down one of our men who had been killed during
the day. They hurry along quite in a different way when they are
carrying a dead and not a wounded man. I think they break step and
hurry along like lamplighters to avoid getting caught by a stray bullet
themselves. It's curious how the mere fact that in a certain direction
there really are the German lines, seems to alter the feeling of a
landscape. You unconsciously orient things in reference to it. In peacetime, each direction on the road is as it were indifferent, it all goes on
ad infinitum. But now you know that certain roads lead as it were, up
to an abyss.

When we came back from this fatigue it so happened it was very
quiet no bullets about at all, and we strolled back exactly as though
we were walking home late from a party on a moonlight night. These
fatigues are not always so lucky. Last week the tennis player Kenneth
Powell was killed carrying up corrugated iron. (It seems curious the
way people realize things. I heard a man say 'It does seem a waste,
Kenneth Powell carrying up corrugated iron.' You see he was interested
in games.) This is a curious life – in that there is nothing certain or
fixed. You never come back to the same billets. You can never leave
anything. You have no place that belongs to you. You really are as
nomadic as an animal. You never depend on any routine. You may be
there 4 or 6 or 10 days. You may come back to a different place
altogether. The only fixed thing seems to be the letters you get from

home. It's very difficult to describe anything to you, to at all make you realize what it is *actually* like. Not that it is above the common place, and too difficult to describe, for that reason it isn't. But just actually in its own peculiar way. If I describe a tiring day in the trenches to you and the weary march back at night to the farm, in the dark, you go wrong at once, because when I use the word farmhouse, you have some fixed idea in your head of a farmhouse, which isn't at all the [. . .] of the one we [. . .] in.

We have not gone back to the trenches to-day as we generally do, the 4 days rest being up, but are to stay up here an extra 2 days. I suppose it will mean that when we do go to the trenches it will be for 6 days, so it's not as pleasing as it might otherwise have been. So that we shouldn't enjoy the extra rest too much, they had us out in the middle of a field to do company drill – we were all drawn up to hear an announcement – we all expected something dramatic, but it was only to say that Gen. Smith Dorian was very pleased with us, or something equally uninteresting, finishing up by saying that they hoped we should continue to uphold our reputation 'till the end of the campaign.' This fell very flat as all everyone hopes is that we shall get back as soon as possible. I am afraid we are in for it. We may get a fortnight's rest but there's no chance of us getting back at all. It still continues wonderful weather and the country looks absolutely different. One can see now how it will look in the Spring. I don't suppose any of us ever waited for the Spring with so much interest. One does notice physical things here tremendously. You reckon up when it will be full moon, it means a very uncomfortable clear walk up to the trenches. Today it's frosty, but a hard wind, everything is very clear and bright. Along the crest of a hill I have just seen a lot of Indians, leading donkeys and mules, leaning forward to meet the wind, and silhouetted on the sky line, looking just like the conventional illustrations of the East. You have no idea what a difference the hard weather makes.

Must stop here.

March 21st, Sunday

I think I told you that for the first nine days we were continually in a kind of reserve trench. The second morning there we saw what so far I think has been the most complete war scene yet. I mean the most conventional, shut off, the most like war in a theatre as it were. Just below us about 300 yards away was a large farm with its buildings (on a position very like that of Gratton (on a hill, below another hill) looking at it from Dunwood[7] but about half the distance away). To make the thing comprehensible I must explain that after 24 hours in the trenches, troops go back for the next 24 hours to what are called 'close billets' i.e. places where they are still under shell fire and so where they must remain invisible all the time. It is the business of the artillery on both sides to shell likely 'close billets,' sometimes getting the information as to which farms and villages are close billets from spies. Most of the farms round about have been destroyed only the walls standing and another man said early in the morning that it was curious that this farm was entirely untouched looking very peaceful (and as I say exactly like Gratton about the same size.) In the middle of the morning we suddenly heard a shell whistling over which burst just over the roof. Then a second, whose smoke was all red showing that it had hit the roof, the red tiles broken up into dust mixing with the smoke. Three or four more shells and then we saw two pigs rushing out of the courtyard. We thought the place was empty and that the Germans were wasting their shells. Then we saw one figure going across a field on the other side of the farm but we couldn't tell whether a soldier or perhaps a Belgian civilian. The shelling went on dropping all over the roof till one caught fire. Then we caught sight of about 30 bent figures creeping along the road along the ridge from the farm. To make you realize the actual scene, there was a hedge on this side of the road and an avenue of trees. There were more shells and finally the whole of one roof burning. More and more groups of men creeping along the road (at this distance we could only see a kind of bent silhouette). This went on till I should think several hundreds more had left (they were probably all asleep resting after the trenches). Then there was a fearful row of ammunition popping off sounding exactly like continuous rifle fire in the trenches. Then another building caught fire (in which I suppose those wounded by the shells had been put). One man came out of an open door and ran across a field behind a haystack after a minute another followed, then there were about ten there, when the Germans dropped a few shells over it. Then along the road men began to come back and fetch out the wounded from the burning barn. As they came back along the road very slowly helping the men along they were spotted and got German rifle fire at them. The place went on burning for nearly two days. The whole scene being extremely depressing. Enormous red flames, exactly like a poster of war and destruction and then miserable looking black figures and probably very tired people crawling out. What happened later in the week I can't tell you about for it would probably be crossed out by the censor. I was on sentry one night and saw a whole regiment passing up in single file to take their position for an attack. One man was shot about 20 yds from me. I saw in the dark, the line stop and people cluster round him, the line pass on and then finally stretcher bearers carry him off. I saw his equipment [. . .] in the place where he had fallen. I had myself too one night up there the unpleasant job of carrying down one of our men who had been shot dead through the heart. This is a very unpleasant job when you have to go in pitch darkness a way you don't know very well over mud and ditches. I'm glad it wasn't a man I knew but it's very queer as you carry him down shoulder high, his face is very near your own. One day after an attack I saw a man come staggering across a field as if he were drunk, holding his head, finally falling down just outside our barbed wire entanglement. It turned out to be a Tommy who had been blown right out of our trenches by our own artillery. All that day there had been a terrific bombardment, English shells whistling over our heads every second.

Must stop now.

If you don't hear from me again, you will know I have gone to the trenches again for 4 or 6 days.

April 19th 1915[8]
We left the filthy barn we are billeted in about seven o'clock, marched down a side road over a hill about three miles to a smashed up village just behind the new trenches we were going to. We were marched up to a chateau all blown to pieces. When we got there we had to wait about 2 hours outside while they tried to find places for us inside. That's how they do things in the army. They never seem to think 5 minutes before they do a thing. Eventually some of us were stowed in a dug-out just deep enough for us to crawl through, just like a rabbit hole and told we were to stay there for 48 hours, a perfect nightmare for people of my size. Eventually they came and after looking round had found us a room in a house in a village that had a roof on it. The room had no windows and was filled with layers of straw which we daren't move for fear of what might be underneath. However it was very comfortable after the dug-out. Here we stayed for 48 hours, the second night being out from 10 till 2 carrying barbed wire up to the trenches. This was a hideous affair. When we got there nobody knew where they were to go and so we stopped there for 30 minutes behind the firing trench while they found out, a very uncomfortable time. One bullet hit the trestles the fat man was carrying and a piece of the wood flew up his arm. It's the kind of footling unnecessary business which makes one so fed up. After 48 hours we went up to the trenches. A wretched night continually soaking and through a blunder the [. . .] fully equipped as we were carrying up boxes about 1000 rounds of ammunition over ditches and soaked fields. I don't know how some of the men ever got up. We got into an open trench about 1:30 having started at 10, so you may tell what sort of a job it was, to go along 2 miles. There were no shelters and it poured continually for several hours. Fortunately the next 36 hours it was finer and then we marched back about 10 p.m. to a rest barn. After going about a couple of miles we stopped at some cross roads for nearly an hour and a half absolutely tired out. It's the kind of thing [. . .] you more than anything. You try to sleep on the side of the road but it's too cold. And now for our rest here. Every night we have had to march back to the trenches about 4 miles and dig. The night before last we were out from 8 p.m. till 4 in the morning. We have only had a proper night's rest in the last three

weeks. This isn't a proper diary I have just told you in a hurry what we have been doing. I'll write a proper account in the trenches directly. I've no time here, as [. . .] to sleep all day. We are back again to the trenches to-night for four days continuously. We shall be glad when we do get our rest, this three weeks is all for some special reason when that is over I hope we shall go back to the old system. This is a curious thing, we move as you know always at night and troops going always in the same direction make definite paths. One of our snipers walking about in the daylight discovered that one of these paths that we walk over led right over the chest of a dead peasant (Belgian).

12

Interregnum

What Hulme was describing in this laconic and fairly detached way was a view from the mud of the inaugural phase of the four years of virtual stalemate that characterized the fighting on the Western Front, with the fluid manoeuvring of the earliest part of the campaign over and the trench lines that ran from the North Sea to Switzerland more or less established. The first period of action described in the 'Diary' covers the HAC's role in occupying the 'F' trenches of Kemmel, to the right of the line and facing the spur of Spanbrock Moelen in the Petit Bois area, one of the strongest centres of the German line and a position from which the Germans were able to dominate the Allies' trenches completely. The weather was atrocious, with frost and snow at intervals but mostly continuous rain. The trenches occupied by Hulme's B Company had been made by the French and were little more than ditches of liquid mud. There was no wire in front of them nor communication trenches of any kind behind. Where present, the parado – the mud-wall raised behind the trenches to prevent men being silhouetted against the skyline – was often built around and over dead bodies, and the mud parapets in front had the consistency of butter and bullets passed through them as easily. In some trenches they were no more than chest high and in order to get any cover at all during the daytime men had to squat down in the mud.

On 7 February B Company were moved to take over the 'K' sector to the left of the line, where they remained working four days in and four out, in the fashion described by Hulme, until 19 February, when they were ordered to resume their occupation of the 'F' trenches. The military focus of the action at this time remained the attempt to take Spanbrock Moelen and end the German domination of the line. In the wake of a partially successful attack on Neuve Chapelle on 10 March, during which many German prisoners were taken, an all-out attack on the spur of Spanbrock Moelen was staged two days later. Delayed until late afternoon by heavy fog, the attack was an utter failure. With the support of the HAC the Worcesters attacked on the right and the Wiltshires on the left. The attack of the Wiltshires was gallant but, in the military parlance of the time, it 'dissolved' in front of the enemy's wire. On the other flank the Worcesters managed to take a small section of the enemy's front line, but on moving forward to consolidate the gain their supporting companies came under 'friendly fire' and suffered such heavy casualties that the attack had to be aborted.

The First Battalion expected to be relieved after this, but heavy fighting broke out in the neighbourhood of St Eloi and they were forced to remain where they were until 16 March, when they went into billets at Westoutre. They had then spent twelve consecutive days and nights in the trenches, losing eight men killed and thirty wounded. They were then marched to new headquarters in Vermizeele, making their base in the convent described by Hulme in the 'Diary', a mass of ruins lying about 1,000 yards from the front line, shelled by day and bullet-swept by night.

From here B Company was sent out to secure the 'RB' trench, so-called because it had been retaken by the Rifle Brigade after the German capture of St Eloi. The trench was opposite the notorious 'Mound' at St Eloi, immediately facing it and sixty yards away. The trench was enfiladed[1] from the Mound and the men had to work at night, digging traverses to make themselves less of a target and being greatly hindered in their efforts by heavy frost. On 25 March shelling destroyed the little that was left of the convent and two days later the men were relieved and went into billets at Dickebusch. Even here they got little rest and were on fatigue duty all night carrying material up to the trenches.

On 29 March the battalion returned to the line for another two days, then took turn and turn about with the Wiltshires, four days in and four out, holding a trench that was part of the line from the Viertstraat-Wytschaeete Road on the right to within a few yards of the St Eloi mound on the left. They held this until the end of May, a period of fifty-six days, at the cost of two officers wounded and 125 other ranks killed or wounded.

Hulme was among those shot. On 14 April he was wounded in the elbow by a bullet that passed through his arm and killed the man behind him.[2] On 19 April he got his blighty[3] (the term in Hulme's unit was to get a 'blue ticket') and returned to England for treatment and convalescence at St Mark's College Hospital, Chelsea.

References Hulme made to the wounding later were largely jocular. He told Kate Lechmere that he had purposely lain heavily in the trench until the corpsmen came to get him because it was 'good for them to be under fire once in a while',[4] and that if he had to be wounded then he was glad it was only his arm. He maintained that it would be better to lose an arm than an eye, because a man who had lost his sight would no longer be able to skip his way through a book. An ideal wound would be the loss of an arm up to the elbow. This could be replaced by a metal hook which would be very useful in arguments – 'one thump on the table and you could hook your foes'. It also amused him to pretend to Dermot Freyer that his comrades in B Company were disappointed that the bullet that merely wounded him should have killed the man behind him. The dead man had been a good footballer, he said, and they would all much rather the philosopher had been killed and the footballer taken the flesh wound.[5] Having realized that his decision not to apply for a commission had backfired slightly he had alarmed other members of his company by openly voicing his contempt for the sheer stupidity of much of what went on around him in the trenches.[6]

Hulme had already, on 9 January, made out a will in which he left 'all the money I now possess' to Dolly, with a provision that she get half the interest on any money he might inherit after this date for the rest of her life, the capital and the other half-share of the interest to go to his mother.[7] No doubt every soldier was encouraged to make such a will; but even if this were the case, trench warfare seems neither to have horrified nor greatly surprised him. Perhaps it was because, in the visionary glimpses recorded some years earlier in the 'Cinders' notebook, he had already seen it before, 'all the mud, endless, except where bound together by the spectator', a place of 'primeval chaos' where 'the eye is in the mud, the eye *is* the mud', in which the well-adapted man never forgets that what really matters is to 'always think of the fringe and of the cold walks, of the lines that lead nowhere'.[8]

*

At St Mark's Hulme shocked the nursing staff and excited the admiration of the visiting Ezra Pound by openly reading books by German philosophers. Pound also later admired Hulme's refusal to 'maudle into the rubbish of "war art"',[9] limiting himself instead to the composition of 'Trenches: St Eloi', the austere verse which he had 'refused to write down' and which Pound obligingly did so for him.

By early June Hulme was up again and from now on, when not on active service, divided his time between London and Lake House in Macclesfield, with Alice Pattinson and her brother Thomas. Almost immediately he received news of the death of Gaudier-Brzeska on 5 June at Neuville St Vaast, after months of fighting and two promotions for gallantry. He passed the news around the Café Royal and it was he who delegated to Robert Bevan's Polish wife Stasia de Karlowska the difficult task of going to Gaudier's studio in Fulham Road and breaking the news to Sophie Brzeska.

Sophie's response to the tragedy was to make a concerted but chaotic attempt to gather all of Gaudier's unsold drawings and sculptures. One package of drawings and sculpture had been left with Hulme at Frith Street for safekeeping, a second was with Pound. In the first instance she approached Pound and asked him to make a list of everything in his possession. She also asked him to put pressure on Hulme to hand over to her the work left at Frith Street. From the start there was confusion over Gaudier's estate and Hulme soon found himself caught up in negotiations involving Gaudier's relatives in France, who had never accepted his liaison with Sophie, and Sophie herself. Matters were complicated by a suspicion on both sides that Gaudier's work was about to increase dramatically in value as a result of his death in action.

After several meetings with Sophie, Hulme was still disinclined to hand anything over to her and the paranoia that was part of her personality began to show itself. At some point she must have accused him of filching material from the parcel of work sent to him by Gaudier. He wrote to remind her that she had in fact promised to let him choose one or two things himself, but that if she had changed her mind she was welcome to have these as well:

I forgot to let you know that I took four drawings out of the parcel – you said Mrs Kibblewhite and I might choose (one of the ducks and one of a man on horseback) and two others which I told you I wished to buy, a small phallic one which could not be exhibited of a man and woman and a little design of a love charm which I wondered whether it would be possible to get carried out. If you want these I will return them also. Otherwise the parcel is exactly as it was sent to me.[10]

Sophie did indeed insist on the return of the whole package. She also asked Hulme to go on her behalf to the French Embassy in London and speak to the cultural attaché there, a M. Morand, to get clarification of her position under French law. Pound had apparently already tried to do so and failed. Hulme did as he was asked, confirming at the same time that he was in touch with Gaudier's family and had sent off a trunkful of personal effects to France:

I have sent things off to the father, the carriage which I paid in advance was twelve shillings.

I have seen Morand. He wants to see the document left by Gaudier giving total status to you. He wants either you or I to send it to him. He will show it to someone in the Embassy who will advise him as to the legal position under French Law. He thinks that if he wrote to the father as you suggest, it would only make the father suspect that the statues are worth much more than £50. If you don't want to let the document out of your hand will you make a copy of it, send both to me, and I will then forward the copy alone to Morand certifying at the same time that it is an exact copy of the original document.[11]

Sophie declined Hulme's offer of help, informing him that the document was not in her possession but in a safe place somewhere outside London 'for fear of the Zeppelins'. She was still insisting that Hulme return everything from Gaudier's package, including the drawings she had apparently offered him:

You told me you would keep them for three or four days, you have had them now for weeks and that should be sufficient. If you want to buy drawings you can come to me in four days after they are returned.

Now I am a wilful creature and the more you insist on keeping them the more I want to have them and will have them. I must sell some drawings to assist those that are in need. I understand that those eventual purchasers (foreigners) do not know much about good drawings, so there is an opportunity of pushing out the weak ones. Please leave the necessary instructions so that I may take the drawings on Thursday morning between 11.a.m. and 1.p.m.[12]

By mid-December she was at last satisfied that everything had been returned to her. The cost of her insistence was perhaps the goodwill of those who might have helped her in the difficult times she now faced. She was keeping a diary in which she addressed herself to the dead Gaudier, and on 26 March 1916 told him that 'your friends only persevere in their efforts to convince me that I am an imbecile, simple and stupid. Hulme, who at first offered to find me a place where I could rest and be quiet, openly mocks me. Pound, less lazy, is willing enough to occupy himself with your affairs, because they are so closely allied with his own interests, but he treats me as an inferior.'[13]

Both Hulme and Pound tried as best they could to help Sophie, but with Gaudier's death began a slow process of mental disintegration which eventually led to her incarceration and death in a mental hospital. Her paranoia elicited in both men a difficult mix of pity, frustration and impatience that finally set them against each other and brought to an end the uneasy friendship that had survived, with ups and downs, since early 1909 and the Poets' Club. In March 1916 Pound wrote to the American art collector John Quinn regretting that he had become 'more or less involved in the quarrel between Miss B. and Hulme, with whom I *had* been in friendly relations for six years'.[14] 'Hulme took a great dislike to Pound,' Kate Lechmere said later, 'but he always loved Gaudier,' implying perhaps that Hulme suspected Pound's conduct over the handling of the dead sculptor's estate.[15] Hulme summarized the whole business in a letter to Edward Marsh, explaining that he had experienced a 'good deal of trouble about the affair, trying to arrange things between the father and Mlle Brzeska, but finally the latter became so difficult to get on with that I chucked the whole thing.'[16] He had evidently enjoyed the experience of living under the same roof as the Gaudier drawings at Frith Street. Some of those depicting horses he had shown to the French painter Maurice Asselin, who found their technical ability 'really extraordinary'. Sophie had let him keep as a souvenir a little clay statuette of a woman, about four inches tall, which he had had cast and which he offered to copy for Marsh.

Nine days after Gaudier's death, on 14 June, Hulme formalized his discharge from the HAC and was appointed to a commission as a temporary 2nd lieutenant in the York and Lancaster Regiment. For the matter to have proceeded this swiftly it is clear he must have applied to return to the fighting even before his wound had healed properly; but the death of someone from his own immediate circle gave him a harsh lesson in mortality that the mass death of strangers in the trenches had not. It led him to advise his brother Harold most urgently to keep out of the infantry,[17] and it became a matter of some importance to keep himself out of the trenches too. It also inaugurated later on a striking display of concern for his admired friend Jacob Epstein in his struggle to stay out of the front line.

The tone of Hulme's observations of the conduct of war from his worm's eye view in the trenches conveys a manly and attractive response to mortal danger. The repetitive crack of the tripod-mounted rifle and the bullets that smack into the mud close to his head elicit nothing stronger than 'it's very irritating', and irritating is the strongest word in all the letters, a reticence all the more remarkable in a man with a well-documented love of strong language. But two of his observations in particular reveal much about the anxieties festering inside him at the time. One is the remark that 'it's not the idea of being killed that's alarming, but the idea of being hit by a jagged piece of steel', a devastatingly clear summation of the fear of a painful death. The other is the observation, 'That's how they do things in the army. They never seem to think 5 minutes before they do a thing.' In peacetime this might just be a normal bit of squaddies' chaffing. In wartime, as he knew perfectly well, and as the death of young Gaudier vividly confirmed, the stupidity of others might well cost him his life.

Hulme now reflected on the unacceptable nature of his position. He liked the company of the common man, the informal rudeness of male camaraderie, perhaps also the lack of responsibility that went with being an enlisted man; but he had probably never before found that a position in which he was relieved of the responsibility of authority had so few advantages to offer by comparison with the sacrifices. Enlisted men had no say in what was going on. Fools and incompetents might decide their destinies and there was nothing they could do about it. Two incidents involving Hulme's battalion in their engagement in front of the Spanbrock Moelen illustrate the dangers. In the first, in the 'K' trenches, at dawn on 14 February, the officer in charge of the front line, 'wishing to annoy the enemy', ordered five rounds of rapid fire per man. There was no visible target, nothing was seen to be hit, and the enemy responded with a heavy shelling which wounded twelve men. The second was that major assault on the Spanbrock Moelen in which partial success turned to fiasco when the supporting companies moving up to consolidate gains came under 'friendly fire' and suffered such heavy casualties that the action had to be aborted. The horrific idea of dying merely because the man in charge is a fool struck Hulme with particular force. He might joke to Dermot Freyer that his complaints about the general level of stupidity among his commanding officers made him unpopular; but after his wounding, and the death of Gaudier, it became less of a joke and more of a real fear.

He now ridiculed the romantic enthusiasm for the war of his friends in London – 'Why do you want to go out there?' he would say. 'It's awful.' At the same time he remained thoroughly convinced of the need for the war and for Germany's expansionist tendencies to be thwarted. To the tactician and mathematician and lover of Go in him, trench warfare now seemed a fatally crude tactic with which to pursue the legitimate ends of the war. Accordingly he turned his attention to finding a way that would satisfy his desire to contribute to the war effort, and to do so without almost inevitably costing him his life. In its summer issue his old school magazine *The Fire-Fly* proudly listed his commission to the York and Lancasters, but Hulme was already taking steps towards finding a more obscure berth, and when Edward Marsh contacted him with a query arising from the book he was writing about Rupert Brooke Hulme took the opportunity in replying to raise the question of his getting a commission in the Royal Marine Artillery:

I wouldn't mind going to the R.M.A. as a private, if there was a chance in several months of getting a commission. I don't necessarily want to be an officer if that is difficult. I can drive a car, if I could get into the Naval Air Service as a private, I should be satisfied. The air service seem[s] difficult to get into unless you know someone and then it is easy. I want to avoid the infantry again. I have had my share of the trenches, I think.[18]

Marsh at this time was private secretary to the First Lord of the Admiralty, Winston Churchill, and his presumed influence made him a magnet for such approaches. Hulme was by no means the only friend from his artistic circles who turned to him for help – Harold Monro was another. Marsh did promise to do what he could, but then Hulme heard nothing for a while and, fearing that he might not have impressed upon his patron how strongly he felt about the matter, he wrote an apologetic letter of reminder:

> 67 Frith Street
> Soho Square

Dear Marsh

I am taking the liberty of writing to you again to ask if it will be possible for you to let me know how soon you are likely to hear about my chance of a commission. I am very sorry to trouble you in this way, but the thing is very worrying to me and I did not perhaps emphasize enough to you how extremely important to me the result will be.

It would be extremely depressing to me to start again as a private at this stage of the war. It was very different in the first months of the war, when one was excited about the thing. Besides, even impersonally, I do think I am suited to have a commission of this kind. Mathematics was always my subject and I should pick up all the theoretical part, the calculations etc of which there is quite a bit in connection with the very big guns of the R.M.A. much more easily than most people, and should enjoy the work. I am also about the build for heavy gun work. I think it is rather a waste (considering the kind of people who have got artillery commissions) that I should have to go through the mill again as a private.

I see there is a rule now that no commission is to be given except to people who served with the Brit. Exped. Force. I had five months in France, and I have a sort of testimonial letter from my C.O. whilst out there, saying I was quite satisfactory.

I must again apologise for troubling you, but the thing is very important to me. I want to get something settled, I don't like being out of it any longer. And as you are the most influential person I know, you are my only hope in the matter.

Yours sincerely

T. E. Hulme

The second thoughts occasioned by the death of Gaudier about returning to the infantry and the trenches and his subsequent campaign to rejoin the fighting in a more appropriate and tolerable capacity probably account for the persistent rumours of Hulme's having been 'lost' for several months by the War Office. He was not lost, only convalescing and busily trying to arrange matters so that having come so close to giving his life for his country he might yet continue to serve it in a way that would be as effective but involve less direct risk. 'I don't like being out of it any longer,' as he told Marsh. Epstein confirmed the strong sense of honour and duty that drove Hulme in this matter, claiming that if indeed he had slipped through the War Office's bureaucratic net after his wounding then it was entirely his own choice to be 'found' again. He need never have reported back to the War Office, said Epstein, adding that he 'could have stayed in England indefinitely'[19] had he chosen to do so.

Hulme spent the time waiting for news of his commission living a life that superficially resembled his pre-war existence, in C. K. Ogden's phrase 'hanging around the Café Royal and waiting on the War Office'.[20] His involvement in the dealings over Gaudier's estate took up some of his time that summer. Another involvement was the reappearance of Dolly's estranged husband Gilbert, who turned up in London with a regiment of the Australian Army. According to Peter Kibblewhite he and Dolly met at least once in order to arrange for their divorce. It seems she entertained hopes of marrying Hulme, but his views on divorce were those of the Catholic Church and marriage to a divorcée was ruled out. Besides, his attachment to Kate Lechmere was holding and seemed under the stresses of wartime life to be getting deeper. She had enlisted in the auxiliary nursing unit known as the Volunteer Aid Detachment, and for the middle years of the war had the luck to be stationed near Macclesfield, where Hulme's Aunt Alice lived and where Hulme spent much of his time. This enabled him to see Kate away from London, away from Frith Street and the reproving glare of friends such as the newly married Ashley Dukes and his wife who, in the recall of Robert Bevan's daughter Halszka, 'always resented K.L. [Kate Lechmere]; they were definitely supporters of the Kibble White [sic] menage'.[21] Hulme was always, said Kate, 'very careful that she [Dolly] should not know about me'.[22]

Kate considered that she and Hulme were already engaged and that it was at Hulme's insistence they were waiting until after the war to get married. He looked on marriage as a sacrament, he told her. Once married he would under no circumstances contemplate divorce and would never fall, no matter how great the temptation of another woman might be. Should his wife be unfaithful to him he would not respond in kind but simply cease to take any interest in her. A particular concern he voiced to her was that women might get tired of sex after the age of forty, although he was certain this would not be her fate – 'You'll never get tired of sex,' he told her. He loved the idea of lovers getting old and fat together, swelling up until they were both of them twenty stone and 'fine examples of middle-aged spread'. As regards work, he told her, he was putting everything off until he was past forty. He intended to live a long life, so there was no need to hurry.

*

In a Supplement to the *London Gazette* of 22 December 1915 Hulme's appointment as temporary 2nd lieutenant with the York and Lancaster Regiment was cancelled and on 20 March 1916 he was successfully commissioned to the Royal Marine Artillery as temporary 2nd lieutenant:

> 67 Frith Street,
> Soho Squ.

Dear Marsh

I passed my medical exam today – the A.A.G. (?) told me that I should get my commission in about 5 days (subject to the approval of the Admiralty – but I suppose this is purely formal).

I am very delighted to have got it, and extremely grateful to you. I am sure that I stood no chance whatever of getting it if it hadn't been for your help. Again thanking you very much for the trouble you have taken.

Yrs Sincerely
T. E. Hulme[23]

He also wrote to tell Kate Lechmere his good news and try to fix up a date, proudly informing her that the RMA was 'very swell and very difficult to get into'. He told her he had been ordered to report for training to Eastney Barracks in Portsmouth in a week's time. Before that, however, he was planning a trip to Macclesfield: 'Is there any chance of seeing you?' he asked. 'I *should* like to.' He urged her to wire him her answer at once by return. He also hinted that he might be given leave the weekend after, but this would only be to attend the wedding of his sister Kate at St Luke's Church in Endon.

13

Heroic Values

Hulme also wrote a great deal during these months in London and produced two series of articles that showed a new and focused seriousness. One was a series on philosophy written for *The New Age* as 'A Notebook';[1] the other, entitled 'War Notes', ran concurrently with the 'Notebook' and was likewise published in *The New Age*. He was also able to enjoy the long-delayed publication of the translation of Sorel's *Reflections on Violence*, by Allen and Unwin, with his own 'Translator's Preface'. 'I have been working hard,' he wrote to Richard Curle in the autumn of 1915, 'and have written my preface to Sorel (in this week's New Age) and am now half-finished thing on Clive Bell.'[2] At the time of his firm's collapse in 1912 Stephen Swift had been advertising the publication of the translation as imminent, with an introduction by Graham Wallas, an early member of the Fabian Society who taught at the LSE and went on to become professor of politics there. Wallas disappeared from the picture after Swift's failure and the job of introducing the book passed to Hulme. His published preface was a slight reworking of the *New Age* piece he mentions in the letter to Curle. Along with the 'Complete Poetical Works' printed as the Appendix to Pound's *Ripostes*, this was the only piece of Hulme's writing that T. S. Eliot could recall having read until the appearance of *Speculations* in 1924.

The preface includes a number of lengthy footnotes that distract attention away from the author and towards the translator, which may be why the American edition did not carry it and why a subsequent English reprint in 1925 dropped it.[3] Hidden among these discursive footnotes, however, is an interesting harbinger of a change in Hulme's views. In referring to the sympathy between Sorel and the writers of

Action Française, which he said Sorel's opponents were using as a way of discrediting him, he concedes that Sorel's ideology does resemble that of Charles Maurras and his supporters, but maintains that his application of it differs from theirs in that he expects the return of the classical spirit to come about through the class struggle. The footnote reads:

It is this which differentiates Sorel's from other attacks on the democratic *ideology*. Some of these are merely dilettante, having little sense of reality, while others are really vicious, in that they play with the idea of inequality. No theory that is not fully moved by the conception asserting the equality of men, and which cannot offer something to all men, deserves or is likely to have any future.[4]

This surprisingly trenchant affirmation of the equality of men was surely the direct result of Hulme's experiences in the trenches, and it forms part of a larger attempt he seems to have been making at this time, in both 'A Notebook' and 'War Notes', to bring his most important ideas and beliefs into some kind of focus.

'A Notebook' was published in *The New Age* in seven parts between 2 December 1915 and 10 February 1916, under the signature 'T.E.H.'. It has something in common with the 'Notes on Bergson', being a further account of his autodidact's odyssey through philosophy and written in a similar 'speaking' style, with italicized words to mark his verbal stresses. His expositions mix mathematics and metaphor in a helpful and lively way as he uses an account of his own struggle towards understanding difficult matters written in difficult language to achieve a disarming and convincing impression of directness and honesty.

A major aim of the expositions was to define and contrast what Hulme called the humanist and the religious attitudes towards life, and in pursuing this end he also gave an account of the most directly philosophical advance in his thinking since his discovery of Bergson. Two writers in particular were important. The first was the Cambridge philosopher G. E. Moore. Apart from an undatable passing reference to 'Moore' among the 'Notes on Language and Style' the references in the 1915–16 series of articles are the first time he mentions him. Understanding and acceptance were evidently not overnight processes, and the almost religious enthusiasm with which he had acclaimed Bergson in the *New Age* articles five years earlier is not in evidence in 'A Notebook'. But there is no doubting the importance of Moore's thought for him:

Having lived at Cambridge at various times during the last ten years, I have naturally known that the only philosophical movement of any importance in England is that which is derived from the writings of Mr. G. E. Moore. I now find these writings extremely lucid and persuasive, yet for years was entirely unable to understand in what lay their value.[5]

His first difficulty had been a general one with the whole concept of moral philosophy. Along with the majority of young people, he wrote, he had found it hard to see the point of this study. At best ethics appeared to be little more than a listing of strictures regarding sexual behaviour, having scant relevance there and none anywhere else, since no one anyway would want to kill or steal from others. When Moore turned his attention to the language in which philosophical propositions were couched as a way of trying to get at philosophical truths this seemed to Hulme merely a form of neo-scholasticism. He failed to see

how the study of such an apparently relative and trivial thing as the nature of propositions, the study of the accidental characteristics of human speech should be an indispensable preliminary to philosophy.[6]

Taking 'what is good' as the central question of ethics, Moore addressed the confusion caused by the two possible ways of understanding the question to mean either 'what *kinds* of things are good', to which the answer was an immense variety of things, including 'the pleasures of human intercourse and the enjoyment of beautiful objects', or 'what things are good', which sought to establish the meaning of the word 'good' in an absolute sense. Bertrand Russell followed Moore in his scepticism, pointing out that it was adjectives and substantives that had dictated the course of philosophy. Verbs and propositions, equally influential, had so far been overlooked. Only a fundamental linguistic analysis of the language in which propositions were couched could solve this problem.

Moore's strict approach to the problems of philosophy led him to attack the Naturalism of nineteenth-century thinkers such as T. H.

Huxley, who argued that the theory of evolution was so complete that it also accounted for the arising of thoughts, ideas and values in the human brain. The implication of this for ethics was that statements about the goodness or badness of things must be rooted in the natural world and could have no reference to a region of special values located beyond the reach of scientific understanding. If courage was to be regarded as 'good' it was because 'goodness' was a natural property of courage, in the same way as yellowness is a natural property of buttercups. In the *Principia Ethica* Moore argued against this, maintaining that the use of concepts which were not specifically ethical to define ethical concepts led one into what he termed the 'naturalistic fallacy'. Values were in fact objective entities, beyond the ken of science.

Hulme's initial difficulties in accepting the importance of what Moore was saying were overcome with the help of the German philosopher Edmund Husserl:

A few years ago I came across similar views [to Moore's] differently expressed in the work of Husserl and his followers. I then began for the first time, if not to agree with these views, at least to understand how they came to be held.[7]

Husserl also offered something of his own, the rigorously intellectual approach of 'phenomenological' analysis which treated philosophy as an exact science devoted to the study of 'essences', abstract entities which are present to the mind but are not themselves states of mind. The aim of the analysis was to penetrate to the level of bare consciousness by leaving aside the contents of consciousness. Over the years the mathematician in Hulme had clearly been troubled by the way in which philosophers whom he liked and admired – such as Moore – or simply respected – such as Russell – had attacked the lack of rigour in Bergson's philosophical method. Husserl's analytical method enabled him to entertain the idea that philosophy did not *have* to be a form of art in order for him to continue to practise it. It could be a science without necessarily running into the determinist cul-de-sac:

The best account I know of the sense in which Philosophy may be a science is that given by Husserl in 'Logos' in 1911 – 'Philosophie als strenge Wissenschaft'. One definition would be that of philosophy as the science of *what is possible* as contrasted with the *science of what is*. [. . .] Philosophy may be a patient investigation into entities, which although they are abstract, may yet be investigated by methods as objective as those of physical science.[8]

Putting together the lessons of Moore and Husserl Hulme saw how they might be used to bolster his claim that the anthropocentric and subjective ethics of humanist philosophy was on its way out:

Logic does not deal with the laws of human thought but with these quite *objective* sentences. In this way the anthropomorphism which underlies certain views of logic is got rid of. Similarly ethics can be exhibited as an objective science, and is also purified from anthropomorphism.[9]

Other aspects of Moore's approach that Hulme does not directly touch on in his writing were probably attractive to him – the promotion of common sense against idealism and the insistence that when philosophical findings and common sense collide it is philosophy that must give way, as well as the conscious attempt to keep his language simple in discussing difficult and abstract matters – but it was Moore's rejection of Naturalism in ethics that was the key concept for the development of Hulme's own views. It persuaded him that ethics was a real subject and not a relativist illusion caused by playing with language. It gave him the confidence to formulate his own understanding of values as objective and 'beyond life', inhabiting a world freed of the empirical prejudice in which love and other 'higher concepts' could be thought of more easily, and to work this into the picture he had already formed, from his observations in the fields of poetry, painting and sculpture, of a civilization on the brink of seismic change.

Hulme saw Husserl and Moore as indicating, albeit in a 'slight' way, what the sculpture of Jacob Epstein, the painting of David Bomberg and the Vorticist group and his own poetry and that of the other Imagists had already given unmistakable sign of. One of the footnotes to the Sorel preface made the point specifically:

It is promising to note signs of the break-up of this period in art, and there are some slight indications of a corresponding anti-humanistic movement in thought and ethics (G. E. Moore, Duguit,[10] Husserl and 'Phaenomenologie').

But Moore and Husserl were less satisfactory witnesses to his prediction than the artists were. Neither man went far enough in his analysis.
Hulme identified two shortcomings in particular:

A complete reaction from the subjectivism and relativism of humanist ethics
should contain two elements: (1) the establishment of the *objective* character
of ethical values, (2) a satisfactory ethics not only looks on values as *objective*,
but establishes an order or *hierarchy* among such values, which it also regards
as absolute and objective.

Now while the school of Moore and Husserl break the humanist tradition
in the first matter, they seem to continue it quite uncritically in the second.[11]

To illustrate the second partiality he wrote that humanist philosophy
had assumed the function of acting as what he called a 'pale substitute'
for religion. Husserl and Russell both insisted on a separation between
pure philosophy and *Weltanschauung*, and Hulme agreed with
them. But he went further, claiming that humanist philosophers
were not in fact free and objective seekers of truth but in thrall to
something he termed the 'canons of satisfaction'. On this theory every
apparently independent, unprejudiced and objective line of philosophical enquiry was in fact subverted from the outset by the existence
of a preferred goal located beyond the end of the thought process
and exerting a magnetic attraction upon it. Such enquiries always
unconsciously shaped themselves to the demands of the preferred goal,
the personal and subjective *Weltanschauung* which is Humanism.
Hence, for example, the perpetuation of the humanist myth of inevitable progress. Husserl, according to Hulme, fell into this trap. He
refers to Husserl's discussion of the difference between impersonal
science and personal *Weltanschauung* and quotes Husserl as saying
that a personal *Weltanschauung* can only spring from the 'highest
possible development of personality' – proof, says Hulme, that for
Husserl *Weltanschauung* philosophy was inevitably an uncritical
Humanism.

In spite of this, however, Hulme hailed the work of both Moore
and Husserl:

In so far, then, as they free ethical values from the anthropomorphism involved
in their dependence on human desires and feeling, they have created the

machinery of an anti-humanist reaction which will proceed much further than they ever intended.[12]

Hulme himself states at one point in 'A Notebook' that these were 'rambling notes', and owing to the origin of the expositions (weekly articles) and the circumstances of their composition (convalescing from a wound, waiting to hear about his commission in the RMA) he had not the leisure, even if he had had the capacity, to mount long and logically constructed lines of argument. But it seems fair to suggest that the practical relevance of the résumé he gives of his understanding of Moore and Husserl was to give authority to the claims, made in pursuit of the Notebook's main aim of distinguishing Humanism and the religious attitude, that values are objective entities, and to use this fact to deepen and strengthen his prediction that the humanist era was over and a new era dawning which would see the return of the religious attitude. This would not be a new Middle Ages, nor would it come about as the result of some inevitable pendular swing. It would transpire because the values and world-views implicit in the religious attitude are, in an absolute sense, the true ones.

The point he returns to again and again is that Humanism, with its belief in progress, is a subjective *Weltanschauung*, not to be confused with a real philosophy. It is doctrine felt as facts, not the discovery of a scientific reality such as gravity. It is one option among many. To support the contention he argues that the cultural manifestations of the Renaissance period from Pico della Mirandola onwards, from its philosophical theory to its economic theory, its literature and its art, despite superficial dissimilarities, share deep, familial resemblances. By the use of contrasts taken from the world of art he shows that this resemblance becomes apparent once we acquire a knowledge of the art of epochs and cultures outside the historical period of the Renaissance – the art of the Byzantines, the Egyptians, the Africans – art so very different from that of the European Renaissance as to force at once a recognition of the deep-seated familial likeness that invests all of its culture. To the possible objection that much of the art of the Renaissance was religious and not anthropocentric he replies that the religious art of the Renaissance was only 'so-called' religious art; human emotions, not religious feelings, were its true subjects. He contrasts humanist art with the austere and ahuman religious art of the Byzantine period and asserts that all of its common presuppositions are actively denied by the forms of the Byzantines.

Having established that Humanism is, after all, only a cultural preference he turns to the practical consequences of the ideology, the most harmful of which has been the location of the concept of perfection on the human plane instead of somewhere beyond it, where it really belongs. Hulme describes what happens next:

> To illustrate the position, imagine a man situated at a point in a plane, from which roads radiate in various directions. Let this be the plane of actual existence. We place *Perfection* where it should not be – on this human plane. As we are painfully aware that nothing *actual* can be *perfect* we imagine the perfection to be not where we are, but some distance along one of the roads.[13]

The search for perfection gets under way. We believe that the restrictions imposed upon us by external authority block our progress along the road and in our efforts to remove them we embark on a life of endless and pointless revolutionary activity, forever striving towards a goal that does not exist. This misplacement of perfection on the human plane, says Hulme, is the essence of all romanticism. The other side of this falsification of the human is that the divine, too, is falsified.

His task, then, is to make people aware of these perceptual errors. A Herculean effort is required to remove the spectacles placed on us all at birth, through which we see not reality itself but reality conditioned by these glasses, whose existence and effect we do not suspect. To bring about such awareness would be gratifying if the result were to reveal Humanism as a choice, and not as the inevitable and only way to see life. Real success, however, would be if awareness functioned as a prelude to the return of the lost capacity to take seriously the religious attitude.

The heart of the conflict between the humanist and the religious attitudes lies in the answer to the questions, who owns the values, and who locates them? Hulme introduces the supposition that there are three regions of reality. There is (1) an inorganic world of mathematical and physical science; (2) the organic world dealt with by biology, psychology and history; (3) the world of ethical and religious values. Between these three regions real discontinuities exist. There is a chasm

between ourselves and the world of absolute values. A defining characteristic of the religious attitude is its assurance that values are both
beyond life and permanent. Humanists, with their earthbound and
relative values, cannot comprehend this. In bringing religion into
the forefront of the discussion Hulme carefully avoids making any
statement that might make it easy for a humanist to dismiss his arguments as mere expressions of blind faith. Neither God nor Christ is
mentioned and the Church only once – dismissively – to say that even
within the Church there are few who realize the overriding importance
of the dogma of original sin, the dogma that man 'is in no sense perfect,
but a wretched creature who can yet apprehend perfection'. It is for
the sake of the dogma, he says, that he is prepared to swallow the
sentiment. He also refers his humanist objectors to the paradox that
men of the Middle Ages, who did not believe in personality, yet believed
in immortality, and in doing so reminds them of Humanism's most
striking failure: that having dethroned God and established man in
God's place it has been able to offer nothing against the fear of death
but more fear.

As a younger man, in Canada, Hulme had experienced 'the fright
of the mind before the unknown [that] created not only the first gods,
but also the first art'. Men created gods because they needed them. It
seems a respectably logical and humanist explanation for the existence
of gods. But he had travelled a long way since then. Now he identifies
'the source of religion' as being the question, 'what is finally
satisfying?', and finds his own satisfaction in locating values beyond
life and in feeling their nature as tragic, in contemplation of a life lived
without the luxury of hope but not in hopelessness. Perhaps the horrors
of trench warfare and a bullet through the arm gave him a second
'fright of the mind' that was the catalyst for this deeper response. 'I
hold,' he writes, 'quite coldly and intellectually as it were, that the way
of thinking about the world and man, the conception of sin, and the
categories which ultimately make up the Religious attitude, are the
true categories and the *right* way of thinking.'

He evens sketches out a future for a world that has exchanged
the humanist for the religious attitude. It will not involve a new
medievalism. The only thing it will have in common with medievalism
will be the subordination of man to absolute values. The best aspects

of Humanism, which he finds to be its honesty in science and 'a certain conception of freedom of thought', will be part of this future mind. But men themselves will not change, because men of different sorts exist in constant proportion throughout different generations. It is just this constancy of man, a notion abhorrent to believers in the inevitability of progress, which 'provides perhaps the greatest hope of the possibility of a radical transformation of society'. Close to the end, casually thrown away, is a reference to 'a couple of thousand years', which is the closest he ever comes to mentioning the name of Christ. This, he says, is all the time it takes for the confused human mind to work itself out clearly into every separate attitude possible for it to assume.

In the seventeen weekly articles printed as 'War Notes' in *The New Age* between 11 November 1915 and 2 March 1916 Hulme showed that the abstract ideas considered in 'A Notebook' also had application in the specific and fraught context of war. Again, his observations reflect their journalistic origins and purpose, with repetitions and recapitulations and a hopping back and forth between themes in response to the changing political and military situation. The 'War Notes' were of course not the only articles critical of the conduct of the war published at this time. For many months the *British Review*, a literary and political publication which Hulme read and in which several of his friends including Squire, Padraic Colum and Edward Storer had work published, ran a series of articles by a Major G. W. Redway under the title 'The True Story of the War'. But where Redway's main concern was to correct the triumphalism of the *Daily Mirror* and *Daily Sketch* and to get his facts and figures correct no matter how unpalatable they might be to the public, Hulme's criticisms were of a more fundamental kind.

Although all the articles appeared under the *nom de guerre* 'North Staffs', the first three in the series, those appearing in *The New Age* on the 11, 18 and 25 of November, were not actually written by Hulme himself but by Orage: Hulme states as much in a scrapbook containing the articles that passed into Jacob Epstein's possession. Inside the front cover is a listing in his hand of all the articles in the series, with his own key-word titles. Underneath he writes:

There are 3 articles written by Orage (after interviews)
Nov 11. General
Nov. 18 Strategy of war
Nov. 25 Conscription[14]

'Orage comes round every Thursday now to interview me about the war,' he wrote to Richard Curle in November, 'first was yesterday.'[15] This might be further evidence of his legendary laziness and his ability to get others to do work for him; what is more probable is that in view of the nature of some of his comments on the conduct of the war he was unsure of his legal position as a serving member of the armed forces in writing so critically of the way things were being done. He might also have worried that if the articles came to the attention of anyone at the War Office and his authorship was revealed it might prejudice his attempts to get his commission in the RMA. Physical incapacity from the wounding can be ruled out. Indeed, after it his handwriting became, if anything, slightly more legible.

Orage did a good job as amanuensis, reproducing both Hulme's characteristic opinions and his characteristic way of expressing them. He was in any case well suited to the task, being still considerably under Hulme's influence and sharing both his repudiation of Fabian socialism and his belief in the doctrine of original sin as the only theory that could adequately account for 'all those cross purposes of the world'.[16] Unlike Hume, he also believed in redemption. For whatever reason, the arrangement lasted only until the 25 November article, and from the article of 2 December onwards, 'Staff Work', everything appearing under the name 'North Staffs' was actually written by Hulme.

Hulme's concerns in the 'War Notes' were to provide a critique of the tactics followed in the first months of the war; to expose the inefficiency of the General Staff and of the gerontocracy in the army, which prevented the acceptance of creative thinking; to offer an ongoing consideration of the moral basis for conscription; and to formulate an overarching argument for the regrettable necessity of the war which analysed the flaws in the pacifist argument against participation.

Hulme's criticism of Allied tactics reflected his keen interest in the whole subject, whether at the chess or Go boards or in the field of combat. His main argument was that the catastrophic trench stalemate on the Western Front of 1915 was caused by the way the Allies were allowing the Germans to dictate the terms of combat. As the defending force the German Army could maintain its position with only a third of the numbers of the attacking force, leaving the rest of its strength free for outflanking manoeuvres. The German plan thus combined a fairly small containing defensive force with a comparatively large attacking and mobile force which they used to outflank the Allies whenever possible, their aim being to lengthen the line on every arc of the overall front and to employ every possible man in it. Instead of concentrating on the creation of a heavy, fixed line the Allies should have copied this tactic and substituted a long, thin, flexible line around Germany, a tactic which, with their superiority in numbers, would have enabled them to stretch the German line until it became too weak to defend. He ridiculed the view expressed by some politicians that 'we shall free Serbia in Flanders', and argued that trench warfare, as it was currently being waged, was not only a prolongation of the war but a prolongation of it to infinity. The only way out of the stalemate was a change in the military culture of the British Army that would substitute mobile for stationary warfare.

Hulme's criticisms became more agitated when discussing the dangerous inefficiency of the General Staff. As a private involved in the attack on Neuve Chapelle he had experienced at first hand the terrible consequences of poor supply. There were at that time no mortars on the Western Front, nor did the British have the rockets and the star shells which the Germans had in abundance and which enabled them to light up the night sky and expose British troop movements that were supposed to be taking place under cover of darkness. A line in the poem 'Trenches: St Eloi' fleetingly makes the point – 'The Germans have rockets, the English have no rockets'. The General Staff was moribund and antiquated. What was needed was a complete restructuring along German lines, with specialists who dealt with nothing but Staff work all their lives, who wore civilian clothes and had no titles. It was the British cult of the amateur he was attacking, the attitude of bumbling through. For the same reason he criticized a military culture in which the average age of generals was between fifty and sixty, comparing this unfavourably to the figure of thirty among Napoleon's generals. Men of that age were too set in their ways to improvise and adapt, too little receptive to new ideas. He might personally have found the tripod-mounted trained rifles merely 'irritating' as the bullets splattered over and over again into the mud beside him, but he recognized the inspired nature of the invention, a weapon that kept its targets in a constant state of terror, and asked rhetorically, 'Why is it that the smaller ingenious ideas for which this kind of warfare offers so many applications seem to spring from the other side?' His answer was that, like the Staff, the system needed an overhaul and a rejuvenation. Replace the gerontocracy with a meritocracy. A related problem he attacked was the class-based standards of military justice. Privates might be shot for desertion or cowardice but generals were shielded in anonymity from the consequences of their incompetence. This was both unjust and bad for morale.

On 6 January 1916 a bill was passed in the House of Commons making all men between eighteen and forty liable to military service, with single men to be conscripted first. The morality of this was one of the most keenly debated issues of the war. Hulme recognized the pacifist argument that conscription was an almost intolerable infringement of individual civil liberties. He recognized the almost surreal horror involved in knocking on a man's door, removing him from his daily life and introducing him to a situation in which he might very possibly lose his life. Nevertheless he affirmed the necessity of conscription, at the same time as he urged the political and military authorities to take their proper share of responsibility when things went wrong, and to be seen to be doing so. Only when this was the case, he argued, could an *implied contract* arise in which men might be willing, in principle, to give up their lives to defend their country and its liberties, on the understanding that everything possible was being done in terms of efficiency and organization to prevent such a sacrifice being necessary. On the very day the war ended, he said, the government's first act should be to repeal the Defence of the Realm Act.

At the heart of the 'War Notes', and its most urgently argued theme, was Hulme's long assault on the ethical basis of pacifism and his attempts to explain to his pacifist readers precisely why they were wrong in their beliefs and why this particular war had to be fought.

He did this by trying to force them to see the real consequences of a refusal to fight it, and by demonstrating to them how they had been misled by their innocence and idealism to misunderstand completely the real nature of the threat posed by German aggression. Beyond this he provided a more abstract but still relevant disquisition on why pacifists had no right to claim that the principled opposition to all war was an inescapable consequence of holding democratic views.

It was necessary, he wrote, to fight the war against Germany because a German victory would mean 'the end of Europe as a new Hellas, a society of nations'.[17] It meant a Europe under German leadership. A country occupied or in some way existing in a dependent relationship with a stronger power never accepts such a situation and its political life becomes an endless series of conspiracies to restore the former state. Hulme offered the examples of Ireland and Poland, beaten but unassimilable nations. Unless she fought this war, Britain would presently find herself a subservient country in the same situation of ceaseless preoccupation with the politics of revolt. To the common pacifist contention that defeat and colonization would be only temporary inconveniences, since progress towards democracy was a kind of preordained condition of human evolution to which even a Germany steeped in military culture must presently succumb, Hulme replied that Germany was not remotely interested in democracy. Her ambition was, on the contrary, the colonization of Europe. In support of this claim he quoted extensively from the anglophobic and proto-Nazi writings of the German philosopher Werner Sombart, and from the more intelligent but equally threatening rhetoric of Max Scheler in *Der Genius des Krieges und der deutsche Krieg*. Scheler was a thinker whom Hulme respected and with whom he shared an interest in Husserl's phenomenology, but in the writing of *Der Genius des Krieges* his concerns were to point out that the aim of the war was 'the creation for the first time of a solidarist Continental Europe under German military leadership', and of a 'new Mediterranean culture grounded on the military power of Germany'. England's entry into the war was inevitable, wrote Scheler, for 'her whole existence as an Empire was threatened by the building of the German fleet'. Moreover, the 'only possible aim in the building of that fleet was directed against England'. Germany's primary object must be the destruction of English naval supremacy, for it was this that stood between Germany and 'the fair division of the earth'.

To Hulme's way of thinking there was nothing glorious about responding to such a direct threat to European security, it was simple necessity: 'I never met a soldier who ever thought of this war as anything but a stupidity,' he wrote, '. . . a necessary stupidity, but still a stupidity.'[18] To those who did glorify war, and to those pacifists who always sarcastically claimed that supporters of the war were driven by their 'Prussian instincts', he responded that the war was not being fought for any great and wonderful end. He likened the work of fighting it to that of men repairing sea-walls whose sole aim is to prevent a bad situation from growing worse. He could offer his readers – and those about to be conscripted – no great and positive 'good' for which they might all be said to be fighting:

But it is not necessary that we should; there is no harmony in the nature of things, so that from time to time great and useless sacrifices become necessary, merely that whatever precarious 'good' the world has achieved may just be preserved.[19]

*

Early in 1916 Bertrand Russell publicly took issue with some of the arguments Hulme was putting forward in the 'War Notes'. Russell's activities with the Union of Democratic Fellowship and, after conscription, with Clifford Allen's No-Conscription Fellowship, led to his being popularly regarded as the most gifted, convincing and passionate defender of pacifist beliefs. A series of lectures on 'The Principles of Social Reconstruction' delivered in London between January and March 1916 confirmed this perception. Russell had recently changed from the belief that ethical values were objective to the view that they were subjective, and the change prompted him to offer society his new vision of social reconstruction in which the energies wastefully diverted into war could be channelled towards properly constructive ends. All of this made him an exponent of the best arguments against which Hulme wished to pit his own. Even before the lectures Hulme had already referred to Russell's representative views several times in the 'War Notes'.

Prior to the war of 1914 pacifism had been associated with the religious beliefs of groups such as the Quakers and the Plymouth Brethren. It was only with the advent of the war that it began to appear in the form advocated by Russell and others as a tenet of humanist belief. The provisions in the conscription act took account of this changed situation. They were liberal in the exemptions allowed for people doing work of military importance, and for those with a conscientious objection to bearing arms, and there was no insistence that such objections be grounded in religious beliefs. A series of military tribunals were established to hear cases, with the power to grant absolute exemption, or exemption from combat duties, on condition that the objector agree to do work of 'national importance' instead. Hulme described their proceedings as 'the only example in our time of public disputation about abstract questions of ethics',[20] but he was disappointed in them once they became operative, calling them a sham and denouncing them as unfair. Were he a pacifist, he said, he would certainly refuse to appear before one.

Russell was, of course, already a familiar figure to Hulme both as president of the Aristotelian Society during Hulme's brief period of membership there, and as one of the most hostile and dismissive opponents of Henri Bergson's philosophy. Early in 1912 Hulme had devoted space and some furious verbal energy to refuting Russell's dismissal of Bergson in the 'Notes on Bergson' for The New Age. By 1916 Hulme had settled on G. E. Moore, 'the commonsense revolutionary' of twentieth-century philosophy, as his favourite English thinker, but he was pardonably proud to have attracted the attention of such an influential and well-known philosopher as Russell, the author of Principles of Mathematics. He and Russell had a mutual friend in C. K. Ogden, editor of the Cambridge Magazine and as president of the Heretics Society the man responsible for inviting both to address the members in 1912. It was Ogden who had written the detailed précis of Hulme's lecture on 'Anti-Romanticism and Original Sin' that appeared in the magazine afterwards.

Early in 1916 Ogden asked Hulme if there was anything he particularly wanted to say in the Cambridge Magazine about the war. He said he would have no objection if Hulme were simply to give him edited versions of the articles Orage was running in The New Age, since he felt there was no overlap between the two circulations. Hulme took up the offer and used his own copies of the *New Age* articles to carry out the editing for the versions that were to appear in the *Cambridge Magazine*. All six 'War Notes' printed in *The New Age* from 27 January 1916 to the end of the series on 2 March, when Hulme was ordered to report for training at Eastney, were written in direct or indirect response to Russell's campaign against the waging of the war in general and against conscription in particular, although it was in reply to the edited versions in the *Cambridge Magazine* that Russell's two rejoinders were written.

Hulme had already called Russell 'the only man of any real distinction among the English pacifists'[21] and when Russell's first response appeared in the issue of 12 February he was distinctly curious: 'Did Russell say anything when sending in his letter?'[22] he asked Ogden. Russell's interest made him more self-conscious about the quality of his writing. He apologized for the next set of 'Notes' sent to Ogden, telling him they were written in a great hurry and 'they are very poor – I should cut them dramatically'. He also chided Ogden for his lax editing: 'You might correct my English a bit, and *spelling*.'[23] But he was glad that Russell had replied, 'particularly as it is a letter that quite gives him away'. He told Ogden that he intended to finish dealing with Russell in the following set of 'War Notes'.

Russell's letter had referred sarcastically to the title given to Hulme's article, 'The Kind of Rubbish We Oppose', a line from the last 'War Note' but taken out of context. Hulme offered Ogden a mild rebuke on this account – 'you know, you oughtn't to have put that heading, for it didn't refer to Russell'.[24] An exchange of such clearly cut opposing views was good for the circulation of the magazine and it seems Ogden was doing his best to dramatize the encounter.

Perhaps it was to guard against this that Hulme began his next letter to Ogden with a firm injunction that if he intended to publish any of the most recent 'War Notes' in the next issue of the *Cambridge Magazine* he must 'be sure to say *nothing* about my being wounded'. He went on to suggest that, if he was going to write a second article on Russell, then 'I think I ought to have free tickets for the next lecture';[25] but he had obviously already decided to write about him anyway, telling Ogden that 'next week may interest you more, when

I intend to talk about the view that we make a mistake in fighting Germany because Germany "will *inevitably* evolve towards democracy"'.

Evidently he did get his free tickets and attend the lecture, in company with Ramiro de Maeztu. In one of his responses Russell wondered whether 'North Staffs' was the man in the audience he had observed at his most recent lecture, 'ostentatiously' reading the *Daily Express* throughout, a charge which Hulme disdainfully rejected.

*

The differences between Hulme and Russell were fundamental and numerous. As Herbert Read put it,[26] what Hulme provided in his encounter with Russell was 'an intellectual defence of the militarist ideology which caused surprise not only to the militarists, to whom it was as strange as it might be deemed unnecessary, but also to the pacifists, who had regarded themselves as constituting a close corporation of the intelligentsia'. Russell was an outstanding example of this surprised intelligentsia, an idealistic man who found it scarcely credible that something as foolish as the war was actually taking place. Hulme's first reference to him in the 'War Notes' was to a pamphlet by Russell in which he had spoken of the outbreak of war as 'a shock' that had shattered the hopes of all 'liberal-minded and humane men'. While not denying that Germany's aggressive foreign policy was largely to blame for the outbreak of the war, Russell's view was that Germany's failure to have acquired much in the colonial adventure was reason enough for her complaint and a cause of justifiable anger. As a free-trader he thought the colonies a costly error, and that to appease Germany by handing some of them over would constitute no great loss.

To Hulme the relevant lesson of the colonial adventure was to remind pacifists of the fact, 'consistently glossed over by school histories', that Britain's acquisition of a colonial empire was not the accidental and undesired result of the triumph of virtue over vice, but an undertaking that had involved a great deal of deliberation and brute force. In his view a similar undertaking, using similar means, was what the Germans had in mind now, only with Europe as their prospective empire.

For Russell liberty was an inherent right, for Hulme it was something that had to be fought for in the sense that it had to be defended against attack. For Russell there was no higher goal than peace, and if German hegemony and a *Pax Germanicum* were the best means of preserving peace in Europe then it was to be welcomed. For Hulme German hegemony meant not a peaceful future but the disappearance of democracy and a future of endless subversion and intrigue.

For Hulme certain values were 'more important than life',[27] the heroic or tragic values that recognized that certain things were worth dying for. In an almost cruel exposure of Clive Bell's haplessly snobbish pamphlet 'Peace at Once' he had dealt earlier in the 'War Notes' with the argument that there was effectively nothing at all worth dying for, a position that he called the ethics of 'hedonism and comfort', with personal survival at any cost as its highest goal.[28] He was aware that in the 'close corporation of the intelligentsia' his occasional references to the unfashionable concept of honour would provoke 'giggling'. Then, as rationalists came to understand 'instinctively' (for in Hulme's analysis a process of reasoning could never reveal the existence of values located beyond life) that the conception of honour was the central nerve of the ethic they opposed, they would attempt to destroy it with ridicule. But he was also aware that Russell's views were more subtle than those of Bell and the all-purpose straw-man pacifist to whom he usually addressed his arguments, and that Russell's need to build sound rational defences for his beliefs and principles was quite as strong as his own. He knew that Russell was not guilty of the worship of life and comfort as the ultimate goods that characterized many of his fellow pacifists, and that Russell did not subscribe to the belief that 'progress' was an inherent part of the human evolutionary process. In fact, Russell had considerable admiration for heroic or tragic values. He felt that mere opposition to war was not enough, and that the aim of pacifism was not to produce people with no wildness in them at all but to produce a society able to utilize their wildness in some way that would be, to use William James's phrase, the 'moral equivalent of war'.[29] Here he was echoing Proudhon, a pacifist who could yet warn, in a passage quoted by Hulme, 'Philanthropist, you speak of abolishing war, take care you don't degrade the human race'. It was because he did not want to dissociate himself completely from heroic values that Russell was keen to point out, in a postscript to his second letter to the *Cambridge Magazine*, that the maintenance of his own unpopular position in the country could be said to require them.

The 'War Notes' revealed a changed Hulme. Religious beliefs are never explicitly a part of what he says, but a belief in God seems everywhere implied in his insistence that the facts of ethics are 'as objective as the facts of geometry',[30] and that their nature is tragic. It was this absence of overtly religious arguments that made him a difficult and interesting opponent for Russell to deal with. Another problem for Russell was the evident fact that 'North Staffs' was manifestly neither a warmonger, nor even a militarist, if the word be used to mean someone who regards military efficiency as the supreme ideal of the state to which all other interests ought to be subordinate. Russell's second contribution was headed 'North Staffs' Praise of War'; but praise of war is precisely what Hulme mocked in Sombart's writings, ridiculing his assertions that 'militarism is not merely an institution, it is the German spirit itself', and that 'war is an unavoidable accompaniment of all State life that is really living'.

Kate Lechmere noticed that Hulme's experiences in the trenches had made him more tolerant and more democratic. The footnote in the Sorel preface was probably the first sign of this, and scattered across the 'War Notes' are further statements that support the truth of the observation. Indeed when he writes at one point that 'this war has greatly, to their own surprise, converted many men to democracy'[31] the likelihood is strong that it is his own conversion, and his own surprise, to which he is referring.

It was, of course, a severely conditional acceptance of democracy, and he was anxious to point out the conditions. His particular objection was to the tendency among those who were opposed to fighting the war to requisition pacifism in the name of democracy by insisting that it was impossible to be both a good democrat and at the same time in favour of fighting the war:

The pacifists should cure themselves of the habit of thinking that pacifism is another name for democracy. [...] I am opposed to *pacifism* as a *democrat*, but I beg leave to point out that democracy is a little older than the tabernacles in which these people imbibed it. If I could correct their tenets by Ireton's[32] belief that 'men are born corrupt and will remain so', I should prefer to call myself a *Leveller*; for not only did they think '*liberty* a right inherent in every man . . . meaning by liberty . . . definite participation in whatever political arrangements the community finds it desirable to make',[33] but they were prepared themselves to fight for this right.

This was seventeenth century democracy, the source of all modern democracy. It had a certain virility and had not then fallen into the sentimental decadence of *humanitarianism*. The truth is that there are two ideas of democracy. The pacifist founded on *sympathy* and the other founded on the conception of *Justice*, leading to the assertion of equality. To the latter conception, I must subscribe whether I desire to or not, as I must to an *ethical* conception. The inferiority of democracy founded on sympathy depends, however, also on a practical question. It seems demonstrable to me that the kind of ethic it fosters will never develop the force which is likely to radically transform society. That is only probable in movements which, like the democracy of the seventeenth century in England, or the Socialism of Proudhon, are founded on the idea of Justice.[34]

Socialists and liberals had long claimed a monopoly on the Levellers as their political ancestors, and for Hulme to requisition and invert his opponents' enthusiasms for use against them like this was an almost Burkean manoeuvre.

Hulme made his point over and over again in the 'War Notes': the fight was only necessary to prevent bad from getting worse. Military heroism was not a virtue in isolation and an act of heroism not enough to turn a bad war into a good one; he does not have an ounce of bellicosity left in him, he writes, and his desire for peace is as intense as that of any pacifist. The war was a stupidity, a necessary stupidity, but still a stupidity. In all his defence of the need to fight there is no whiff of pleasure, no trace of hatred of the Germans as people, no desire to 'teach them a lesson'; only an attitude in which he can be seen increasingly to cherish the liberal institutions and traditions of his country, and a conviction that to refuse to fight would lead inevitably to their disappearance and replacement by the rule of German bureaucracy backed by Prussian militarism. The result of these convictions was this compelling and tragic defence of the need to fight the war of 1914, in the construction of which he came at least close, in his deep acceptance of the implications of his values, to finding a rock upon which he could stand securely and face the prospect of his death.

*

Russell obtained no personal impression of his opponent 'North Staffs' from these articles. In later life[35] he was under the impression that he had met Hulme on one occasion during the war, through Vivien Haigh-Wood-Eliot, T. S. Eliot's first wife, and that Eliot knew Hulme 'well' at this time. Eliot, however, never met Hulme. Writing in 1954 he said he was 'pretty confident' that his wife had never met him either. Vivien Eliot was an admirer of Hulme's poems and Eliot took this to be the source of Russell's confusion, if such it was, that it was the poems and not the man he had been introduced to.[36] Certainly there is nothing in Hulme's skeletal correspondence to confirm a meeting. Lunch with a 'Russell' does crop up in an undated letter to Ogden, but it is overwhelmingly likely that the reference is to Edward Stuart Russell, the biologist and philosopher who was among the British contingent with Hulme at the Bologna Conference in 1911 and with whom he remained in sporadic contact afterwards.

Recalling their exchange some forty years later Russell suggested that Hulme was 'just seizing an issue rather than speaking out on a subject specially close to his heart',[37] thus confirming Hulme's repeated complaint that his liberal-humanist-pacifist opponents could never take seriously any views but their own. Russell turned out to be a good example of the tendency, nurturing into old age his memory of Hulme as an 'evil man who could have created nothing but evil', and in his aversion to Hulme's views declaring that he 'would have wound up an Oswald Mosley type'. Epstein, who was probably Hulme's closest friend, explicitly excluded the possibility. Hulme was 'a conservative, but not a Fascist,' he said, adding that he 'couldn't have endured a fool like Mosley'.[38]

14

The Epstein Book

Hulme left London for training at the Royal Marine base at Eastney near Portsmouth in late March and remained stationed there for the next eight months. He took his library with him – in Richard Curle's phrase, his 'thick German books' – in a wooden box which he had custom-made for the purpose and which now went everywhere with him. He was pleased with his posting and towards the end of his period at Eastney again wrote to thank Marsh for his help in getting him into the Marines:

Sunday Sept. 24th

Dear Marsh

I have been down here six months now and am very grateful to you for getting me into them. I have nearly finished my lowers now and expect to go out in about a month or three months. I think this place is much the pleasantest to spend the war in for nobody ever refers to it and no training has any reference to it. [. . .][1]

There was a reasonable train service between Portsmouth and London and on leave he was able to continue to visit Frith Street and to see his family in Endon and Macclesfield, whiling away the time on the train journeys by playing Go against himself on a specially made miniature board which used cribbage pegs instead of counters. Kate Lechmere's VAD unit was still stationed near Macclesfield which made it easy for them to continue seeing each other there. Although Hulme's surviving letters to her are not detailed enough to give any clear picture of how the affair was conducted, it seems they met sometimes in London, where they would spend the night together in a hotel, and sometimes at a hotel in Macclesfield, where Hulme would be visiting the Pattinsons' home at Lake House. The vagaries of the train service often disrupted their plans, the inconvenience only partially compensated for by the frequency and speed of the postal and wire services. On one of his leaves Hulme's train arrived seven hours late at Stoke, stranding him there, depriving him of his night with Kate and on his return to barracks obliging him to resort to a cold bath as a way of calming himself. However, he was on leave again the following week and asked if she could manage a night with him then. In the meantime he exhorted her to write him a 'nice *hot* letter' as a form of consolation.

Hulme still insisted on their relationship being kept secret, a fact Kate might have found harder to understand once Dolly had obtained her divorce from Gilbert and Hulme had made it clear that he did not want to marry a divorcée. She was already deeply in love and certain that she wanted to marry him, but he put her off, insisting that they wait until after the war. Later Kate implied that he was still troubled by thoughts of having let his family down, that he had in some way not yet proved himself to his family and was anxious to do something about this before committing himself to marriage.

The wedding of his sister Kate might have made the question pressing. It took place at St Luke's Parish Church, Endon, on 8 April and Hulme had obtained leave to attend. As a gift he had bought her a Gilman interior for which he had paid the artist £12, with the message that if she did not like it she was to give it back to him, since he did.[2] He tried to arrange the weekend so that he and Kate Lechmere would be able to spend a night together:

Dear K.D.

This is the position.

I have only managed to get leave from Friday noon to Sunday night.

I cannot get up to Macclesfield before 9.47 on Friday night which is no use to us. I therefore propose coming up on Sat. morning to my home, and shall have to return immediately after the wedding to London, as there are no trains back on Sunday. I shall therefore not come to Macclesfield at all. Now, will you stay the night with me, otherwise we cannot meet at all for some time. You might (1) meet me in London about 10 p.m. Friday night and return with me on Sat. morning. Or (2) come to London on Sat.

night – Now I'm dying to f.you – Wire me to 12A Torrington Square, where I will call on Friday about 6.

p.s. I have received one letter, but the hot one has not been forwarded. I shall get it I suppose tomorrow when I call for it.[3]

It seems that she chose the first option, for the unidentified smiling figure standing beside Hulme in the wedding photograph is surely her. In the same photograph Hulme himself is scarcely recognizable as the athletic young man who had enlisted as a private in the HAC some eighteen months earlier. The moustache and cap give him the appearance of a typical officer and in the months of convalescence and lazy near-civilian life in London he has put on weight. His brother officers at Eastney Barracks nicknamed him 'Hindenburg' and Kate Lechmere estimated his weight at the time as somewhere between fifteen and seventeen stones. She was proud of his bulk. 'Lengthways and breadthways he overpowered other men,'[4] she recalled. Hulme seems to have been quite free of personal vanity and unconcerned by the increase in his weight and jokingly referred to himself as a 'heavy philosopher'.

During these snatched nights together Kate Lechmere got to know him better and heard his confidences. She noted the newfound respect for democracy and the growing tolerance, but as he was still carrying the knuckleduster in his trouser pocket she thought it wiser not to question him about these developments, certain that to have done so would only risk a blow to the shoulder and a repetition of his favourite injunction, 'Forget you're a personality.'[5]

Jacob Epstein's career had continued to advance during the war. *Rock Drill*, which in its drawn form Hulme had praised in 'The Critics and Mr Epstein' in *The New Age*, continued to surprise and impress critics when Epstein exhibited it as sculpture at the London group show in March 1915, by which time it had become a nine-foot tall robot in white plaster, visored and holding on to a black-painted rock drill of the type used for blasting through rock in coal mines. Fascinated by its form Epstein had bought the drill second-hand in 1913 and cast the robot on the drill's tripod of stilts. The art critic of the *Manchester Guardian* wrote that Epstein had 'accepted it all, the actual rock drill is here in the art gallery', the bald statement itself indication enough of the aesthetically sensational nature of exhibiting what was in effect a 'found' object as a work of art. Later in the war Epstein stylized the driller and turned the sculpture into a stunted and armoured monster as his interpretation of the image evolved, under the influence of the war, from being a tribute to mankind's power over both Machine and Nature into a bitter admission that it was the Machine that had somehow gained control over mankind and was enabling the mass slaughter.

In his first article about art for *The New Age*, on 'The Critics and Mr Epstein', Hulme had referred to *Rock Drill* as a 'magnificent drawing' but chose not to elaborate, since it seemed to have been found intelligible 'even by the critics'. He preferred to defend the Epstein that interested him most and in the least intellectual way, as the artist of sexual frankness and creator of superb erotica. It was these aspects of Epstein's work that caused the real controversy among hostile critics, whose references to them as 'medical' or 'anatomical' drawings gave them a resonance far beyond the enclosed world of art. Comments he made later on in his letters to Kate Lechmere about Epstein's sexually explicit sculptures confirm the profound significance these had for him, and the deep personal satisfaction he felt in contemplation of the way in which these stone objects were able to render solid something as abstract and elusive as sex.

Aesthetically *Rock Drill* was probably the most extreme creation of the brief Vorticist era. After reducing it to a torso with a monstrous foetus Epstein seems to have felt he had gone as far as he wanted to in the direction of exploration and thereafter began a slow journey of return to the artistic mainstream, as the number of portrait busts of notables and friends he worked on from this time onwards indicates. These included the Admiral Lord Fisher; Iris Tree, the daughter of Sir Herbert Beerbohm Tree; Marie Beerbohm, the daughter of Max; Elizabeth Scott-Ellis, the daughter of Lord and Lady Howard de Walden; the Duchess of Hamilton; and the painter Muirhead Bone. Hulme was another in this assorted group of sitters, fitting in his sessions on periods of leave spent in London. 'I have been up in town lately a lot,' he told Marsh in his letter of 24 September, 'as Epstein has just finished doing my head.'

Although he was personally flattered to have his bust done by the artist he admired above all others, this perceptible change in Epstein's artistic development made it necessary for Hulme to practise a possibly unconscious ambivalence in his usually clear and concise judgements of works of art. He had attributed far-reaching significance to the return of geometrical or abstract art in the years immediately before 1914, seeing in it the dawning of a reawakened sense of original sin in Western man, and announcing it as the harbinger of a new era of epistemological modesty and heroic values in the service of a revitalized classical or religious view of life. Epstein's slow return to conventional representational work cannot have fitted easily into this vision. He had cast himself as John the Baptist to Epstein's Messiah, but it looked now as though Epstein had gone as far as he wanted to in the direction of revolution. On the other hand, Epstein remained committed to a frank sensuality in his work that transcended genres and styles, and this was at least as important a part of Hulme's intense admiration as the philosophical significance he had projected on to the work. Kate Lechmere, assessing the relationship, felt that the most likely scenario was that Epstein had embarked on the period of abstraction that led to *Rock Drill* and *Carvings in Flenite* directly under the influence of Hulme's conversation and theories, at a time when all his natural artistic instincts were those of the modeller; and that the Hulme-inspired Epstein was a magnificent aberration rather than the real Epstein, who was now, with the portrait busts, picking up again where he had left off before starting work on the Wilde monument. She obviously goes too far in suggesting that Hulme 'used Epstein as his medium to express his abstract art'; but it is easy to believe her when she suggests that Hulme 'became cross when Epstein created too many busts',[6] even when one of the busts in question was of himself. It was probably during the sittings in London that the idea of their doing a book together arose. This was to be, in Hulme's phrase, 'an essay on abstract sculpture'[7] to accompany a portfolio of photographs of Epstein's work, and it became the last thing on which he worked.

On 14 November 1916 Hulme was promoted to temporary 2nd lieu-tenant, attached to the *Crescent*[8] and sent to South Sutor in Cromarty in north Scotland. He wrote in telegrammatic haste to Kate to make a last date:

Dear K.D.

My affairs moving rapidly, very busy, may be off any minute. Had better go London Saturday. I must see various people, may be last leave. Can you meet me 6 London, Café [illegible . . .], then go to Atkinson's.[9] Meet me again at 11 p.m. in hotel. Will pay fare. Don't tell Atkinson. Keep it quiet. Do want you badly. Liked letter. Write again. I'll write properly to-morrow.

Yr. K.D[10]

A week later, contemplating the long hard stint of sexual abstinence that lay ahead in remote South Sutor, he renewed his membership of the London Library which he had allowed to lapse back in 1908.[11] Along with his books and his Epstein essay he planned to pass the time by resuming his contributions to *The New Age*. Shortly after arriving in Cromarty he wrote to thank Ogden for forwarding the latest issue of the *Cambridge Magazine* and giving him the new address to which to send subsequent issues. 'Now I have time to write,' he told him, 'I propose starting writing in the New Age again and am starting off with Russell's book, which seems very poor to me.'[12]

Hulme spent the next five months 'guarding the fleet in a little hut on top of heather cliffs'.[13] By early 1917 the total personnel of the garrison was over 600 men from the RMA and the RMLI whose primary duty was to man the heavy 9.2-inch guns and the 4-inch anti-submarine guns and searchlights covering the entrance to Cromarty Firth. With the outbreak of war most of the active service officers and men had to be withdrawn and substituted by reservists, officers and men who had returned wounded or invalided from the front, and temporary officers and others promoted from the ranks. Hulme had been posted as part of this latter group. No threat to the fleet base from the German submarines ever materialized, but the garrison was maintained in a high state of readiness. None of Hulme's surviving letters from South Sutor mentions daily life on the base at all, but a description written anonymously by an officer in March 1917 suggests that, despite the absence of danger, the posting was a rugged enough experience:

I wonder often how the medical officers who classify men as Class 'B' visualise this place. I would like to have one here and work with him for twenty-four hours. I would choose a typical winter day, blowing hard and raining. Meeting him at Cromarty, I would hustle him up three hundred feet over rough paths across the heather to – Battery. Then down a precipitous staircase to the sea-level and up about eighty or ninety feet to the lights: back up the aforesaid staircase, and down a very good imitation of the King Charles V steps at Gibraltar to the battery where they never see the sun from November to February and everything consequently drips and sweats. Thence back to Cromarty, taking *en route* a very secret building where about forty unfortunates live in a marsh.

Across the firth to the other side, and up an even rougher path to – Battery; down again to the water's edge as before by winding and precarious steps. Up to – Battery, four hundred feet, and down again to the water.

I would then let him rest till dark, when I would take him over the same ground without a light, for fear of enemy submarines at sea. There are other things I would show him: the bunks at the lights where men sleep and the spray comes in; the light gun shelters made of canvas, nice and breezy in the long winter nights. Finally I would get him to measure the cubic air space in a few huts, and then guess how many men had to be put into them.

I think I would then have convinced him that this is not a health resort, nor a suitable asylum for the aged and infirm. I know we are the 'nth' line and cannot expect the best men, but it is rough on some of the poor old gentlemen who are sent here.[14]

For recreation the men boxed and played quoits, with football and cricket in and out of season despite a rocky cricket pitch that dropped steeply to the sea at one end. Half a mile of potatoes were grown on a hillside, and wherever the mountainous terrain allowed it there was terrace gardening.

Quite how actively Hulme would have participated in all this is a moot point. He knew before the posting that his time there was not limitless and that he would be out in France again in a few months, so much of his free time would have been spent working on the essay about Epstein. Epstein had for some months been trying to interest publishers in the proposed book, and in the wake of the acclaim for his exhibition in the autumn of 1916 at the Leicester Galleries he found Grant Richards interested in the project. Richards had enjoyed his greatest success with various editions of A. E. Housman's *A Shropshire*

Lad. More recently he had published C. R. W. Nevinson's *Modern War* and was obviously hoping to do well with another book on art. On 1 January 1917 he wrote to Epstein:

Dear Mr Epstein,

thank you for your letter. I was talking to Mr Rider about the suggested book on Friday and told him how much the idea interested me. If anything is to come of it we ought to hurry, so I have to-day written to Mr Hulme. As I told Mr Rider, the first thing to do would be to get a collection of photographs and to see what would be available for use.

Sincerely yours
Grant Richards[15]

On the same day he wrote to Hulme:

Dear Sir,

Mr Epstein has written to me suggesting that I might care to consider the publication of a book of reproductions of his work, and he tells me that you already have the text for such a book in preparation and suggests that I should write to you. Might I see the manuscript and might I also see the collection of photographs of Mr Epstein's work which he tells me you have made? The book would I suppose be issued in form similar to Mr C. R. W. Nevinson's 'Modern War' which I have recently published.

Faithfully yours
Grant Richards

Although much of the ensuing three-way correspondence between Richards, Epstein and Hulme is missing there is enough to form a tentative idea of what kind of book this might have been, and to suggest a reason beyond his congenital laziness why it took Hulme a fatally long time to finish it. Replying on 5 January to questions in a lost letter from Hulme, Epstein informed him that he wanted him to stick to their agreed classification of works, which would be '1. Realistic works including portraits. 2 Decorative works. 3. Plastic and abstract essays.'[16] Referring to the portfolio of photographs Hulme had and which he was using as a reference in writing the essay, he said that he wanted to include among the portraits the bust of Hulme and the bust of his own mistress, Meum Stewart. Of later abstract works he proposed to include two photographs of the Venus carving.

Richards had suggested a frontispiece in colour, and Epstein was suggesting either the granite carving of the Venus or the head of Iris Tree.

Meanwhile Hulme, on the same day, had written to Richards giving a detailed list of the twenty-five illustrations he wanted to see in the book, referring him to page numbers in the portfolio which he was sending him by registered post. He wanted the book back to enable him to finish his writing, but promised to have a set of copies made for Richards. It is not clear whether Hulme himself took the original photographs, but his offer to have these 'specially printed darker to reproduce better' suggests at least some knowledge of the technical aspects of photography.

Either in a missing letter, or in conversation with Epstein, Richards had been given some idea of the final length of Hulme's accompanying essay, as well as a contractual proposal he did not favour:

January 8 1917

Dear Sir,

thank you for your letter. Since I wrote to you I have seen Mr Epstein, as you know. Twenty-five pictures is just the number that we want, unless – and this I should certainly like – we omit one and include instead of it the portrait of Mr Epstein – the one which Francis Bate did, in which he is represented by the side of a block of marble.

The length you propose is rather more than we wanted, but I daresay that can be overcome. But what we could not agree to is your reserving the American rights. The British public is not receptive and the sale of the book would not, I fear, be great, and the likelihood of our selling a certain number of copies in the American market is valuable. And as a matter of fact it is only a likelihood, and I am not by any means sure that an American publisher would want the book: that is to say, it would want some selling. I speak here from experience.

Your photographs have not yet arrived but I thought I had better write to you immediately.

Faithfully yours
Grant Richards

The answer does not seem to have satisfied Hulme. In another (lost) letter he seems to have pressed the point about the American rights as well as sought clarification of his financial position in the drafting of the contract. Richards would not be swayed:

January 17, 1917

Dear Sir,

I am sorry to say I could not insert in the agreement for Mr Epstein's book such a clause as you suggest. But I have talked the matter over with Mr Epstein and I understand he is willing to agree to pay you some share of whatever he may get out of the book in the way of royalties. That of course would be a matter between you and him. He suggested it as a way of getting over the point you raise.

The £10 would not be paid to you in advance of royalties; it would be paid for the copyright of your essay. May I now have the essay to read if, as I hope, it is finished?

Faithfully yours
Grant Richards

It was being made clear to Hulme that in the publisher's eyes he was very much the junior partner in the enterprise. There is an unmistakable touch of impatience in Richards's final request to see the essay, and at some point Hulme became anxious that he might be displaced as the writer of the text. Epstein had also raised these fears, perhaps unconsciously, when in the space of one letter he twice asked Hulme if it would not be possible for him to get leave to travel to London for a couple of days to talk about the illustrations and the book, complaining that in Hulme's absence 'it seems to me impossible to do this job properly and indicate definitely what photographs should be included'.[17] He felt under pressure from Richards to get on with things and capitalize on the interest in the Leicester Galleries show. He reassured Hulme on both counts, however, affirming that he would, as soon as he got the contract from Richards, 'look into it and see that the American part of it is safe-guarded, that is that I receive royalties on the American sales. I will share with you the royalties both here and in America.' In the event of disagreement he would take Hulme's advice and seek out his old friend J. C. Squire, whose career as a writer had taken off by this time and who had considerable experience in resolving contractual difficulties with publishers.[18] And he gave short shrift to the suggestion that someone else might be brought in to do the writing:

23 Guildford St. W.C.

My dear Hulme. I'm sorry you have not finished the foreword for the book but I've no notion of 'letting you down'. Grant Richards is naturally impatient at the delay as there is tremendous interest in my show. I will not consent to anyone but you doing the foreword for the book. At present G. R. is quite willing to go on but if he should drop it then we can get another publisher and certainly I don't much care for G.R.'s idea about making it a 'popular' book. I've looked forward to something better than that for my own satisfaction and perhaps publishing with Lane[19] or on our own will give us a better book [. . .][20]

Neither Hulme nor Epstein was impressed by what Richards had done with the Nevinson book, Epstein dismissing it as 'cheap in get up and the sort of popular monograph that there's been too much of ',[21] and it may have been, in the first place, an increasing sense that what Richards wanted was another 'popular monograph' that was holding Hulme up. In the second place, he may have been trying to fathom the ambivalence in his own attitude to Epstein's work, as well as interpret it properly. Did Epstein have some sneaking awareness that Hulme, as his devoted apologist, now felt that he was producing too much figurative art, that he was 'cross with him', as Kate Lechmere put it, for doing all these busts? The Epstein Hulme had written about so passionately in 1914 was not the Epstein he was trying to write about in 1917. His head might have been willing to write about the numerous busts, but his heart made it a struggle to do so with the proper enthusiasm.

Epstein seems to have sensed that Hulme was in a dilemma and to have tried to help him resolve it. He wrote telling Hulme that Richards was 'appalled' by the abstract works, but 'all of them will go in' – the three flenites, the two photos of *Rock Drill*, the doves. Richards had made no secret of the fact that 'the important things were the portraits, from a "popular" point of view'. Epstein had told him that a book of portraits alone was of no interest to him. Richards was set on the Iris Tree bust as the coloured frontispiece, Epstein was adamant that it should be the *Rock Drill* torso as more representative of his work – and, presumably, more relevant to Hulme's own idea of what he was writing, an 'essay on abstract art' that focused on Epstein's work. He offered Hulme some specific and supportive advice, telling him he would like his text to be as 'comprehensive as you can make it, and to dwell mostly on my abstract works and "plastic aims" in sculpture, referring to my realistic works as a beginning or foundation for the others'. Somewhere in among all this Hulme may have found himself caught between his desire to write about an idealized Epstein whose work he could use to get his visionary ideas across to a wider audience than he could ever have reached with his *New Age* articles, and his respect for Epstein's understandable desire for a book that was mainly concerned with his own development as an artist. This dilemma may be the best explanation for the long delay in producing an essay that could surely have amounted at the most to a hundred pages of prose.

The last surviving communication between Hulme and Richards is a brief note of 26 February 1917 from Richards relating that he is, in accordance with instructions in a telegram from Hulme, returning the book of photographs to him. That seems rather final, but it need not have any significance beyond Hulme's still needing the pictures to write his text. Certainly the project was still very much alive in March, when Hulme wrote to Kate Lechmere and proudly referred her to a supplement devoted to Epstein in the *Sketch*, a weekly paper with a profile not unlike that of today's *Country Living*, which had an article on the Leicester Galleries exhibition and a portfolio of illustrations of Epstein's sculpture. The article called Epstein 'the greatest sculptor in England today' and announced that 'a book dealing with his art and the theory of his latest works, written by Lieutenant T. E. Hulme and illustrated with photographs is to be shortly published by Grant Richards under the title "The Sculpture of Epstein" '.[22] Writing to Edward Marsh in April Hulme told him that he had 'practically finished' the essay. And on his last leave, during his final tour of duty in France, he told Kate Lechmere that he had 'finished his manuscript for his Epstein book'.[23]

*

After five months in the highland remoteness of Cromarty Hulme was recalled to Eastney at the end of March 1917. He had caught the eye of his commanding officers both at Eastney and Cromarty, who wrote on his military record that he was 'very promising. Should do well with more experience in handling men.' His exceptional talents as a mathematician were also noted and he was to be recommended for advancement 'in due course'.

It was probably the mathematical skills that were responsible for his being handpicked for the task of manning the heavy guns of the Royal Marine Artillery Siege Train on the beach at Dunkirk. After six weeks of waiting at Eastney he was told, on 19 May, that he was being posted to the *Attentive II*, the supply ship for the siege train guns, and that he was to leave for France immediately.

15

Art, Sex and Death

Three months after the introduction of conscription, in the summer of 1916, Epstein had received his call-up papers. Almost at once Hulme had become involved in a campaign mounted by the sculptor's wife and friends to secure his exemption; failing that, to make sure that if he was compelled to join up he would at least be kept out of the firing line.

Three aspects complicated the issue: Epstein had been a British citizen for only three years; he was at the outbreak of a 'young man's' war already thirty-five years of age; and the campaign was mounted in the face of growing public unease about the way in which artists were being granted exemptions, not as pacifists (although they almost invariably were), but on what were seen as the questionable grounds that an artist's life was in an absolute sense worth more than that of an ordinary working man. Hulme became involved through his friendship with Edward Marsh at the Admiralty and the possibility that he might be able to persuade Marsh to use his influence once again on Winston Churchill. Other figures engaged in the campaign by Epstein's wife Margaret included Orage, Muirhead Bone, E. P. Scott, who was editor of the *Manchester Guardian*, and the Admiral Lord Fisher, whose bust Epstein had recently completed. The novelist John Buchan on the HQ staff of the British Army was another, as was the Duke of Marlborough. Epstein's wealthy American patron, John Quinn, was also asked to write letters. Frank Newbolt, brother of the poet Henry whom Hulme knew from his poetry-writing days, was employed to represent Epstein at the Military Tribunal.

The series of letters Hulme wrote to Marsh, some of the longest and most legible to have survived ('I have tried to write as legibly as possible'), were no doubt as effective as anyone else's in procuring for Epstein the series of short-term exemptions which carried him through until a final rejection of his appeal in September 1917, by which time he was effectively assured of surviving the rest of the war without having to face danger. They cast light on Hulme on two counts: by confirming the profound and almost religious faith he had in the value of art, and by extension the exceptional status of artists; and by their moving display of concern for the fate of another which far outweighs any concern ever expressed over his own safety. In this light they give a quite different meaning to the one intended by Wyndham Lewis when he coined his mantra 'Epstein is Hulme, Hulme is Epstein' as a way of trying to persuade Kate Lechmere to stay away from Hulme.

The first letter was sent from Eastney Barracks on 24 September 1916, a few days before Epstein was due to appear before the tribunal at Holborn:

[. . .] I really do think this case is on an entirely different footing to the others. It is not like the case of a young artist who *might* do something. He is I believe about 37. Moreover, he is doing something in an art in which nobody else is doing anything. There will unfortunately always be plenty of writers, but there are not more than 3 or 4 sculptors. He is not a conscientious objector, and if he is not exempted will serve I suppose in infantry. If everyone were really serving there might be less of a case here, but considering the kind of people who do get exemption and the reasons they do get exempted for, I do think it would be scandalous if he got killed [. . .][1]

The throwaway remark that 'unfortunately' there will always be 'plenty of writers' contra the '3 or 4 sculptors' establishes clearly Hulme's order of precedence in the arts. Nevertheless he found it politic to assure Marsh, whose tastes in sculpture were conventional, that he was certain he would like Epstein's 'later work', a reassurance Marsh took up in his reply to the letter when he referred to Epstein's having journeyed 'into regions where I had no hope of following him', and his delight at Hulme's assurances that Epstein was 'returning to the tradition', which seems to be slightly more than Hulme was saying. He told Hulme that direct interference by the government was obviously out of the question, but that he was not unduly alarmed at

Epstein's prospects – 'I can't imagine they wd. send a fat middle-aged man into the firing line. I do think he's almost certain to be kept for Home Defence.'[2]

Hulme's next letter, also written from Eastney, but after his five-month sojourn in Cromarty and just a few weeks before he was sent out to join the siege guns, was again written at the request of Margaret Epstein with a view to influencing the outcome of the tribunal that was due to hear Epstein's next appeal, in May 1917. In this he laid stress on the possibility of getting Epstein to do some work of national importance 'eg membership of one of those Red Cross committees that get up art shows, or anything of that kind would be sufficient'.[3]

The May appeal failed. The tribunal ordered that Epstein be called up in three days' time, recognizing his contributions to society as an artist and expressing the hope that he would win 'fresh laurels in the trenches'. Frank Newbolt again won leave to appeal the decision, and at the rehearing on 6 June Epstein was granted another three months' exemption. The newspapers had a field day in reporting the verdict. In an interview in the *Evening Standard* the painter Sir Philip Burne-Jones expressed indignation at the spectacle of Epstein's repeated exemptions, noting that 'some of our most gifted artists have, without protest, or the publicity of two continents,[4] gone quietly and ungrudgingly to the Front to make the supreme sacrifice' and hinting strongly that it was Epstein's fashionable status that was protecting him. The Burne-Jones article whipped up a dozen or more indignant responses from artists who rejected the use of the word 'genius' in describing Epstein and wrote to various newspapers demanding that he do his duty and join up like anyone else. G. K. Chesterton in the *Sunday Herald* pointed out that a dangerous principle would be established, if one were to say that 'because a man is a great artist' he should not be called upon to share the duties of ordinary citizenship. There were many in Epstein's circle, including Hulme, who believed that the responses were largely the result of a campaign orchestrated by a man named Horace de Vere Cole who had a great personal antipathy towards Epstein. Be that as it may, the paradoxical result of the newspaper articles and letters was that it was the outraged artists rather than the outraged public who finally compelled the military to announce that they would be reconsidering Epstein's exemption. At a rapidly convened hearing in July

ART, SEX AND DEATH

his appeal for further exemption was refused, no more appeals would be entertained, and his call-up date was irrevocably set for 6 September.

Epstein assumed that Hulme could not be counted on to pull his Marsh-string after this. He wrote to Bernard van Dieren, 'Hulme, of course, is indignant and says he will write but he is in a busy part of Flanders and I know how dilatory he is in any case'.[5] But he was wrong. Hulme's last letter in support of the Epstein campaign turned out to be the most closely considered of all his contributions:

> Royal Naval Siege Guns
> Barbara Camp
> A.P.O S (10)
> B.E.F.
> Thursday July 26

Dear Marsh,

I expect you are rather tired of hearing from me about Epstein, but the news that *Winston* is again in the Cabinet[6] makes me think it just possible that the position you told me of in your last letter might have ended, and that you might again be able to do something.

You will probably have seen in the papers that Epstein's appeal for exemption has been refused and that he has been called *up on September 6*. The circumstances of the thing make me more angry than the fact itself. Epstein was given, a short time ago, three months exemption by the Law Society Tribunal. Upon this there appeared in the Daily Mail, Daily Sketch etc what looked to me even out here a series of protests against his exemption having all the appearance of an *organised conspiracy* – in which amongst the names of a lot of artists, like Brangwyn, who naturally protested at anyone else getting more mentions than themselves, [was] a note from G. K. Chesterton saying that the artist should no more be immune than anyone else.

I have since found out that the whole thing was a conspiracy. Horace Cole, the man who did the Dreadnought hoax,[7] wrote to the military representative whom he happened to know and to Phillip [sic] Burne-Jones and organised the whole series of protests in the papers. The spectacle of Burne-Jones solemnly giving interviews to half a dozen papers, in the name of art, and giving his views on what Epstein ought to do, is you must admit exasperating. Even if Epstein ought to go in the army, I don't think that this beastly little type of conspiracy is the means by which he ought to be forced in. There is something I think fearfully revolting in the spectacle of all these people in reality giving vent to their private spite and being able to do it in patriotic phrases. I'd willingly give a year's pay, or undergo an extra day's shelling in order to be able to beat these beastly people.

Of course Chesterton is quite right on the general principle that the artist has no more claim to immunity than anybody else. We're all equal in that sense I suppose. But that isn't the point. Is the state making an economical use of its material and ought it not to preserve a sculptor like E. in exactly the same way that it would preserve the only man who was capable of making some particular kind of instrument – not because instrument-makers were as men more valuable than anyone else.

However all these kinds of arguments need not be brought in. It isn't as if we were really a country *in extremis* and calling up our last men. I know a young man of 22 in Macclesfield whose father makes silk ties and makes some of them for the navy. He gave himself one of the badges intended for the workmen and has not even had the necessity to go before the tribunal at all. I know personally of many similar cases. That being the case, I think one ought to do all one can, even to the extent of pestering an acquaintance, to see that Epstein is not wasted, like Gaudier was, when these kind of people escape.

I don't know whether you have read any of the many casual notices of the affair, in papers like the Bystander and so on. They really make me feel quite uncomfortable, and make me believe that after all the Germans may have something in their chatter about our hypocrisy. A nation that took 2 years to get conscripted, that even now is less conscripted than any of the allies, need not raise a complacent hue and cry because a Polish Jew living in America till he was well over twenty and then after that fairly cosmopolitan, who has only been naturalised about a year or so before the war, probably to please his wife – does not show the same anxiety to interrupt his natural life and waste his time.

I feel convinced that if something is not done he will be drafted in the ordinary way to infantry and I want at all costs to prevent that.

Do you think that anything could be done for him now – not to get him out altogether of course, that is not possible, but to ensure that he gets some kind of job that will at any rate keep him out of infantry – I don't know how of course, but I thought that in some way Churchill might help – if his articles are anything to go by, he certainly has very *intelligent* pessimistic views about the war, and was never one of the idiots who have drivelled about winning the war on the Western Front.

[...]

I hope you will excuse my bothering you with all this. I have tried to write as legibly as possible. But the thing worries me very much – the feeling of impotence against such a stupid situation. I shall be more grateful than I can say if you can do anything – I might even present Churchill with an Epstein, or Epstein might do a head of him.

But *do* if you possibly can – the thing is really tragic, I think.

Yours sincerely

T. E. Hulme Lieut. R.M.

Some months before it happened, in a speculative moment that turned out to be prophetic, Ezra Pound had written that if the Germans succeeded in killing Gaudier-Brzeska they would have done more harm to art than they already had by the destruction of Rheims Cathedral, for a destroyed building could with some ease be restored, 'but the uncreated forms of a man of genius cannot be set forth by another'.[8] Hulme's attitude to the prospect of Epstein's death was identical. Three times in the course of his letters to Marsh he mentions Gaudier's fate as a terrible cautionary reminder of the likelihood of being killed in the artillery. Nor was his support for Epstein inconsistent with his opposition to pacifism. He would have been quite happy to see him involved in the war effort in some way, so long as his life was not put at risk. Hulme's letter was actually shown to Churchill,[9] but by that time Hulme had heard from Margaret Epstein that Epstein had enlisted in Colonel Patterson's Jewish Battalion. In the same long and grateful letter of 7 September informing him of this development Margaret Epstein acknowledged receipt of his last cheque on 3 September,[10] a reminder that Hulme was still diligently paying off instalments on the Epsteins he had bought.

Writers were plentiful. Painters too, presumably. Real sculptors were rare enough to warrant the status of protected species. Hulme's argument brought him curiously close to a position taken by Bertrand Russell on the issue of pacifism, but which Russell saw from the reverse angle. Russell advocated the extreme anti-realist position that there was no natural right to violence even in self-defence. The only case in which killing in self-defence might be justified would be that of a man uniquely in possession of an important mathematical theorem which would increase the sum of important truths in the world and would be irrevocably lost to the world should he fail to survive the attack.[11] Epstein was as important to Hulme and to the world as his hypothetical mathematician was to Russell.

*

In the absence of regular female company at Cromarty Hulme, like any other soldier, had struggled with the problems of sexual abstinence. Faced with the choice of ignoring his needs completely or indulging them in some way that gave at least some slight approximation to normal sexual life he opted for the latter. Tentatively at first, later with a focused abandon that at times verged on the pathological, he wrote letters of compellingly intense desire to Kate Lechmere, and with all the gratitude of a drug addict received similar letters from her in return. Just occasionally they contain news, and one or two mingle in an almost surrealist way the pornographic and the aesthetic, reflecting perhaps the pressure of his continuing attempts to get the Epstein monograph written. Most of them are in pencil, most are in large part illegible. None is dated, but in a letter from Cromarty there is an example of this surreal mixing of themes in what is evidently a reply to the first letter he received from Kate in which she has fully understood his needs. It shows very clearly the extent to which the sexuality of Epstein's art was an important part of Hulme's admiration for it, as well as refining the reactionary simplicity of his attitude towards women: he wants Kate as his sexual equal, as shameless and open in her sexual curiosity as he is himself shameless and open:

Dear K.D.

I liked your letter immensely. Do write to me by return again like that. I like anything that makes sex seem solid just as I like heavy pieces of sculpture which make fugitive things seem fixed. Your letter made sex seem solid because it was frank and healthy interest in the possession of your C. That's good. Solid and exciting. I feel like that too. I liked Epstein's statue with the C. like a pillar and I like to think of the knuckleduster for the same reason. It fixes our sex in a solid way. I think your letter makes sex seem solid because it is good healthy sensuality [illegible . . .] I wish I could put my hand on it. I like more than anything what you do in the morning. Do you do it every morning really. I like to think that you do – that is a good solid sensual excess. I like that. Tell me if you do. I like to close my eyes and imagine it every morning. I hate to think of women graciously giving themselves, as if it were a condescension. I like to think of them as wet and straining for it. Actively taking steps to get it. You know the way one hand with fingers outstretched can interlace with another with hand similarly outstretched. I like to think of our bodies like that, the x limbs being the interlacing fingers holding us close together with that whatever electric thing in the middle and with our bodies and legs as a sort of web or shield, made safe for the time being. A kind of sheltered glove for the time being inside which the delicate sucking, pumping operation can go on.

Your letter being for the first time really frank in the way I like excited me so much that it brought back the atmosphere and almost the smell of very early sex when about 16 [illegible . . .] wandering about in a wood in the country and with a delicious aching and the desire to go it hot in the hay or in a loft. Do you understand what I mean by early sex here. When did you first think of it. I want the soft sucking sponge all round the pillar now. Up and down, drawing it up and down. Do write by return. Of course, I came before I got to the end of the letter.[12]

In another letter he returns to the sexual element in Epstein's work:

[illegible . . .] I like them because they show how our own imaginings about sex-symbols are the same as those that lay behind religious myths. It appears that the way of getting fire by rubbing pieces of wood together,[13] the top one rotating as it bores into the lower one, is sexual and part of all religious rites. Very like Epstein's Rock Drill, isn't it. A [illegible . . .] stick into soft wood and the fire that comes of it.

Later in the same letter he refers to a sexual dream in which he saw a woman on the wall 'like a Byzantine mosaic', with outstretched hands and fingers tipped with red knots that suggested multiple vaginas to him.

By writing to her in this obsessive way Hulme was able to make himself a constant and vivid sexual presence in her mind. He describes the smell of his sperm to her, he imagines her sitting under the table and taking him in her mouth, he imagines the sperm flowing into her mouth, sees her floating in the air in front of his face with her legs apart and his tongue inside her. At one point he borrowed a copy of the *Arabian Nights* from the London Library and, having studied it himself, sent it on to her. In the next few letters he asked for her reactions to the book: after she read page sixty, did she lay the book down on the bed or on the floor? Did she pull up her nightgown? Did she masturbate under the sheet or did she throw back the bedclothes first? He wants to know everything. 'Tell me exactly how often,' he instructs her. 'I love to think of women being lascivious.'

None of Kate's letters to him survive, but from Hulme's responses it is clear that she now and then felt alarmed by the intensity and monotony of his letters and sought some assurance that she was something more to him than just an assemblage of holes. He answered as honestly as he could:

I like to feel real mechanical lust and lasciviousness in my muscles. It seems more real and permanent then. You want to know if I like your cunt because I like *you*. I always want to feel certain that you don't like *it* because you like me, but that you like *it* because you *do* like it.

In a later letter answering yet another request for some kind of assurance he goes slightly further, telling her that 'Of course I feel very friendly to you apart from sex, but sex makes the thing burn.' And the letter that informed her of his posting to France on 19 May contained what was by now the standard mingling of the factual and the sexual:

> R.M.A.
> Heavy Siege Train
> c/o G.P.O.

Dear K.D.

Came over here last week in fearful rush . . . [illegible . . .] So you won't see me for three months at least. Ordered away suddenly, no warning. No time to see you. Write me long hot letter. Last night it was in a delirious state, a sort of film of aching all over the surface of it. I loved last time. I like the noise you make – the more excited you seem, the more excited it makes me. So you see I must have an attraction. Don't tell Mrs Bevan I am here, let her find out some other way.[14]

Dear I want to f.you badly.

Yr K.D.[15]

*

Following the German occupation of Ostend in 1915 a number of guns had been landed and positioned on the coast to counter the German batteries mounted in the south-western suburbs, including four 11-inch guns with a range of 30,000 yards, and a huge 15-inch gun, the 'Leugenboom', which posed a constant threat to Allied shipping off the Belgian coast. This original Royal Naval Siege Train consisted of four 9.2-inch guns and one 12-inch gun, the 'Dominion', which was operated from a farm, with a skeleton barn built over it as camouflage. The 9.2s were mounted well forward near Nieuport Bains, two of them, the 'Eastney' and the 'Barbara', in concrete gunpits near Groenendijk, with the other two, the 'Carnac' batteries, about 400 yards to the rear of them. These four, with two 6-inch guns and another 9.2 on a railways mounting, formed the unit known as the Royal Naval Siege Guns.

In February 1917, as part of the preparations for the Passchendaele offensive in July, several more guns were added and the unit separated into the Royal Naval Siege Guns and the RMA Heavy Siege Train. Both were under the admiral of the Dover Patrol and both were borne on the supply books of the *Attentive II*. Hulme was sent out to join the siege train and the crew manning the 'Barbara',[16] one of the two forward 9.2-inch guns. He described the latest cindery landscape to Kate:

I am with big guns. We get shelled almost every day, but are well protected. The man I relieved was killed by a shell, but I don't think this is at all likely to happen to me. We are very comfortable. (Don't tell Atkinson all this as everybody's own affairs are quite private.[17]) I am in the sand dunes on the Belgian coast. It's a very curious life [illegible . . .], all surrounded by a landscape of sand.

Two more letters written at about this time from Barbara Camp describe a very different kind of war from the one he had experienced in the trenches with the HAC. One is the sole surviving letter written to his mother:

Royal Naval Siege Guns
Barbara Camp
A.P.O. S.10
B.E.F.
Wednesday

Dear Mother

I have been out here now for over a month, and though it is unlike what I expected, I must say that so far I am very well satisfied. I may later on get a different job which will be even better, as it will be one where my knowledge of mathematics will be useful.[18]

I am over two miles behind the front line trenches, but of course in this war that as far as shelling is concerned is no protection. We get shells at us nearly every day [missing lines . . .] hit us continually and do no damage. The only place we are likely to get hit is in the open on our way down. But there is a chance now that our way of life may very soon be altered considerably whether for the better or worse we do not know. Everything here of course depends on the weather, the worse it is the better for us, for though the Germans know to a yard where my gun is, yet they can't hit it unless there is an aeroplane up to tell them whether their shells are getting near it or not – and in cloudy weather of course they can see nothing. When therefore we get up in the morning and see the sky completely covered with clouds we say 'What a beautiful day'. But it is only in the last few [missing lines . . .]

At night I come back from the gun and live in quite a comfortable camp. A long wooden building, kind of long, flat bungalow, with a veranda and quite a nice view over the sands. After dinner we sit there on easy chairs. I have electric light in my cabin and read in bed. Of course all this comfort is very insecure. Every now and then a shell comes near and we have ignominiously to leave the place. But that doesn't happen often. The most disagreeable things here are the gas alarms. Sometime about 2.a.m. you hear great horns blowing all over the country like New Years Eve at home. You have to jump up, put on your gas mask, dress and go down to the guns, ready for the attack. Of course you can't see very well in them, the goggles get dimmed, you feel you are being choked and the whole thing is rather a nightmare. But I'd rather spend a year here than a month in the trenches I used to be in. I have plenty of time for my own private work. Then again I like being in a French section (we are the only English here) and meeting French officers. It's all much more amusing.

Remember me to Father and Kate

Yr affectionate son

Ernest

The memory of New Year's Eves appears to be only the second such reference to home in all Hulme's surviving correspondence, along with the brief allusion to Gratton Hall in one of the 'Trench Diary' letters in 1915.

The other letter was that of 26 July to Edward Marsh already quoted, in which his main concern was for Jacob Epstein's safety. Apologizing for the frequency with which he was raising the matter Hulme goes on to mitigate his intrusion by giving Marsh some rare personal news, including an explanation of the fact that he is now with the Royal Naval Siege Guns rather than the Marines Siege Train:

[...]
I personally, compared with the life I led in the infantry out here in 1914–15, lead a very agreeable life. I am entirely with Naval people – my 'mate' at the gun is a man called Bill Adams,[19] who was Shackleton's second in command in the South Pole expedition and then went into Labour Exchange work.

We are right on the sea, and there is something about sand, whether it is the suggestion of promenades, piers and bands I don't know, which entirely takes away the sordid quality of the war. It was also very amusing when I first came out being with the French as part of their artillery. I had lunch with the French commandant of heavy artillery the day before they left and he said 'I should like to remain here, very much, as a spectator'. He no doubt anticipated exactly what has since happened. Unfortunately the English army seems so constructed that it has not yet realised what an extraordinary discovery language is and what a lot of trouble can be saved by acquiring information that way, instead of by knocks on the head. [...]

In June 1917 the British had taken over the sector in preparation for the Passchendaele offensive and both the RN Siege Guns and the RMA

Heavy Siege Train came under the control of the Fourth British Army. Hulme's dislike of this development was repeated to Ashley Dukes, who came into the same part of the line in June. Dukes visited him a number of times in his mess and recalled his uneasy certainty that the relatively quiet war he had experienced so far under the direction of the French was about to come to an end. He was still teetotal and never touched the rum served to his unit as part of the rations. He was the only abstainer in the unit, an oddity that caused some to suppose that he was treating a venereal disease; Dukes knew that the real explanation was his desire to remain in control of his faculties at all times. His belief in the truth of heroic values involved no desire for a hero's death, and on the walks they sometimes took together he ridiculed the crudity and brutality of trench warfare, affirming that long-range gunnery was the way to win the war, 'eliminate Germans scientifically, at a range of nine miles'.[20] Dukes recalled his careful and life-preserving routines, how he had never even walked as far as Nieuport, a mile in front of his guns, 'because he objected to coming under rifle fire'. Accompanying Dukes one day on his way into the line he took his leave of him at a ruined dairy along the road, explaining that this was 'the utmost limit of his constitutional'.

Hulme's surmise that life was about to become more dangerous after June turned out to be correct:

Friday

Dear K.D.

You will have seen from the papers that the English have taken over the line from the French, so that our whole situation and life here changes – in many ways for the worse as far as comfort is concerned – leaves little time for writing.

I was walking along a road here which was in full view of [missing lines . . .]

I am at the present moment sitting in a little dug out, which I have assisted to make, in view of the [illegible . . .] time we now expect. It has about 12 feet of sand on top of it. Contains two little beds and is about 8ft square – a telephone and a little table. I hope to work but the working all day with the spade makes it difficult for me to hold the pen properly [end missing . . .]

268

In the intensified fighting the Germans mounted a major attack on Nieuport and Lombartzyde on 10–11 July, with the 15-inch 'Leugenboom' still the great opponent, establishing themselves so close to the British guns that the 'Eastney' and 'Barbara' batteries became untenable, with their crews repeatedly coming under machine-gun fire that prevented them working. Several of the guns received direct hits and one 9.2 was cut in two by an 11-inch shell. The whole crew of the 'Carnac' were killed or wounded by a single shell, and there were serious losses from repeated gas attacks. Even in their sand-bedded dugouts the crews took a terrible pounding. Wyndham Lewis was also stationed near Nieuport at the time and was able to see the siege gunners, 'big specks across intervening fields', as they dodged the debris flung far and wide by the shells coming over from the naval guns at Ostend. 'The life of war is conducive to a certain clannishness, if not exclusiveness,' he wrote in *Blasting and Bombardiering* to account for the fact that he and others in his unit never thought to fraternize with their British comrades – in his case especially not once he found out that Hulme was among them.

Hulme, in the midst of this hell, carried on writing fevered letters to the woman who had come between Lewis and himself. Could she send him a photograph of herself naked? She must write to him at once, send him another 'awful' letter. And in a passage of tormented longing he conjures up for her a picture of where he would much rather be and what he wants to do with her when the whole thing is over:

I like being in the country. We could go one afternoon one summer, you with a cotton skirt on, *nothing* above your stockings. We'll swim like ducks and then do it. I like the hot feeling of summer . . .

Hulme was on leave in the middle of September. From a brief note,[21] in which he asked Frank Flint to come along to Frith Street and bring with him the French poet Jean de Bosschère, whose work Flint was translating, it seems that he managed to keep this remarkable salon going to the very end, albeit in greatly reduced form. He travelled to Endon to see his family, where his sister noticed a great change in him, as though he realized it might be his last leave. Back in London he spent the night at a hotel with Kate Lechmere. In the morning he had to get up early to go to Victoria to catch the train for the Channel and France. He stood in silence in the doorway for about a minute as she lay watching him from the bed. 'I can't swallow,' he said before he left.[22]

Some two weeks later, on 28 September 1917, four days after his thirty-fourth birthday, Hulme suffered a direct hit from a large shell which literally blew him to pieces. Apparently absorbed in some thought of his own he had failed to hear it coming and remained standing while those around threw themselves flat on the ground. What was left of him was buried in the Military Cemetery at Koksijde, West-Vlaanderen, in Belgium where – no doubt for want of space – he is described simply as 'One of the war poets'. His name is also remembered on the Hulme family vault in the newer part of the cemetery at St Luke's Church, Endon Bank. Four years after his death a memorial window designed by Dolly Kibblewhite's father, Thomas Curtis, was installed in the North Aisle of St Luke's, showing the soldier and the scholar, St Michael and St Augustine, with a text from The Commendment of the Book of Common Prayer which was found written on a piece of paper in the pocket of Hulme's uniform at the time of his death. It seems an appropriately cindery farewell:

> Thou only art immortal
> The Creator and Maker of Man
> But we are mortal formed
> Of the Earth and unto Earth We
> Shall return for so didst
> Thou ordain when thou
> Created me saying Dust
> Thou art and unto Dust shall
> Thou return All We go down
> To the Dust and weeping o'er the
> Grave we make our song
> Allelujah.

Epilogue

Hulme's essay on Jacob Epstein disappeared at his death and has never reappeared. It seems reasonable to suppose that he was carrying it on his person at the time and that it was blown up with him. Epstein himself preferred another explanation, which he offered in a letter to his American patron, John Quinn:

You ask me about Hulme and the book he wrote on my work. Alas, all is lost. In some mysterious way everything disappeared. He had the finished manuscript with him in France; also a large and carefully selected book of photographs of my sculptures which he intended to use for the book. The manuscript he had worked on for over a period of two years and it was a very careful and original statement of my aims in sculpture and an estimate of my achievement and it would have fulfilled for me what I have desired, a serious and non-journalistic account of my sculpture without any deferring to the taste of the editors or public. Hulme's effects all disappeared and no trace of them can be found. To think that not only his body and brain was smashed up but also the work of his brain is appalling for as well other manuscripts which I know he was writing also were lost. Mind you these things were lost in his billet. Hulme was killed outside his gunpit, and the disappearance of Hulme's effects have nothing to do with any shell hit.[1]

Epstein was writing just five months after Hulme's death and, as he made clear on many occasions in later life, he had lost a friend he loved dearly and a critic with a profound understanding of his artistic vision. He was also in the middle of long-running difficulties with the military tribunals which were undecided whether to send him to the front or allow him to remain at home in some other capacity as an enlisted man. He seems to have been alone in suspecting that Hulme's belongings had been stolen, and it is possible that his distress and his troubles fomented a paranoid explanation to accompany his disappointment.[2] The disappearance of the monograph remains a matter of regret for art historians. Richard Cork, art critic of *The Times*, calls its loss 'deplorable' and the essay itself one of the 'missing links in the history of early British modernism'.[3] An enigmatic and tantalizing survival of the project is a portfolio of photographs, battered and brown-speckled, in the archives of the Brynmor Jones Library at Hull, with Hulme's own handwritten list identifying the various pieces to be used in the book.[4]

Epstein, of course, went on to fame and the respectability of a knighthood. Pound and Lewis became famous for their contributions to the world of art and, in the fullness of time, notorious for their political views. Orage, losing his residual faith in Guild Socialism, closed *The New Age* in 1922 and took up the thread of mysticism that had always been part of the magazine's profile under his editorship. He left for America to become a disciple of the Russian mystic George Gurdjieff and did not return to England until 1931, when he founded another literary magazine, *The New English Weekly*, which he edited until his death in 1934. Of the old Poets' Club group, Francis Tancred developed a mental illness shortly after the war and died in an institution. Dermot Freyer published a volume of short stories, *Not All Joy*, in 1932, but his name remains unknown to historians of Irish literature. F. S. Flint stopped writing verse after 1920 and began a career in the civil service at the Ministry of Labour. He continued to translate and comment on French poetry until his death in 1960. Hulme's friend and former landlord Ashley Dukes pursued with some success his career as a dramatist, critic and theatre manager. He published an autobiography, *The Scene is Changed*, in 1942, but is largely remembered now for his comedy *The Man with a Load of Mischief*. He died in 1959. To all of them Hulme remained a vivid memory throughout their lives. All, in memoirs or letters, spoke of how much they missed his stimulating presence. Most would have concurred in the sentiments expressed by Richard Curle in regretting the paucity and brevity of Hulme's letters, that it was 'a pity, because they convey the merest shadow of his personality, which was, I am inclined to think, the most remarkable one I have ever come across'.[5]

Dolly Kibblewhite and Kate Lechmere, the only two 'named' women in Hulme's life – if one can put it like that – would probably have nodded their assent too. The will Hulme made out in Dolly's favour in 1915 seems to have been lost at the time. A letter of administration dated 27 July 1921 states that Hulme 'made and duly executed his last Will and Testament and did not therein name any Executor or Residuary Legatee or Devisee' and his estate, valued at £232 5s 4d, duly passed to his father, his mother Mary having died of cancer of the spine in 1920. Dolly fortunately had no need of the money, having considerable private means. After a brief court appearance in 1930 as a witness in a case involving Epstein and the sale of some allegedly forged works of art that was reported in the national press[6] she dropped out of artistic circles and left London to live quietly in a succession of West Sussex country cottages in Heyshott and Pulborough, gardening, cycling and looking after her two Siamese cats. In old age she had the pleasure of overseeing a reconciliation between her own two children and those of her husband Gilbert's second marriage, contracted in Australia. If the magical act of burning Hulme's letters was intended to help her forget, she made certain to sabotage the gesture by hanging on to a sturdy pair of boots that had once belonged to him. Some thirty years after his death, and shortly before her own in 1947, she ceremoniously handed them on to her grandson Martin, who recalls with fond admiration that he got several more years' wear out of them before they finally turned up their toes in Sweden in 1955.[7]

Kate Lechmere never married, and it seems safe to say that Hulme was the love of her life. The letters written to Michael Roberts in the 1930s as Roberts was preparing his study of Hulme have an almost therapeutic intensity as she recalls in reckless detail the intimate memories of the time she and Hulme spent together, in ways that both she and Roberts knew could never possibly be used in his book. Roberts, a sympathetic and understanding correspondent, was a good foil for her grief. After a professional life as a milliner she retired and enjoyed a role as a living witness of the birth of Vorticism, Wyndham Lewis's early career, the Rebel Arts Centre and, of course, Hulme and the beginnings of the Imagist movement in poetry. In the early 1950s Samuel Hynes befriended her in London, when she was living in a house in Oakley Gardens, Chelsea, near the Albert Bridge, and taking in lodgers. Hynes enjoyed many a drink with her as she freely and frankly reminisced about the old days in London. She told him of a simple, touching dream she had had just after the war, in which she saw Hulme 'standing in the sun, looking happy'.[8] It was at Hynes's suggestion she finally parted with her collection of erotic letters, creased and faded almost to the point of illegibility, to the Harry Ransom Humanities Research Center in Austin, Texas. She died in 1976 at the age of eighty-nine.

Hulme once told Kate that his important work lay ahead of him and that he did not expect to write anything of real profundity until he had reached middle age. In a characteristically sculptural way he made the same point in 'A Notebook':

At any rate, I prefer people who feel a *resistance* to opinion. Except for the gifted few, this may be the best method to pursue in philosophy up to forty. It might be argued that a concentrated direct study of such matters should be postponed to this time, when a man really has prejudices to be moulded. There is, perhaps, more chance of getting *shape* out of stone than out of undergraduate plasticine.[9]

One difficulty in assessing Hulme's achievement and influence is that we have to deal with the little he had time to achieve rather than the lot he planned to achieve. Even with this restriction, however, enough remains to make it clear that his reputation as a figure of considerable significance in the development of twentieth-century culture is warranted. As the growth of his posthumous reputation sketched in the Introduction shows, poets did indeed begin writing the kind of poetry he wanted to see written. Painters and sculptors too began to make the kind of work he wanted to see made, and the abstract art which he helped to nurse through its difficult early days went on to become the new orthodoxy. Developments in the plastic arts, however, on which he theorized more specifically than in the field of poetry, outstripped his predictions and in doing so exposed the paradox at the heart of his position, that in hailing the abstract art of Epstein, Bomberg, Lewis and the Vorticists he was greeting the return of an ancient tradition rather than the dawn of a new one. He chose to see this as being prompted by the same psychological needs that had motivated the first, primitive makers of abstract art, as modern man felt once again the need to withdraw from the complexity and uncertainty of his times into the security of unchanging and permanent shapes. But even if this were true of abstract painters at the start of the twentieth century, as art headed back towards its roots in geometrical shapes it passed through what Hulme seems to have assumed would be its stopping point and carried on downwards into a sub-atomic chaos of personality-driven happenings, concept and installation art that had little apparent connection with his theory.

The accuracy of the predicted end of the humanist era which he claimed to see writ in the poetry, art and philosophy of his time, and its replacement by a neo-classical *Zeitgeist* founded on a bedrock of original sin, is equally difficult to assess. Certainly the record of wars and persecutions since the time of his writing contains nothing to suggest that he was mistaken in his belief that there is no such thing as moral progress; but perhaps any other period of history would show the same. Over the years since 1948 the United Nations' Universal Declaration of Human Rights has acquired an increasingly scriptural authority, but using neither God nor the Bible as its moral reference point its acceptance cannot be used to demonstrate the longed-for return of the 'religious attitude'. As for original sin, an argument might be advanced to the effect that the environmental movement that arose in the latter half of the twentieth century provides evidence of the return of a belief in original sin, in that the movement tends to view man as an innately evil force whose activities inevitably threaten the earth with destruction; but again, this is not quite the sense in which Hulme meant it. In philosophy the influential Structuralist movement, with its origins in Freud, Marx and Saussure, showed strongly anti-humanist tendencies in its descriptions of human consciousness as neither free nor rational but controlled by sexual, political or linguistic processes of which the mind itself is largely unaware and over which it has little control; but Structuralism nowhere proposed that God be returned to fill the space left vacant at the centre by man after this analysis.

On the whole it seems safer to suggest that, just as divisions into artistic periods and styles are finally no more than historical conveniences, so sweeping cultural predictions about impending changes in the *Zeitgeist* are made ultimately for the serious fun of the argument itself, and in the full knowledge of the fact that the accuracy or otherwise of such predictions can only ever be a matter of opinion. Hulme hinted as much when he observed that the covers of a book are responsible for 'much error' in creating the illusion of a connection between things that might, in reality, have no necessary connection at all.

Perhaps Hulme's greatest value lay in this, that he articulated in a clear, simple and direct way the difference between the two most fundamentally opposed types of human being, those for whom the idea of a world without constant change is unendurable, and those for whom it is the most desirable prospect imaginable, and proposed himself as the firm embodiment of the latter. He epitomized the conservative character at its best, austere in complaint, modest in epistemology, healthy in scepticism, honest and open in appetite, willing to listen and learn, to attack the views of others and to have his own attacked. A talented debunker, boisterous, rude and domineering but never, it seems, a bully, never sinister, he had a developed understanding of the severe limits to human kindness, and of the need to deal with this without invoking revolution and the dream of a better future. Despite the apparent pessimism of his intellectual vision he had an enormous and infectious appetite for life, and yet was prepared to risk and finally give his own for his country. As the analyses of the 'War Notes' make clear, he knew that he was doing so in defence of a democracy whose values he found diffuse and at times almost invisible.

Notes

INTRODUCTION

1. Michael Roberts, *T. E. Hulme* (London, 1938), p.259.
2. T. E. Hulme, *Speculations*, ed. Herbert Read (London, 1924), p.225.
3. Ibid., p.243.
4. See, for example, Patricia Rae, *The Practical Muse: Pragmatist Poetics in Hulme, Pound and Stevens* (Lewisburg, 1997).
5. Richard Cork, in his standard work *Vorticism and Abstract Art in the First Machine Age* (London, 1976), devotes two chapters to Hulme's influence.
6. See Jerry Z. Muller (ed.), *Conservatism: An Anthology of Social and Political Thought* (Princeton University Press, 1998), where one of Hulme's 'Essays on War' is reprinted.
7. Herbert Read, letter to C. K. Ogden, 15.2.1923, McMaster University Library.
8. Roberts, *Hulme*.
9. Edwin Muir, *The Present Age from 1914* (London, 1939), volume 5 of Bonamy Dobrée (ed.), *Introductions to English Literature*.
10. Raymond Williams, *Culture and Society: 1780–1950* (London, 1959), p.192.
11. Ibid., p.191.
12. Frank Kermode, *Romantic Image* (London, 1957), p.120.
13. Ibid., pp.130–31.
14. Read's arrangement of the material was, in fact, largely back to front.
15. The BBC have no surviving tape of the programme. Dickinson's own manuscript is among the Dickinson papers in the Special Collections department of the University of Birmingham Library.
16. Both Roberts and Jones wanted illustrations for their books but were overruled by their publishers.
17. Michael H. Levenson, *A Genealogy of Modernism: a Study of English Literary Doctrine, 1908–1922* (Cambridge, 1984), p.81.

18. Karen Csengeri (ed.), *The Collected Writings of T. E. Hulme* (Oxford, 1994).

19. Patrick McGuiness (ed.), *T. E. Hulme. Selected Writings* (Manchester, 1998).

20. Richard Curle, letter to Samuel Hynes, 17.6.1954, Harry Ransom Humanities Research Center, the University of Texas at Austin (HRHRC).

21. Ethel Kibblewhite, letter to Michael Roberts, 4.8.1937, University Library, Keele.

22. This was in general another world of discretion. In the 1930s Kate Lechmere wrote frankly to Roberts of her relationship with Hulme during the war, with both parties assuming correctly that none of this personal material would be used in Roberts's book. Hulme's relationship was kept secret from Ethel Kibblewhite, however, and out of consideration for Kibblewhite's feelings Lechmere would not even allow her name to appear in Roberts's Acknowledgements. This was twenty years after Hulme's death.

23. Sir Herbert Read's son, the art historian Ben Read, assures me that the material really was all handed back and that, contrary to rumours, there is no hidden trunk of papers still waiting to be discovered.

24. Kate Lechmere, letter to Michael Roberts, 10.2.1938, University Library, Keele.

I THE WHIP

1. *The Criterion*, II, 7 (April 1924), p.231.

2. Bertrand Russell, talk with Samuel Hynes, 9.12.1953, HRHRC.

3. A family tree several feet long, commissioned by Thomas Hulme of Dunwood Hall, is held in the archives of the Society of Genealogists, Charterhouse Buildings, Farringdon.

4. Author interview with Geoff Perkin of Endon, son of the village blacksmith, 29.4.2000.

5. Kate Auchterlonie, letter to Michael Roberts, 23.6.1937, University Library, Keele. Her short letter to Roberts gives neither dates nor ages for these reminiscences.

6. In 1918 the hall was renamed 'Memorial Hall', from the tablets commemorating former pupils who died in the war.

7. F. S. Adams, talk with Samuel Hynes, 23.2.1954, HRHRC.

8. Alfred Haigh, letter to Michael Roberts, 18.7.1937, University Library, Keele.

9. Sandow was a contemporary celebrity, a professional strong-man whose regimes of physical culture were widely practised at the time.

2 THE DISCORD CLUB

1. Letter to Michael Roberts, 3.12.1937, University Library, Keele.
2. The 'Little Go' was an internal examination; to be 'plucked' meant to fail the exam.
3. St John's College Archive, Cambridge.
4. Ibid.
5. The reference to Clerkenwell is obscure. Possibly Yearsley was thinking of Hulme's court appearance and assigning it to the magistrates court at Clerkenwell rather than Marlborough Street.
6. St John's College Archive, Cambridge.
7. Ibid.
8. *The New Age* (23 November 1911), pp.79–82.
9. In *T. E. Hulme*, Michael Roberts included the observation that while in Toronto Hulme 'used to go to St Thomas's, a church of Anglo-Catholic tendencies', but the assertion is rendered problematic by the fact that Roberts's informant dates this churchgoing to 'the year prior to the war', in other words 1913. Hulme was definitely not in North America in 1913. His younger brother Harold equally certainly was, and a case of mistaken identity seems likely.
10. Charles Gimblett, letter to Samuel Hynes, 22.3.1954, HRHRC.
11. The school has no records of teachers from the period.
12. Sense seems to require a stress of disbelieving wonder on 'like'.
13. Karen Csengeri (ed.), *The Collected Writings of T. E. Hulme* (Oxford, 1994), p.53.
14. T. E. Hulme, *Speculations*, ed. Herbert Read (London, 1924), p.73.

3 THE COMPLETE POETICAL WORKS OF T. E. HULME

1. Henry Simpson, letter to Michael Roberts, 5.9.1940, University Library, Keele.
2. Wyndham Lewis, *Blasting and Bombardiering* (London, 1937), p.105.
3. Karen Csengeri (ed.), *The Collected Writings of T. E. Hulme* (Oxford, 1994), p.49.
4. Gustave Kahn, *Premiers Poèmes* (Paris, 1897), p.23.
5. *The New Age* (24 August 1911), p.400.
6. Oscar Wilde's friend and, after Wilde's death in 1900, the executor of his

estate. The dinner, on 1 December 1908, was to honour Ross's work in keeping Wilde's name alive and paying off his debts. Hulme was presumably there but makes no other reference to the occasion.

7. 'A City Sunset' was reprinted for the first time in Michael Roberts's book on Hulme in 1938, in a version that uses 'coquettes' for 'reigns' in the second line, and heaven's 'wanton' instead of 'jocund' in the tenth. Roberts's version also has the smooth 'thighs' of Lady Castlemaine, not her 'flesh'. Roberts's editors at Faber, T. S. Eliot and later Richard de la Mare, were nervous about this reference. Faber's legal department discovered there was a living holder of the Castlemaine title and this probably explains Roberts's choice of version.

8. Csengeri (ed.), *Collected Writings*, p.56.

9. Notebook entitled 'Notes', Hulme Collection, University Library, Keele.

10. *Egoist*, 1 May 1915.

11. The notebook at Keele containing Hulme's poems has 'Free Verse' written on the cover in Hulme's hand.

12. Hulme refers to 'the last but two' of the sonnets, which would be CLII. However CLI suits his own title better, although the almost illegible roman numeral could be either.

13. Ezra Pound, talk with Samuel Hynes, 31.8.1953, HRHRC.

14. Ibid.

15. Jacob Epstein, *Epstein: An Autobiography* (London, 1955), pp.59–60.

16. Ezra Pound, *Make It New* (London, 1934), p.361.

17. E.g. Karen Csengeri in *The Papers of the Bibliographical Society of America*, volume 80, first quarter, 1986, p.108; and Samuel Hynes in *Further Speculations*, p. xix.

18. Ezra Pound, letter to Michael Roberts, 30.8.1937, University Library, Keele.

19. Ezra Pound, letter to Samuel Hynes, 15.2.1954, HRHRC.

20. Among his stray couplets and lines Hulme has: 'Here stand I on the pavement hard/From love's warm paradise debarred'.

21. Quoted in Csengeri (ed.), *Collected Writings*, p.458. The poem referred to is 'The Man in the Crow's Nest'.

22. Hulme Collection, University Library, Keele.

23. The term seems to derive from the conception of divine power and authority in Polynesian religion. Hulme may have come across it in the vocabulary of friends, such as Florence Farr, who were interested in the syncretic teachings of Theosophy.

24. *The New Age* (22 February 1912), pp.401–3.

25. Joy Grant, *Harold Monro and the Poetry Bookshop* (Berkeley and Los Angeles, 1967), p.79.

26. T. S. Eliot, *To Criticize the Critic and Other Writings* (London, 1978).

27. T. S. Eliot, letter to Samuel Hynes, 23.3.1954, HRHRC.

28. T. S. Eliot, *Selected Letters. Volume One: 1898–1922*, ed. Valerie Eliot (London, 1988), p.311.

29. Eliot, *To Criticize the Critic*, pp.185–6.

30. T. S. Eliot, 'A Commentary', *The Criterion*, II, 7 (April 1924), p.231.

31. Ezra Pound, talk with Samuel Hynes, 31.8.1953, HRHRC.

4 THE NIGHTMARE OF DETERMINISM

1. *The New Age* (25 May 1907), p.453.

2. Orage quoted in Philip Mairet, *A. R. Orage: A Memoir by Philip Mairet* (New Hide Park, 1966), p.40.

3. Alfred Haigh, talk with Samuel Hynes, 19.2.1954, HRHRC.

4. Wallace Martin, *'The New Age' under Orage* (New York, 1967), p.137.

5. *The New Age* (3 August 1911), pp.328–31.

6. Quoted by Hulme in *The New Age* 10/5 (30 November 1911), pp.110–12.

7. Bergson was awarded the Nobel Prize for Literature in 1927.

8. *The New Age* (23 November 1911), pp.79–82.

9. *The New Age* (30 November 1911), pp.110–12.

10. *The New Age* (23 November 1911), pp.79–82.

11. H. Bergson, *An Introduction to Metaphysics*, translated by T. E. Hulme (New York, 1912), p.67.

12. Hulme seems to have had a kitten himself at the time.

13. *The New Age* (26 October 1911), pp.610–11.

14. *The New Age* (30 November 1911), pp.110–12.

15. Bergson, *An Introduction to Metaphysics*, pp.15–16.

16. Karen Csengeri (ed.), *The Collected Writings of T. E. Hulme* (Oxford, 1994), p.54.

17. *The New Age* (23 June 1910), p.187.

18. *The New Age* (29 July 1909), pp.265–6.

19. *The New Age* (27 April 1911), pp.607–8.

20. *The New Age* (22 June 1911), pp.189–90.

21. *The New Age* (22 February 1912), pp.401–3.

5 1911

1. Richard Curle, talk with Samuel Hynes, 5.4.1954, HRHRC.

2. Unpublished memoir by Peter Kibblewhite, kindly sent to me by Martin Kibblewhite.

3. Diana Poulton in tape-recorded conversation with Ian Harwood, kindly loaned to me by Ian Harwood, n.d.

4. Kate Lechmere, talk with Samuel Hynes, 9.1.1954, HRHRC.

5. Kate Lechmere, letter to Michael Roberts, 10.2.1938, Hulme Collection, University Library, Keele.

6. Ashley Dukes, letter to Michael Roberts, 11.2.1938, Hulme Collection, University Library, Keele.

7. Hulme Collection, University Library, Hull.

8. *Cambridge Magazine*, 4 March 1916.

9. *The New Age* (2 December 1909), pp.107–8.

10. *The New Age* (27 April 1911), pp.607–8.

11. *The New Age* (9 November 1911), pp.38–40.

12. Paul Hulme's archive.

13. *The New Age* (27 April 1911), pp.607–8.

14. H. Wildon Carr's report on the conference to the Aristotelian Society, 1.5.1911.

15. Hulme Collection, HRHRC.

16. D. L. Murray, letter to Alun R. Jones, 3.2.1956, University Library, Hull.

17. Ibid.

18. In Endon during Hulme's time there was in fact someone who bore the name baptismally, Thomas Gratton the tailor.

19. Paul Hulme's archive.

20. Ben Read's archive.

21. The talks were not published until *Speculations*, where an essay based on them appeared under the title 'The Philosophy of Intensive Manifolds'. The title was Herbert Read's.

22. *The New Age* (2 November 1911), pp.15–16.

23. Ibid.

24. *The Commentator* 4 (3 April 1912), pp.294–5.

25. *The Commentator* 4 (15 May 1912), pp.388–9.

26. *The Commentator* 2 (19 April 1911), pp.357–8.

27. Probably the Austrian economist Carl Menger (1840–1921). Hulme may be referring to his *Gründsätze der Volkswirtschaftslehre* (1871) in which Menger formulated a theory of subjective value based on the usefulness of goods.

28. *The Commentator* 3 (8 November 1911), p.388.

6 ORIGINAL SIN

1. Letter to Ogden, 12.11. prob. 1911, McMaster University Library, Hamilton, Ontario.
2. 'Syndicalist' translates roughly as 'trade unionist'.
3. Georges Sorel, *Reflections on Violence*, translated with an introduction and bibliography by T. E. Hulme (London, 1916), p.22.
4. Ibid., p.23.
5. Ibid., p.131.
6. Letter to Ogden, 12.11. prob. 1911, McMaster University Library, Hamilton, Ontario.
7. Ibid.
8. Ashley Dukes, talk with Samuel Hynes, 19.1.1954, HRHRC.
9. Ashley Dukes, letter to Michael Roberts, 11.2.1938, University Library, Keele.
10. Letter to *The New Age*, 9.11.1911.
11. Hulme writes 'Tonquebec'.
12. Kate Lechmere, letter to Michael Roberts, 10–11.2.1938, University Library, Keele.
13. The notes are undated.
14. The nuns of Stanbrook are by tradition always so titled.
15. 'House Chronicle', Stanbrook Abbey, 13.1.1924.
16. Letter to Ogden, 27.11.1911, Ogden Archives, McMaster University Library, Hamilton, Ontario.
17. There is no surviving manuscript of the Clifford's Inn Hall lecture.
18. The spiral as an image of progress was originally used by Goethe.
19. Presumably a reference to John Middleton Murry's arts and literary magazine *Rhythm*, which was devoted to the images and ideas of the Fauves and was a consistent promoter of Bergson's ideas.
20. *Cambridge Magazine*, 9.3.1912.
21. T. E. Hulme, *Speculations*, ed. Herbert Read (London, 1924), p.111.
22. Ibid., p.118.
23. Named after the British theologian Pelagius, who taught in Rome in the late fourth and early fifth century. He held that man could take the initial steps towards salvation by his own efforts and independently of divine grace – a more or less proto-humanist position.
24. Hulme, *Speculations*, p.115.
25. Ibid., p.117.
26. Ibid., p.129.

27. Ibid., p.126.
28. Ibid., p.131.
29. Ibid., p.137.
30. Ibid., p.131.
31. Ibid., p.137.
32. Ibid.
33. Ibid.
34. Ibid.
35. Ibid., p.140.
36. Wyndham Lewis, *Blasting and Bombardiering* (London, 1937), p.104.

7 CAMBRIDGE REVISITED

1. St John's College Archive, Cambridge.
2. Ibid.
3. 'It is my pleasure to confirm that I consider Mr T. E. Hulme a man of outstanding worth. He brings rare qualities of discrimination, energy and penetration to the study of philosophical questions. Unless I am very much mistaken, he is destined to produce interesting and important work in the field of philosophy in general and perhaps particularly in the philosophy of art.' T. E. Hulme, *Speculations*, ed. Herbert Read (London, 1924), Introduction, p. x.
4. Hulme Collection, n.d., HRHRC.
5. *The Granta* (4 May 1912), p.359.
6. Ibid., pp.358–9.
7. Ezra Pound, letter to Michael Roberts, 20.8.1937, University Library, Keele.
8. Sir John Squire, letter to Michael Roberts, 11.8.1937, University Library, Keele.
9. *Cambridge Magazine*, 2 March 1912.
10. Hulme Collection, HRHRC.
11. Omar Pound and A. Walton Litz (eds.), *Ezra Pound and Dorothy Shakespeare – Their Letters 1909–1914* (New York, 1984), p.108.
12. Joan Tomlinson, *On a May Morning* (Guildford, 1977), p.4.
13. Sir John Squire, letter to Michael Roberts, 11.8.1937, University Library, Keele.
14. St John's College Archive, Cambridge.
15. Flint Archive, HRHRC.
16. Ibid.
17. *The Poetry Review*, 1 (December 1912), p.537.

18. Joan survived the episode unscathed. Less than three years later she met and married a man named Andrew Tomlinson, who shared her passion for progressive education. Together they founded and ran the Beltane school, raised a family and remained happily married for fifty-seven years.

8 THE FRITH STREET SALON

1. The French psychologist Théodule-Armand Ribot (1839–1916), author of *Diseases of Memory* (1882).
2. T. E. Hulme to E. Marsh, n.d., Berg Collection, New York Public Library.
3. This may account for the presence of some curious homophones in the typed manuscript versions of Hulme's poems. 'Read', for example, appears several times for 'red'.
4. Arundel del Re, 'Georgian Reminiscences', Part 2, p.464. In the quarterly *Studies in English Literature*, Volume XII, 1932.
5. *The Poetry Review*, 1 (January 1912), pp.10–13.
6. In a letter to Edward Marsh, 25.11.1912, quoted in Christopher Hassall, *Edward Marsh: Patron of the Arts* (London, 1959).
7. Ethel Kibblewhite, letter to Michael Roberts, 12.11.1937, University Library, Keele.
8. Hulme to F. S. Flint, n.d., from Germany, HRHRC.
9. *Poetry and Drama*, 2 (June 1914).
10. Ibid.
11. Ibid.
12. Hulme to Flint, n.d., HRHRC.
13. *The Quest*, volume 4, no. 4, p.784.
14. Flint to Hulme, n.d., HRHRC.
15. *The Quest*, volume 5, no. 1.
16. Paul Selver, talk with Samuel Hynes, 1.12.1954, HRHRC.
17. Ashley Dukes, *The Scene is Changed* (London, 1942), p.40.
18. Unpublished draft in McMaster University Library, Hamilton, Ontario.
19. De Maeztu and Hulme seem to have been close, but apart from a letter of condolence sent to Kate Lechmere on Hulme's death there is no documentary evidence of their friendship. He credited Hulme, his junior by several years, with the influence of an older brother and in his book *Authority, Liberty and Function in the Light of War* (1916) wrote that it was Hulme who had taught him the idea of 'the political and social transcendency of the doctrine of original sin'. Maeztu was a Roman Catholic, later Spanish Ambassador to the Argentine. He died fighting for Franco in the Spanish Civil War.

20. Hulme's table-hopping often took in Japanese officers who frequented the Café Royal for a further game of Go.

21. Jacob Epstein, talk with Samuel Hynes, 26.2.1954, HRHRC.

22. Ashley Dukes, talk with Samuel Hynes, 19.1.1954, HRHRC.

23. D. L. Murray, letter to Alun R. Jones, 3.2.1956, University Library, Hull.

24. Richard Aldington, letter to Samuel Hynes, 15.5.1953, HRHRC.

25. Henry Slonimsky, letter to Samuel Hynes, 25.5.1954, HRHRC.

26. C. R. W. Nevinson, *Paint and Prejudice* (London, 1937), p.63.

27. H. J. Massingham, *Remembrance* (London, 1942), p.33.

28. Omar Pound and A. Walton Litz (eds.), *Ezra Pound and Dorothy Shakespear – Their Letters 1909–1914* (New York, 1984), p.323.

29. Jacob Epstein, *Epstein: An Autobiography* (London, 1955), p.60.

30. Joy Grant, *Harold Monro and the Poetry Bookshop* (Berkeley and Los Angeles, 1967), p.101.

31. Ibid., p.99.

32. Robert Frost, *The Trial by Existence* (New York, 1960), p.101.

33. Elaine Barry (ed.), *Robert Frost on Writing* (New Brunswick, 1973), p.83.

34. Joseph Cohen, *Journey to the Trenches: The Life of Isaac Rosenberg 1890–1918* (London, 1975), p.95.

35. Curle gives no date for the meeting, and the biographies of Conrad make no reference to it either.

36. W. H. Davies, *Later Days* (London, 1925), p.97.

37. *Abstraktion und Einfühlung* was not translated into English until 1940.

38. David Bomberg, talk with Samuel Hynes, 6.2.1954, HRHRC.

39. The draft is in the Tate Gallery Archives, document no. 8135.35.

40. *The New Age* (18 December 1913), pp.213–15.

9 HULME AND MODERN ART

1. Worringer is not included in Hulme's undated 'Plan for a Book on Modern Theories of Art', which Read reproduced in *Speculations*, suggesting that the 'Plan' was outlined before this trip.

2. T. E. Hulme, *Speculations*, ed. Herbert Read (London, 1924), p.vii.

3. Noel Carrington (ed.), *Selected Letters of Mark Gertler* (London, 1965), pp.71–3.

4. Quoted in Joy Grant, *Harold Monro and the Poetry Bookshop* (Berkeley and Los Angeles, 1967), p.67.

5. 'Flenite' was Epstein's own amalgam of flint and granite.

6. *The New Age* (25 December 1913), pp.251–3.

7. Jacob Epstein, *Epstein: An Autobiography* (London, 1955), p.61.

8. *The New Age* (15 January 1914), pp.341–2.

9. Denys Sutton (ed.), *Letters of Roger Fry*, vol. 2 (New York, 1972), p.378.

10. Herbert Read changed the title in *Speculations* to 'Modern Art and Its Philosophy', on the grounds that the phrase 'the new art' sounded 'passé'.

11. Karen Csengeri (ed.), *The Collected Writings of T. E. Hulme* (Oxford, 1994), p.283.

12. Ibid., p.282.

13. Ibid., p.284.

14. *Observer*, 1.2.1914.

15. *The New Age* (16 April 1914), p.753.

16. *The New Age* (26 March 1914), pp.661–2.

17. Jacob Epstein to Hulme, n.d., in David Auchterlonie's archive. It is possible the word 'genius' followed 'creative' in Hulme's original ms., but was lost in the printed article.

18. Until he decided on a career in art, Bomberg's own family had expected him to become a mathematician.

19. *The New Age* (9 July 1914), pp.230–32.

20. Ibid.

21. There is coincidental irony in the way Hulme's own 'Cinders' and 'Notes on Language and Style', as well as the 'Plan for a Book on Modern Theories of Art', exist almost as 'abstract' books, a series of ideas fleetingly sketched and shaped which the reader needs to work to put together for himself.

22. Possibly his friend Robert Bevan.

23. *The New Age* (9 July 1914), pp.230–32.

24. David Bomberg, letter to Samuel Hynes, n.d. Punctuated for sense. HRHRC.

25. The drawing is reproduced in Richard Cork, *David Bomberg* (Yale, 1987), p.109.

10 KATE LECHMERE

1. W. K. Rose (ed.), *The Letters of Wyndham Lewis* (Norfolk, Connecticut, 1963), p.48.

2. Wyndham Lewis, *Blasting and Bombardiering* (London, 1937), p.100.

3. Jacob Epstein, talk with Samuel Hynes, 26.2.1954, HRHRC.

4. Lewis, *Blasting and Bombardiering*, p.33.

5. Ibid., p.105.

6. Ibid., p.106.

7. Kate Lechmere, talk with Samuel Hynes, 9.1.1954, HRHRC.

8. Kate Lechmere memoir, 'Wyndham Lewis from 1912', in *Journal of Modern Literature* 10/1 (March 1983).

9. Lewis, *Blasting and Bombardiering*, p.36. To his considerable credit this last detail of the fight stems from Lewis himself: 'I seized Hulme by the throat; but he transfixed me upon the railings of Soho Square. I never see the summer house in its centre without remembering how I saw it upside down.'

10. Epstein, talk with Samuel Hynes, 26.2.1954, HRHRC.

11. Lechmere, 'Wyndham Lewis from 1912'.

12. Kate Lechmere, 'Recollections of Vorticism', in *Apollo* (January 1971), pp.52–3.

13. Kate Lechmere, letter to Michael Roberts, 10–11.2.1938, Keele University Library, Keele.

14. Ibid.

15. I have been unable to identify who 'Maxwell' might be.

16. Richard Curle, letter to T. E. Hulme, 1.5.1917, HRHRC.

17. Richard Aldington, letter to Samuel Hynes, 30.4.1954, HRHRC.

18. Hulme to Curle, n.d., Lilly Library, Indiana University, Bloomington, Indiana.

19. D. L. Murray, letter to Alun R. Jones, 3.2.1956, University Library, Hull.

20. Nina Hamnett, *Laughing Torso* (London, 1932), p.72.

21. Lechmere Archive, HRHRC.

11 DIARY FROM THE TRENCHES

1. This 'Diary' consists of letters sent by Hulme to members of the family. They were first published as 'Diary from the Trenches' by Samuel Hynes in *Further Speculations* in 1955. I have added two letters from Hulme to his father. The 'Diary' letters exist only in typescripts made by the family. Square brackets are used here to indicate material that was illegible.

2. Probably Alice Pattinson.

3. Jack Johnson was the world heavyweight boxing champion at the time.

4. Stanbrook Abbey, where Alice Pattinson's two sisters were nuns.

5. Hulme's younger brother, who served as a despatch rider during the war.

6. Hulme's sister.

7. Dunwood Hall, where Hulme's paternal grandmother lived.

8. Army records state that Hulme was wounded on 14 April, so the date is probably a mistake in the family's transcription.

12 INTERREGNUM

1. The term means to be fired at along the whole length of a line. An angle of 90 degrees gave the most devastating line of fire.

2. The HAC war diaries that might give exact details of the incident are missing.

3. The term comes from the Hindu word 'bilayati' meaning 'home-place'.

4. Timothy Materer (ed.), *Selected Letters of Ezra Pound to John Quinn 1915–1924* (Durham, 1991), p.160.

5. Kate Lechmere, talk with Samuel Hynes, 9.1.1954, HRHRC.

6. Dermot Freyer, letter to Michael Roberts, 28.3.1938, University Library, Keele.

7. Ibid.

8. Public Record Office, Kew, PRO reference WO 339/4640.

9. T. E. Hulme, *Speculations*, ed. Herbert Read (London, 1924), p.236.

10. Quoted in Roger Cole, *Gaudier Brzeska: Artist and Myth* (Bristol, 1995), p.124.

11. Ibid., p.125.

12. Ibid., p.126.

13. Ibid., p.139.

14. Materer (ed.), *Selected Letters of Ezra Pound to John Quinn.*

15. Kate Lechmere, letter to Michael Roberts, 10–11.2.1938, University Library, Keele.

16. Letter to Edward Marsh, n.d., Berg Collection, New York Public Library (NYPL).

17. Kate Auchterlonie, talk with Samuel Hynes, 8.4.1954, HRHRC.

18. Letter to Edward Marsh, n.d., Berg Collection, NYPL.

19. Jacob Epstein, talk with Samuel Hynes, 26.2.1954, HRHRC.

20. C. K. Ogden, letter to Samuel Hynes, 16.12.1953, HRHRC.

21. Halszka Baty, letter to Michael Roberts, n.d. but early 1938, University Library, Keele.

22. Kate Lechmere, letter to Michael Roberts, 29.3.1938, University Library, Keele.

23. Letter to Edward Marsh, n.d., University Library, Keele.

13 HEROIC VALUES

1. Reprinted in abridged form in T. E. Hulme, *Speculations*, ed. Herbert Read (London, 1924) as 'Humanism and the Religious Attitude'.

2. Letter to Richard Curle, n.d., Curle Archive, Lilly Library, Indiana University. The Bloomsbury art critic Clive Bell was the subject of another of the 'War Notes'.

3. The American edition was published by B. W. Huebsch in November 1914.

4. *The New Age* (6.1.1916), p.234.

5. Ibid., p.235.

6. Ibid., p.234.

7. *The New Age* (16.12.1915), p.159.

8. *The New Age* (6.1.1916), p.235.

9. Hulme, *Speculations*, p.259.

10. Léon Duguit (1859–1928), French legal and social philosopher.

11. *The New Age* (27.1.1916), p.307.

12. Ibid.

13. Hulme, *Speculations*, p.33.

14. Hulme's *New Age* scrapbook, Jacob Epstein papers, Henry Moore Institute, Leeds.

15. Letter to Richard Curle, n.d., Curle Archive, Lilly Library, Indiana University.

16. *The New Age* (29.6.1911), p.203.

17. *The New Age* (20.1.1916), p.270.

18. *The New Age* (30.12.1915), p.199.

19. *The New Age* (10.2.1916), p.341.

20. *The New Age* (2.3.1916), p.413.

21. *The New Age* (3.2.1916), p.317.

22. Letter to C. K. Ogden, n.d., 'Haven't written for two weeks . . .', Ogden Archives, McMaster University Library.

23. Letter to C. K. Ogden, n.d., Ogden Archives, McMaster University Library.

24. Letter to C. K. Ogden, n.d., 'I wrote these war notes . . .', Ogden Archives, McMaster University Library.

25. One in Russell's series on 'The Principles of Social Reconstruction'.

26. Hulme, *Speculations*, Introduction, p.xi.

27. *The New Age* (17.2.1916), p.365.

28. In the course of his argument with Bell he made the point that the rich in any war were morally obliged to be the first to volunteer, as a mark of gratitude for the comfort they have enjoyed as members of society.

29. Richard Rempel et al. (eds.) *The Collected Papers of Bertrand Russell*, vol. 14 (London, 1995), p.145.

30. *The New Age* (2.3.1916), p.414.

31. *The New Age* (30.12.1915), p.197.

32. Henry Ireton, Oliver Cromwell's son-in-law, was a general on the Parliamentary side in the English Civil War. He later became a politician.

33. The ellipses in this quotation are Hulme's own. Hulme's definition of the Levellers' idea of liberty and his version of Ireton's quotation both seem to be freely adapted from formulations used by G. P. Gooch in his *History of English Democratic Ideas in the Seventeenth Century* (Cambridge, 1898). I am grateful to Michael Whitworth for drawing my attention to this point. See *Notes and Queries*, vol. 241, no.4 (December 1996).

34. *The New Age* (23.12.1915), p.174.

35. Bertrand Russell, talk with Samuel Hynes, 9.12.1953, HRHRC.

36. T. S. Eliot, letter to Samuel Hynes, 23.3.1954, HRHRC.

37. Bertrand Russell, talk with Samuel Hynes, 9.12.1953, HRHRC.

38. Jacob Epstein, talk with Samuel Hynes, 26.2.1954, HRHRC.

14 THE EPSTEIN BOOK

1. Hulme Collection, University Library, Keele.

2. She did like it and kept it. The painting is reproduced as Plate 61 in Wendy Baron, *Perfect Moderns* (Aldershot, 2000).

3. Hulme Collection, n.d., unsigned, HRHRC.

4. Kate Lechmere, letter to Michael Roberts, 10–11.2.1938, University Library, Keele.

5. Kate Lechmere, talk with Samuel Hynes, 9.1.1954, HRHRC.

6. Kate Lechmere, letter to Michael Roberts, 10–11.2.1938, University Library, Keele.

7. Letter to Edward Marsh, n.d. but probably April 1917, Berg Collection, NYPL.

8. A shore-based supply ship, not a seagoing one.

9. Probably the painter Lawrence Atkinson, with whom Lechmere was friendly.

10. Card, n.d., HRHRC.

11. His resumed membership is dated 22 November 1916. The library's borrowing ledgers were kept only until 1850 so that it is not possible to trace Hulme's borrowings.

12. Hulme to C. K. Ogden, n.d. but probably late 1916. Hulme does not

specify which book he means. Ogden Archives, McMaster University Library.

13. Hulme to C. K. Ogden, n.d., but probably late 1916. Ogden Archives, McMaster University Library.

14. Unattributed quotation in Edward G. Fraser and L. G. Carr-Laughton, *The Royal Marine Artillery 1804–1923*, vol. 2, 1859–1923 (London, 1930).

15. All the Grant Richards letters are in the Grant Richards Archives, Rarebook and Special Collections Library, University of Illinois, Urbana-Champaign.

16. Letter dated 5 January and postmarked 24 January. David Auchterlonie's archive.

17. Letter, 5.1.1917, University of Illinois, Urbana-Champaign.

18. Letter, n.d., David Auchterlonie's archive.

19. John Lane of the Bodley Head.

20. Letter, n.d., David Auchterlonie's archive.

21. Ibid.

22. *Sketch*, 21.2.1917, page x.

23. Kate Lechmere, letter to Michael Roberts, 10–11.2.1938, University Library, Keele.

15 ART, SEX AND DEATH

1. Hulme Collection, University Library, Keele.

2. Letter of 26.9.1916, David Auchterlonie's archive.

3. Letter, n.d. but probably April 1917, Berg Collection, NYPL.

4. A reference to American interest in Epstein's case.

5. Stephen Gardner, *Epstein* (London, 1993), p.170.

6. On 16 July Churchill was appointed Minister of Munitions in Lloyd George's government.

7. Cole was well-known in London for his practical jokes.

8. *The New Age*, February 1915.

9. Christopher Hassall, *Edward Marsh: Patron of the Arts* (London, 1959), p.382.

10. Letter of 7.9.1917, David Auchterlonie's archive.

11. The whole Hulme–Russell debate on pacifism is discussed in Chapter 3 of Alan Ryan, *Bertrand Russell: A Political Life* (London, 1988).

12. Lechmere folder, HRHRC. The letter is unsigned and may be incomplete.

13. Here Hulme inserts a small drawing.

14. Presumably Robert Bevan's wife Stasia de Karlowska. Apart from his natural secretiveness, there are no indications as to why Hulme should write

this. He wrote a lot of letters from the front to the Bevanses' eighteen-year-old daughter Halszka. 'I destroyed them, I regret to say,' she told Michael Roberts, 'but what he wrote to a girl like me would not have any philosophical interest.'

15. Lechmere Archive, HRHRC.

16. St Barbara is the patron saint of gunners.

17. Another example of Hulme's secretive nature.

18. This may refer to the possibility of his joining the officer responsible for ranging the guns, Captain J. H. Hollingsworth, in his work. Hulme was said by his sister Kate to be working with another officer on a book on gunnery at the time of his death and it is possible Hollingsworth was his unknown co-author. In the introduction to *Speculations* Read mentions finding many notes – now lost – among Hulme's papers on the technical problems of artillery practice.

19. Jameson Boyd Adams, who had been with the Shackleton team that left for the Pole on 29 October 1908.

20. Ashley Dukes, talk with Samuel Hynes, 19.1.1954, HRHRC.

21. The envelope is postmarked 19.9.1917.

22. Samuel Hynes, recalling a conversation with Lechmere, in a letter to the author of 13.4.2000.

EPILOGUE

1. Jacob Epstein, letter to John Quinn, 2.3.1918, NYPL.

2. In a postscript to the same letter to Quinn Epstein informed him that he had already found, in the composer Bernard van Dieren, a successor in admiration to Hulme, and that John Lane had agreed to publish a book with photographs accompanied by an essay by van Dieren. This appeared on 21 May 1920.

3. In a letter to the author, 3.9.2001.

4. It was found by Alun R. Jones in a bookseller's in Vigo Street, London in 1955. Jones bought it and presented it to the University Library at Hull.

5. Richard Curle, letter to Samuel Hynes, 17.6.1954, HRHRC.

6. *Daily Telegraph*, 17.10.1930.

7. Martin Kibblewhite, telephone conversation with the author, 24.1.2001.

8. Kate Lechmere, talk with Samuel Hynes, 9.1.1954, HRHRC.

9. *The New Age*, 6.1.1916, pp.234–5.

Bibliography

1 BOOKS BY OR ABOUT HULME

Speculations by T. E. Hulme, ed. Herbert Read, London, 1924, 1960
T. E. Hulme by Michael Roberts, London, 1938. With an Introduction by Anthony Quinton, Manchester, 1982
Further Speculations by T. E. Hulme, ed. Sam Hynes, University of Minnesota, 1955. Revised edition, Lincoln, 1962
The Life and Opinions of T. E. Hulme by Alun R. Jones, London and Boston, 1960
The Collected Writings of T. E. Hulme, ed. Karen Csengeri, Oxford, 1994
T. E. Hulme. Selected Writings, ed. Patrick McGuiness, Manchester, 1998

2 UNPUBLISHED MATERIAL

The following collections of unpublished letters and notes by and about Hulme were used. Other sources are given in the Notes:
Hulme Collection, University Library, Keele University
Hulme Collection, University Library, University of Hull
Hynes Papers, Harry Ransom Humanities Research Center, the University of Texas at Austin (HRHRC)
Flint Papers, HRHRC
Richard Curle Papers, Lilly Library, Indiana University, Bloomington, Indiana
Ogden Papers, McMaster University Library, Hamilton, Ontario
Peter Kibblewhite's memoir. Private collection
Paul Hulme's archive. Private collection
David Auchterlonie's archive. Private collection
Ian Harwood, two tape-recorded interviews with Diana Poulton, n.d. Private collection
Ben Read's archive. Private collection

3 SELECTED REMINISCENCES, BACKGROUND AND CRITICAL WORKS

Aldington, Richard, *Life for Life's Sake*, New York, 1941

Allen, R. F., *Literary Life in German Expressionism and the Berlin Circles*, Göppingen, 1974

Bridgewater, Patrick (ed.), *The Poets of the Café des Westens*, Leicester, 1984

Brodsky, Harold, *Henri Gaudier Brzeska 1891–1915*, London, 1933

Buckle, Richard, *Jacob Epstein: Sculptor*, London, 1963

Clapham, H. S., *Mud and Khaki – the Memoirs of an Incomplete Soldier*, London, n.d.

Cohen, Joseph, *Journey to the Trenches: the Life of Isaac Rosenberg 1890–1918*, London, 1975

Cole, Roger, *Gaudier Brzeska: Artist and Myth*, Bristol, 1995

Cork, Richard, *Vorticism and Abstract Art in the First Machine Age*, 2 vols, London, 1976

Curle, Richard, *Caravansaray and Conversation*, London, 1937

Davies, W. H., *Later Days*, London, 1925

Doyle, Charles, *Richard Aldington: a Biography*, Basingstoke, 1989

Dukes, Ashley, *The Scene is Changed*, London, 1942

Ede, H. S., *Savage Messiah*, New York, 1931

Epstein, Jacob, *Epstein: An Autobiography*, London, 1955

Fletcher, J. G., *Life is My Song*, New York, 1939

Fraser, E. G., and Carr-Laughton, L. G., *The Royal Marine Artillery 1804–1923*, London, 1930

Gallup, Donald, *A Bibliography of Ezra Pound*, London, 1963

Garnett, David, *The Golden Echo*, London, 1953

Goold Walker, Major G. (ed.), *The Honourable Artillery Company in the Great War, 1914–1919*, London, 1930

Grant, Joy, *Harold Monro and the Poetry Bookshop*, Berkeley and Los Angeles, 1967

Hamnett, Nina, *Laughing Torso*, London, 1932

Hassall, Christopher, *Edward Marsh: Patron of the Arts*, London, 1959

Hibberd, Dominic, *Harold Monro – Poet of the New Age*, Basingstoke, 2001

Hogg, Ian V., *Allied Artillery of World War One*, Crowood, 1998

Hutchens, Patricia, *Ezra Pound's Kensington*, London, 1965

Jerrold, Douglas, *Georgian Adventure*, London, 1937

Kermode, Frank, *Romantic Image*, London, 1957

Krieger, Murray, *The New Apologists for Poetry*, Minneapolis, 1956

Lehmann, John, *Rupert Brooke: His Life and His Legend*, London, 1980

Levenson, Michael, *A Genealogy of Modernism*, Cambridge, 1984

Lewis, Wyndham, *Blasting and Bombardiering*, London, 1937

Lipke, W., *David Bomberg: a Critical Study of His Life and Work*, London, 1967

Marsh, Edward, *A Number of People*, London, 1939

Martin, Wallace, *'The New Age' under Orage*, New York, 1967

Massingham, H. J., *Remembrance. An Autobiography*, London, 1942

Monk, Ray, *Bertrand Russell: the Spirit of Solitude*, London, 1997

Muir, Edwin, *The Present Age, from 1914*, London, 1939

Nevinson, C. R. W., *Paint and Prejudice*, London, 1937

Powell, L. B., *Jacob Epstein*, London, 1932

Rae, Patricia, *The Practical Muse: Pragmatist Poetics in Hulme, Pound, and Stevens*, Lewisburg, 1997

Reid, B. L., *The Man from New York: John Quinn and His Friends*, OUP, 1968

Rempel, Richard et al., (eds.), *Bertrand Russell, Prophecy and Dissent, 1914–1916*, London, Boston, 1988

Ryan, Alan, *Bertrand Russell: a Political Life*, London, 1988

Selver, P. P., *Orage and the New Age Circle*, London, 1959

Silber, Evelyn, *The Sculpture of Epstein*, Oxford, 1986

Speake, Robert (ed.), *The Old Road to Endon*, Keele, 1974

Squire, J. C., *The Honeysuckle and the Bee*, London, 1937

Steele, Tom, *Alfred Orage and the Leeds Arts Club, 1893–1923*, Aldershot, 1990

Stenlake, Frances, *From Cuckfield to Camden Town*, Cuckfield, 1999

Tillyard, S. K., *The Impact of Modernism. The Visual Arts in Edwardian England*, London, 1988

Tomlinson, Joan, *On a May Morning*, Hickey Press, 1977

Tytell, John, *Ezra Pound: the Solitary Volcano*, London, 1987

Wees, W., *Vorticism and the English Avant Garde*, Manchester, 1972

Williams, Raymond, *Culture and Society: 1780–1950*, London, 1959

Index

In this index, works by T. E. Hulme appear under their titles. All other literary and artistic works appear under their originators. References to notes have the suffix 'n' or 'nn'. Where there are two notes with the same number on the same page, the relevant chapter number is given in brackets to differentiate between them.

'Above the Dock' 40, 61, 62
abstract art *see* modern art
Action Française 108, 114, 118, 222
Adams, Jameson Boyd 267
Adams, F. S. 5–6, 7, 16, 17, 34, 35
African art 153 155, 156, 157, 185
Aiken, Conrad 147
Die Aktion (German newspaper) 138
alcohol *see* drink/drinking
Aldington, Richard 64, 85, 86, 143, 144, 182–3
Alexander, Samuel 80
Alexandra, Queen 22–3
'Anti-Romanticism and Original Sin' 112–13, 114, 236
Aquinas, Thomas 109, 176
Arabian Nights 264
Aristotle 109
Aristotelian Society, London 79, 86, 92, 125, 128, 236, 242n14
art
  aesthetics of 94, 101–2, 123, 150–51, 152–71

African 153, 155, 156, 157, 185
Byzantine 93–4, 153, 227, 228
decay/decline of 165
Hulme on value of 257–62
Hulme's interest in 142–3, 150–51, 152–71, 173, 177, 247, 274–5
Ludovici's review of 151, 156–7, 160–61
modern *see* modern art
philosophy of 75, 127, 153, 155, 163–5, 168, 169–70, 225–6, 275
pornographic 161
Post-Impressionist 150, 162, 165
religious 227–8
sculpture *see* sculpture
sex in 155–6, 161–2, 173, 246, 262–3
art history 153–4, 227–8
Asselin, Maurice 215

Atkins, Frederick A. 67
Atkinson, Lawrence 179–80, 248,
    291n8
Auchterlonie, Kate *see* Hulme,
    Catherine (Kate)
'Autumn' 48, 50–51, 52, 61, 62

Ballet Russes 94
Baron, Wendy
    Perfect Moderns 291n2
Bax, Ernest Belford 76–7
    Roots of Reality 77
de Beaunier, André
    La Poésie nouvelle 47
beauty, Hulme on 36, 60–61, 62
Beckett, Samuel 36
Bell, Clive
    Hulme on 221, 239, 290n28
    'Peace at Once' 239
Belloc, Hilaire 99, 105
Bellow, Saul 113
    Herzog xvii
Benn, A. W. 101
Bennett, Arnold 99, 105
Bergson, Henri 69–70, 78, 80 176
    Essai sur . . . la conscience 69–70,
        71, 77
    Hulme on xiv, 34, 62, 69, 70–75,
        77, 78, 79, 84, 96–9, 103,
        104–5, 107, 120, 141, 236
    on Hulme 121
    Hulme, meetings with 87
    Hulme's lectures on 96–7, 125
    ideas/themes 70, 71–6, 88, 89,
        107
    Introduction to Metaphysics,
        Hulme's translation of 6, 75–6,
        77–8, 96, 103, 120, 124–6,
        140–41, 281n11
    Lasserre on 88

'Notes on Bergson' xiv, 34, 62,
    71–5, 79, 97, 236
    opposition to 126
    publications 69–70, 94–6
    Bertrand Russell on 125, 236
    University College London
        lectures, 1911 97–9, 103
    'Bergson Lecturing' 96–9, 103
Berlitz School of Languages,
    Brussels
    Hulme as teacher of English 35,
        70
Besant, Annie 162
Bevan, Halszka (Robert Bevan's
    daughter) 219, 292n14(15)
Bevan, Robert 143, 150, 166, 175
Bevan, Stasia (Mrs Robert Bevan)
    175, 176, 212, 265
Blake, William 32
*Blast: The Review of the Great
    English Vortex* (journal) 179
Blavatsky, Madame 43
Bloomsbury Group 150, 166, 172,
    173, 174
Blunden, Edmund 136
Boer War 41
    Hulme on 12–13
Bomberg, David xiv, 149, 150, 167,
    173, 182, 225, 287n18
    Hulme on 94, 168–70
    on Hulme 170
    In the Hold 168
    Zin 169
Bone, Muirhead 256
de Bosschère, Jean 269
Bridson, D. G. 60
British Army 256, 267–8
    conscription 8, 233, 235, 256–62
    General Staff 231, 232–3
    see also First World War

British Review (journal) 230
Brooke, Rupert 134–5, 136–7, 147
　'Grantchester' 136
Brussels, Hulme in 35, 70
Brzeska, Sophie 58, 176, 183–4
　Gaudier-Brzeska's death and
　　212–14
　mental illness/death 214
Buchan, John 256
Bullough, Edward 152
Burne-Jones, Sir Philip 258, 259
Bushe-Fox, L. K. 120, 121, 131, 133
Byzantine art 93–4, 153, 227, 228

Café Royal, London 143
Cambridge Daily News 27, 28
Cambridge, Girton College 125
Cambridge Independent Press 22
Cambridge Magazine 120, 126, 236,
　240, 248
　Hulme's association with 8, 112,
　　124
Cambridge New Theatre 24–5, 27,
　30, 31, 45
Cambridge, St John's College
　debating society 21, 31
　The Discord Club *see* The Discord
　　Club
　Eagle (college magazine) 20–21,
　　31
　examinations 22
　Hulme at 18–19, 20–31;
　　expulsion 29–32; failure to take
　　degree 133; return to 103, 104,
　　120–33; rustication 22, 25, 29
　Hulme's lodgings 121, 122–3
　reputation 21
Campbell, Joseph (Seosamh
　MacCathmhaoil) 55, 58
　Hulme on 56–7

Canada
　Harold Hulme in 279n9
　T. E. Hulme in 34–5, 39–40, 59
Carr, Geraldine (née Spooner) (Mrs
　　Herbert Wildon Carr) 128, 130
Carr, Herbert Wildon 79, 130
　Hulme and 127–8, 131
　in Italy 86–7, 92, 129, 282n14
Carr, Joan Wildon (Herbert Wildon
　　Carr's daughter) 127–8
　Hulme and 94, 127, 129–31
　in Italy 86, 129
　On a May Morning 128, 131
Carr, Ursula Wildon (Herbert
　　Wildon Carr's daughter) 130
Carr-Laughton, L. G. *see* Fraser,
　　Edward G. and Carr-Laughton,
　　L. G
Cavalcanti, Guido 59
Celtic culture 42–3, 55–6
Cézanne, Paul 162, 165
Chesterton, G. K. 43, 48, 99, 105,
　258, 259, 260
children, Hulme's love of 84
Churchill, Winston 134, 217, 256,
　259, 260–61
'Cinders' xv, xix, 31–2, 35, 36, 63,
　85, 86, 118, 156, 211, 287n21
'A City Sunset' 48, 49–50, 60,
　280n7
class structure 41
classicism
　Hulme on xvii, 9, 39, 112
　romanticism and xvii, 9, 112,
　113–19
Clifford's Inn Hall, London 112
Cohen, Joseph
　Journey to the Trenches . . .
　286n34
Cole, Horace de Vere 258, 259

Coleridge, Samuel Taylor
    Biographia Literaria 114
Colum, Padraic 49, 55, 58, 230
The Commentator (journal)
    Hulme's articles in 94–103, 104,
        111
'The Complete Poetical Works of
    T. E. Hulme' xiii
    contents 61
    publication xv, 64–5, 113, 127,
        140, 221
    reviews of 140
    see also individual poems
Conrad, Joseph 149
conscription 235, 256
    Epstein's 256–62
    Hulme on 8, 233, 256–62
    see also British Army
'Conversion' 59, 60–61, 62
Copernicus 163
Cork, Richard 272
    David Bomberg 287n25
    Vorticism and Abstract Art . . .
        277n5
Cram, Marion 51
creative process, Hulme on 114–15
The Criterion (journal) 65
'The Critics and Mr Epstein'
    156–61, 245, 246
Csengeri, Karen (editor)
    Collected Writings of T. E. Hulme
        xvii, 279n13(2), 280n17,
        287nn11–13
Curle, Richard xviii, 34, 81, 85,
    109–10, 140, 143, 149, 181,
    182, 183, 221, 231, 243, 272
Curtis, Dora (Ethel Kibblewhite's
    sister) 81, 83
Curtis, Mary (Mrs Thomas Figgis
    Curtis) 81, 83

Curtis, Thomas Figgis (Ethel
    Kibblewhite's father) 81, 82, 83
    on Hulme 121
    his memorial window to Hulme
        270

Daily Mail 172
Davies, W. H. 149–50
    Later Days 286n36
de la Mare, Walter 136
de la Mere, Richard 280n7
debating/debates
    Hulme's interest in 7–15, 21, 76,
        77–80, 143–50, 269
democracy, Hulme on 240–41
Derby Day, 1914 181–2
Dessoir, Max 152
determinism 74–5
Diaghilev, Sergei 94
'Diary from the Trenches' xvi,
    185–208, 209
Dickinson, Lowes 101
Dickinson, Patric xvi, 159
van Dieren, Bernard 259, 293n2
The Discord Club (St John's
    College, Cambridge) 29
    farewell dinner for Hulme 25, 26
    Hulme as founder/president 22
    riotous behaviour by members of
        23–8
divorce, Hulme's attitude to 218
Dolmetsch family 83
Doolittle, Hilda ('H. D.') 63, 64
drink/drinking, Hulme's attitude to
    11, 85, 268
Drinkwater, John 135
Duguit, Léon 225
Dukes, Ashley 84–6, 108, 142, 143,
    178, 181, 182, 272
    in First World War 268

marriage 219
publications 272
Duncan, Revd T. A. (Hulme's uncle)
121

Edward VII, King 22–3, 41
Egoist (journal) 54, 63
Eliot, T. S. 2, 118, 242, 280n7
  To Criticize the Critic . . . 281n26
  on Hulme 1, 65, 221, 242
  Hulme's influence on xiii, xv,
    64–5, 113
  on Imagist poetry 64
  'Love Song of J. Alfred Prufrock'
    147
  'Reflections on *vers libre*' 65
  The Wasteland 136
Eliot, Vivien (T. S. Eliot's first wife)
  242
'The Embankment' 59–60, 61, 62,
  65
England
  Hulme on future of 10–11
  Orage on socialism in 68–9
English Review (journal) 68
Enriques, Professor 91
Epstein, Jacob xiv, 142–3, 145–6,
    154–6, 173, 225, 230, 272, 273
  Epstein: An Autobiography
    280n15, 286n29, 287n7
  Carvings in Flenite 157, 161, 247
  conscription 256–62
  in First World War 215, 245,
    256–62
  Hulme on 94, 155–61, 167, 171,
    173–4, 245, 256–63
  on Hulme 167, 171, 218, 242,
    271–2
  Hulme's proposed book on 247,
    249–54, 271

Kate Lechmere on 247
Ludovici on 151, 156–7, 160–61
Marsh on 257–8
his portrait busts 246–7, 253
Rock Drill 18, 245–7
Speculations, his Foreword to 142
style 246–7
Twenty-One Gallery show, 1913
  150–51, 161
Venus 161, 250–51
Epstein, Margaret (Mrs Jacob
  Epstein) 256, 258, 261
'Essays on War' (series) xvi
Etchells, Frederick 167, 174
ethics 236, 240
  see also philosophy
Evening Standard (newspaper) 258
evolutionary theory 105
Exmouth, Hulme in 56–7, 61
Expressionism 138

Fabian Arts Group 67, 76
Fabian Society 42, 43, 67, 68, 173,
  221
Farr, Florence 43, 55, 83, 97,
  280n23
Fascism 102
Figgis, Darrell ('Michael Ireland')
  112
First World War, 1914–18
  casualty figures 201, 202, 210,
    269
  declaration of 182
  'Diary from the Trenches' xvi,
    185–208, 209
  Dukes in 267–8
  Epstein in 215, 245, 256–62
  Gaudier-Brzeska in 183–4, 212,
    218, 261
  Harold Hulme in 199

First World War – *cont.*
  Hulme in xiii, xix, 12, 40, 182–3,
    184, 185–208, 209–12; death
    xiii, xv–xvi, 270; wounded
    211, 212
  Hulme on conduct of 12, 215–17,
    230–35, 267–8
  Hulme's support for xiv, 216,
    218, 234–5, 238–42
  Kate Lechmere in 218–19, 220
  Marsh in 214, 216–18, 219–20,
    243, 256–8, 259–61
  pacifism xiv, 13, 233–4, 236,
    238, 239, 241, 261–2
  Passchendaele offensive 265,
    267–8
  shelling, effects of 189, 196–7,
    201, 205–6
  trenches, conditions in 191, 192,
    194–5, 197–9, 203, 205,
    207–8, 209
  'War Notes' 221, 222, 230–35,
    238–42, 276
  see also British Army
Fisher, Admiral Lord John 246,
  256
Fitzgerald, Desmond 55, 58
Fletcher, John 156
Flint, Frank S. xiv, 52–3, 58, 63,
  148, 161, 272
  'History of Imagism' 54, 63–4
  Hulme and 53–5, 56–7, 61–2,
    70, 124, 131–2, 136, 140, 141,
    269
  on Imagist poetry 54, 63–4
  New Age column 56
Ford, Ford Maddox 57, 68
France 41
  Action Française 108, 114, 118,
    222

Hulme in 87–9
  see also First World War
Fraser, Edward G. and Carr-
    Laughton, L. G.
  The Royal Marine Artillery 249
Frazer, James 20, 21, 60
French language, Hulme's ability in
  6, 87–8, 103, 124–5, 131
French philosophy 87, 100
  see also Bergson, Henri; Sorel,
    Georges
French poetry 118
  Imagist 64
  medieval 57
  vers libre 46–7, 51, 56
French Revolution 88, 115–16
Freyer, Dermot 20, 51, 55, 159,
  211, 216
  Not All Joy 272
the Frith Street salon 143–50, 269
Frost, Robert 148–9, 156
  North of Boston 149
  Robert Frost on Writing 286n33
  The Trial by Existence 286n32
Fry, Roger 150, 162, 164, 166
  Lewis and 172–3
Further Speculations, edited by
    Samuel Hynes
  contents xvi, xviii, 288n1
  publication xvi
  see also Speculations
Futurist movement 150, 157, 164,
  174–5
  manifesto 175

Gardner, Stephen
  Epstein 292n5
Garnett, David 85
Gaudier-Brzeska, Henri 58, 143,
  159, 161, 175

death 212, 218, 261
estate, difficulties over 212–14
in First Word War 183–4
Hulme on 94, 162, 167, 183, 260, 261
Pound and 212–14
Pound on 171, 261
Gaudier-Brzeska, Sophie *see* Brzeska, Sophie
de Gaultier, Jules 88
Geiger, Moritz 152
genealogy
of Hulme family 278n3
Hulme's interest in 32–3
geometric art 166, 247
see also modern art
Georgian poetry 135–6, 137, 147
'German Chronicle' 137–40
German language 138
German philosophy 87, 100
Germany 41, 42, 135, 238–9
Hulme in Berlin 131, 133, 134–40, 141–2, 152–3
see also First World War
Gertler, Mark 149, 156
Gibson, Wilfred 135
Gill, Eric 156, 162
Gilman, Harold 244
Gimblett, Charles 35
Ginner, Charles 165, 166
Das Gnu group 138
von Goethe, Johann Wolfgang 100, 112
Gooch, G. P.
History of English Democratic Ideas . . . 291n33
Gore, Spencer 172, 173
Grafton Group (of painters) 162, 165

Grant, Duncan 162, 172
Grant, Joy
Harold Monro and the Poetry Bookshop 280n25, 286nn30–31, 286n4(9)
The Granta (journal) 120
Hulme's articles in 123, 124
'Gratton, Thomas', as Hulme's *nom de plume* 94–5, 97
Gurdjieff, George 272
Gwynne, C. W. 9

Haigh, Alfred 5–6, 7, 8, 9, 16, 17, 34–5, 69
haiku poetic form 56, 76
Hamann, Richard 152
Hamilton, C. J. 167, 174
Hamnett, Nina 183
Laughing Torso 288n20
Hannay (publisher) 141
Hardie, Keir 102
Harrison, Frederick 10, 11
Harwood, Ian 282n3
Hassall, Christopher
Edward Marsh . . . 292n9
Hay, J. Stuart 76
Heath, George (the Moorland Poet) 1
The Heretics (Cambridge philosophical society) 111–13, 114, 120, 125, 236
Hermetic Students of the Golden Dawn 43
Hicks, George Dawes 128
Hiller, Kurt (editor)
Der Kondor 137–8
Hobson, Mrs (Hulme's Cambridge landlady) 121, 122–4, 133
Hollingsworth, J. H. 293n18
Hollinshead, Edward (Hulme's uncle) 29–30, 122

honour, concept of 239
Honourable Artillery Company
  (HAC) 209–10
  Hulme in 182–3, 184, 185–208
  Hulme's discharge from 215
Houseman, A. E.
  A Shropshire Lad 249–50
Hueffer, Ford Maddox *see* Ford,
  Ford Maddox
Hulme, Catherine (Kate) (Hulme's
  sister) 1, 2–3, 33–4, 93, 199
  T. E. Hulme, relationship with 33
  marriage 220, 244, 245
Hulme, Harold Washington
  (Hulme's brother) 1, 93
  in Canada 279n9
  in First World War 199, 215
  T. E. Hulme, relationship with
  32
Hulme, Mary (née Young) (Hulme's
  mother) 1, 2–3
  death 273
  Hulme and 266–7
Hulme, T. E. [Thomas Ernest]
  (Tommy)
  achievements *see* importance/
  influence *below*
  appearance 35, 45, 245
  arrest at Empire Music Hall,
  Leicester Square 28
  awards *see* prizes/awards *below*
  birth/baptism 1
  character/personality xiii,
  xvii–xviii, 3, 6, 7, 11, 14, 15,
  16–17, 18–19, 20, 22, 27–31,
  35, 58, 84, 95, 103, 104,
  120–21, 122, 127, 129, 142,
  144, 159, 175, 176, 181, 182,
  231, 240, 272, 276
  childhood 2–5

childhood writing 5
correspondence *see* individual
  correspondents; papers/
  manuscripts *below*
dating his work xvi, xvii
death/burial xiii, xv–xvi, 270
education 5–19; *see also* at
  university *below*
Epstein's portrait bust of 246–7
financial problems 43, 49, 69, 97,
  124, 132, 141
handwriting xviii, 6, 231, 262
health problems 92–3
holidays 4
ideas/themes xiii, xv, xvii, xix, 14,
  17, 20, 64, 72–5; *see also*
  individual works; philosophy;
  political philosophy
importance/influence *see*
  reputation *below*
Ethel Kibblewhite's sketches of
  84
his knuckleduster 159, 180, 245
memorial window to 270
papers/manuscripts xiv, xvii, xviii,
  xix; *see also* Csengeri, Karen:
  Collected Writings . . .
personal habits 20
personality *see* character/
  personality *above*
prizes/awards 17–18
publications xiii, xiv, xvi, xvii; *see
  also* individual publications
reading habits 32
as rebellious/aggressive 18–19,
  22, 24–5, 27–31, 35, 84, 103,
  104, 159, 175, 182; *see also*
  character/personality *above*
reputation xiii–xiv, xv–xvii, 167,
  171, 173, 174, 274–6

testimonials to 121
thought *see* ideas/themes *above*
at university 18–19, 20–32, 103,
    104, 120–33; *see also*
    education *above*
walking, love of 32–4
his will 211, 273
women, relationships with
    xviii–xix, 34, 37–8, 129–31,
    176–7, 180; *see also*
    Kibblewhite, Ethel; Lechmere,
    Kate
Hulme, Thomas (Hulme's father) 1,
    2, 25, 273
T. E. Hulme, correspondence with
    188, 198–9
T. E. Hulme, relationship with 25,
    29, 32, 34, 95
on T. E. Hulme 121
Hulme, Thomas (Hulme's
    grandfather) 278n3
Hulme family xviii, 1–2, 4
genealogy 278n3
homes 1, 2
T. E. Hulme and 29–30
politics 3
see also Pattison
'Humanism and the Religious
    Attitude' *see* 'A Notebook'
Humanism
Hulme on 222–30
pacifism and 236
Husserl, Edmund, Hulme on
    224–7
Hutchinson, Mary 65
Huxley, T. H. 71, 79, 223–4,
Hynes, Samuel 60
    Hulme: *Further Speculations*
    edited by xvi, xviii, 280n17
    Kate Lechmere and 272–3

'I Love not the Sunset' 50
Ideal Home Exhibition, 1913,
    modernist room 172–3
Image, Selwyn 51
Imagist poetry 55, 64, 145, 147,
    225
Eliot on 64
Flint on 54, 63–4
French 64
Hulme and 63–6
Pound and 63, 64
tenets of 64
Des Imagistes (poetry anthology)
    63, 148, 161
immigration, Hulme on 11–12
interior design 172–3
International Congress of
    Philosophy, Fourth, Bologna,
    1911 80, 86–7, 89–93
*International Library of Psychology
    Philosophy and Scientific
    Method*, Ogden as editor of xiv
'Introduction to Bergson' 141
Introduction to Metaphysics see
    Bergson, Henri: *Introduction to
    Metaphysics*, Hulme's
    translation of
Ireland
Celtic culture 42–3, 55–6
Home Rule 42, 58
Ireland, Michael (pseud.) *see* Figgis,
    Darrell
Ireton, Henry 240–41
Irish Literary Society 49, 55, 76
Italy, Hulme in 80, 87, 89–93

Jackson, Holbrook 67, 68
James, William 239
    A Pluralistic Universe 77
Japan, *haiku* poetry 56, 76

John, Augustus 161
Johnson, B. S.
  A Few Short Sentences 35
Jones, Alun R. 95, 293n4
  The Life and Opinions of T. E.
    Hulme xiii, xvii
Jones, E. E. Constance 94, 125

Kahn, Gustave 46, 47, 51, 56
Kandinsky, Wassily 166, 168
de Karlowska, Stasia see Bevan,
    Stasia
Kermode, Frank
  on Hulme xvi, 113
  Romantic Image xvi
Kibblewhite, Diana (Ethel
    Kibblewhite's daughter) 82, 83,
    84, 282n3
Kibblewhite, Ethel (Dolly) xiv, xix,
    81, 124, 135, 159
  character 81-2, 278n22
  divorce 218, 244
  Hulme, correspondence with
    xviii-xix, 273
  Hulme, relationship with 81,
    83-4, 94, 103, 127, 142, 179,
    181, 219, 243, 272-3
  Hulme, sketches of 84
  under Hulme's will 211, 273
Kibblewhite, Gilbert (Ethel
    Kibblewhite's husband) 82, 83,
    218, 244, 273
Kibblewhite, Martin (Ethel
    Kibblewhite's grandson) 273,
    282n2
Kibblewhite, Peter (Ethel
    Kibblewhite's son) 82, 84, 218,
    282n2
Kitchener, F. E. 5
Klemataski, Alida 176

'The Knuckleduster' (BBC Third
    Programme documentary) xvi,
    159
Kongress für Ästhetik und
    allgemeine Kunstwissenschaft,
    Berlin, 1913 152-3
Konody, P. G. 165, 172, 177

Labour Party, formation of, as
    Labour Representation
    Committee 41
Lalo, Charles 152
Lane, John 293n2
language
  French 6, 87-8, 103, 124-5, 131
  German 138
  Hulme on use of 9, 38, 118
  Hulme's speaking style xiii, 45,
    159
  Hulme's written style 9, 38, 56,
    58, 60, 61, 71-2, 77, 78, 118,
    160
  use of 8-9, 223
  see also debating/debates
Laplace, Pierre 71, 72
Lavrin, Janko xiv
Lasker-Schüler, Else 138
Lasserre, Pierre 88-9
  Hulme, influence on 97, 108, 114
  Le Romantisme française 88
Lawrence, D. H. 63, 161-2
Leathern, J. G. 22
Lechmere, Kate ('KD') 83, 159,
    179-80, 211
  character 180
  on Epstein 247
  in First World War 218-19, 220
  on Hulme 159, 240, 245
  Hulme, relationship with xix,
    133, 177, 178, 180-81, 184,

218–19, 243–5, 247–8, 262–4, 268, 269–70, 278n22
Hulme's erotic letters to xix, 262–4
Hynes and 273–4
Lewis and 175, 177, 178, 179
memoir 288n8
'Lecture on Modern Poetry' xvi, 45–8, 51, 76
Leeds Art Club 67
the Levellers 241
Levenson, Michael
  A Genealogy of Modernism xvii
Lewis, Wyndham xiv, 45, 156, 159, 161, 272
  Blasting and Bombardiering 104, 119, 173–4, 176–7, 269, 279n2(3), 288n9
  Fry and 172–3
  Hulme and 172, 173–9
  Hulme on 94, 166–7
  Kate Lechmere and 175, 177, 178, 179
  on modern art 164, 179
Liebich, Mrs Franz 96, 97, 120
literature 42
  Hulme's definition of 36
Lloyd, H. M. 126
logic 224–5
  see also philosophy
London 41–3
  Bergson in 97–9, 103
  the Frith Street salon 143–50, 269
  Hulme in 33, 34, 35, 39–40, 43, 54, 81, 84, 94, 103, 142, 172, 269
  Marinetti in 174–5
London Group (of painters) 165–7, 173
  see also the Vorticists
London Library 33, 248, 264

London School of Economics 221
Ludovici, Anthony
  art exhibitions review, 1913 151, 156
  Hulme on 160–61
  Nietzsche and Art 160
Lyttleton, Kathleen 33

MacAlister, Dr (of St John's College, Cambridge) 18, 19, 22, 25, 30–31, 120
  on Hulme 120–21
MacCathmhaoil, Seosamh *see* Campbell, Joseph
McGuiness, Patrick (editor)
  T. E. Hulme. Selected Writings xvii
machinery as art 164, 166, 174
Macmillan (publisher) 140–41
de Maeztu, Ramiro 143, 181, 285n19
  Authority, Liberty and Function . . . 285n19
Mairet, Philip *A. R. Orage: A Memoir . . .* 281n2
Mallarmé, Stéphane xvi, 52
'Mana Aboda' 37, 61–2, 63
Manchester Guardian 245, 256
Marinetti [Emilio] Filippo 150, 157, 164
  in London 174–5
marriage, Hulme's attitude to 219
Marsh, Edward 134–5, 137, 147, 149, 254, 267
  on Epstein 257–8
  in First World War 214, 216–18, 219–20, 243, 256–8, 259–61
Martin, Wallace
  'The New Age' under Orage xvii, 281n4

Marx, Karl 102
Massingham, H. J.
  Remembrance 286n27
mathematics, Hulme's ability in 6,
  17–18, 22, 72–3, 266
Maurras, Charles 107, 114, 222
Mead, G. R. S. 141, 163
Menger, Carl 102, 282n27
  Gründsätze der
  Volkwirtschaftslehre 282n27
metaphysics, Hulme's interest in
  75–7
Miller, Paul 23–4
Minchin, H. C. xv
della Mirandola, Pico 115, 158,
  163, 227
modern art 172–3, 245–7
  geometric 166, 247
  Hulme's interest in xiv, 142–3,
    151, 152–71, 173, 177, 247,
    274–5
  Hulme's *New Age* articles on 162,
    165–71
  Lewis on 164, 179
  Ludovici's review of, 1913 151
  machinery as 164, 166, 174
  as non-evolutionary 165
  Pound on 177
  realism in 163, 165
  Worringer on 150, 152–4
'Modern Art and Its Philosophy'
  153, 155, 163–5
Modernist poetry 61
  Hulme's importance to xiii, xvi,
    xvi
Monro, Harold 113, 135, 137, 140,
  146–7, 176, 217
  'The Future of Poetry' 136
Monroe, Harriet 64
Moore, G. E. 79, 126

Hulme on 222–4, 225–7, 236
  Principia Ethica 224
Morris, Revd 121
Mosley, Oswald 242
'Mr Balfour, Bergson and Politics'
  88
Muir, Edwin
  on Hulme xv
  The Present Age . . . 277n9
Muller, Jerry Z. (editor)
  Conservatism . . . 277n6
Murray, D. L. 79, 94, 95, 144, 183
Murry, John Middleton 140,
  283n19
music 42
Myers, Charles 152
mysticism 43, 75, 272

natural history, Hulme's interest in
  15–17
Nature (journal) 90, 92, 94
'nature of man' debate 105, 173,
  223–4, 225
Neuve Chapelle, France, attack on,
  March 1915 210, 232
Nevinson, C. R. W. 143, 145, 167,
  174, 175
  Paint and Prejudice 286n26
  Modern War 250, 253
The New Age (journal) 67, 99, 142
  book reviews 52–3
  closure of 272
  Dukes as drama critic 84
  Flint's column in 56
  Hulme's association with xiv, 8,
    52–3, 59–60, 62, 65, 67,
    69–79, 87, 88, 89–90, 97, 105,
    113, 127, 151, 161, 162, 248
  Hulme's 'Contemporary
    Drawings' series 167

Hulme's modern art articles
published in 162, 165–71
Ludovici's art exhibitions review,
1913 151, 156–7, 160–71
'A Notebook' published in
222–30
Orage as editor xiv, xvii, 68–9,
89–90
'War Notes' published in 221,
230–35
New Age scrapbook 230–31
'The New Art and Its Philosophy'
see 'Modern Art and Its
Philosophy'
The New English Weekly (journal)
272
'The New Philosophy of Art as
Illustrated in Poetry' 63, 77,
112–19
Newbolt, Frank (Henry Newbolt's
brother) 256, 258
Newbolt, Henry 43
Newcastle High School 5
Debating Society 7–15, 78
The Fire-Fly (school magazine) 6,
7, 8, 10, 11, 12, 16
Hulme at 5–19
Hulme as librarian 15
Harold Hulme at 32
Natural History Society 15–17
prizes/awards 17–18
No-Conscription Fellowship 235
'North Staffs', as Hulme's *nom de
guerre* 230
'A Notebook' 119, 221
contents 222–30, 274
published in *New Age* 221, 222
'Notes on Bergson' xiv, 34, 62,
71–5, 79, 97, 236
'Notes on Language and Style' xvi,

xix, 35–9, 104, 139, 153, 222,
287n21
women/sex discussed in 37–8
'Self-delusion' section 38

Observer (newspaper) 165, 174,
175
Ogden, C. K. 218
as *Cambridge Magazine* editor
236–7
Hulme and 107–8, 111–13, 125,
236–7, 242, 248
as *International Library of
Psychology . . .* editor xiv
Russell and 236–7
Omega Workshops 172
Orage, Alfred R. 67, 256
as author of three of the 'War
Notes' 230–31
as *New Age* editor xiv, xvii, 68–9,
89–90
as a socialist 67, 68–9, 102, 272
original sin, doctrine of 108, 109,
111–19
'Over a large table . . .' (untitled
poem) 39

pacifism
Hulme's attitude to xiv, 14,
233–4, 238, 239, 241
Humanism and 236
Russell on 235–6, 261–2
see also First World War
Pattinson, Alice (Hulme's aunt) xix,
198, 218–19
Hulme's allowance from 43, 49, 69
Hulme's correspondence with
48–9, 60, 86
Hulme's relationship with 33, 34,
111, 212

Pattinson, Florence
  as Dame Ursula of Stanbrook
    Abbey 33, 34, 109, 110, 111,
    194
Pattinson, Helen
  as Dame Barbara of Stanbrook
    Abbey 109, 110–11, 194
Pattinson, Thomas (Pattinson
    sisters' father) 110
Pattinson, Thomas (II) (Alice
    Pattinson's brother) 121–2,
    212
Pelagian heresy 115
Perkin, Charles 2
'A Personal Impression of Bergson'
    84, 94, 95
phenomenological analysis
  in philosophy 224–5
philosophy 86–7, 89–93
  of art 75, 127, 153, 155, 163–5,
    168, 169–70, 225–6
  determinism 74–5
  ethics 236, 240
  foreign influences on English 146
  French 87, 100; see also Bergson,
    Henri; Sorel, Georges
  German 87, 100
  Hulme's interest in 33, 35, 36, 70,
    72–5, 79, 87, 104–5, 112–19,
    120, 134–5, 143–51, 274–6;
    see also 'A Notebook'
  logic 224–5
  political xiv, 3, 10, 98, 99–103,
    104, 107–8, 113–19
  rationalism 73–5
Pickford, Mr (mathematics teacher
    at Newcastle High School) 13
  on Hulme 18–19, 31
plagiarism 56–7
'Plan for a Book on Modern

Theories of Art' xv, 286n1,
    287n21
Poètes d'Aujourd'hui 52
poetry
  French 57, 64, 118
  Georgian 135–6, 137, 147
  German 137–40
  haiku 56, 76
  Hulme on 137–40
  Hulme's desire to write 39–40,
    62–3
  Hulme's lectures on xvi, 45–8,
    51, 113–18, 136
  Hulme's method of writing 56,
    58, 60, 61–2, 64
  Imagist see Imagist poetry
  Modern xiii, xvi, 61
  Symbolist xvi, 64
  vers libre 46–7, 51, 55, 65
Poetry (journal) 64
Poetry Bookshop 112, 135, 147,
    148, 172, 176
Poetry and Drama (journal) 147
  'German Chronicle' published in
    137–40
The Poetry Review (journal) 133,
    136, 137, 140
Poetry Society 147
Poets' Club, London 43, 47–63, 75,
    144, 147
  The Book of the Poets' Club
    59–60
  breakaway (Secessionist) group
    54–63, 64, 117, 172
  Flint and 52–3, 54–5
  For Christmas . . . 48, 51, 56
  Pound and 57–9
  rules 43–4
  as a workshop 64
Pogson, F. L. 71

political issues 41–2, 88–9, 99–100
  Fascism 102
  socialism 67, 68–9, 76, 99–103,
    106, 107–8
  syndicalism 106, 107
political philosophy
  Hulme family's 3
  Hulme's xiv, 10, 98, 99–103,
    104, 107–8, 113–19
pornography, Hulme's liking for
    161, 173
  see also sex
Post-Impressionist art 150, 162,
    165
Poulton, Diana (née Kibblewhite)
  see Kibblewhite, Diana
Pound, Ezra 57–9, 124, 135, 137,
    145 148, 159, 272
  A Lume Spento 57, 58
  Catholic Anthology 65
  correspondence 284n11, 286n28
  Gaudier-Brzeska and 212–14
  on Gaudier-Brzeska 171, 261
  Hulme and 127, 211, 140, 144,
    214–15
  Hulme's influence on xiii, 58–9,
    64
  Imagist poetry and 63, 64, 161
  Make It New 280n16
  on modern art 177
  Personae 57
  Poets' Club and 57–9
  Ripostes 60, 64, 65, 140, 221
  'Sestina: Altaforte' 58
  style 58
  'To Hulme (T. E.) and Fitzgerald
    (A Certain)' 58
  Vorticism and 175
Powell, Kenneth 203
progress, Hulme on 112

Proudhon, Pierre Joseph 239, 241
G. P. Putnam (publisher) 140

The Quest (journal) 141, 163, 285n15
Quest Society 153, 155, 163
Quinn, John 214, 256, 271

Radford, Ernest 55
Rae, Patricia
  The Practical Muse . . . 277n4
rationalism 73–5
del Re, Arundel 135
Read, Ben 278n23
Read, Herbert 113
  Hulme: Speculations edited by
    xiv–xv, xix, 32
realism, in modern art 163, 165
Rebel Art Centre, London 175, 178
Redfern, W. B. 24–5, 28, 30
Redway, Major G. W.
  'The True Story of the War' 230
Reeves-Smith, Janet 128–9, 130
religion 3
  history of 106
  Hulme on 222–30, 240
  Hulme's interest in 108–9
  Pelagian heresy 115
  Roman Catholicism see Roman
    Catholicism
religious art 227–8
Rhys, Ernest 55
Rhythm (journal) 140, 283n19
Ribot, Théodule-Armand
  Diseases of Memory 134
Richards, Grant 249–50, 251, 252,
    253–4
Roberts, Michael 60, 180, 273
  T. E. Hulme xv, xvi, xvii, xix, 32,
    33, 111, 137, 273, 277n1, 277n
    22, 279n9(2), 280n7

Roberts, William 162, 166, 167, 174
Roman Catholicism 105, 106–7, 108–11
 Hulme's interest in 109
 original sin, doctrine of 108, 109, 111–19
romanticism
 classicism and xvii, 9, 112, 113–19
 definition of 9
 Hulme on xvii, 9, 100–102, 108
 Lasserre on 88
'Romanticism and Classicism' 112, 113
Rootham, Cyril 29
Rosenberg, Isaac 149
Ross, Robert 48, 49
Rousseau, Jean Jacques 100, 116
Royal Marine Artillery 216–17
 Hulme in 219–20, 243, 248, 254–5, 265, 267, 268–9
 siege train guns 255, 265, 267–9
Rundall, G. W. 5
Ruskin, John
 Modern Painters 116–17
Russell, Bertrand 80, 223, 224, 226
 on Bergson 125, 236
 on Hulme 1, 125, 240, 242
 Hulme on 78–9, 238–9
 Ogden and 236–7
 as a pacifist 235–6, 261–2
 'The Principles of Social Reconstruction' 235, 237–8, 240
Russell, Edward Stuart 94, 242
Russian Revolution, 1917 106
Ryan, Alan
 Bertrand Russell . . . 292n11

Sackville, Lady Margaret 51, 52
St Eloi, France, in First World War 210
Sandow, Eugene 14
Scheler, Max
 Der Genius des Krieges . . . 234–5
Schiller, F. C. S.
 'Error' 92
Scott, E. P. 256
Scott, Forsyth 131
sculpture 150
 Hulme's interest in 150–51, 171, 173
 see also Epstein, Jacob
 'The Sculpture of Epstein' 254
 see also Epstein, Jacob: Hulme's proposed book on
'Searchers After Reality' (series in New Age) 77, 87
Secession Club 83
Selver, Paul 142
Sertillange, R. P. 109
sex
 in art 155–6, 161–2, 173, 246, 262–3
 Hulme's attitude to 85–6, 129, 155–6, 159, 176–7, 180, 181, 219, 262–4, 269
 reality and 38
Shackleton, Ernest 267
Shakespeare, William
 sonnets 57
Shaw, George Bernard 42, 55–6, 67, 68, 105, 128, 155
Sickert, Walter 150, 179
Simmons, Mr (a correspondent in New Age) 78
Simpson, Henry 43, 48, 51, 144
Sketch (newspaper) 254
Slonimsky, Henry 144–5

social change 88–9
socialism 76, 99–103
    Hulme as a socialist 102–3
    Orage as a socialist 67, 68–9,
        102, 272
    Sorel on 106, 107–8
Sombart, Werner 234, 240
Sorel, Georges 105–6
    as anti-intellectual 107
    Hulme's interest in 105, 107, 173
    ideas/themes 106–8
    Reflections on Violence, Hulme's
        translation of xv, 102, 103,
        105, 124, 131–2, 141, 221; his
        preface 221–2, 225–6, 240
Speculations, edited by Herbert
    Read 221, 238, 277n1,
    279n14(2)
    contents xiv, xv, xix, 65, 112,
        142, 282n21, 284n3,
        286nn1–2, 287n10, 290n1
    Epstein's Foreword 142
    publication xiv–xv, xvi–xvii, 104
    reviews xv
    sales xv
    see also Further Speculations
Spencer, Stanley 146
spiritualism *see* mysticism
Spooner, Geraldine *see* Carr,
        Geraldine
sport
    Hulme on importance attributed
        to 13–14
    Hulme as sportsman 6–7, 20
Squire, J. C. [Sir John] 20, 21, 31,
        92, 124–5, 129, 140, 230,
        252–3
'Stamford Hall or The Prevented
    Robbery' (short story, written
    as a child) 4–5

Stanbrook Abbey, Worcester,
    Pattinson sisters as nuns in
        109–11, 194
Stewart, Meum 250
Storer, Edward 55, 58, 64, 230
strike action, Sorel on 106
Strindberg, Frida 172
Stubbs, Dr, Bishop of Oxford 110
Stephen Swift and Co. (publisher)
        96, 105, 120, 126, 132, 140,
        141, 221
    bankruptcy 140, 141
suffragette movement *see* women's
        rights
Sunday Herald (newspaper) 258
Symbolist poetry xvi, 64
syndicalism 106, 107

tactics, Hulme's interest in 231–2
Tancred, Francis W. 51–2, 55, 56
        58, 97, 133
    'A Brief Account of Myself' 52
    death 272
    'On finding Selwyn Image not at
        home . . .' 56
Theosophical Society 42
Theosophy 163, 280n23
The Thrush (journal) 57
The Times 272
Times Literary Supplement 68,
        80
    on *Speculations* xv
De Tongedet 109
'A Tory Philosophy' 112
'Trenches: St Eloi' 65–6, 212,
        232
Tunnicliffe, Charles 33, 111

Union of Democratic Fellowship
        235

University College London
Bergson's lectures, 1911 97–9,
103
Hulme at 33, 34
Unwin, T. Fisher 95
Upward, Allen 145

values, Hulme on 228–9
vers libre poetic form 46–7, 51, 56,
65
de Visan, Tancrède
L'Attitude du lyrisme
contemporain, Hulme's review
of 47
the Vorticists 173, 175, 180, 225,
246
Manifesto 179
see also London Group

Wadsworth, Edward 167, 174, 175
Wallace, Lewis 68
Wallas, Graham 221
'War Notes' 222, 276
published in New Age 221,
230–35, 237, 238–42
three written by Orage 230–31
Ward, Dudley 134, 135

Ward & Hughes, Ecclesiastical
Stained Glass Manufacturers 83
Welby, Lady 112, 126
well-dressing 3–4
Wells, H. G. 42, 101, 105, 173
Westminster Gazette (journal),
Hulme's articles in 84, 94
'White, T.K.', as Hulme's nom de
plume 84, 94–5
Whitworth, Michael 291n33
Williams, Raymond 113
Culture and Society . . . xv–xvi
on Hulme xv
women's rights 41–2, 55, 180
Worringer, Wilhelm
Abstraktion und Einfühlung 150
Hulme's interest in 150, 152–4

Yearsley, Claud 29
Yearsley, Ralph 29
Yeats, W. B. 42, 43, 55–6, 57, 75,
83, 136
'The Death of St Narcissus' 61
'The Lake Isle of Innisfree' 60
York and Lancaster Regiment,
Hulme in 215, 219
'Young Sex' or Puberty 57